Also by Michael Ballé and Freddy Ballé
The Gold Mine

THE LEAN MANAGER

a novel of lean transformation

by

Michael Ballé *&* Freddy Ballé

Foreword by Jeffrey K. Liker

Published by the Lean Enterprise Institute
lean.org

Lean Enterprise Institute ®

© Copyright 2009 Lean Enterprise Institute, Inc. All rights reserved.
Lean Enterprise Institute and the leaper image are registered trademarks
of Lean Enterprise Institute, Inc.
ISBN: 978-1-934109-25-0
Design by Off-Piste Design, Inc.
July 2009
Library of Congress Control Number: 2009927190

Lean Enterprise Institute, Inc.
One Cambridge Center
Cambridge, MA 02142
617-871-2900 • fax: 617-871-2999 • lean.org

For Roman and Alexandre

FOREWORD

You can sense the frustration as Jenkinson explains to his young ward Andy: "Customers come first. Deliver good parts on time. Reduce your costs. Work with your people so that they solve their own problems." Very original and unexpected, right?

Those of us who have been in the business of translating Toyota's revolutionary system to others have felt a similar frustration. How can we make this any simpler while still communicating the elegance of the Toyota Production System (TPS)? I have been in the business for almost 25 years. In that time there was the quality movement, an employee-involvement movement, a six sigma movement, and then a lean movement. Now there is a lean six sigma movement. Each of these movements viewed Frederick Taylor's scientific management as the villain. We need to look beyond local efficiency and consider the whole system of people and processes. That understanding has been there, at an abstract level, but getting it embedded in the organization seems to be an overwhelming challenge.

I first became a fan of Michael and Freddy Ballé when I read *The Gold Mine*. I liked the idea of a business novel, but did not expect an awful lot. As I read it I grew more and more excited. This is what I have been trying to communicate to my associates and clients for years. I immediately urged everyone I knew to read the book. Admittedly, my immediate enthusiasm that the book would transform their thinking was misplaced. That only happens by doing, a central message in the book you have before you, but we can all dream.

What got me so excited about *The Gold Mine*, and what *The Lean Manager* builds on, is that they are both good novels. Each grabs you and pulls you into the story. As you get immersed in the story you relate. You see your own problems in a different way. In short, you identify. What I have been trying to communicate to my clients and students is that TPS is a living system. It is not a toolkit or road map. You have to live it to understand it. It evolves. Yet companies find it overwhelmingly seductive to have a clear toolkit and road map. Consulting companies feed on this need and are all too happy to provide what their customers want. If I had to list the top five mistakes in learning from Toyota, they would be:

1. Giving it a name, e.g., lean six sigma, and making it a program.
2. Trying to PowerPoint and road map your way to lean.
3. Assigning the program to middle managers to deploy.
4. Failing to see this as a major cultural change that takes a lifetime to effect.
5. Senior management failing to take responsibility for leading the culture change.

Michael and I have had endless discussions about how to help organizations avoid these mistakes and move down the path of true cultural change. It is enormously complex, yet unbelievably simple. The most complex part is that you can only learn this system by doing the work. Yet people want to be convinced intellectually before they are willing to make a commitment to doing it.

In *The Lean Manager*, Jenkinson does what he has to do. As the CEO, he has the power to force people to do it or leave the company. He uses that power selectively. He clearly is focused on profitability, even if it means closing plants and letting employees go. In fact, he insists that when plants kaizen out a person that person (or equivalent) is out the door, especially if that person is not buying into change.

This is contradictory to the Toyota way that aims for mutual prosperity and trust with team members who are protected from layoffs if at all possible. The message from Jenkinson seems to be that the ship is so far off course that its very existence is threatened, and righting it through downsizing is essential to survival.

At the same time Jenkinson is clearly committed to developing people. He has learned the Toyota lesson of the value of investing in people. He also has learned a thing or two from his sensei—that you have to identify people with the motivation to improve themselves, give them challenging goals, let them fail here and there, and support them as they learn. He is willing to let Andy struggle, but then periodically shows up to help Andy see new options. He asks Andy questions instead of giving him answers. This is very Toyota-like. The Socratic method is preferred over teaching by offering conclusions. The result is that even as CEO of a good-sized company, Jenkinson is able to penetrate down to the working level and change the culture. It also becomes clear in this story that without Jenkinson's leadership at the CEO level the plants would have no chance to find their way on their own. The Alnext Business System was a lifeless exercise because it lacked the drive and commitment of the former CEO.

To the employees who have not experienced the journey it seems contradictory that Jenkinson keeps talking about customers and investing in people and quality, while he is ordering them to reduce the quality department and shift authority from sales to engineering. In their paradigm, quality is the responsibility of the quality department, and customer satisfaction is the responsibility of the sales department. Jenkinson needs to be dictatorial to move the organization in fundamental ways and get them out of the bureaucratic rut they are in. As they experience real kaizen, they start to move themselves, and Jenkinson can shift from a role of dictator to one of coach and adviser.

How did we get to the point where we need someone at the top of the company to fundamentally rebuild the culture? Why do we need the CEO to tell us that we are in the business of deeply understanding our people and processes and focusing first and foremost on satisfying customers? We get a refreshing contrast through the eyes of Andy's wife, Claire. As a small-business owner who grew up in the business, she knows exactly what her small riding center is about. She is intimately familiar with day-to-day operations and each person she has hired. She does not need to go to the "safety department" to look up the statistics on who is hurt as she takes a personal interest in each of her employees. She also knows the strengths and weaknesses of each and every horse. She understands what it takes to satisfy customers. She is the type of "lean manager" her husband needs to become.

All over the world there are small companies that have no trouble understanding that they depend for success on customer satisfaction, consistently delivering a value-added product or service, and they depend upon willing and able people to accomplish this. Something unhealthy happens as businesses grow and become increasingly bureaucratic. They lose their way. The secret to Toyota is that it managed to grow, become quite bureaucratic, and *not* lose its way. It may stray from time to time, but then leaders always pull it "back to basics," as we now hear from Akio Toyoda.

Value-stream mapping is a great tool for "learning to see." It helps you find the lost organization. Where is the organization that adds value to the customer? It gets lost and buried in layers of bureaucracy. Is it still there? Through value-stream mapping a team of open-minded people can sort through the mess they helped create and find the hidden value-added process. Then the future state dusts it off and puts it in the proper perspective as front and center rather than hidden by the staff organizations and layers of management. Unfortunately, value-stream mapping often becomes part of the bureaucracy and loses its power to help people to see.

I can intellectualize all this over and over, but there is nothing like living it. A novel like this comes closest to that experience. As we are progressing on the "lean journey," companies are maturing from process-improvement toolkits to lean value-stream management, to employee engagement in problem-solving, to aligned culture focused by self-aware leadership on the right business problems. The companies I teach are begging for guidance on leadership. They have had enough discussion of tools. They understand that path is a dead end. It is the right time for this discussion, but how do you have the discussion?

A business novel that illustrates the struggles of real people to change and learn and adapt to an unforgiving business environment is priceless. Once again I am excited and have hopes that this book will enlighten readers about what it really means to live a business transformation that puts customers first and does this through developing people. People who do the work have to improve the work. There are tools, but they are not tools for "improving the process." They are tools for making problems visible and for helping people think about how to solve those problems. Whether it is kanban or standardized work or 5S, these are tools to set a standard and make the deviation from the standard visible to the work group. Then the work group must develop problem-solving skills to identify the root cause and solve the real problem. Any solution is an experiment that is "right half the time." If the tools do not change the way people who do the work think about their own processes, the tools are a failure. If leaders do not understand how to use the tools to unleash the creativity and motivation of people, they are not leaders—they are just administering a bureaucratic process.

If this is only about leadership and focusing on the right business problems, then is there anything really new about Toyota and lean and six sigma? That is a good question, and we could have a healthy debate. If this is just another framework that reminds us of the basics of an excellent way of organizing people to accomplish a defined goal, that is fine with me.

Foreword

I have great admiration of Freddy Ballé's deep experience as a true lean leader. I also admire and am secretly jealous of Michael's novel-writing abilities (though Michael will swear he is a bad novelist). As a duo they have made an invaluable contribution to the movement that I have devoted my career to. They make the intellectual points in a way that makes you feel like you are living it. Now we all hope that more people will really live it!

– Jeffrey K. Liker
  Professor, University of Michigan
  Author of *The Toyota Way*

Chapter One

CUSTOMERS FIRST

"He's closing the plant!"

Closing the plant meant losing his job. Losing his job meant losing Malancourt. Losing Malancourt didn't bear thinking about.

Driving blindly through the heavy spring rain, Andrew Ward rehearsed how he was going to break the news to his wife. He had dreaded this moment since taking on the job three years ago, but as months and then years had gone by, the fear had receded. Now the monster had suddenly sprung, showing him up for the failure he was.

Ward once had been a successful consultant. For a few good years, just out of University, he had lived the high life. Sharing an expensive flat in central London with a few yuppie mates, he made good money flying around the world to audit clients and recommend ways to improve their supply-chain effectiveness. Asia was waking up. Corporations were globalizing furiously. Oil was cheap, transport costs easily dismissed. Ward wore the suit and the bright-eyed smile, full of boyish charm, just as comfortable in the glass-and-steel headquarters from Prague to Singapore as the gritty warehouses in remote industrial zones. He dazzled management with his presentations. He palled around with material handlers in dusty distribution centers. And he threw back pints with the lads in city bars anywhere. Ward was born and raised in Richmond, London's well-to-do suburb, where bankers and music-business execs met in pubs on the Thames. He had grown up in cities, lived in cities, and traveled around the globe from one major city to another. He enjoyed the bright lights and the crowds, the high streets, the bars, the working days, and the lively nights.

He had become the plant manager of a French factory near the German border, on the outskirts of the Champagne region for the simplest and most confounding reason of all: true love. He'd fallen absurdly in love with a girl whose dreams had been about horses: riding horses, caring for horses, trading horses, breeding horses. She was working at a posh London riding club and moonlighting as a French translator. Because he had spent summers as a kid in his parent's Provence retreat, Ward had become accidentally fluent in French and was asked to supervise when she got hired to translate a corporate brochure for the Paris practice. Bang! Lightning had struck. In no time, they had moved into a dismal studio on Earl's Court. They were young, beautiful, and in love in London. Life was a ball.

Claire's father owned and operated the Malancourt Riding Center, a modest equestrian club not far from Metz, where she'd fallen in love with the big dumb brutes with whom she'd grown up. He often joked she'd been born in a manger. When her father had a bad accident, from which he recovered slowly, physically diminished, Claire decided that she could no more abandon the center than she could wipe out her childhood, and decided to take it over. While she had always considered this to be a distant possibility, Claire found herself totally unprepared when suddenly faced with the stark choice of committing to Malancourt there and then or selling or closing it completely. Worse, as she finally managed to have a heart-to-heart with her father, she discovered the whole business was heavily mortgaged, never made much in the first place, and that her parents' spending income had always come from her mother's wages as a school principal in town. Still, she'd resolved to save Malancourt. Ward could follow if he liked, but she would not be coming back to London.

Blame it on love. Still reeling from this abrupt change of affairs, two months into Claire's moving out of their pad, Ward had realized two basic truths. First, he couldn't live without her. It might sound terribly melodramatic, but he felt that this was a straightforward fact. Second, nothing in his high-flying, global consulting job had qualified him for a paying job in rural France. For a few frustrating months, he'd tried shuttling between London and the middle-of-nowhere village of Malancourt, where Claire was learning the difference between actually running a riding center as opposed to just working there. A city boy, he'd found the sticks terrifying beyond words, but a man's got to do what a man's got to do. At the time, Ward had been part of a long-term mission for the Alnext Corp.'s automotive division, working for Lowell Coleman, the VP in charge of logistics. Coleman had been asked to rationalize the flow of parts through a division where one component could easily travel twice around the world before reaching the customer. In one of the projects Ward had worked on, they discovered that one part was assembled in 21 steps spanning 18 countries (counting components manufactured by suppliers). On several occasions, Coleman had hinted that he would like to hire Ward for his supply-chain office, but Ward had had no motivation to make the switch. Eventually, however, Ward shared his dilemma, and Coleman proposed a solution. Alnext's automotive division had a plant in eastern France whose plant manager was soon retiring. Since Ward had been trained as a lean/six sigma black belt, he could take the job of the plant's CIO (continuous-improvement officer) for a few months, with the aim of learning the ropes and taking over as plant manager when the older guy retired. Vaudon was a 40-minute drive from Malancourt. There would be no more traveling abroad. It was the perfect setup.

Everyone more or less expected this to be a stopgap solution. Coleman thought that Ward would tire of the operational role and eventually rejoin the corporate supply-chain team. A little hands-on experience couldn't hurt. Ward feared he would fail miserably at running anything as complex as a plant, but was buying the time he needed to find another job in the region. Once settled in France, he reasoned, it would be easier to look for work locally.

In the end, what was designed as a temporary solution evolved into something more permanent and satisfying. Jean Blanchet, the retiring plant manager, an old hand in molding injection, had taken an unexpected shine to the easygoing, hard-working young Englishman. Ward's engineering background became useful as he discovered, much to his surprise, that he liked working with machines and technical processes. He did well with various six sigma projects during his first year at the plant. Furthermore, due to the rapid turnover among managers, most of the management team was fairly young. They accepted Ward's nomination from corporate with an equal measure of equanimity and cynicism, not protesting too loudly over his ascent. After all, "parachuting" rising stars from central headquarters to completely screw up local operations was well established in both French industry and politics. And to be fair, Ward had turned out to be a decent plant manager.

Then Philip bloody Jenkinson took over the business and ruined it all, deciding to close the Vaudon plant without further ado! Goodbye job. Goodbye income. And goodbye Malancourt, Ward lamented. He could never find employment with the same pay grade in this godforsaken part of France, and there was no way Claire could keep the stable financially viable in the coming years. They'd survive it, but she would be devastated.

"Lowell?"

"Hi, Andy. I was expecting your call. He told you?"

"Yeah. He's closing the plant. You knew?"

"I did. Phil asked me not to say anything. He wanted to tell you himself, face to face."

"Well, he did. Do you think it's final?"

"What do you mean?"

"Jenkinson. You've been working with him? Is he really that tough?"

Ward heard the pause, and the indrawn breath.

"Yes, he's pretty tough. But he's not completely the madman people would have him be. He's not very good with people, you know, chitchat. But he's quite clever. What happens is no one sees him coming. People here are starting to take him seriously, but it's so political that ... the usual."

"How so?"

"See, when he arrived, he didn't do anything for the first four or five months. No announcements, no decisions, nothing. He spent most of his time with engineering, and people figured out that he was an engineer. He ran *kaizen* improvement events in person—that threw some. He'd ask the entire plant management to attend, but never commented if some people didn't show up. He also started visiting customers directly at every complaint. Not with sales, though. He went straight to the lines, to understand how our products were fitted on the car. And then, suddenly, he starts a war on every front."

"The whole deal of selling the headquarters building and relocating every one in the plants?"

"That was just the tip of the iceberg. The real thing is he took program management away from sales. He fired most of the program managers who used to report to Wayne Sanders and put technical engineers in charge of programs. Remember that Sanders is the guy who brought the Univeq equity partners in. He was always considered more powerful than the CEO himself because he had his grip on all customer relationships—not to mention the investors. Now Phil tells him that the sales force is there to support the engineers, not the other way round. There is talk that Sanders blew up over this, but then he had to back down."

"Wow. I never realized. But relocating the engineers? These guys hate being told what to do. Didn't they quit in droves?"

"Not so much. Remember, he's been hunkered down with them for months, and he's given them a lot more latitude, so what's relocation compared to that? In any case, the move was only the start!" exclaimed Coleman, mixing outrage and wonder. "Then came the sale of the Toluca plant."

"The crown jewel, right? High-margin parts for SUVs?"

"Again, the tip of the iceberg. Phil wants sales to go after more parts for small cars. It doesn't make any sense because margins are so tight on the small-car market, and we think that the company *really* needs to improve its operating income right now. But Phil is adamant, and Wayne is fighting him every inch of the way. Wayne's argument is that we need to keep focused on products with the higher margin, even if it means less volume. Phil's point is we have overcapacity everywhere, so we need volume first, and that it's his job to get the cost down to make operations profitable."

"The Toyota thing, right?"

"How do you mean?"

"Well, uh, profit equals price minus cost," stammered Ward, trying not to sound like a know-it-all. "You know, that lean slide we used to have in the presentations. Rather than calculate your cost, add the expected margin and try to sell at that cost, you sell at market price, and lower the costs until you make your profit target. Which is how Toyota attacks markets. They start with small cars, where margins are slim, but where the competitors don't fight very hard because they consider the segment unattractive in the first place. At least that's what we were told in the lean training."

"No, no, you're right. You're right. That's how he thinks. I wish he'd be more explicit about it, but that's his strategy. In any case, Wayne is not having any of it, so engineering is now pulling toward pitching for smaller cars in the new bids, and sales is confused as hell. It's a real awful mess. But I'll say this about Phil, he doesn't give up easily."

"And what about his lean reputation?" wondered Ward. "He barely looked at any of the stuff we installed with the Alnext Business System."

"Yeah, I know. Just doesn't seem to care. Remember that we used to have a group of 15 high-potentials going around the plants and leading *kaizen* events? He's closed that office, and given them all one month to either go back to line functions or leave the company. Claims that *kaizen* is the plants' business, not corporate. There's only Jared Sims left in charge of ABS now, and the poor fool is completely clueless. Every time he asks a question, regardless of the topic, Phil answers, 'Teach the plants to run their own *kaizen* events,' as if that was completely self evident."

"You mean no more ABS audits?"

"Not in the near future, that's for certain. Don't get me wrong. Phil is a fanatic for the Toyota stuff. We supply a couple of small parts to Toyota's Georgetown plant for the Camry from the Bethany site, and Phil's fired the plant manager over service to Toyota. He's promoted some guy simply because he had experience supplying Toyota. The point is that whatever Toyota asks for, Toyota gets. Phil's attitude is do it first, figure it out later. I believe he's trying to develop more of a relationship with Georgetown, but he always plays his cards pretty close to the vest."

"So, how come he's not interested in our lean work?"

"Beats me! For my money, I suspect that what he means by lean is very different from what we meant by it. He never talks about 'lean' in any case, so it's hard to know. Every time we'd tried showing him something from our lean program he just stares back, shakes his head, and moves on. Makes us all feel like complete idiots. But he's certainly asking everybody to work completely differently, and no one is quite sure whether their job will still be there when they turn up in the morning," Coleman said.

"He's certainly asked me to look at the supply chain completely differently. He's asked me to reevaluate all our parts-localization decisions from a lead-time perspective. He wants to have a picture of what the total supply chain would look like from the point of view of truck routes and frequency. This is different from our usual focus on unit transport costs, and I still haven't figured out how to get reliable numbers out of the system."

"Mean and lean, huh?"

"He's tough, all right. I don't know about mean. He's a cold guy, for sure. Not the chatty type at all. He listens, and even appears to hear, what he's being told. People underestimate him because he seems so slow and doesn't speak up very often. He asks a lot of questions, but never lets you know exactly what he thinks. It's unnerving, but make no mistake, the guy is very bright and he's got the memory of an elephant. He's making a lot of enemies right now, for sure, but I don't think it's intentional. He's just difficult to work with because he's got a clear idea of what he wants, but won't tell you. Or when he does, it's hard to hear. As a result, there's a lot of resentment building up in U.S. operations. I suspect you're about to find out over there in Europe, now that he's looking your way."

"Indeed. I wish you'd warned me. He caught me completely by surprise."

"He does that," agreed Coleman, laughing quietly. "Listen, some people are keen on demonizing the guy, but my experience is that he tends to be a straight shooter. He does what he says."

"So the plant is screwed? He is going to shut us down? Is that what you're saying?"

Another long pause. Ward imagined he could literally hear the VP think it through, across the Atlantic.

"He closed the Peterborough site," Coleman finally answered.

Ward said nothing, digesting that. Peterborough had been one of the large, historical automotive plants of Alnext.

"I'll tell you what," Coleman added carefully. "Phil is determined, but he's also open-minded."

"Yeah, right!" exploded Ward, still smarting from the day's mortifying plant visit. Jenkinson had fired off questions without even waiting for the answers, or showing any interest in what he was being told.

"No, no," insisted Coleman. "He is. I've seen him change his mind. He's got this weird theory from reading the early texts of Taiichi Ohno, you know, the guy who's supposed to have invented all this lean stuff ..."

"I know who you mean."

"Anyhow, Phil believes that all of us are wrong half of the time. Himself included."

"For real?"

"Believe it. That's why he's so hot on trying things out. He's convinced that the only way to figure out whether you're right or wrong is by experimenting, trial-by-fire sort of thing. He's a real old-fashioned engineer in that way, and he treats every problem in the same manner. Data won't convince him, but any genuine attempt at doing something, no matter how small, will give him pause. He needs to touch it to believe it."

"I don't understand," muttered Ward. "Is he open-minded or not? This sounds awfully close-minded if you ask me!"

"Think of it this way. Making an abstract case for something just doesn't move him. He isn't interested. And as an arrogant son-of-a gun, he's generally convinced his reasoning is better than yours. But show him a bona fide experiment, a *fact*, and he'll listen. I've seen him radically revise a position on the spot when someone demonstrates by *doing* that there's a better explanation or way of doing things. So if you want to convince him of anything, don't build a paper case. Don't argue. Show him something."

"Thanks for the tip, Lowell," Ward replied, deflated. "But I don't quite see how this can help. If he's made up his mind that the plant should be closed, what could we possibly show him?"

"I don't know, kid," Lowell answered. "I really don't know, and I don't have enough influence with the man to do anything about it at this stage. I wish I could help. If worse comes to worse, there's always a place for you here on my team. We could use your help."

"Thanks again, Lowell. You're awfully kind. But you know Claire would never move."

"How are they in any case? How's the boy?"

"We're fine. Charlie is going on eight months. Thanks for asking."

"Hang in there!"

Ward had been excited yet apprehensive about the new CEO's plant visit. He had heard about Jenkinson's reputation as a tough customer and genuine lean hero. In his continuous-improvement role, Ward found it frustrating relating his book learning to the realities of a living, breathing plant. He was looking forward to seeing a "real" lean expert in action. He had carefully prepared the visit with his management team, making sure that all the Alnext Business Systems standards were in place, and creating slick PowerPoints detailing the results of its lean six sigma projects.

And all to waste. Jenkinson had barely spent an hour in the plant. He had driven a rental from Frankfurt and returned there after his whirlwind visit, leaving Ward standing numbly in the plant's lobby feeling like he'd been crushed by the passing tornado. Ward had slowly stirred himself up from his daze, intending to go back up the stairs to debrief with his management team, but then changed his mind. He didn't feel fit to face them. The shock had to wear out first. Instead, he crossed the soulless lobby and passed through the heavy doors that led to the shop floor. At that moment he had to admit how shabby the plant looked, with its yellowish walls full of impact traces, dirty skylights that made the light so dim, and aged presses working as well they could, given that there had been no investment that he could remember, and never enough staff for maintenance, let alone daily care.

Jenkinson had brushed off the prepared presentations. "Let's go to the shop floor," he said, without bothering to step upstairs into the meeting room to meet the management team. Embarrassed, Ward phoned his assistant to tell the other managers not to wait for them, and followed the big man into the press hall.

Ward was tall and thin, almost gangly, with a mop of straight black hair and boyish blue eyes. Jenkinson was even taller, and much wider. A large, ponderous man, he wore a studious frown behind his glasses and spoke infuriatingly slowly, with a lazy Californian twang that made you want to finish all his sentences for him. He had short, graying blond hair, square Nordic features, and the kind of rough skin leftover from youthful acne.

Jenkinson had walked slowly through the plant with Ward at his side, stopping here and there to look, asking question after question about operational details, most of which Ward hadn't known how to answer without getting someone to find out. Every time he obsequiously suggested he could ask for the answer, Jenkinson waved him away and walked on, leaving him standing with a sinking feeling in the pit of his stomach.

"You're making about 250 million euros in sales, right?" Jenkinson had finally checked. "That's about $360 million."

"Just about," agreed Ward, his apprehension growing. "Our EBITDA is at 4.5 percent, which is on budget—but I realize it's far too low," he'd added hastily. "Our costs ..."

"Remind me, what are your customer ppms like? Bad parts per million?"

"Around 400," winced Ward. "We've got several visible parts ..."

"And internal?" interrupted Jenkinson.

"We're not even counting in ppm," Ward replied, "we've got between 3 and 4 percent scrap."

"I bet that's half your margin—no wonder your financials are so terrible."

Jenkinson stopped in front of a press, watching the robot hand slide in and out of the mold, picking up the finished part and dropping it on the conveyor, where an operator would deburr the part and place it in the customer packaging.

"Weekend shifts?'"

"At the moment, we've had some press breakdowns so we need to catch up, and we've still got the parts that were supposed to be transferred to Romania. We're running seven days a week on those."

"Come on!" the CEO had exclaimed irritably, with an outstretched hand encompassing the press area. "Look around you, a third of your presses are standing idle!"

Ward kept his expression carefully blank, and said nothing. What was there to say?

"Inventory?"

"Overall, about 20 days."

"Work in process?"

"I'd have to check. But I'd say about three days—four at the most."

Jenkinson had stared at the plant manager then as if looking right through him, and Ward suddenly realized how bad things were, how poor his numbers sounded, how unkempt and messy his plant looked. He had managed to tap-dance his way out of trouble many times before but, in that instant, he knew the game was over. This was not the kind of senior exec he was used to. This was not a man who was satisfied with ballpark numbers and nutshell briefings. He *saw* the plant in a way Ward himself didn't. This was different. Ward could see that the stakes were far higher than he suspected.

"Our benchmark plant in Bethany," the CEO said, looking away, "has less than 15 customer ppm, three days of inventory overall with two hours of WIP, and an EBITDA of 20 percent of sales."

"We need to talk," he added. "Better do it in your office."

"And then he tells me he's closing the plant," Ward said so softly that his wife didn't hear him. He ended up getting directly into his car and driving home without a word to anybody, arriving just as Claire was giving their son his bath. He kept blathering on about the visit, finding it hard to get to the point, the end point, and its consequences.

"Most painfully humiliating day in my life," he babbled on angrily. "He shows up at the plant with hardly a 'Hello,' ignores the presentation we've spent ages putting together, walks straight to the shop floor without a word, and just stands there looking."

Ward pulled a long swig from his beer and sighed as his wife wrestled Charlie into his pajamas. She glanced at him from the corner of her eye, wondering what could possibly have happened. He was generally a happy soul who didn't take work—or himself—too seriously.

She couldn't remember the last time she had seen him so dejected. Something was terribly wrong, but she had not yet realized what it was.

"'What was your last customer complaint?' Phil asks. And to my total embarrassment, I can't tell him. 'Let me find out,' I say, but he just shrugs. 'What was your last lost time accident?' I can't answer either. 'Okay,' he says, and starts walking down the alley of presses. The third press he sees is not running, and there's no one around. By now I know what's coming, and I cringe. 'Why is this press stopped? Is it not loaded? Breakdown?' I don't know. 'Right this instant, how many of your 20-so presses are running or stopped?' I felt like a complete jackass."

"Hey, babe, you're the plant manager, you're not expected to know all the details, right?" Claire appealed, carrying the baby into the living room. When they'd moved into the farmhouse, they had pulled down walls to form two small bedrooms at the other end of the building and a large open living space with an American kitchen. Claire plonked the baby in his pen and turned to Andrew.

"Well," he hesitated. "That's what I thought on the spot. I'm supposed to have the big picture, yeah? I've got people to know the small stuff, right? But that's not quite true, is it? You would certainly know which one of your riders had an accident last. Hell, I can probably tell you that goose Melanie sprained her ankle a couple of weeks ago."

"Three weeks ago," she corrected absentmindedly. "And Frédéric Hainault cricked his neck badly on Monday."

"See? And you probably can tell exactly what sort of shape every one of your nags is in, right now."

"Darling, this is what I do. I take care of horses. You run a factory for heaven's sake! It's not the same."

"Isn't it? Isn't that the point?" asked Ward, staring up at Claire in a rare moment of self-doubt. "You've got more horses in that stable than I have presses in my plant. Surely I should be able to tell which one's up and running and which is not? And why?"

"In any case, that's all moot," sighed Ward. "After beating me into the ground all around the plant, Jenkinson tells me he wants to talk one-to-one. So we get to my office, and he hits me with the good news: he has decided to close the plant."

"He can't be serious!" Claire started, aghast.

"Oh, he is. The plant's been barely breaking even for the past three years."

"But you've been on budget every year!"

"Yes, and we both know how weak the budgets were. He's not blaming me, well, not as such. But he knows the numbers better than I do. And he tells me that, first, the budgeted sales for the plant are going to keep dropping this year, since the engine covers will move to Romania any time now, and then next year's pipeline is empty."

"But I thought they were committed to find work for the plant?" Claire protested, waving her arms in dismay.

"That was before the sale," Ward muttered, rubbing his face. "Jenkinson's argument is that plant costs are way too high, he's got overcapacity in Europe, and spare capacity in either the Polish or Czech plants. In any case, our quality and delivery performance are not good enough to try making a special commercial effort to get products in."

"Ouch!"

"Ouch indeed," Ward concurred as he picked up Charlie, who had started crying, fed up with all the serious parent talk.

"You have to hand it to the guy, he gave it to me straight. It's one of three things: He's aware of how complex it is to close a factory here in France, so I can stay on to help him shut the factory down and do so in the best or the least-worse conditions for everybody involved, or he can fire me and find an interim manager to close the plant."

"You mentioned three options," Claire said, as Ward sank back in gloomy silence, absently playing with the baby, who gurgled happily.

"Yes, well," he stirred, turning down his mouth in distaste. "I could also resign in anger—which would save the company coughing up severance pay."

"Did he actually say that?"

"No, not as such. He didn't have to. But why would he sock it to me like that! No, the bastard wanted me to quit right then and there," he snapped.

It must have been bad, Claire realized anxiously, watching Ward swing from dejection to anger and back. He was one of the most even-tempered men she'd ever known, with a generally easygoing disposition and a self-deprecating humor she loved. She saw true rage and bitterness building up in his pale eyes and, suddenly, that scared her, sending a cold shiver up her spine.

"When he took over as a CEO, you used to think he was a good guy?"

"Just serves to show," he muttered sullenly, passing Charlie to her and crossing the room toward the kitchen.

She heard him slam the fridge door and rummage for the bottle opener. This was so unlike him. She was normally the one to fly off the handle at the drop of a hat, to make a scene, complain and blame ... in his words, to be French. It unnerved her to see him so upset.

Ward finally fought the bottle cap off, and continued to brood. True, Jenkinson had been welcomed as a savior when the Alnext Corp. had decided to spin off its loss-making automotive division in what had largely been considered a firesale. Jenkinson had come in with something of a reputation. Ward remembered the PDF copies of *Forbes* being emailed around with Jenkinson on the cover and the caption, "The Lean Manager." The man was hailed for turning around an electrical equipment company and multiplying its market value by a factor of 10 in seven years. Some academic had even written a book about the whole "lean" transformation that Ward had never bothered to look up. The main theme, he remembered reading somewhere, was that lean is "all about people." Yeah, right!

With hindsight, Ward felt a fool for not having seen it coming. Far away from the corporate decision centers, he had first heard of the creation of Nexplas Automotive through the press. At the time, he had been overwhelmed by the birth of Charlie, not paid attention, and kept his head down. Nothing had changed much for European operations at first. The deal had been set up by Univeq, a private equity group that had snapped up the division at a ridiculously low price. Under heavy Wall Street pressure, Alnext's top management had been scrambling to refocus on its profitable segments, and decided to spin off automotive. Jenkinson was rumored to have been handpicked as CEO for his turnaround track record as well as his willingness to sink a serious chunk of his own money in the venture, supposedly owning up to 20 percent of the stock.

For months on end, nothing much had been heard from Jenkinson, and operations went on with business as usual, no worse, but certainly no better. Ward had doggedly continued to struggle with his impossible customers, useless suppliers, and the nonstop demands for more reporting from corporate. He had abandoned all hope that the critical investment he needed to fix his struggling presses would ever be approved. After all, it had been refused for three straight years as the automotive division's numbers had melted away and corporate had pushed one wave of penny pinching and cost squeezing after another.

Then, out of the blue, Jenkinson had made a big splash with three sudden strategic moves. First, he had sold the Toluca, Mexico, plant, which had traditionally been considered a jewel in the crown of the division. He had come under intense fire because of this. The plant sold SUV bumpers very profitably to U.S. automakers, and was considered one of the few cash cows left in the company. Then, he'd closed one of the four U.S. plants, and announced the merger of two more, intending to halve the number of plants in North America by the end of the year. Far from the frontlines, Ward had been amused and cheered him on. But then Jenkinson took the third step of selling off the sprawling corporate headquarters and engineering complex in Ann Arbor, relocating all functions to the plants.

Throughout all of this, Europe had largely been spared. Reporting lines had remained unchanged. In the days of Alnext, the division had been organized along product lines, separating plastic engine parts (the bulk of the Vaudon plant's activity), external parts such as bumpers, and a third branch that specialized in dashboards and all the involved fittings. To be sure, many execs had left the U.S. side of the business as a result of Jenkinson's changes, but Ward knew few of them personally. And since becoming a lowly plant manager he had made a point of keeping his nose clean and avoiding corporate battles. Now he was kicking himself. The war had finally come to Europe, and he had just become one of its first casualties.

He had met Jenkinson on a couple of occasions since the birth of Nexplas. In the early months, the new CEO had conducted a grand tour of all the facilities. This had been a formal affair, with Jenkinson constantly surrounded by apparatchiks. His hulking size, faded jean shirts, used chinos, and quiet demeanor couldn't have stood out more in the midst of the self-important suits who seemed to spend most of their time telling him how things really worked in automotive, or rather Automotive with a capital "A." What would this nerdy guy from a little electrical product company in a little equipment industry know about this industry of industries? Ward had also caught a glance of him at the companywide hoo-hah held in Fort Lauderdale to announce the changes to all executives. Jenkinson had introduced himself as the new CEO, and delivered an appallingly boring speech about people being the main asset and quality above all. Yeah, sure.

The dust had barely settled in the U.S. when Jenkinson dropped another bomb. Program managers would report to the engineering VP and no longer to sales, which, in a sales-driven company was a true revolution. Furthermore, he was doing away with the product line organization. He had attached the smaller plants to regional managers, essentially the plant manager of the largest regional site. Financial and administrative responsibility would remain region-based, which meant that Vaudon still depended on Neuhof for most corporate functions. It was all rather confusing. Klaus Beckmeyer, the manager of the Neuhof plant would become Ward's direct boss, but Jenkinson would oversee plant operations directly. The CEO had explained he would visit plants regularly by himself, as he did that day, and would phone each plant manager once a fortnight, on Friday mornings. "I'll be looking forward to that," groaned Ward under his breath. Even his favored Corona tasted sour as he blamed himself for not realizing that eventually Jenkinson would do to Europe exactly what he'd done in the U.S. Press overcapacity had been the elephant in the room all along, but none of the previous top management team had been willing to face this issue. And now the bill had come due.

"Here," said Claire, pushing a cup of bubbly in his hand as he stood staring numbly into space. "Charlie's asleep, so I thought we'd have a quiet drink."

"Are we celebrating something?" asked Ward, with a puzzled smile.

"I don't know," she smiled back in forced good cheer. "Are we?"

"He means it. The Vaudon plant is history."

She shrugged, and touched her glass to his, looking him in the eye. "You know what my father always claimed. The quicker you're back in the saddle after being thrown, the faster the pain will fade—and the fear. 'If you can talk, you can ride,' the man said."

"Oh, what the hell," he submitted. "You're right. I'll get a fire going, and we can get drunk, you and I."

"That sounds like a plan!"

Ward carefully placed the firewood in the ancient fireplace, and set a match to it. The flame stirred and crackled. A few minutes later, a cheerful blaze was warming the hearth. Claire had switched off the lights, and lit the row of orange candles she kept on the mantle.

Ward wasn't fooled. In the flickering light of the fire, he could see the drawn lines of her face, the false smile. She was putting a good front on it, but they both knew the score. Since they'd taken over the old, fortified farmhouse and the adjacent stables, they'd been sinking a steady flow of cash into their upkeep. They'd already started converting one of the abandoned buildings into bed and breakfast guest rooms. Without his paycheck, they'd probably have to give up their dream of restoring the place to its former grandeur.

"You'll find another job, you'll see. We'll be fine."

He sighed heavily and took another long sip, savoring its bite. Another perk of living so close to the champagne region, he thought. We couldn't afford anything half as good anywhere else. And with the taste of the wine chasing that last thought, the anger and frustration he'd been carrying all evening finally came together, congealing itself in a form of reckless defiance. It wasn't just the material implications for his family, for the plant, and everyone who would have trouble finding another job in this region. He couldn't remember ever feeling as ashamed at work as today. His pride and self-confidence had been cut to shreds by the unsavory certainty that he should have done better. Jenkinson had been brutal.

But, Ward had to admit, he had not been wrong. The plant was losing money. They had too many delivery and quality problems. It was getting by, but just barely. He had felt lucky to survive in the job, happy to be good enough and fly under the radar. Well, his luck had finally run out. He'd have to work at it now.

"I'm not closing the plant," he told Claire, with more confidence than he felt.

"What do you mean?" she wondered, clearly puzzled. "What can you possibly do?"

"I don't know yet," he admitted. "But, to start with, I can try reasoning with the man. Bloody hell, closing a plant in France is a mighty pain, so surely it can't be high on his agenda. There must be a way to buy some time."

Here's what I'll do," he resolved, rolling over the carpet to rest his head on his wife's legs. "He's visiting the Neuhof plant tomorrow. I'll drive to Frankfurt and try to talk him around. What can it hurt?"

As he cooled his heels in the Neuhof lobby, Ward thought to himself, here's a real plant. In the spacious reception area, several sleek, glass displays were showing off the products, a model of a car with the bumper and dashboard fittings tastefully accented by well-placed spotlights. Two pretty, uniformed *frauleins* smiled sweetly as a voice told him they were trying to locate the plant manager. Numerous cost-cutting exercises at Vaudon had long ago done away with live receptionists; visitors signed themselves in and called from a phone booth to get picked up.

Against his better judgment, he felt vaguely intimidated. The three-hour drive had been rather harrowing, particularly on the German highway where keeping pace with speed racing under the pouring rain had left him somewhat shaken. Time enough to have second thoughts about showing up uninvited. The enormous plush reception sofa was making Ward feel smaller and smaller, and he hoped that nobody would notice that he was shrinking by the minute.

"Herr Ward," one of the girls suddenly seemed to say, "Herr Ackermann will shortly come for you."

That was a relief. Hans Ackermann was the plant's continuous-improvement officer, and they'd slogged through several six sigma and lean training courses together. He was a big, buff chap with a drooping moustache. He had been promoted to his current job from being a mold maintenance technician. He had long given up on getting any lean started in Neuhof, but had taught Ward more about molding than any one else.

"Andy! Good to see you!" Ackermann beamed, pumping his hand vigorously. "Come through, they're at the paint plant."

Neuhof was about three times larger than the Vaudon plant. It had historically been the European administrative center for the Alnext Automotive division. Most of the European engineers were based there, as well as admin staff for all three units. Ward wondered about the current status now that Jenkinson had abandoned the branch concept, but things traditionally moved slowly in Neuhof, so he suspected the tsunami had not hit yet. He didn't know the plant very well, as most parts made here were bumpers and dashboards. The other engine parts in Europe were largely in the Wroclaw site, in Poland, and some in the Czech site. Neuhof had a large everything: large press shop, large assembly shop, and, of course, large paint plant, the pride of the factory.

"How's it going?" Ward asked cautiously.

"A bloodbath!" answered the big man heartily, with an undercurrent of amusement. "We just spent at least two hours in shipping trying to figure out the *real* service rate."

"I know how it feels," agreed Ward. "I was through it yesterday."

"Logistics maintains that our service rate is 98 percent, citing data in the MRP. But it is unclear whether this refers to orders served in the day, week, month; how they count negotiation with the customer; and so on."

"Sounds familiar."

"So, Herr Jenkinson had them list all 27 of yesterday's trucks one by one, and made them detail customer orders per truck. Then he had them compare the data with what was actually sent in the truck, and count only the trucks with exactly what the customer asked for in the truck—no more, no less."

"And?"

"Four out of 27," Ackermann answered knowingly, "and 15 percent on-time delivery. He had Herr Kastner, the logistics manager, write it large on a whiteboard: 15 percent. Then he asked what they expected these numbers to be today. How many trucks would have exactly what the customer ordered in it? Herr Beckmeyer looked like he would blow up," Ackermann continued. He had been put in the role of CIO because corporate had requested a continuous-improvement office in every plant, but clearly no one in Neuhof had been very interested. He'd gone into the job full of enthusiasm and optimism only to discover he'd walked right into a dead end. He'd bitterly resigned himself to keep up all the paperwork required by Alnext's Business System, the so-called "lean" program, but had mostly given up on the shop floor.

Ward imagined that Beckmeyer would indeed be ready to explode if he were getting the same treatment from Jenkinson that he had received in Vaudon. The man was generally considered to be a competent administrator, even if widely disliked as supercilious. Ward couldn't deny that he shared this sentiment. Suddenly, coming all the way here sounded like a much better idea.

Nonetheless, Ward felt humbled by the quality of operations in the German plant. He envied its clean, neatly color-coded zones and indications helping people throughout. Where he thought he had made an effort in applying the corporate "lean" standards, this plant had done twice better. Large panels of Alnext's official "roadmap" to lean were posted along the gangways, as were huge boards displaying flurries of indicators. As they walked through the injection shop, he breathed in the familiar smell of burnt plastic, and marveled at the huge tonnage the presses needed for bumpers and dashboards. He had to admit that, at first glance, their machines appeared to be in much better conditions than his own, with none of the oil and water leakage one could find pooling around Vaudon. On the other hand, seeing the plant differently since yesterday's dressing down, he now noticed the waste of large numbers of people walking around, moving parts and equipment, or simply standing idle next to the presses, and generally keeping busy with non value-added work.

They had to don special coveralls to enter the paint installation, which was a massive white box in the center of the plant, surrounded with racks and racks of shining, colorful bumpers waiting to be fitted with components. The paint installation was kept under positive pressure to keep dust contamination down. Dust is one of the main enemies of industrial painting. Every little grain can show up in the paint as a defect in the finished product. Consistent with Alnext's previous strategy of delivering specialty parts to high-end vehicles, the plant catered to the German power cars, and quality was of the essence. Which, it turned out, was exactly what was being debated there.

Ward and Ackermann caught up with the group on the far end of the painting installation, in front of a steadily moving conveyor. Workers were picking the painted bumpers off the conveyor's jigs, inspecting the parts for paint defects, directing the bad parts to the rework stations, and placing the good ones in buffer racks from where they would be picked for assembly. Various fittings were assembled at individual stations there before being inspected again and then stored in a large, supermarket-like series of neatly marked shelves, where they would be picked in the right sequence to deliver to customers.

Klaus Beckmeyer was standing rigidly, looking livid. He was surrounded by a bevy of aides and managers, a few of whom Ward recognized. Ward could read volumes from their body postures alone: Jenkinson's tall frame seemed to lean over them all, as they wilted, like trees bending in a storm.

"What do you mean, you can't count the percentage of parts that are good on their first pass through the paint process?" Jenkinson was asking slowly.

"This is not what I said," Beckmeyer replied sharply. "All these figures are in the computer. As I said, I shall call the paint technical expert, and he will be able to answer exactly what you ask."

"I am not interested in what the computer thinks. And I am not interested in what the technical expert thinks," said Jenkinson, with exaggerated patience that bordered on being patronizing. "I am trying to find out whether the people doing the actual work know if they are producing good parts or bad parts. Look at how many parts you're reworking. No one is even counting. Do *they* know how well they are producing good parts for their customers?"

"Herr Jenkinson," replied the German general manager, clearly exasperated. "These are just rework operators. What would they know about the operation of a robotic paint plant? In any case," he added, clipping his words, "our quality is irreproachable!"

Ward noticed that Jenkinson had a nervous tick of pushing his glasses with his forefinger on the bridge of his nose when flustered, a nervous movement he repeated a couple of times while listening to Beckmeyer. He frowned, and stood there with wide eyes, as if he had never seen the man before. The entire group felt the tension rise between them, and the operators could no longer just glance at them furtively: many of them stopped work to witness this showdown.

"First of all," said Jenkinson, breaking the silence, "your quality is not irreproachable. Have you counted your customer claims lately?"

"Impossible expectations," huffed Beckmeyer. "These are German OEMs. Their standards are the highest in the world."

"Impossible or not, I've spent hours listening to your sales manager complain about how hard it is to try to discuss price or pitch a new program with a customer when the first thing he encounters is hell from the client for your poor quality. You should try it, some time, Klaus. In fact, I strongly suggest," he added with a long pause for emphasis, "that you personally visit your customer about *every* quality complaint."

"Second," he pursued relentlessly, "your level of quality is higher than the other plants in the group. Much higher, I'll grant you that. But you must understand that this quality is extremely costly. Look behind you."

Jenkinson gestured for every one to turn around.

"Don't look at me. Look at what they are doing. Rework and rework and rework. Quality here is purchased through inspection and rework. I cannot afford this any longer, and neither can you. This company is on the verge of bankruptcy because of *this*, everywhere!"

Unlike everyone else in the small group, Beckmeyer refused to turn around, standing his ground and glaring at Jenkinson. Considering his own poor level of quality, Ward felt like he should disappear into thin air. And yet he couldn't help enjoying Beckmeyer's misfortune with guilty pleasure. Especially after the beating he'd taken the day before, this felt like justice.

"Herr Jenkinson," Beckmeyer said venomously, "if you care to reproach me, I would appreciate the courtesy that you do this in private and not in front of my staff."

"These are not reproaches, Klaus," snapped back the CEO. "These are *facts*. And I expect this plant and this company to work as a team. We *are* going to confront our problems, and we *are* going to solve them together. Any one not happy with this can leave right now," he added, looking at each of them challengingly, as if expecting immediate resignations. Ward had half-a-second of a wild fantasy of doing so, followed by Beckmeyer, but, of course, no one even breathed.

"Now. Let me be very clear about this," Jenkinson continued. "Making money is what we do. We make money when we service our customers by delivering the parts they want exactly when they want them and with the quality they require. Every time we send them a part they don't like, we're giving them an electric jolt, saying go and buy elsewhere. We make money every time we send them a part they can use, a part that has passed through our process without a hitch, which means first time through. This is how, and only how, we make money. Every time a part is reworked or repacked we lose money! Is this very clear for all? Because, in this company, every one, from the CEO to the janitor, must be obsessed with this simple idea: We make money when parts are RIGHT FIRST TIME. And we are going to make money together by putting ... our ... customers ... first.

"By customer I mean the *next person in the process*," he continued after a moment's silence. "Not just the end customer. This is going to be our obsession—all of us. Customers come first, before job descriptions, rules, systems, whatever. I expect every working area to track its own on-time delivery and defects, and to discuss them with the next step in the process. We need to understand what the next step needs from each of us to be able to do their work correctly: We need to work as a team, across departments and process steps. If everyone in the company does this, our final customers will be well served and we'll finally have a chance to turn this thing around! No ifs. No buts."

Ward had not heard Jenkinson make such a long speech before. It gave him time to reflect on the Vaudon operation from this point of view. The infuriating thing was that he actually made sense.

"Now," the tall American continued with a deep breath, taking his glasses off and cleaning them on a pocket handkerchief, "if we're all quite clear about this, I'd like to show you why we need to understand this together, starting with operators. Let's go back into the paint area."

The small group followed him through the pressure lock. Within the positive-pressure paint area, white-clad operators were inspecting and cleaning the black plastic bumpers and then placing them on the conveyor that would take them through the automated painting process. To Ward, paint plants had always been reminiscent of James Bond secret bases, with their technicians in lab coats buzzing around in the glaring light of the glossy white room. They all climbed a set of narrow stairs and walked in single file along a tight corridor where they looked through large windowpanes at the gee-whiz robots spraying the parts on the conveyor in gleaming metal booths. After coming down another set of stairs on the other side of the robots, they entered the paint mixing room, where they were overwhelmed by the strong chemical smell.

"I wonder what he's seen," whispered Hans Ackermann as he held the door for Ward. "We've been here before, and he said nothing."

In the paint area, a network of tubes ran from giant vats to the paint robots. The place was covered with remains of dry paint, but seemed otherwise reasonably clean and well maintained to Ward. Jenkinson went straight to a low rack where paint pots were lined up. An operator was busy unloading more pots from a pallet truck.

When the little group had assembled around the rack, Jenkinson deliberately passed his finger over the cover of one of the paint pots, leaving a shiny trail on the lid where he wiped away the thin layer of dust.

Without commenting on this obvious problem, Jenkinson politely asked the German team to ask the operator to demonstrate how he opened a paint pot. After a lengthy discussion, the confused operator finally understood what was expected of him. He picked up a screwdriver, and undid the lid of the next paint pot.

"Stop!" ordered Jenkinson in mid-operation. The operator froze, like a child playing a game of statue. Right then everyone could clearly see how in the movement of opening the can, he briefly tilted the lid over the liquid paint in the pot. With an emphatic finger jab, Jenkinson showed how the ill-fated dust would fall straight into the paint. Ward swore he felt the group wince, as everyone knew that every particle of dust could create a grain in the paint, causing the part to be reworked.

"Let's go and see where you store the paint pots," he instructed.

As expected, the paint pots were methodically lined in the storage racks of the incoming-materials warehouse, where dust motes could be seen lazily swirling in the light slanting through the high windows.

"*Results*," lectured Jenkinson, "are the outcome of a *process*. What we want are *good* results from a *controlled* process, because they will be repeatable. Bad results from an uncontrolled process simply mean that we're not doing our job. Good results from an uncontrolled process, however," he added with a rare smile, "only mean we're lucky. And in automotive, luck ran out years ago. Today, bad results from a controlled process just says that we're stupid: we expect different results from doing the same thing over again.

"Now, I know that corporate has traditionally been interested only in financial results, regardless of how you deliver them. The guy with the results gets the bonus, right? And here, in this plant, you've been mainly concerned with controlling the process through increased automation, conveyors, and other methods like this. Yes?"

The Neuhof team shifted uneasily, wondering where this was going.

"What I expect," he explained carefully, "is that every employee understand the link between their results and the process they use to get them. You are convinced that only the paint specialist can improve the paint plant quality, and if he can't, no one can. But I tell you that only the operators that live and work here every day fully understand how the process works.

"Any operator could have told you about the dust contamination from the paint pot lids, if you had asked the right question," Jenkinson said. "So what I expect from management is to get the paint specialists and the operators working together to fix problems and paint parts right first time, so that we can satisfy our customers *and* make money!"

The opulent meeting room was deathly silent as the group settled down for the visit's final debriefing. Coffee and cookies stood untouched in the center of the lacquered wood conference table. Although Ward was dying for a cup after his early morning start, he was reluctant to break the spell of immobility that seemed to have settled on the German team.

"Where is the HR manager?" asked Jenkinson upon entering the meeting room. "How the hell are we supposed to progress without HR involvement?" They had all looked at each other in confusion wondering what HR had to do with anything that had happened earlier on. Ackermann had finally picked up the company phone to locate the human resources director. Now they were all waiting for him to show up. Jenkinson sat slumped in one of the plush leather chairs, wearily rubbing his eyes. Beckmeyer stared obstinately at the distant pine-clad hills out the window.

The HR manager finally arrived, a mousy little man with a startled look on his face. He seemed to enter the room in segments— his head first, as if checking he'd really been asked to be here, then a hesitant torso, and finally dragging the rest of himself into the room. He took a seat next to his general manager. Jenkinson acknowledged him with a nod, and straightened up. He addressed the group, most of whom had sat as far across the polished table as possible.

"Three things," he began slowly, while looking straight at Beckmeyer, as if no one else were in the room. "First, I want an ergonomic assessment of the plant from the HR department. I've noticed that the plant's employees' overall age seems high. And there's a lot of handling of large and heavy parts, even with the conveyor, which, for other reasons, we will discuss again later. This assessment needs to be done quickly, and I expect to be copied with the report personally by the end of the month. Furthermore, now that the plants report directly to me, I'll ask you to notify me of every lost time accident within 24 hours of its occurrence. This is not debatable."

Ward couldn't stop himself from nodding: Jenkinson had asked the same things from the Vaudon plant, although its operator population looked, on average, much younger than Neuhof's.

"Second, you will immediately stop the implementation of your new MRP system."

"You can't mean ...," blurted one of the execs.

"I do mean it. Listen carefully. Stop the implementation. Send the consultants home. Don't pay a penny more."

"But the contract? The sunk cost? The ..."

"The bank is closed. There is no more money for IT. Period. So you break out of the contract, and you write off the sunk cost. Clear?"

"Herr Jenkinson," insisted the production manager, who seemed as confused as he was annoyed. "We have many problems with the current system. We need an improved version."

"This is precisely the point. You need to learn to solve your own problems, and not expect the computer system will do it for you. It won't. You've been producing parts well enough with what you've got. Keep on doing so. Learn to solve your problems. In any case, the decision has been made at the entire company level, so, again, no debate."

Ward thought the stunned silence was a sight to see.

"Third, the cost of protecting the customer from the plant's quality problems is simply too high, and needs to be reduced radically. To start with, I'll ask you to cut the quality department by a third."

This actually elicited gasps from around the table, and Ward wondered for a second whether he had heard correctly.

"Yes. I want you to shrink the quality department, while also lowering the number of quality incidents to customers."

"Impossible!" exclaimed Beckmeyer out loud, as the room erupted in German.

"Maybe," replied Jenkinson evenly. "But I've heard you use this word before, about your customers' expectations. We can't prove whether these things are possible or impossible in this room. We can only pursue this goal. And if this management team can't do it, I'll find one that can. As I mentioned earlier, using the same method and hoping for different results borders on insanity. This company needs a radical improvement of its quality, with an equally radical reduction of its cost base. Therefore, I am not asking to do more of the same and reduce quality complaints through your current approach. I want to clearly shift the responsibility for quality from the current quality department to production."

The production manager, a thin, intense man sporting a shaved head and an ear-stud, looked shell-shocked. He opened his mouth to say something, but no words came out. The quality manager's face was pale. Surprisingly, Ackermann seemed to wink slyly at Ward—or maybe he'd dreamed it. At least someone was having some fun. Ward guessed that for the continuous-improvement officer, after years of being under fire to "improve," only to be blocked by the resistance of line management on one hand and the lack of interest of the support function on the other, today's massacre must have been a satisfying comeuppance.

"Production is directly responsible for its quality," repeated Jenkinson. "I don't give a damn about any quality procedures or any quality-management systems you might have. It's completely up to you whether you keep them or not, but I'll now expect each area manager to answer for their quality performance, no one else."

"You tell us!" exploded the production manager with a thunderous scowl. "How can we do that? You tell us? You say customers come first, and now you want us to cut the quality department! You tell us how!"

"Red bins," answered Jenkinson evenly. "Or red racks. Every cell must have a specific location to place bad parts as they occur. Then you must conduct an analysis of every nonconforming part. To start with, I suggest, that you create a quality task force led by yourself, the quality manager, engineering manager, and whoever else you might think relevant. Tour all the red bins every shift to understand where and what your quality problems really are. This isn't hard, it just demands organization and determination. And it always pays."

"Pfff! Red bins!" scoffed the production manager, with an exasperated hand gesture. He then crossed his arms tightly and scowled at the table, refusing to look up.

"In any case," continued Jenkinson unflustered, "let me be extremely clear. Production will take responsibility for its own quality. And you will take the heads out of the quality department, and the cost out of the business. What is more, I'd like you to do this smartly."

Turning back to the terrified HR manager, he continued to drive his point relentlessly.

"I want human resources to provide the names of the real quality experts you have in this plant by next Monday. People who can recognize the difference between a good part and a bad one and know what part of the process causes what kind of defect. Even if they turn out to be the older people who are most likely to take a severance package. HR needs to explain to me how these people will be retained, not lost. So to make myself crystal clear: The quality department must be cut by a third, and none of the people leaving should be real process experts. Beyond that, who goes and who stays is completely up to you. Again, you can reshuffle people as you like internally, but I'll expect the heads out of the business. Any questions?"

The strain in the room had become so high that it was almost palpable. Ward struggled to hold back a nervous giggle, as he found himself wondering whether being told the plant was to be closed was not the easier way after all. This was the hard way. The silence pulled and stretched, as Jenkinson sat there looking at people one by one, doing nothing to alleviate the tension.

"Is there a timeframe to this?" Beckmeyer finally asked tersely, visibly struggling to contain his fury.

"The ergonomic assessment and the hold on IT development are to be acted on immediately," Jenkinson answered without emotion. "In the next two weeks I'll want to review your proposal of how you intend to carry out the quality streamlining. As for actual implementation, there is no deadline yet—we'll discuss that when you've got a working plan.

"That more or less covers it, gentlemen," he concluded, standing up. "If you have any questions, don't hesitate to email. Remember, there will be a fortnightly call for the plant manager to discuss specifics. In any case, I'll be coming back soon. Thank you for your welcome, and good luck."

"Andy," he turned to Ward, acknowledging directly his presence for the first time. "Did you drive up here?"

Ward nodded mutely, cursing himself for feeling so intimidated. I'll be saluting next, he thought wryly. And calling him "sir."

"Do you mind driving me back to the airport, then? I'm due on a flight home this evening. We can talk on the way."

As the miles passed by on the way to Frankfurt, the CEO remained quiet, lost in thought. Jenkinson didn't look much like a millionaire, casually wearing a navy blazer over a faded jean shirt and beige chinos, which Ward found rather tasteless. The only sign of real wealth the man sported was the flashy Rolex on his wrist. Other than that, he looked more like an archetypal engineer than a CEO, down to the nerdy collection of pens in his shirt pocket. More than anything else, he came across as *earnest*, in that particular way that Ward associated with Americans. The man also suddenly looked exhausted and jet-lagged.

The rain had stopped, but the weather remained moody and gray, and the road was still wet enough to force Ward to concentrate on his driving. As the airport got closer, he was feeling increasingly flustered, trying to work his nerve up to confront Jenkinson, reluctant to intrude into his obvious brooding.

Finally Jenkinson stirred, muttering to himself, "Why does it have to be so damn hard!"

"You could try explaining more," answered Ward impulsively.

"You think?" asked Jenkinson, stretching in the passenger seat. "Probably. Never was much good at it. Too me, it feels like that's all I'm doing: explaining, explaining, talk, talk. The more I explain, the more they find reasons *not* to do."

"Maybe it's because what you say is not what people expect."

"That so?" Jenkinson asked with a chuckle. "Customers come first. Deliver good parts on time. Reduce your costs. Work with your people so that they solve their own problems. Original and unexpected, right?"

"You know what I mean," insisted Ward, speaking more cautiously. "I certainly expected you to come with some lean stuff, you know, value-stream mapping, improve the flow, and that kind of thing. And there you are hitting us over the head with quality. I'm not saying you're wrong. It's disconcerting, is all."

"Lean, lean, lean," grumbled Jenkinson. "What the hell is lean? All I know is that Toyota didn't get to where they are today by simply improving their flow and reducing costs. They build cars people buy, that's the real trick. They build them better, faster, and cheaper. Lean is customer satisfaction first, before getting into eliminating waste. And in any case, the only way to do this is through people."

"Customer satisfaction, eliminating waste, developing people," repeated Ward. "I buy that. But what about flow?"

"Oh, don't get me wrong. Flow is important. *Leveling,* flow when you can, pull when you can't. Of course it is. But that's just technique, it's a way to reveal problems, nothing more. The fundamental issue is attitude. People have to be determined to put their customers first.

They have to be fanatic about developing people. They must understand that everything they do is ultimately all about the product—the product that costumers buy. And this product must solve more problems for the customer than it creates. If we want customers to purchase from us, we should work tirelessly at keeping the inconvenience cost down. And for that, you need people."

"You mean that people need to improve products to solve customers' problems?"

"Yeah, making people before making parts, that's what it's about. Name of the game. But it is sure hard to get across."

"Were you serious about that stuff back there?" asked Ward, after mulling it over.

"Usually am," replied Jenkinson, rubbing his face tiredly. "What stuff did you mean, in particular?"

"Getting them to cut their quality department by a third. If you'll excuse me for saying so, that sounded fairly ... radical."

Jenkinson didn't answer right away and, for a moment, Ward feared he had pushed his luck too far. He cursed inwardly as he almost missed the Frankfurt Airport exit.

"A few years ago," his passenger eventually said, "I had the opportunity of visiting Toyota's Cambridge plant in Ontario. The tour was nothing special, just industrial tourism. They put my group in a small train, sort of like a theme-park ride, and gave us the standard tour through the plant. Obviously, there is nothing more like an automotive plant than another automotive plant, and nothing looks more like a Toyota plant than another Toyota plant, so I didn't expect to see very much, other than confirming what I'd seen in their other plants. But I did wonder about one thing.

"You see, that plant builds the Lexus, Toyota's luxury high-end car. Now, legend had it that only Japanese plants had the necessary rigor and discipline to maintain the level of quality required for the Lexus. So, as we toured the plant, I wondered, what is so special about this plant that they get to build Toyota's most demanding product?

"So in the end, I asked them. The guys giving the tour weren't execs. They were retired employees showing the tourists around, regular joes. But their answer really struck me.

"It's because of the *kaizen* by team members and team leaders, they said. They believed that Toyota had given the plant its top product because of the problem-solving activities of their operators! In all my time in industry, I had never heard anything like this. Not because of superior engineering. Not because of new investments. Not because of better management. The plant earns the right to build the very profitable, high-end product because of the continuous-improvement activities of its operators. The idea is that in order to build the company's most demanding product, what was needed were operators who would constantly seek small improvements and, hence, spot minute problems and find ways to solve them."

"In a way, it's common sense," agreed Ward. "The most demanding product is given to people with the proven ability to solve all the small problems. Hell, I wish someone said that about my own plant."

"*Sense*, certainly," said Jenkinson, giving him a quizzical look, as if to say that he had been saying that all along. "*Common*, unfortunately not. Look, I don't know if it's true, and I certainly have no idea of how Toyota's senior management actually makes its product allocation, but these guys certainly seemed to believe it. So I asked them how they did it. How come they had all this *kaizen* activity?"

"And?"

"Because of the work of the team leaders and supervisors. They have five to seven team members to a team leader, 25 to a group leader, and the leader's job is to sustain *kaizen* efforts. 'We are organized for problem-solving,' they said.

"And that's when the light bulb went on. You see, as managers, that's what we do. We organize things. This is the one thing we should know how to do."

"Yeah," nodded Ward, but having serious private doubts about his ability to organize in that way.

"But our understanding is that we organize ourselves to deliver product, nothing more," Jenkinson said. "Ship the product out the door; provide the service. Use the minimum resources, have clear job descriptions, build integrated systems, and deliver. Toyota was doing something radically different; it was organizing for problem-solving. Think about it. Is the problem-solving activity organized in your plant?"

"I guess, no. It's sort of assumed that people solve problems as part of their work. Nothing special."

"Exactly!" exclaimed Jenkinson, warming to his subject. "Problem-solving is not organized. Jobs are. Consequently, any issue is always someone else's problem—particularly at interfaces and exchanges. And so the restrictions of the job become more important than serving customers first. I had been doing lean for years, but suddenly I saw the light. The line management had to be taught to recognize, address, and solve problems: customer problems, operator problems, process problems."

Just as Ward was about to ask for clarification, Jenkinson pursued his thought, in full lecture mode.

"I think I've figured it out. I researched this topic all the way back to the late 19th century. In the old days, business owners used to be managers. They surrounded themselves with a few trusty people and ran the business centrally, with a strong line, few chiefs and many Indians, and very little structure. Sort of like having a secretary handling personnel files rather than a full-fledged HR department that does who knows what. As Peter Drucker explained, Frederick Taylor then arrives and convinces owners to delegate the running of their companies to professional managers, who will organize work scientifically."

"Scientific management, right?"

"Yep. Taylor persuaded the bosses to invest in specialist functions to organize the shop floor. This meant paying for an engineer, staff, special equipment designed by an engineer, and getting back direct labor productivity. And it worked spectacularly well! This is how we ended up with the corporations we know, with Finance running the show, IT organizing everything, and a weak line management whose main job is to deal with the unions and fight the fires. This enabled us to create mammoth global corporations. But it's incredibly *wasteful*."

"How so?"

"Taylor taught us to gain productivity by applying knowledge through staff structures. This is far better than not applying knowledge at all. But ultimately it relies on specialists whose knowledge of day-to-day, real-life conditions is tenuous at best. The solutions they invent might work, but they work very inefficiently. Come on, have you ever had an IT system that actually helped you? Or a quality department that solved quality problems?"

"Pass," answered Ward, chuckling.

"What specialist staff structures produce are *system*s: IT systems, quality procedures, human-resources manuals, automated lines, and so on. As a result, line management can't resolve any real problem because what is mainly asked from them is to implement the systems. Compliance, compliance, compliance, often at the expense of competence. Systems are far too general and devised too far away from local work conditions to be effective at improving detailed work."

"So, what's the alternative?"

"Applying knowledge through the line rather than through staff structures. This is what Toyota hit upon. It's the line management's job to *improve* operations day to day by working with operators, not just to implement systems invented by eggheads. This is a lot leaner because, first, all processes are improved by the very people who run them, and, second, staff structures are now composed of real experts rather than specialists. I don't need an IT department to run my system for me. I need one guy who can teach me how to really use my existing IT system. I don't need a quality department to produce quality procedures. I need someone who can explain to me exactly what goes wrong where in my process so that I can see how it creates specific quality problems. I don't need a financial function to run my ratios and tell me what I can spend or not spend. I need a real financial expert who can teach me how to use my budget to manage my plant effectively. Overall, I need far fewer people, but with greater *expertise*. The key to a lean operation is that management organizes people to develop knowledge continuously."

As they neared the airport they hit traffic, giving Ward time to chew this over. He wasn't certain he understood or even agreed with what Jenkinson was saying, but he recognized true belief when he heard it. The guy had a vision, that much was certain. It was maybe a totally crackpot theory, but he sounded sincerely convinced. Ward didn't know whether to be reassured by this or more worried. True believers tended to give him the jitters.

"You see," Jenkinson started in again, "for years I've studied lean with various *sensei* who kept saying in one form or another that lean is not about applying lean tools to every process but about using the lean tools to develop *kaizen* spirit in every employee. When you're on one side of the mountain, it's so hard to see how the valley looks on the other side. Applying lean tools to every process is simple for us. We create a new structure, call it a lean office, staff up continuous-improvement officers, and then dispatch them to apply lean tools to every area. And meanwhile line management continues to do what it does, uninvolved, and uninterested. And then we are surprised that after gathering the low-hanging fruit, the whole thing sinks in the mud. And the whole effort is abandoned until the next program of the year comes along.

"Believe it or not, this company is far better organized than my previous business was. People have clear job descriptions. You have far better, more integrated systems. Procedures are much clearer. As a result, however, no one owns problems because they always belong to somebody else. It's precisely because the division was so good at doing the wrong things that it didn't make money for Alnext, and could be bought so cheaply. If I want to make this work and make money from it, if we all do for that matter, then I need to break you guys from your hope that clearer organizational charts, more structure, and neater systems will improve the situation. The only thing that will make things better is a radical change in attitude, in which people learn to recognize problems and try things out until they're solved. And to understand what a problem is, you've got to put customers first."

"A lean company is an outfit where *everybody contributes directly to adding value to customers*. Adding value starts by solving problems. How do you get there? Start by making all your managers spend as much time as possible solving customer problems and eliminating waste as they fight fires and organize the problem-solving in their areas. Then you need to convince all your operators to contribute their ideas and suggestions so that the company is using their heads as well as their hands. And you need to do all of this before the customers pull out or the automotive market slides even lower, before materials inflation puts us out of business, before the banks call in the loans or increase interest rates, and before the board kicks me out of this job. Simple really. Not easy, but simple."

"Wow."

"So, here, I've explained," Jenkinson said, sounding amused. "Let's test your theory. You suggested that I need to do more explaining. Well, I just did. Does it help?"

"Yes," Ward said uncertainly, and added, "and no."

"There you go. What's the point of explaining? One only learns by doing."

"It does help in one way," Ward ventured. "It helps to feel that you know what you're doing. I mean, even if I don't get it all … it's good to know there's a plan."

It sounded good, but he still worried about Coleman's comment that Jenkinson was taking program responsibility away from sales and placing it in engineering. Just as with cutting the quality department in Neuhof, the man seemed to have a strange way of putting customers first. Ward had always heard Alnext's honchos claim that "customers came first," Sanders in particular. What that usually meant is accepting any kind of crazy request and blaming production for not delivering. Jenkinson seemed to have a different take on the phrase. What Ward understood was to solve existing customer problems or problems for the next step in the process rather than imagine extravagant solutions to vague customer wishes. One more troubling notion he needed to think through.

"In any case," Jenkinson said, switching gears and turning to face Ward directly. "I'm sure you didn't drive all the way here to hear me pontificate about lean. What did you want to talk about?"

"Ah," hesitated Ward. "How should I put it?"

"Just shoot."

"Now, then. Lowell Coleman says you believe you are wrong half of the time. Is that right?"

"He said that, did he?" chuckled the CEO.

"Indeed."

"The trouble is knowing which half," he laughed. "But that's right. This is a core assumption of lean: No matter how confident we sound, we are all wrong at least half the time. The only way of knowing is by testing our beliefs, our hypothesis. This is nothing more than basic scientific thinking. Theories must be backed by empirical evidence. What makes you ask?"

"How can I convince you that you're wrong about closing the plant?" asked Ward.

"Ah," Jenkinson sighed, and then fell silent.

Ward took the slip road to the airport terminal while his passenger said nothing, and he worried again he might have overstepped the line.

Eventually he pulled the car into the passenger dropoff lane and cut the engine. Jenkinson just sat there, in no hurry to get out, mouth pursed in deep thought.

"What's the plant's problem?" he eventually asked.

"You told me. It's not making any money right now and you don't know how to put any new products in it."

"And I've got overcapacity across the company," completed Jenkinson. "So what's the plant's problem?"

"Its quality reputation is not good enough to earn the right to produce more parts for the company, and its operating costs are too high to run it as a second-tier job shop. I can see that. But I can fix it. I just need some time. And some help."

To Ward's surprise, this actually drew a smile from the man. Not a put-down sneer, but more of a genuine, somewhat wistful grin.

"Andy," he said looking straight at him. "*You* are the help. *You* are the plant manager. *You* are all the help the plant needs. There is no cavalry to the rescue. We have no cavalry. The plant's got *you*—and that's it."

"What about time?" asked Ward, taken aback by the man's sudden intensity.

"Here's the deal," Jenkinson replied, after another pause. "People who know Europe better than I do tell me that closing a plant in France takes time and requires a lot of administrative work. Convince me that you're working seriously at coming up with a feasible plan to shut the place down, and I'll be willing to listen to alternatives. For starters, fix your quality problem. No more customer complaints. No more missed deliveries. If you can do that, it might not save you, but it'll buy you some time. And sometimes, miracles can happen if you survive long enough.

"Remember," he added with another slow grin, "80 percent of success is showing up. You showed up today. Now show me results."

Put customers first by getting line management to own and fix quality and delivery problems. As compared to the current approach of relying on job descriptions, systems, and procedures, this definitely sounded like a shock to the system. Maybe it was exactly what Ward needed to stir things up at the plant. He also realized he'd have to start with the obvious: immediate, concrete complaints rather than some abstract notion of "customer satisfaction." Delivering on-time, defect-free products sounded like a pragmatic place to get started, as opposed to whimsical notions of what "customers" in the abstract would like in absolutes. The next process is the customer. Indeed.

Ward felt both reassured (slightly) and more worried (enormously) by his chat with the boss. He realized that he had to do something drastic. Otherwise the same causes would lead to the same results, and Jenkinson would not tolerate failure for long. To be sure, this would mean changing a lot of minds, starting with his own, he thought gloomily. Ward had never considered lean to be a management issue. It always struck him as a useful operations method. He'd always assumed that his management was basically sound, and that lean techniques reinforced this by smart cost-cutting. Disturbingly, Jenkinson seemed to think the entire management approach needed to be questioned. Probably the most startling takeaway from this conversation was the implied challenge thrown down by this way of seeing lean. Ward would have to rethink fundamentally his whole approach to everything that every person did in the plant in order to start building the kind of management in which everyone could contribute directly to adding value for customers.

To save the plant, Ward concluded sarcastically, he only needed to completely revolutionize its management approach as well as fighting the 1,001 daily fires. A walk in the park.

He was not surprised to see the light on in the old stone stables on the left side of the farmhouse. The house and adjacent barn were the best of what remained of the old fortified farm, with two other buildings linked by a ruined wall on the other side of a central pond. Over the years, Claire's father had kept the barn more or less in shape to hold three stalls, where he kept a few horses apart from the main modern stables across the road.

As he turned the corner to park the car, the headlights painted Claire in stark light, standing by the first stall, brushing a dappled gray horse. She was grooming Pagui, an aged hunter who had been her favorite show jumper when she'd been a young girl.

"Hey."

"Hey yourself," she answered with a quick, anxious smile. "How did it go?"

"I'm not sure," hesitated Ward. "Not at all what I expected."

Pagui nickered and nuzzled her back, eliciting an automatic slap. Whenever she turned her back on him, he had the habit of butting his forehead between her shoulder blades.

"I've been thinking about it," she said, brushing away a stray lock of dark hair with the back of her hand. "All of this. We can do without, you know. It's not our life. We can move. Do something else."

He saw her involuntarily shudder in the dim light as she actually voiced the thought out loud, trying to put a brave front on it all. Malancourt had become their joint passion, their impossible dream, and simply hearing her mentioning the possibility of defeat broke his heart.

"Remember when you used to kid me about all these 'just so' stories I told to liven up my presentations?"

"Some of them were awful," she smiled.

"Remember the one from Herodotus, the old Greek guy?"

"The one about the thief and the horse?"

"Yes, just before being executed, the thief makes a bargain with the king. In one year he will teach the king's favorite horse to sing. The other prisoners all laugh at him—how can he teach a horse to sing? No one can. 'Well,' the thief replies, 'I've got a year, and who knows what might happen in that time? The king might die, the horse might die, and—perhaps the horse will learn to sing.'"

"Will you sing for me, Pagui?" she laughed, stroking the old warhorse's forehead.

"That's how I feel now. I think I've gained some time, so who knows what might happen? Jenkinson might leave, the plant might get sold again, or, perhaps, I'll manage to get it lean!"

Chapter Two

EVERYBODY, EVERY DAY

It took all of five minutes back at the plant to do away with Andrew Ward's post-holiday glow. That's when he was told of the accident that had occurred while he was away. And suddenly all warm memories of sun, sea, and shining white houses perched improbably on the hilltops of the Greek islands melted away into the noise and smell of the factory.

It was late September, and Ward had just returned to work after a week of holiday with his family. They chose September over August, the traditional French holiday, for two reasons. First, August was gorgeous at the farm. Most patrons of the riding club were away in August, but horses still needed to be fed and cared for. The other was that Ward had gambled a sizeable chunk of cash on the major overhaul of two of his presses. So while the plant usually shut down for two weeks in August, a mix-up with customer demands forced them to keep certain products running. This mini-crisis turned out to be a small gift, for it gave Ward an excuse to continue the work of the past months and finish the progressive overhaul of the main equipment. The slower pace of work enabled him to actually enjoy taking the time with the maintenance team to learn more about the machines. The only drawback had been that since most key people took their holiday at this time, Ward had to deal with a crew of mostly unsupervised temps in the shop. Ward had left for Greece delighted to recharge his batteries, but had worried about the quality level resulting from the undertrained temps. Sure enough, customer complaints about quality had been building up during his absence.

The relaxing time had given him time to steel himself mentally for his return to the siege situation caused by his boss's impossible demands. Since Jenkinson's visit, he had never worked so hard in his life. It was a constant struggle keeping up with all the changes he had called for while wrestling internally with fits of self-doubt. Every trip to the shop floor was a new adventure. Ward would be faced with yet another problem needing a fix. And he usually had no clue where to start.

As he walked down the steps from the management offices, he swore to himself again that he would move all managers adjacent to production. The plant extended through three halls. The first one housed the injection-molding presses, some of them with a few assembly stations attached. The second hall had mostly assembly cells, and the third hall was dedicated to storage and loading docks. In the first hall, presses were neatly aligned on both sides of a central alley, with small tonnage and maintenance areas on the left side, and the larger machines on the right. Ward frowned as he passed the first high-tonnage press, which was standing idle. He couldn't recall whether the production plan called for it to be running or not. Instead of losing time on this distraction, he chose instead to find Mathilde Régnier, the operator who had been hurt last week. She was supposed to be back at work that day. He vaguely remembered her as one of the younger employees working in the press shop, a shy, hard-working woman he rarely dealt with and who was never any trouble.

Jenkinson's marching orders still stung, but Ward was determined to follow them as literally as possible, figuring that he had nothing much to lose. It couldn't hurt kissing up to the man who determined the future of his plant. And, who knows, maybe some of his "advice" could actually help. Ward launched "Operation Suckup" by asking the supervisors to warn him first thing after any accident. Next he e-mailed Jenkinson the moment there was any accident that was bad enough to account for lost time or keep an employee from returning to work within the shift. Each time he did so Ward got a Blackberry message within 24 hours, with the same deceptively simple question: Why did this happen? The first few times, Ward couldn't reply immediately and had to fish for answers from his own management team. Frustrated by this approach, he began to conduct the interviews and do the accident analysis himself.

To his amazement, their main tracking measure, the number of consecutive days without a lost-time accident, improved twofold immediately. Ward was delighted to realize these gains, though he knew there were still too many incidents. He also was puzzled over why the performance had soared so quickly—until the human resources manager, Jean-Pierre Deloin, cynically commented that the measure improved because there were no more Monday morning accidents. When Ward had asked him to explain what "Monday morning accidents" were, Deloin suggested that a pulled muscle first thing Monday morning following a local football match on Sunday evening was, perhaps, not so accidental. He would not say more, but Ward understood that when people hurt themselves during the weekend, they'd declare it as a work accident on Monday morning. This was exactly the kind of sly innuendo and jaundiced worldview that Ward found irritating and counterproductive, but he had to admit that the figures bore it out. Since he had personally been conducting the inquiry into each accident, Monday mornings had become almost accident-free.

Ward could not bring himself to like Deloin, with whom he spent many hours wading through the administrative and legal requirements of a credible timetable to shut a site in France. Deloin was a short, tubby man in his late 50s, with a face like a wrinkled apple. He had sparse white hair, a white beard, yet no moustache—like an ancient mariner, thought Ward. The man was a skilled survivor. He had started his career nearby, working for another company in a neighboring plant. That plant had closed long ago, and after a series of restructurings and acquisitions his former employer had become part of the U.S.-based group Alnext. In the heyday of la Française de Plasturgie, Deloin had moved up the corporate ladder methodically, becoming second-in-command to the group HR director. Dodging the witchhunt that followed the acquisition by Alnext, he wisely took the job of Vaudon HR manager. There he found a kindred spirit in Jean Blanchet, the ex-plant manager, and together they had maneuvered tirelessly to keep Vaudon open while its sister plants were closed, one after the other.

Deloin had accepted Ward's nomination as plant manager with world-weary skepticism, and mostly kept his thoughts to himself. He did the job with minimal fuss and occasional acerbic comments about the beyond-belief stupidity of the universe, capitalism, management, and plant managers, though not always in that order. Ward had to admit he had never caught the man being forthrightly obstructive. In fact, Deloin's knowledge and experience were invaluable. He had a lifetime's practice in dealing with the fractious French unions, the yearly ritual strike, and the constant strain of a working culture in which every negotiation started with conflict rather than discussion. Ward still got surprised by the French tendency to start with a show of force and then back down toward a compromise, rather than simply try to talk it through upfront. In the beginning, this had really thrown him. Indeed, three years ago, Ward's promotion to plant manager had been duly greeted by a general strike, which Deloin had handled deftly, compensating for many of Ward's own beginner's mistakes, with long-suffering and all-knowing little smiles that grated on Ward's nerves. Yet, in the course of the dispute, they'd hammered out something of a working relationship, and Ward had learned to take the other man's side comments at face value.

Ward was depressed by Deloin's knack of always suspecting the worst in people. In this particular instance, he knew that nobody could think poorly about Régnier. She was a fresh-faced woman with curly brown hair and an open, toothy smile. She had been working afternoon shifts at the end of the hall in one of the massive, 2,000-ton presses. Ward had asked to be called when the mold was being changed. He wanted to observe Mathilde's normal cycle of trimming and packing the parts coming off from the press. As two setters used the overhead crane to lift the large metal cube of the mold out of the press, Régnier swept up fallen cores and plastic dust from the area around the press.

"Hello, *Mademoiselle* Régnier," he called. "Are you all right?"

"Oh, *M'sieur* Andy," she answered, blushing slightly. "It's *Madame* Weber, now. I just got married."

"Ah, congratulations, Mathilde," Ward said, kicking himself—he'd known that, having signed the company check for a wedding present. It seemed to him time spent on the shop floor only opened up the number of opportunities to make a fool of himself, what with all the things he should have known and, evidently, didn't. He felt he lived with his foot in his mouth these days. "Can you tell me what happened last week?"

"Oh, it was such a stupid accident, *M'sieur* Andy," she answered sheepishly. "Completely my fault. I was distracted and stepped in front of a moving forklift. Like this."

Along the wide alley dividing the press hall a steady stream of forklifts were picking up containers of finished parts or dropping off pallets of components. Within this area a narrow strip of faded green paint signaled a pedestrian alley. Ward could immediately see how the proximity to the operator's station made it so easy to back into the path of a lift truck.

"The driver honked," she continued, embarrassed, "and I stepped back. But I stumbled and fell …," she hesitated, "flat on my bum."

"Ouch," he said, trying to keep a straight face as he visualized the scene. "Must have hurt a lot." Accidents are stupid by nature, and she could have injured herself seriously, either by being hit by the truck or by the fall.

"Oh, yes," she nodded emphatically. "The nurse feared I'd broken my tailbone, and I had to go to the hospital and have x-rays and so on. They said I'd be fine, but it would be painful for a while."

"I'm sorry to hear that. But what made you walk into the alley without looking?"

"Oh, I'm so sorry. I don't know what I was thinking. I was so preoccupied, you see?"

Although perfectly fluent in French, and having lived among the natives for years, Ward still felt like a fish out of water when it came to casual chitchat. The French were so bloody difficult and contrary that he never knew when compassion was going to be interpreted as patronizing, friendly curiosity as an invasion of privacy, or, on the contrary, tact seen as aloofness. He was about to extricate himself with a "carry on," when she jumped the gun anxiously.

"*M'sieur* Andy, may I ask you a question?"

"Certainly. Anything."

"Is it true that the plant is going to close?"

He nearly did a double take, but had the presence of mind to frown and answer "No! Absolutely not!" with as much certainty as he could muster. "Where did you get that idea?"

"At the bank. They told me the plant would close soon."

"At the *bank?*" he exclaimed, totally bewildered now.

"Yes, sir," she said, wincing, probably thinking she'd talked too much. Social relations in the plant were not bad per se, but private conversations with the plant manager on the shop floor were definitely unusual. "You see, my husband and I, we went to the bank. There's this nice housing project in a village a few miles out of town, and we'd like a home of our own, now that we're married."

"Sure. Great idea."

"The man at the bank would not let us have the loan," she spoke softly, her face flushing. "He said that our income was too low. And, more importantly, he said our status was too uncertain to qualify. 'Uncertain?' I asked. 'I work at the Vaudon plant,' I tell him. 'Everyone knows it's going to close soon,' he says. 'No guarantee,' he adds. So is it true?"

"It is not true," repeated Ward guiltily. "We have to work hard, but there are no plans that I know of to close the plant," he lied. "Is that the bank on the main square, next to the Tabac?"

"Oh, yes. I think that's why I was so preoccupied, you see?"

The internal phone he carried on his belt buzzed as he was furiously trying to think of an adequate response.

"Andrew," said Anne-Marie, the management team's assistant, "Philip Jenkinson is on the phone—do you want to take him now?"

"Yes, transfer him in just a second, please." To Mathilde, he apologized. "Mathilde, I've got the CEO on the line, I need to take this call—but we'll talk again, right?"

She nodded without saying anything as he rushed away, her face blank as she returned to her sweeping. "What did I miss now?" muttered Ward to himself, as he told the assistant to put Jenkinson on the line.

"Andy? How are you?"

"Yes, I know," he answered resignedly. "This is the second lost-time accident this month. I was just carrying out the analysis."

"Ah," paused Jenkinson, making Ward realize he was probably not calling for that at all. "The woman who fell, right? What happened?"

"She says she was distracted, and walked into the path of a forklift. The guy saw her in time and honked, and she took a step back, lost her balance, and fell on her tailbone. Must have hurt like hell. They had to send her for x-rays at the hospital."

"So what's the root cause?"

"Hell, I don't know! Not enough training? I thought about putting physical barriers between the machine area and the alley. But, well, then we would run into all sorts of problems getting the containers in and out of the zones."

"Come on, what was the proximate cause of the accident?"

Bollocks! Ward hated when his boss went into these didactic modes. He didn't need Jenkinson's help to feel stupid most of the time. He did quite well on his own.

"What's the but-for cause?" insisted Jenkinson "But for that ... she would not have fallen."

"Her distraction?"

"Okay, that's one, but pretty fuzzy. What else?"

"Uh—the forklift?"

"You got it. Forklifts running around within working areas—what are you thinking about?"

"You mean, no forklifts in the plant?"

"Only in clear, designated areas, of course. Not where you've got plenty of people working and walking along the aisle."

No forklifts?

"Ah, I see," mumbled Ward, although he clearly did not.

"I wasn't calling about that," Jenkinson said. I've got people asking for your scalp here."

What now? Ward thought, prepared for the worst.

"First, we've got PSA screaming bloody murder about a washer problem in a gearbox."

"What?"

"Yeah. Apparently, there are two diameters for the washers. You guys sent them the wrong ones or the wrong label or something, and they installed them without noticing. They found out at final testing, when some cars were already on the park. So they had to go and look for all the cars with washers from this batch, and get back into the gearbox. A real mess. Must've ticked off someone really high up, because they called me directly."

"Jeez, sorry about that!" said Ward feebly.

"Okay. You'll obviously have to go and find out what happened. I'm not sure why PSA went straight to me before you heard anything about it."

"We do have a complaint from them this month, but it's about scratches on an engine cover part. They claim that is a visible part, but in our specs we've got it as a functional part and without the same requirements as a part that can be seen. We're still arguing about it, but it doesn't seem like too big a problem."

"Have you gone and visited the customer line about it?"

"Ah, not yet," Ward winced. Jenkinson really cared about these followup visits for quality complaints. And of course with everything else going on he had not made the time for this.

"Andy, listen carefully," Jenkinson said slowly, in his annoying way of talking as if you were rather dim. "Doing the visits is about understanding the quality issues and developing a *relationship* with your customers. It's about getting to know someone in the customer plant who'll bother to give you a call when there's a problem. Nobody should learn about disasters from their CEO. Got it?"

"Got it," he sighed. He had walked back to his office and was now feeling a powerful urge to simply lay his head on his desk.

"But that's not all. Finance is pissed off with you as well. They say that you've got large, unexplained expenditures in August. And so their projections are off for Europe. Care to let me know what's going on?"

This time Ward had prepared himself.

"I'm still on budget, though."

"I didn't say you weren't. I just want to understand."

"Before we get to that, have you seen that we've cut the cost of nonquality by half in three months? We went from 3 percent of sales down to 1.5 percent. That's about half the ppms."

"Yes, I've seen. You've been working very hard to get these results."

"Second, we've still got the parts the customer wanted us to transfer to his Romanian supplier. Apparently, they haven't succeeded at making the parts right yet, so we're still producing seven days a week. It's going to cause us big problems. The demand is so high that we haven't had time to do any proper mold maintenance. So far, our sales are beating projections with this extra volume but sooner or later we're going to hit the wall."

"Andy, that's fine. Your sales are holding, and you have reduced your nonquality costs. That's very good. Stop beating about the bush: what about these expenditures?"

"I changed the screws on two presses this summer," Ward confessed.

"That costs money," replied Jenkinson noncommittally.

"Yes. We had known for years that two of our main presses were shot, and we'd put the investment request in the budget year after year, but you know how it has always been with Alnext. We kept being refused. And when our quality problems became such a high priority over the summer, I just felt that we would never make real progress until we dealt with this head-on. So I just signed for it."

"Why not tell me about it first?"

"Yes …," Ward hesitated. "I should have. But I know what you would have said."

"Which would be?"

"No investment. *Kaizen* first. And motion *kaizen* before equipment *kaizen*."

Unexpectedly, Jenkinson laughed at that—his long chuckle coming through the line as clearly as if he'd been standing right there in the room.

"I probably would. But give me some credit, man. I might have said 'Yes.'"

"Hell, Phil, you know how it is," Ward exclaimed, suddenly venting his frustration. "Plants are supposed to be autonomous, but the plant manager has got his hands and feet so tied up that he can't buy a bag of peanuts without having to clear it with corporate first."

"We're not talking peanuts in this case, we're looking at some serious money."

"I know, I know, I've spent most of what I've regained from the Romanian stuff and the reduction of nonquality costs. I realize that. As I told you before, I'm going to go down fighting, and I really believed this needed to be done."

"Okay," said Jenkinson after a long, uncomfortable pause. "I'll cover for you. Just this once, however. Please don't do this again: talk to me first. You've created more of a political problem than you know, and I've got enough on my plate already without needing you to add to the list."

Ward hoped his deep exhalation didn't sound as loud over the phone as it did to his own ears. He hadn't realized he'd been holding his breath all the way through the blank in the conversation.

"Now for the real work," Jenkinson continued. "I am serious about *kaizen* before investment. Very serious about it, indeed. In fact, I believe that if we were good enough we should never have to reinvest money on existing processes. Investment should be reserved for new products and new installations. Your job is to keep existing machines and tools running at top level through *kaizen*. Are you clear on that?"

"No investment on existing processes. Results through *kaizen*. I understand the words, and see where you want to go, but I have no idea of how to do this. How can you run old equipment *and* reduce nonquality without reinvesting?"

"It's hard," agreed Jenkinson. "To start with, I want you to make a persuasive case for changing these two injection screws. Not rhetoric, mind you. I want clear before and after data."

"I can try, but what's the point?"

"Learning," replied Jenkinson tersely. "I don't mind mistakes so much if you draw the right lessons from them. Now, I'm not saying that investing in rehabbing your presses is a mistake, but the way you went about it certainly is. So I want a clear *PDCA cycle*."

"*Plan, do, check, act?*"

"Correct. Look, you've planned this, right? Then you've gone and done it—which is to say you bought and installed the parts, yes? Now, I expect a convincing *check*. That will enable us together to draw the proper conclusions when it comes to *act*."

"You mean regarding the other presses?"

"Yes. Let's consider you're changing the screws on two presses is an experiment. The deeper question is: What conclusions do you draw from this about every other press. Also, rather than '*act*,' I often feel '*adjust*' is a better word. If you didn't get the results you hoped for on these two presses, how are you going to adjust your action in order to reach your target. Andy, you need to learn from this!" he emphasized. "The clock is ticking, and *you need to learn*."

"Let's take a step back," Jenkinson continued. "What is your main problem now?"

"My main problem?" sighed Ward. "Where to start?"

"You say you've lowered nonquality costs, correct? Listen to me, that doesn't mean squat. What is the cost of a customer complaint? A few percentage points of sales? Or a whole new program that goes to the competition! The question is, 'Are you producing fewer bad parts?'"

"To some extent," he agreed cautiously, taken aback at the man's sudden outburst. "We're also throwing away fewer good parts."

"How so?"

"Well, when we started looking into the red bins seriously and counting everything, our ppms first went through the roof. We realized many good parts were thrown away as bad. Operators were being overcautious. Then we also fixed a number of obvious problems. I believe we've tackled 167 actions in the first month alone. Maintenance and engineering are still working full time at this, which will cause problems later on because we've completely dropped planned maintenance."

"Okay. But you still have quite a few customer complaints."

"Yes, this is very frustrating. We have fewer customer ppms, that's for sure, and fewer complaints as well, but the effect is far less noticeable. I'm not sure I understand why. There are fewer bad parts in the system, but far too many still reach customers. I'll admit to being stumped here."

"What about on-time delivery? Reports show that it's increasing."

"I've been very brutal about this. I asked logistics to prepare enough parts in advance for an entire shift to have what they need for shipping and to keep a list of missing parts. Doing it this way, we have one entire shift to try to catch up on a late item. As long as it's not a missing supplier component, we usually can do it."

"But you've increased your finished-goods' inventory."

"Yes, there is that."

"So, let's see if I understand," Jenkinson said slowly. "You've reduced the waste of bad parts to some degree, but reinvested these savings into upgrading presses. And you've improved customer service by increasing finished-product stock, am I right?"

"Oh, bloody hell!" exclaimed Ward, unable to bottle up his frustration any longer. "We're doing what you asked! We're improving quality and service! Customers first. Isn't it what you said? What more do you want? Miracles?"

"Take it easy, Andy," growled Jenkinson. "I'm the guy who's trying to save you. You want to save your plant, you start by understanding what's wrong with it."

"You're right, I'm sorry," he backpedaled quickly. Survival lesson number one: don't swear at your CEO. "It gets so frustrating."

"Tell me about it."

Lesson two: don't whine either.

"So, what's your main problem now?"

"Obviously, although I'm improving quality, I am still sending defective parts to customers. And while our delivery has improved, this also has increased inventory, which means I haven't fixed the system. And costs are not significantly better."

"That's how I'd see it, yes. But what is your main *problem*?"

Holding back an impulse to reply "You," Ward snapped, "Phil, I don't know." Trying to calm himself, he continued. "I wish I did, but I don't. I've got problems coming out of my ears, and I don't know how to be everywhere at once."

"Well, that does sound like a real problem," chuckled the CEO. "Okay, what's your main worry then?"

Ward had to think about this for a while.

"Well, we are improving several important things, but the cost of this effort is huge. The technical and maintenance guys have been knocking themselves out fixing quality issues, and, as a result, most of their daily work has had to take a backseat. We've seen impressive numbers in our initial scrap reduction, but we can't seem to produce more enduring results. I'm afraid that chasing after these targets at this pace will eventually burn everyone out—and that neglecting the scheduled maintenance will have terrible consequences sooner or later. I get the feeling I'm fixing the symptoms, not the system itself."

"Sounds likely," Jenkinson agreed, in a surprisingly cheerful tone.

"But I don't know how to do anything else," admitted Ward.

"Knowing that you don't know is half the battle," said Jenkinson, once more infuriatingly patronizing. "Try to figure it out. I'll be traveling to Frankfurt to conduct some *kaizen* events next month, so I'll stop at your plant and we'll discuss it."

No further investment in existing processes? Invest only in new products or processes? And still expect performance improvement from *kaizen* on current stuff? How can that be possible? Of course I had to invest in these presses, they were falling apart. The guy must be nuts, glowered Ward. My real problem is that my CEO is *loco*.

Ward sat vacantly at his desk after hanging up. Then he stood and walked to the window. It was a perfect September day out there, sunny without being stifling. What was he doing here? He should be out watching his neighbors in their tractors preparing the fields for the fall, or listening to the buzz of critters in the grass and frogs in the pond. Having a cold beer in his deck chair. Taking Charlie for a walk through the woods in the new backpack contraption they'd just bought. Jenkinson's call had taken the wind out of his sails. He thought he had been doing okay, improving both his quality and delivery, yet this call did no more than remind him how close he was to losing the plant, his job, and all that went with it.

Six months after Jenkinson's death sentence for the plant, he'd still not been told to carry out the closure plan, so he guessed that, overall, his time-winning strategy was working—by the skin of its teeth! It seemed like every other month something happened that could be construed as one more nail in the coffin. Fortunately, few of Jenkinson's fortnightly Friday morning calls were this bad. They rarely lasted more than 20 minutes, and Jenkinson would usually just ask "Why?" over and over without giving much guidance. In retrospect, Ward felt foolish for not getting clearance for the couple of hundred thousand dollars to refurbish the presses. But what the heck, he thought rebelliously. They intended to close the plant anyway, so why not spend some money. It's not like they weren't making progress.

Had he really been to Greece and back? At that moment it felt like his whole life was nothing but angry customers, defect rates, scheduling woes, carping bosses, and persistent rumors of the plant's imminent closure. Ward suddenly felt the need to pass some of the pain on to someone else.

"Anne-Marie," he asked his assistant on the phone, "could you please call the bank manager of the branch in town. I'd like to talk to him right away."

"*Monsieur* Ward," the call came back a few minutes later. "My name is Antoine Fritsch. I am the manager of the Vaudon branch. Your assistant tells me you wanted to talk to me. What can I do for you?"

"Thank you for calling me back, *Monsieur*. I'm Nexplas Automotive's plant manager. Can you clarify something for me? Has a Mathilde Régnier or Mathilde Weber come to your bank for a loan recently?"

"Ah, I'm sure that this is confidential information," answered the bureaucrat in an obsequious voice. "Is there a problem?"

"The problem is that someone at your bank refused this lady's loan on the basis that her job at the plant was not secure as the plant was scheduled for closure."

"*Monsieur*—"

"Let me finish. First of all, this plant is not closing. Second, as I'm sure you're aware, Vaudon is a small community, and I'd expect your personnel to be more circumspect. Third, I'd very much appreciate it

if you could personally check Ms. Régnier's loan application, and, if
you find the amount requested reasonable, I'd be grateful if the bank
could help her out."

"*Monsieur*," the bank manager answered, full of righteous outrage.
"This is purely a bank matter, and I fail to understand how you could
possibly see fit to influence us in such matters."

"Well," Ward answered, with as much spite as he could muster,
letting full rein to his anger, "as far as I know, our plant keeps its main
account at the regional branch of your bank. Changing banks is totally
at my discretion, and I'm sure that your central office would be most
displeased to hear that they've lost a major customer because of *your
personal failure* to please your customer, and committing an
indiscretion which could in fact trigger significant repercussions given
labor relations today."

Ward smiled wickedly at the hoarse breathing he heard across the
line. He pictured the man furiously balancing out the uniquely French
pleasure in denying a request with the administrative paranoia of
getting central branch involved. Ward was not a bully by nature, but
he had suffered more than his share of petty humiliations when first
settling in the region, and felt no guilt about passing today's baton of
misery to this poor man.

"Of course, *Monsieur*," the tight voice finally answered. "I'm sure
there has been a misunderstanding. I shall personally look into the
matter."

"I'm sure you'll find everything in order," Ward replied coldly.
"Please let my assistant know when Miss Mathilde Régnier—Weber
—when her request has been met favorably. Thank you for your help."

"Well," he reflected after hanging up, "I've done what I could.
Now let's hope we can keep the plant open!"

He tried to get his head around the fact that he'd been that close to
losing his job without ever being aware about it. Far as he was from
corporate, it was hard to know what was really going on. He'd have to
phone Lowell Coleman again to try to get a handle on things, but the

man hadn't warned him this time around either. Admittedly, he'd been away on vacation—but still ... after all the hard work he'd been doing these past months, he felt really let down. Still, he chided himself, no one said it'd be easy. Stiff upper lip and all that sort of thing, old chap. Take the beatings and keep going on. In any case, what had he done wrong?

Like an old movie flashback, Ward thought about the crucial meeting back in May, the day after his fateful trip to Frankfurt, when he had gathered his management team together. They knew Jenkinson's visit hadn't gone well, and Ward's absence the next day had fueled the rumor mill. For once, they had all turned up early in the meeting room, eschewing the customary 15-minute delay for tiered arrival. As he occasionally did, Ward felt proud to have such a good team, and prayed he would not let them all down. Malika Chadid, the recently appointed quality manager; Olivier Stigler, the production manager, with his affected semitinted glasses; Stéphane Amadieu, the young financial controller, the only one for whom suit and tie still seemed *de rigueur*; Carole Chandon, the feisty logistics manager, a pretty 30-something who constantly overcompensated for her looks by bullying anyone and anything; and Matthias Muller, the maintenance manager, a temperamental middle-aged man sporting really short gray hair and a neat goatee.

In Ward's opinion, Muller was one of the most competent people around the table, but also one of the hardest to manage, not a team player. Closing the circle around the U-shaped table arrangement was HR manager Deloin and Franck Bayard, the technical manager, a gifted engineer who thought he deserved better than being stuck in the back of beyond, but somehow was still there, year after year.

"The plan is to close the plant," Ward had announced.

"But we still have a chance to prove ourselves worthy of keeping it open," he'd explained with raised hands, forestalling their various reactions of disgust and dismay. "Before we go any further about what was said with the CEO, I'd first like to hear your thoughts about why he considers the plant has no future."

They'd looked at each other, at a loss for words, wondering who'd go first.

"It's the damn pension funds," Muller reacted vehemently, crossing his arms aggressively on the table, and falling back to his customary rant against profiteering financiers. "It's all about profit, profit, profit."

"We're not cost-efficient enough?" asked Amadieu.

"Profitability is part of the problem," agreed Ward grimly. "But only part. Why would they close the plant, not simply downsize it?"

"What is there to downsize?" grated the HR manager, with a cynical grin. "They've been downsizing for years, we're all that's left. First you cut the fat, then into the muscle."

"We do have more presses than we need," pitched in Chadid, her usually cheerful voice now sounding somber.

"No new products!" exclaimed Bayard. "We're losing volume as the programs end or as the vehicles don't sell, and we've got no new products to compensate. My team's been twiddling its thumbs for the best part of this year. Without new products, we're as good as shut anyhow. The bastards send it all to Poland and CZ. Or even to Neuhof. We get nothing," he concluded bitterly.

"That's right," agreed Ward, trying to read the mood of the room and their individual reactions. Would they rise to the occasion or collapse and blame their circumstances? "We get no new products. Why?"

"Not cost competitive," muttered production manager Stigler, shifting uneasily in his cheap seat. "We know we're too expensive. And it's not going to get better as we're not getting any investment."

"Probably, but that's not the reason I was given."

"Give us a break, Andy. Don't do this!" burst out Chandon. "We're not children here, and we're not going to sit here waiting to stumble on what you want to hear. I, for one, have better things to do."

"You are bloody well going to sit here until you figure it out," Ward snapped back, with more force than usual, surprising them all. "If the future of the plant is not important enough for you to use a bit of your gray matter, we'd better pack up and go home. Think about it."

They just stared at him dumbly, astonished at his sudden vehemence, as if they'd never seen him before. He knew he was considered by some to be almost too easygoing, but he'd never seen the point of rubbing people the wrong way. Yet, for a bunch of bright individuals, they were being frustratingly slow.

"Listen to me carefully," he warned feelingly. "I'm not going through another day like I did with Jenkinson. From now on, he's in charge, whether you like it or not. I, for one, have no intention of seeing this plant shut. So we're going to do things *his* way and that's that. And his way is getting our heads out of the sand and trying to face up to the fact that we have *no new products coming*! So, I ask again, why?"

"Our quality stinks, obviously," chuckled Deloin unexpectedly in the deadly silence that had followed Ward's shouting. Peering at them over his glasses for effect, playing the wise old bird and looking it, too.

"How can you say that!"

"That's not true!" Chadid and Stigler cried simultaneously.

"Yes it is, *les enfants*," replied Deloin. "Of course it is. And we're not servicing our customers either."

Ward sat back, stunned, waiting for more.

"Don't act so surprised. You behave like you've never heard of the automotive industry. The Toyota plant in Valenciennes expects single digit or fewer ppms from their suppliers. And where are we? We're at 40 on good months. They expect better than 99 percent on-time delivery—we're lucky if we do 95 percent. How do we compare?"

"We're not supplying Toyota," replied Stigler sullenly.

"More's the pity. *They* sell cars. Remind me how the latest big hit from our customers is doing."

"Half the predicted volume," agreed Chandon thoughtfully.

"So let's sum up," continued the HR manager, as if he'd enjoyed rubbing it in. "We're too expensive for the French OEMs desperate for cost cuts right now. Our quality is not good enough for the Germans, and we don't deliver well enough for the Asians. Where does that leave us? You tell me. We're not getting a new product because we're not good enough *and* we're too expensive. That's all there is to it. If I were an OEM and had to accept the kind of quality and service we offer, I'd source from Romania. It's not going to be better, but at least it's going to be a lot cheaper."

"Jean-Pierre is right," emphasized Ward to his team, looking at them in the eye, one after the other. "Yes, it stinks. Yes, you don't like hearing it. I sure don't. But we've got to face it—we're not good enough to get more parts. We, you and I, have not been doing our job well enough to warrant the survival of the plant."

"How can we!" cried the technical manager in disgust. "We don't get a penny to invest."

"And we won't get a cent," Ward said. "Remember, their plan is to close us down. But, I'd hate to surrender without a fight. So here are the terms from the CEO. First, Jean-Pierre and I are to prepare a realistic timetable for closure. Don't bitch. It's got to be done. So that you will all know where we stand.

"Second, Jenkinson has dared me to dramatically improve both quality and service. If we can do this, he's agreed to find volume to put into this plant," Ward said, stretching the truth considerably. He knew himself to be a very poor liar. He needed to give them *something*!

"I can do my part easily enough," wheezed Deloin in the stretching silence, stroking his collar of beard thoughtfully, as if satisfied that, finally, his dark foretelling had come true. "Lord knows I've seen my share of site closures. So, boys and girls, tell me how are you going to do your part?"

They erupted in a flurry of conversations, sharing a common theme that without a serious injection of cash back into the plant, nothing much could be done.

"Enough!" bellowed Ward. "No more whining, no more 'It's not my fault.' If we work together, we can do it. I know we can. So here's what we're going to do:

"First, not a word of this conversation gets out of this room. The official take is that we need to improve service and quality dramatically to get new products. There is no point in burdening the operators with our own anxieties."

"And incompetencies," added Deloin snidely.

"Second," pursued Ward ignoring the older man, "we're going to do exactly what Jenkinson says, like it or not. The first step is red containers for nonconform parts in every cell."

"Oh, come on," complained Stigler. "We've tried that already with the Alnext Business System. It never worked."

"No," countered Ward. "*We* never made it work. We've used them as scrap bins, little wonder they fell into disuse. This time around we're going to do what it takes. Starting today, I want this management team to tour the red bins three times a day: midshift at 10 a.m., 4 p.m. and 3 a.m."

"3 a.m." scoffed the engineering manager. "You'll be coming in at nights, I suppose."

"Indeed, I will—I'm committing to being on the shop floor one night a week, and I'd appreciate if you did the same. Fine. I concede we have to work out a system for the night-shift review, but make sure you're there for the two during the day.

"What's more, before we regrind defective parts, I expect a daily detailed breakdown from your quality department."

"Do you mean you want us to count every bad part?" yelped the quality manager. Her expressive face looked aghast, as if he'd just asked for the moon.

"Every single bloody one!"

"Andy! You don't realize. I simply don't have the staff."

"Then drop anything else. And if it's the only thing the quality department does all day, so be it."

"But what about the quality systems and certifications?" she asked, distressed.

"Count first. We need to know exactly what our problems are, and if we don't change *now*, we're finished. So give me a count. If you're taking heat from corporate, let me know and I'll deal with it."

"Aha!" chortled the maintenance manager, slapping his hand on the table. "Good for you, lad. Finally we're talking some sense."

"Third," Ward added, "we need to figure out how to improve our on-time delivery. I have to admit, I haven't got any bright ideas there. Carole, think it over, and make a suggestion."

The meeting wound itself down quietly. Ward knew they were good people, and once they'd digested the news and gotten their heads around the challenge, he was confident they would deliver. They'd been used to him muddling through issues, mostly listening to them debate and argue. This time, he'd called the shots and that surprised them. His apparent determination to hang the systems and get on with the job had puzzled them. Systems were what they did. Making people apply systems was their job, wasn't it? He agreed with them that systems held the plant together, but in the short time he had to give Jenkinson what he wanted. Hang he might, but they'd take him to the scaffold kicking and screaming.

And now, in his office, Ward had to admit that, overall, they'd responded. They had some results to show for it. Chandon had come up with the idea of having all the parts for the trucks ready a shift in advance, and managed to put together a bit of code in the scheduling system that did that. It was painstaking, but she'd gotten logistics operators to physically check the availability of parts in the finished-good stores two shifts before loading, inserting missing parts in the next shift's plan. Chadid had attacked the quality question with her usual vigor, and installed plastic bags in the red bins. After the on-site analysis of what could be found in the bins during the daily review, the defects were collected once a shift, brought to the main meeting room, and tallied before being taken to regrind. They had implemented red-bin reviews immediately after that meeting, though since then the value of this practice had become harder to see. They had been surprised that the number of problems highlighted by the reviews soon vastly overloaded the plant's ability to resolve them. Maintenance and technical departments had rolled up their sleeves and worked like dogs, but still there seemed to be no end to the problems. As a result, they decided to concentrate on the easier, cheapest actions first, but over time, new issues emerged. For instance, it appeared that the amount of regrind in the mix of materials had a large impact on the quality of visible parts. The plant did not use its own regrind, but sold it to a third party. Unfortunately, the plant also had little control on the quality of incoming plastic granules—suppliers were the bailiwick of central purchasing in Neuhof.

Ward was a strong believer in five words he had picked up from a training course in his consultancy days: plan, organize, staff, influence, control. All in all, he felt these five wise men had held him in good stead. For instance, he'd gotten his staff together and they'd planned the red-bin reviews, organized how they would go about it, decided who would attend. At first, he had participated in most reviews to make sure they happened, and they'd gotten an incredible amount of small things to fix out of them. His take on management was to get the right people together, point them in the right direction, and let them get on with it. True, he mostly got the people he was given rather than those he chose, and direction was not always easy to pick, but on the whole he felt he'd done a pretty good job at running the plant.

So what was the problem? *What was the problem?* Ward mulled the question over as he drove home. Throughout dinner that evening, he barely listened to Claire telling him all about the mess she'd encountered upon their return from Greece. Her father had been back in charge during their week in the islands, and she really didn't see how he could have run a business all these years, considering the chaos he'd created in a few short days. What was the problem?

"The problem," he declared suddenly to his wife who, interrupted in mid-sentence, raised a disapproving eyebrow. "The problem is that what we're doing is simply not sustainable."

"What do you mean by that?" she asked kindly.

"Well," he stammered, suddenly aware he had not been paying attention to anything she'd been saying all evening, "we've improved our results, but not through a controlled process. We're not working smarter, we're working harder. And I don't think any of us can maintain this working rhythm in the long run."

She nodded, pouring him the last of a lovely wine her father had left them as a welcome-home present. Charlie had consented to go to sleep early. They had moved outside to have dinner on their front doorstep, watching the sun set far over the open fields. She savored these last golden evenings before the days got shorter and the rains came, announcing the long, bleak winter, and she minded how Andy seemed to bring work home more frequently these days.

On the other hand, she realized how desperate the situation seemed, and could not begrudge his efforts to fix things. She didn't know whether to be relieved or worried about seeing him so involved with the plant. She'd seen him stressed before, but never so deeply engaged with the plant that he could be physically present at home, yet still battling with his injection machines and assembly lines.

"We're more focused," he thought out loud, "but we're not doing anything different. Also, improving our customer service has in fact driven up our costs. In logistics, Carole has hired a temp per shift to help with her counting. She's also keeping more finished-goods inventory. In production, we're using people to do 100-percent checks whenever we have a doubt, which also means more temps. And we still can't seem to stop bad parts reaching customers. And the maintenance and technical guys are working their tails off."

"Is that bad?"

"Serves the engineers right," smiled Ward. "They haven't got any new project to work with, which is the problem in the first place. But it can't be good in the long-term. And the maintenance team is playing ball, but they've started grumbling. I wouldn't be surprised if we start seeing a big increase in sick days."

"So, what can you do?"

"I don't know," he answered miserably. "I really don't. We've done the best we know, but beyond that ... I hope that bloody Jenkinson's got some good advice when he comes. Did I tell you I almost got fired while we were in Greece?"

"Yes, baby, you did," she said, leaning against him and settling into his shoulder.

He sipped the last of the wine pensively. The past months had brought a curious mix of hope and discouragement. They had improved the situation—but this relatively small gain had come at a huge cost. It was like realizing that if you tried hard enough, you could change the course of the Titanic, but not enough to miss hitting the ice. Her hair smelled good and clean from her after-work shower and, as he breathed it in, he noticed the sweet scent of the dusk in the coolness of the rising dew. At long last, as he closed his eyes, he heard the pond frogs sing, and told himself this was the good life. Don't you forget it, matey.

"Listen, Andy," Chadid said barging into his office. "Am I supposed to do the red-bin reviews on my own?" she protested acidly.

"No, of course not. We agreed it would be quality, production, maintenance, and engineering at the minimum. Is there a problem?"

"Yes. No one's showing up, that's the problem," she answered crossly. Chadid was the only management appointment Ward had made himself, although it had clearly been a no-brainer. She was young, full of life, and brimming with contagious good humor, although God help them all when she got into one of her occasional black moods. She was bright, conscientious, and hard-working. She was also great fun, with boisterous laughter that made even the most hardened individuals smile. The daughter of a Paris subway driver, she had grown up in a tough area in the outskirts of Paris. She'd done well at school, and had gone to study engineering at Metz University. She'd been hired as a quality technician by Ward's predecessor, and when the former quality manager had retired he'd given her the job, passing over two people who thought they'd deserved the promotion. She was excellent with customers, who usually liked her, and didn't beat her up as much as the previous guy.

"Let's go and find them," sighed Ward. Ever since they began holding the red-bin reviews regularly, attendance had been an issue. The moment he let the pressure drop, people stopped attending. It was not becoming part of the plant culture fast, that was for sure.

Ward had always felt lucky with the team he had inherited from his predecessor. Stigler, the production manager, was from the mountainous Vosges region farther to the east, and had ended up in Vaudon when Alnext had closed the plant where he had been module manager. While he had been bitterly disappointed when Ward was named plant manager after being there for barely more than a year, Stigler finally accepted the appointment. He often kidded Ward about his fabled corporate contacts (unfortunately not as numerous as all that), and seemed, ultimately, reconciled to wait for Ward to move on to a new top job. He came in early and left late, and kept things together. He was good in a crisis, and liked nothing better than to play hero and save the day, which *had* saved Ward's bacon a number of times. They had never been bosom buddies, but they got along fine.

They found Stigler in his office, in deep discussion with Chandon, the logistics manager. Stigler gave them one look and immediately knew what this was about.

"Yeah, I know, red-bin time," he said irritably. "Do we really have to do this every day? We always see the same things. Right now Carole and I really need to solve this rescheduling problem. Saarlouis is asking for 30 percent more parts over the next couple of pickups, and we haven't got enough in stock."

"You didn't see it coming?" asked Ward, shaking Chandon's hand.

"As if we could," she scoffed. "Their demand is all over the place."

"And what about safety stock?"

"That's what we were looking at," replied the production manager. "How much we've got, and how we can reconstitute it."

"I don't like using safety stock for cases like that," frowned Chandon. "Safety should be for safety." Although they'd been working together for years, Chandon was still a mystery to Ward. She kept herself apart from the rest of the team. She lived locally and returned home for lunch. She was intensely private and had no known close friends at work. Ward knew almost nothing of her private life beyond the fact that her parents lived in the area and that she was divorced with a small child. She kept her desk in the logistics area, on the far side of the plant, and, to tell the truth, Ward rarely saw her other than at the obligatory management meetings.

"You do what you think is best," said Ward, "but now we really need Olivier for the red-bin review. Feel free to join, if you'd like."

"I think I'd better finish this," she answered tersely.

Ward never quite got used to how easy it was for the French to refuse any instruction that was not issued forcefully, in triplicate, and repeated at least thrice a day. As a kid, when his father had told him to "feel free" to do something, that usually meant now, no hesitations, no excuses. Here it definitely meant what it said: feel free.

Ward felt the most comfortable with his core team—the heads of production, quality, and finance. They often got together for lunch at a local dive. It didn't look like much but the food was good and the owners were friendly. He'd realized soon enough that what the four of them had in common was that they all were strangers to the very local town of Vaudon. The financial controller was the baby of the band. Straight out of business school, Amadieu was from the south of France.

Hiring him had been Blanchet's last decision before passing the reins to Ward. He had a sort of Jekyll and Hyde personality that could be a real laugh. At work, he was the perfect young exec, eager to learn his trade in order to step on to bigger and better things—quiet, careful, probably bored. In private he was talkative and brash. He saw himself as something of a ladies' man and both Stigler and Chadid took turns teasing the details of his escapades out of him. Ward couldn't tell whether any of it was true, but the combination of Stigler's needling and Chadid's risqué humor often had them in fits. Professionally, Ward prayed that the guy knew what he was doing, because he spent far too little time involved with the details of the financial reporting, which had grown exponentially more complicated during Alnext's tenure. He made a mental note to look into it more deeply. Jenkinson didn't appear to care much about numbers, but when crunch time came, it turned out that he knew the financials of the plant to the decimal.

Ward didn't know the rest of the management team as well as he knew his lunch buddies. The maintenance manager, Muller, had never shown any inclination to join them for lunch. Not an easy character at even the best of times, Muller gave Ward the impression that he looked down on the lot of them, with the kind of working-class reverse superiority that comes from having dealt with men and machines all one's life. As for the new continuous-improvement officer, he was a diffident young man. On several occasions they had invited him to join them, and he would occasionally come, but more often than not he had a sandwich at his desk. The HR manager, finally, the last remaining veteran of the previous manager's team, was also Vaudon's deputy mayor, and far more active in local politics than he was at work. Ward actually felt privileged to find him in his office and to be granted an occasional audience with his officialness. It irked him once in a while, but, all in all, the man was invaluable when it came to unraveling any tricky local entanglement. He always knew who to talk to and what to say. Overall, Vaudon had enjoyed a long stretch of relative social peace, mostly thanks to his experience and influence, as well as Ward's own innocence in these matters. Basically, he followed Deloin's lead on any thorny people issues.

Ward had never known whether Blanchet had approved of his appointment to plant manager. Blanchet had immediately taken him on as a deputy when Ward became continuous-improvement officer, and made a point of teaching him the basics of running a factory. He'd been both avuncular and distant, increasingly isolated in his own site as the old-timers were replaced by a much younger generation. For instance, he had maintained a separate dining room for management—essentially himself and Deloin—where he invited other members of the executive team. One of Ward's first actions as a plant manager had been to tear down that wall and enlarge the self-service cafeteria. He felt guilty about not taking more of his lunches with the rest of the troops, but he always felt uneasy there, never quite knowing how to react to the odd French mix of formality and informality. Blanchet had always maintained that keeping a proper distance with the frontline workers was essential to the plant manager's authority. "They'll never respect you if they don't fear you," had been his advice. Ward didn't believe in any of it—but still, he'd taken to lunching out most days. Besides, it was good for management teambuilding.

In the end, they managed to drag Muller into the red-bin review. Ward had laid down the law this time. The reviews were *compulsory*, was that clear? Now he was frustrated to find that most of the red-bin issues were familiar, and workers simply didn't have the time to deal with these matters—or they didn't know how to fix them. As a result, the review felt like an empty ritual, a pointless rehashing of old issues.

Ward had discussed this issue with Jenkinson during one of the regular phone calls the CEO had been adamant about continuing. "Yes, we see the same problems every day—so we tend to take them for granted," he'd explained. "Which is precisely why you need to keep the review every day. That way your people don't get used to living with problems without trying to solve them. Whatever you do, stick with it."

Ward had picked up a recurring theme on the calls, and felt he was being tested: Would he stay the course? He wasn't sure he shared Jenkinson's belief that getting people to confront the same problems every shift was the key to getting them to solve them. But he'd committed to it, so he was damned if he would let that particular practice slip. The more he thought about it, the more he felt he should force himself to check every day if the review was happening, or maybe, even, to participate in every single review. That felt like a bit of overkill, as he didn't want his people to feel he was breathing down their backs. But it might come to that yet.

"I'm Amaranta Woods," she said, extending a firm hand with a bright smile. "Most people call me 'Amy.'"

"Andrew Ward," he replied, shaking the offered hand. "Most people call me 'Andy.' He had not known what to expect, but whatever it had been, she wasn't it. Amy was a short, roundish woman with strong Latino features and a force of spirit that radiated out of her as if she had swallowed a 1,000-watt spotlight. She was oddly dressed for work, wearing a formal, visibly expensive, tailored suit jacket over a white blouse, jeans with a wide Western buckle of silver and turquoise, and battered safety shoes. He liked her immediately.

"Here's what that nice man over there gave me as I got out of the taxi," she said, handing over a bright yellow sheet with "SAVE VAUDON" written in large letters across the top. Sure enough, the union leader was standing at the gate handing out his photocopied leaflets to all comers. After a week or so, the bank's comment must have gone around and come home to roost. The only satisfaction Ward derived from this is that, according to Anne-Marie, Weber had gotten her loan.

"Union tract," he apologized. "I never read them," he commented, shrugging off the look she gave him. Then she smiled.

"Phil is really sorry he couldn't make it, so he sent me—I'm the consultant. Don't let me borrow your watch, I'll use it to tell you the time!"

"Yeah, he called. He's in China, right?"

"Oh brother, is he in it," she said easily, as he took her up the stairs to his office. "They're supposed to start production for GM at the end of the month, and, of course, they can't seem to produce a decent part. It's a total disaster." She concluded with a cheerful smile.

"You don't seem too concerned?" he asked cautiously.

"Oh, Phil will sort them out. He's an engineer at heart, that's what he's always been really good at. He thrives on this sort of thing."

"You've known him long?"

"You could say that!" she laughed, saying no more. Her laugh was high and clear, at odds with her curiously deep, throaty voice.

"Ah," Ward cleared his throat. "We weren't sure how this day would proceed, so we've not prepared anything special. How would you like to go about this? Do you want to meet the team? Do you want a presentation of the plant and what we do?"

"Let's do that later, shall we? Let's start with ..."

"A tour of the shop floor," he finished for her, grinning. Her good spirits were infectious.

"I'd love a cup of coffee though," she added impishly.

"Sure, sure," he coughed. "But it has to be from a machine, downstairs. We, ah, have no one making coffee up here."

"Fine with me! Lead on."

Ward nodded at the couple of technicians taking a coffee break in the rest area as Amy closed her eyes and sipped the scalding drink. "Ah, Europe," she said with a slow smile. "Even the coffee out of the machine tastes better than ours."

"You should go to Italy. Their espressos are tops."

"I'm stopping at the Torino plant before flying home. I'm looking forward to it."

He drank his own coffee without much enthusiasm, finding it dreadful and wondering what to do about this woman the CEO had sent to do ... what?

"Now," she said, her large black eyes staring intently at him. "Phil does apologize for not being here himself. He intended to lead a *kaizen* event in Neuhof, and then stop over here, but, anyhow, he tells me you've painted yourself into a corner. What's your side of the story?"

Taken aback, he tried to explain what they'd been doing. Amy listened with total concentration. When he had completed his tale, she asked whether she could observe one of the red-bin reviews.

"Sure," he readily agreed. "There's one at 10. In about 45 minutes."

"Perfect! Let's have a quick look at the shop, then. You wouldn't have a tool change going on right now?"

"Um, I don't know, let me check."

What was it about these people? Ward had been working so hard with the red bins, he'd been pretty certain he would be able to answer obvious questions without feeling like the incompetent blunderer he had looked to be in front of his CEO. Yet there he was, stumbling at her first detailed question. This was going to be another long and painful day.

And indeed, on the floor, she was as inquisitive and incisive as Jenkinson, although a lot nicer about it. They came upon two operators changing a tool on a 1,500-ton press. After asking Ward to introduce her to the two men, Amy smiled broadly at them and then observed them intensely. Ward spent the first 10 minutes trying not to cringe too visibly. His men spent most of this time walking away from the job in search of this or that, untangling jumbled parts, or simply standing idle waiting for their partner—on the other side of the large machine—to complete a task.

"I visited a Toyota factory recently," she said suddenly. "They had a 4,500-ton stamping press. Large as a house. On the side, they had an electronic display showing the changeover time: five to seven minutes. I asked them about it, and they said they had a quality circle working hard on getting the variation out of the change, so that they could be more consistently at five."

"Ah. But the whole installation is set up to make the changes easy, surely?"

"Oh, yes. Imagine the size of the mold—the size of a small truck. They're all on automatic tracks and so on. Actually, it takes them about 50 minutes just to prepare the change. But the point is that if they invest 10 percent of their press utilization in changes, they can run batch sizes of one hour of production. What are yours like?"

"We don't calculate batches like that, but some presses we change once a day, most once every couple of days. Some never."

"Picture the impact on the inventory," she said brightly.

Ward sighed. He knew that! Of course. Because of the cost in terms of loss of injection time and people, batch sizes had been calculated to balance out the cost of holding the inventory of parts. Few mold changes meant large inventories, but little time lost on changes. Conversely, as Ward understood, by reducing the time it took to change tools, you could reduce the batch size, and, thus, the inventory. In his days as a supply-chain consultant, he'd been to all the lean trainings, and had been told all about the SMED technique (*single-minute exchange of die*) aimed at reducing the changeover time, but he'd never considered it seriously in his own plant. Yet.

"The amazing thing is," she carried on, "that apparently Toyota was already changing tools with an average of 10 minutes back in the '70s! They'd even found an American company that built presses designed for quick changeover, which was going bust because this didn't interest anyone at the time, so they purchased all the machines available to be able to study them. Weird how we could be so blind. Let's have a look at the assembly cells, shall we?"

On the way to the assembly hall, she stopped to examine a mid-size press with exaggerated care. As Ward spotted the oil leaks, the dirty pipes, the mass of congealed plastic from the last purge laying on the top of the injection unit, he felt like a criminal whose car was about to be searched by the police. Amy spent a few minutes watching as the mold would open, the automatic hand come down and pick up the part, the hand move back up, and then close again to inject another part. Carefully, she laid her hand on the part just deposited on the moving carpet. Seeing the part was only tepid, she picked it up, looked at it carefully, and passed it to Ward without a word.

Ward gritted his teeth again. The trick to injection molding, he knew, was to get the molds to operate as quickly as possible so as to maximize the press's productivity. The mold's operation could be optimized at two levels. First, minimizing the "unused" open time of the mold needed to get the plastic part out, and, second, reducing the "effective" part of the cycle as the mold was locked closed. The shorter the closed time, the hotter the parts would come out. Mold closing time had a significant impact on the part's quality, and for the plastic to firm up they needed to cool off sufficiently before being extracted. Parts that came out too cool usually indicated that the mold's setting was not optimized, and productivity gains could be made. He didn't know whether this was just a show on her part to impress him, or whether she really knew her way around injection presses. Either way, he could see the mountain of work piling up.

Assembly was even worse. Operators were not organized in cells, rather they stood, or sat, in front of isolated automatic machines that added components to the base part. In some cases, the part would go straight to the customer after going through one machine, but in most cases the parts moved from one machine to the other, piling up work-in-process inventory between each machine.

Amy asked him to introduce her to one of the operators who was loading and unloading an automatic machine for assembling diesel filters. Then she just stood there and observed, without speaking, or looking his way. Just watching. Ward was anxious to move on. His mind was abuzz with all the things they had seen in the shop, and the million and one things waiting back at his office. Earlier that morning, Deloin had cornered him to suggest that if he wanted to try stunts as he'd done with the bank manager, he might want to go through him—this was a small town after all. Ward had shrugged him off. The loan had been accepted. He didn't give a damn about stepping on toes any more. All of this was whirling through his mind, and he almost danced with frustration, wanting to move on. But she just stood there. Finally, he forced himself to take a deep breath and try to see.

"You're looking for the seven wastes, aren't you?" he asked, just to say something.

"Yep. Look," she ticked them off on her fingers:

Overproduction: Is the lady producing too much or too soon? We can't know, because we can't see the *takt time* visualized anywhere.

Waiting: She loads the machine, and then waits for the cycle to finish before unloading the part and loading another one.

Conveyance: When a box is full, she has to carry it all the way around her station to place it on the pallet over there.

Overprocessing: I can see the parts that fail the test accumulating in the red bin. There seem to be a lot. I'd wager that many of them are false positives—they're rejected by the test machine but when you pass them again, they're found to be good. If that's the case, they're being tested twice instead of once.

Inventory: She's got more parts on hand than what she needs to get the job done.

Motion: Draw an imaginary square on the floor, and trace all the foot motion she goes through to pick up that last component. Then, draw another imaginary square in front of her, and look at all the hand motion she has to make in order to place the components in the machine. Finally, check all the eye movements.

Correction: The yellow bin over there is for rework, isn't it?"

"Blimey," blew up Ward. "If you had any idea of the problems we're dealing with! By the time we get to this level of detail, we'll be well ahead. I can't believe this!" he added in sheer frustration.

"That is why you fail," she pronounced in a strange voice.

He just stared at her.

"Oh, cheer up," she said brightly. "That was my best Yoda impression. You know? From *Star Wars?*"

He stared at her for half a second, and then had to laugh. She was right: There he was, in a French plant, being lectured by a Mexican cowgirl quoting *Star Wars*. Life could not get much weirder, could it?

"I mean it, though," she added with a wistful smile, "it's because you don't see the small stuff that you're stuck. That was Phil's hunch, at any rate, and I think he's right."

The red-bin review turned out to be no less embarrassing.

"Where the hell is Olivier?" he asked in French, after introducing Amy to the red-bin review team.

"Better things to do," answered Chadid with a hard-to-read shrug. One more issue, he noted bitterly. The production manager was missing more and more of the reviews, and the quality manager was bitching about it. He'd have to do something about this. Logistics had stopped attending the reviews, and now maintenance was turning up missing as well.

They were back in the press area, examining the scratches on a cylinder head cover. The team was arguing about the origin of the scratches. They looked at the process while the operator picked parts to place them on a large outgoing container. Eventually they concluded that there was nothing to stop the parts from falling off the conveyor where the automated arm places them after extracting them from the press. This led to a discussion about the kind of barrier to install to keep the parts from falling to the floor.

Amy had kept quiet until now, listening to Ward's translation of the discussion. "Can you translate for me?" she asked after a while.

"Sure, go ahead."

She picked up the part from the hands of the technical manager, and walked to the operator. She asked Ward to introduce her, and then asked the operator to show her what was wrong with the part.

Ward felt lucky this wasn't a temporary worker. Adrien Meyer had been with the plant a while, and knew his job. He was a tall, gaunt chap, with protruding blue eyes that gave him a constant hunted look, but, in fact, he was a steady man, who did the job carefully and with few gripes. He pointed to the scratches, and said that he thought they were caused by some parts falling off the workstation.

"And why do you think this happens?" she asked sweetly.

"Well," the tall man hesitated, looking nervously at the management team. His large eyes darted from one to the other, making him look more hunted than ever. "After a certain number of parts, I have to change the container. This one here. The forklift brings a new one, and takes the full one away, but I have to handle the change with the pallet jack over there, and it can take a bit of time. Sometimes, the parts pile on, and some fall. It doesn't happen often," he added quickly, "but it can happen."

"Thank you, sir," smiled Amy. Then turning to the management team, she added, "Now, why do the parts fall?"

"Because the operator is away from the workstation."

"But why?"

"Because he has to change the containers."

"And why is that?"

They all looked at each other, nonplussed. One had to change containers, surely?

"Because the containers are too large and difficult to handle," Ward finally said. "And the size of the containers are specified by the customer, so we can't change them easily."

"Okay. But, you could organize the area better," Amy suggested, grabbing Chadid's notebook. "And have the containers on mobile frames. Here, if you create a square area, you can have a full container for pickup here, one empty waiting there, and the one this gentleman is filling up right now, there. In that way, you minimize the container change operation."

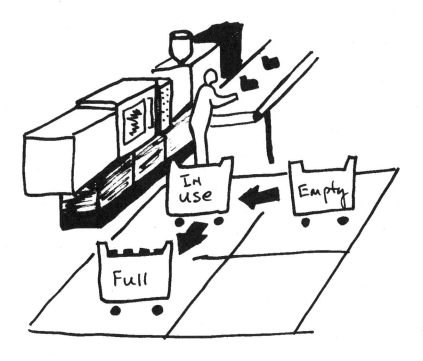

"But essentially, Andy's right. The main problem is that the containers are too large and difficult to handle by the operator."

"What was the real point I was making?" she asked Ward a bit later, as they followed the continuing red-bin review.

"Ask why five times?"

"Yes, but that's not it. Come on, what's the point I'm trying to make? Talk to the operator."

He stopped in his tracks and stared at her.

"Look at your team," she nodded toward the group surrounding the next red bin in the round.

"Just look at them! They're all around the red bin, discussing the parts, with their backs turned on the operator! They haven't talked to the operator once!" She exclaimed, sounding uncharacteristically angry.

"These guys spend their working life looking at and handling the parts. They know a good deal more about what happens to the parts than you ever will. They've got brains, you know?"

The two of them continued this discussion over lunch in the company meeting room.

"You've been having a hard time with the union?" she asked as they munched on ham and cheese sandwiches. The bread at least was good.

"Not really," he answered, chewing. "They collared me after Phil's visit, which was fair enough. I told them that the real problem was getting new products into the plant. They conceded that our quality and service levels were not really competitive, so the threat more or less blew over. There was a silly incident recently, so it started the fire burning again, but nothing too serious. I hope," he concluded, showing his crossed fingers.

"If I know Phil, a strike would be more than enough reason to close the plant," she shrugged, making Ward wince. "Believe it, he'd do it—whatever the cost."

"Tell me something," he said, trying to steer the conversation away from that touchy subject. "You've been conducting *kaizen* events in Neuhof, yes? Instead of Phil? Does he do that habitually?"

"Yep, he conducted *kaizen* workshops with the management teams of most plants in North America, but he's been a bit slow to get to Europe. In the past, he led each *kaizen* personally and made the management team attend with every company he acquired. So, he was seriously annoyed at not being able to attend, but he dislikes postponement even worse, hence plan B: *moi!*"

"How come he never scheduled a *kaizen* here?" Ward complained. "Is he so convinced that the plant's future is a foregone conclusion that he can't be bothered?"

That made her laugh, her girlish giggle so different from her radio hostess voice.

"What?" he asked, slightly peeved.

"Why do you think Phil conducts the *kaizen* himself," she asked, sobering up.

"To make people understand how important it is?" he squirmed. "Leading by example sort of thing."

"That's certainly part of it," she agreed. "But that's about them. Why does *he* do it?"

He shrugged.

"He's looking for people, see? He's looking for leadership, involvement, someone in the management team who'll get it, and he can rely on. He's doing these himself because he can't rely on anybody out there, so he's trying to prime the pump, in a manner of speaking."

"So why not us?"

"Are you just being dense? Because you've tried to do something about your situation already, and he hopes you'll figure it out by yourself without him having to hold your hand all the way."

"Are you serious? But he seems to think I'm floundering."

"He does. You are. Which is why I'm here!" she smiled brightly, brimming with infuriating self-confidence. "Let's try and clarify your problem, shall we?"

"The problem is I'm overloading my technicians, and I can't do that forever, and I'm still not stopping bad parts from passing through to the customer, that's what it is!" he replied, angrily.

"So what's the problem?"

"Lord, you people! ... I don't know what the problem is? ... Okay. If I did, I would tell you!"

"Look at it this way," she continued, unflustered by his sudden anger. "Let's start with the quality issues. You've got a Pareto of problems, yes?"

She began sketching on the whiteboard. "Now, we are all trained to use our skilled resources to solve the most significant problems, agreed?" she said, circling the three bars she had drawn representing 20 percent of the issues that accounted for 80 percent of the total number problems.

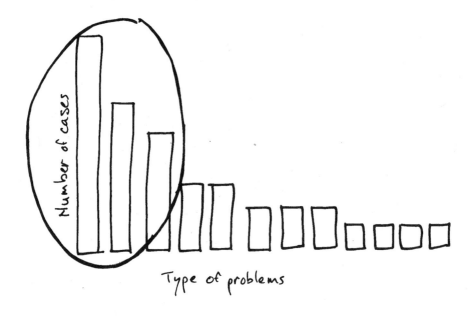

"Right. Most effective use of resources. Focus on the 80 percent. Right?" he said, unsure.

"But what have you been doing with the red-bin reviews?"

He drew a complete blank. Ward, you complete idiot, think, think, he swore to himself. And finally the light came on.

"We've been going down the Pareto curve. We're no longer only tackling the big emergencies, we're starting to worry about smaller problems."

She nodded encouragingly.

"That's it," he continued, excitedly. "We even formalized it. Right in mid-June, we got stuck with a list of actions that increased faster than our ability to carry them out—it got ridiculous. Every red-bin review would add more items to the action plan, and it was always up to the same guys to do something. They simply couldn't. So we decided to keep two separate lists. One with the open actions, and a second weekly one, which listed priorities for the coming week as agreed to on Mondays by the red-bin review. We kind of erased the board every week. So every week, the technical guys had a list of actions to carry out, and they went as far as they could down the list, and then basta!

"We would re-do the list the next week," Ward continued. "I think I mentioned this to Phil, and he seemed to think it was a smart thing to do. In the end, we ended up doing this on a fortnightly basis, because a lot of stuff needed more than one week to be done, with getting replacement parts in and so on. So was that the right way to go about it?"

"Definitely clever," she agreed. "And very smart. But did it solve your problem?"

"It got things done, but I have to agree—it didn't. It paced the work of the technical guys, and at least it killed all the stupid ideas. The remaining items, such as the screws, kept coming back, and so I ended up taking them on as special projects. Ultimately, the technical team is still as overloaded as before. All the pressure is on them."

"Now, what's so frustrating about the customer complaints you've been having lately? Where do they appear on the Pareto curve?"

"Oh, about here," he pointed to the very end of the curve. "They're mostly one-offs, the kind of thing we see once in a blue moon. But they still add up."

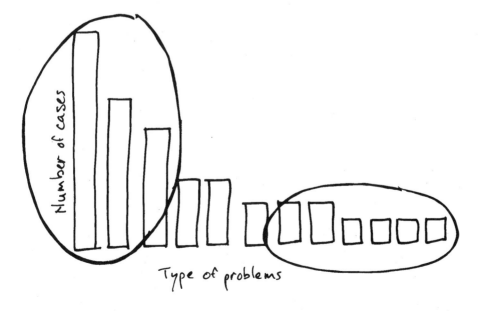

"So what's the problem? Can you clarify it?"

"Beats me! If I wanted to resolve every single problem on that curve, I would need to increase my technical resources exponentially."

"Which wouldn't be very lean, would it?"

"No, it wouldn't," he laughed, suddenly remembering Jenkinson telling Beckmeyer to cut his quality department by a third. He should ask Ackermann whether they'd complied or not. "But I can't see any other way."

"How many people are you in charge of?"

"452 last time I checked."

"Are you using 452 brains? Or only the 10 brains around you and 442 pairs of hands?"

"I don't get it," he sighed.

"Every single person here can solve problems. But you're directing the entire flow of problems to your few technicians. You simply can't sustain improvement with this model."

"But who else is there—operators? You've got to be kidding!"

"Am I? Who had the most sensible things to say during the red-bin review, every time I bothered to ask them?"

"The operator, fine, but ..."

"Why haven't I met your supervisors? I think I spotted one or two walking across the plant. What do they do all day?"

"I've only got one in each hall during the day. There used to be a supervisor per hall per shift, but two years ago corporate had us cut back on indirects."

"Can't they solve problems as well?"

"They do—it's just that ..."

"That they're not solving *product* problems, they're running around sorting out screwups, aren't they?"

"Listen. Stop." He argued, waving his arms irritably. "You're going to have to spell it out for me."

"*Everybody, everyday* solving problems, that's the only answer to the Pareto dilemma. You've got to visualize two flows in the plant.

One: the product flow through the plant, which could be improved by the way. Two: the problem flow to the person who finally solves the problem. Phil's big take on lean management is that you shouldn't funnel all problems to your key technical people. You should protect them to work on the *really difficult* issues. What you have to organize is the problem-solving *in the line*!

"And you're saying I should get operators to solve problems?" Ward asked again, shaking his head in disbelief.

"Why not? They spend their lives with parts and processes in their hands."

"Oh, please! It sounds good in theory, but it simply doesn't work. We do try to get operators' take on issues," Ward protested, "but when we involve them in working groups, they never say anything."

"That's your challenge. Are you asking the right questions?"

He started pacing the floor, shaking his head. To think he'd been a consultant as well. Had he come across just as detached from the realities of everyday operations? Lost in managementspeak la-la land? Probably, yes.

"I mean it," Amy insisted earnestly. "Operators' knowledge is hands-knowledge, not word knowledge. They have lots to tell you about your products and process if you ask them the right questions. Remember the red-bin review in your assembly area? There was an argument because the team found some good parts in the red bin. They pounced on the lady at the workstation, and she said they were from the previous shift. I asked two questions."

"Go on ...," he said.

"Are you often on this workstation? And she said she'd just been moved there because her usual equipment was down. And then I asked her when she'd been last trained on this part. And she said two years ago, when the product was introduced. I remember. That's your issue. In two years, no one has taken the time to work with her and understand what she thinks of the part or how it's made."

"What's the link with training?" he snorted.

"How else are you going to have the conversation? Certainly not by sitting the operator at a desk, turning a spotlight on them, and asking them, 'Tell us all you know about the product.' Don't be silly. You've got to work the product with them regularly. Hands on. As you do, question every gesture. They have practical reasons for how they do things—they'll say so. You've got to make it easy for operators to tell you what the problems are. They're your first line of defense; they're the ones who need to warn you *before* you have a problem. But because this isn't natural, you've got to *organize* it!"

"Let's see if I get it right," Ward muttered, thinking it through. "You're saying that large problems can be solved by engineers, sort of six sigma type problems. But small problems should be solved by operators through *kaizen*?"

"Exactly. If not solved, certainly detected. Your operators are your first and last line of defense between small problems and large problems. Phil keeps arguing that management spends its time fighting fires— that's understandable because if you don't extinguish them then all of production burns down. But if all you do is fight fires, you'll have bigger and bigger ones, more frequently. You need a way to spot the smoldering in the undergrowth before it becomes a fire. You will never have enough technicians to do this. But your operators can. They can put out the first sparks of a fire before it becomes a full-fledged flame."

"I get the theory," he nodded slowly, "but, operators, well, operate. How do I get them to do that?"

"As I said, you've got to set it up. You've got to *organize the problem-solving*, not just the *delivery of parts*. And that starts by *basic stability* in the plant."

"Huh?"

"Let's go back to assembly, I'll show you."

With the brushwood analogy in mind, Ward had to admit that his messy assembly area looked like it could go up in flames in an instant. The assembly machines were neatly arranged in rows, with an operator at most of them, but they were lost in a sea of yellow plastic containers, cardboard boxes, empty wooden pallets and so on—with forklifts coming in and out to pick up the finished-product pallets. Amy looked intently at the hall. Ward smiled, thinking that he preferred the abuse dished out by a friendly, laid-back Californian rather than his own Darth Vader boss.

"Follow the fire analogy," she said, smiling sweetly. "We're standing here. Can we see any fire burning?"

"Not in the least. Any one of these stations could be producing a customer complaint right now," he acknowledged, gritting his teeth, "I know I have problems because I make many bad parts. I've got a hundred places where we check for quality. But the bigger problem is that we still end up being surprised by nonquality in our parts! So that must mean the operator checks and poka-yokes we've got in place are failing us. Damn."

"Uh uh. You might have a fire in the undergrowth, but no way of seeing it, yes? Here?" she pointed to a station. "Or here?"

"Anywhere," he agreed, seeing the area differently. It did get kind of scary when you started thinking that way.

"But, see, the forest is not empty. You've got people working here all day long. The operators at the station—maybe they could call the fire brigade."

"But that's the problem. Since they spend all their time here, they probably wouldn't see it either."

"Precisely. So how can we help them do that?" Amy asked, dragging him to a station. Ward cringed, as it was staffed by Sandrine Lumbroso, a well-known troublemaker who had been in the plant for more years than anyone could say, and whom Ward most definitely didn't want to talk to. As they approached, Lumbroso ignored Amy's cheerful "*bonjour*" and hunched a little more on her work, trying to completely turn her back on them.

"So, if I'm an operator here," Amy asked Ward, "how can I help you spot a problem early?"

"I've got to be very familiar with the parts."

"Or the machine."

"Yes, I've got to be able to tell a good part from a bad part, and to see whether the machine is operating normally or not. Are you saying we need to train operators more?"

"Of course, you need to train operators a whole lot more," Amy smiled. "But not in the way you think. Let's stick with this thought first: how can you, personally, create conditions for operators to be familiar with the parts and the machines?"

"I get it—they should always work with the same parts, on the same machines. To spot problems they've got to know the parts and equipment inside out."

"Basic stability," she agreed emphatically. "You stabilize the value streams through your plant, so that clear product families are always worked on the same machines."

"Many of our assembly machines are dedicated, but that would mean attributing molds to presses. I'm losing flexibility, aren't I?"

"That's MRP thinking," she chided. "The MRP is there to optimize your inefficiencies—"

"Come on," he interrupted. "That's a bit extreme."

"Is it? Think about it: The MRP effectively automates your work-arounds. One press is down, no problem, the MRP routes the product through another press that can take the mold, so that you can take your time to fix the press. One component is missing? No problemo, the MRP programs another part for assembly, so you can take your time in bringing the component in and never have to slow the plant."

"And?"

"Obviously," she told Ward rolling her eyes, "you've got no incentive to keep machines up and running and components stocked. Now consider this: If a product could be routed through a fixed set of machines, and you want to deliver customers without holding stocks, the machine'd better run, and components' had better be available. Don't you think?"

Ward was indeed thinking hard. He nodded. "Rather than make parts with different people on different equipment every day, you're saying I should get the same operators to make the same parts on the same machines. If I did that, you're suggesting that there would be a lot more pressure to keep equipment up and running and to fix quality problems immediately."

"Sure," Amy confirmed. "All the more so if the parts have to be routed through their designated area. As long as the MRP offers you alternatives to making one part at the right time on the right equipment, then your failures, slowdowns, rework, all of this is acceptable. What the *just-in-time* system does, essentially, is force the plant to keep all systems up at all time—if not the entire value flow stops. That's serious pressure."

"You're saying I've got to get rid of the MRP," he blustered in total disbelief.

"For work scheduling? Sure," she answered matter-of-factly. "You'll need it for other things such as getting instructions to suppliers and forecasting and high-level capacity planning, but not within the flow. The MRP is your number one cause of instability."

"Can we park this one for later?" he pleaded. "I hear what you're saying, but, right now, I can't even envisage running this plant without the MRP. If I *did* want to stabilize how parts flow through the plant, where would I start?"

"Product/process matrix."

"Sounds like a consultant answer, all right," he laughed. "When in doubt, draw a matrix."

"Yeah. Here. You vertically list all your products down to the part number, from the high volumes to the low, and horizontally every piece of equipment you've got. Hand me your pad, I'll sketch it for you.

"Then you put in crosses everywhere you can use a piece of kit to work on a part. At first, the matrix looks like a mess. The aim of this is to create stable product families that go through dedicated equipment.

91

You also can do a quick capacity check to see whether the size of the hose is large enough for the flow."

		EQUIPMENT				
		P1	P2	P3	P4	P5
P A R T S	A		X	X		
	B	X	X	X	X	
	C			X	X	X
	D			X	X	X
	E	X	X	X		

"I see what you're saying," Ward agreed carefully. "Not agreeing to it, mind you, because I can't imagine how we'd run without some flexibility to cover for breakdowns and such. But I think I see your point. Next you're going to tell me that the operators should always be at the same station, working on the same parts to gain as much familiarity as they can on the parts."

"And how is that surprising? Do you do any sports?"

"Me?" he laughed. "No, it's against my religion. But my wife trains competition jumpers. Why?"

"Does she? So here's a big puzzle. If one rider is trying to win a specific event, should he train every day on a different horse on a different type of course in order to learn riding 'in general' or would he—"

"Ride the same horse on the same course every day to know the animal's reactions and the terrain by heart. You're right, it's pretty obvious. But we can't keep operators at the same stations all the time."

"Why?"

"Well, any one station doesn't operate continuously. We do two hours of this here, then two hours of that there."

"Why?"

"Because ... okay, I get it. We're not producing at the customer's rhythm, so we're creating inventory as well as moving people around. It's dumb."

"The 'flexibility' you have in mind is not true flexibility. It's keeping for yourself the latitude of moving people around if one station is down, so that you can maintain your efficiencies by working on something else while you take your sweet time fixing the equipment. And so what you really get is 'flexibility' for your production manager, not for your product flows. In effect, it's a license to accept waste."

"Olivier is going to bust a gut," Ward predicted.

"The production manager? They usually do," she said with a smile.

"For argument's sake, say I buy the first part. Say I've stabilized the value streams through the plant ..."

"And clarified them."

"And clarified them," he shrugged, not sure what she meant by that, "and I've stabilized the operators at the machines, which, by the way, may cause ergonomic problems. There's absolutely no guarantee that the operator will be interested in picking up problems." He thought about some of the hard characters he had in the plant.

"That's because they're abandoned."

"Meaning what?"

"Think back to sports. How easy is it to try to work alone on breaking records, you know, solitary achievement?"

"Pretty hard, I'd say. Takes a lot of determination. But," he thought of Claire's riding club, "even if they ride alone, they seldom work alone. They're part of a group, most likely."

"Not a group," she corrected. "A *team*."

"I guess you're right. A team."

"People in the trenches don't go the extra mile for themselves, or their generals, or their pay. They do it for their buddies."

"Teams," he sighed. "Of course. How large is a team?"

"It depends, less than seven, more than three. I tend to think five plus two, minus two. Under three it's not a team, it's a pair. Over seven, the group will tend to splinter. Think of it as having drinks at the pub, how many people can hold a conversation together without it splintering in subgroups?"

"Five probably. A bit more, then it gets really crowded."

"So," Amy said, ticking off her fingers. "First, you've got to stabilize your value streams by having set products go through set equipment.

"Second, you have to organize people so that they work in fixed teams."

"Even if they work on different machines, independently?" Ward asked.

"The ideal is to organize production cells for five people, of course, if you can. If not you just pull the machines together in a clear area— it also helps with the professional illness problem as people can rotate through the cell."

"I dread to think there's a third."

"Good guess. Third, you've got to stabilize the workload, so that your *teams* build the *product families* at an even *pace*.

"Think about it, Andy, if you have a repetitive work plan, and make the products in the same areas, with the same teams, then you can start shifting some of the burden of problem-solving from your technical resources to your line managers. Maintenance should be there for the real fires, the really unexpected crazy breakdowns. Engineering should be focusing on getting new products off to a good start. Your line supervisors should be solving most of the day-to-day issues."

All of a sudden, that made Ward laugh—almost a giggle. The unexpected grasp of the immensity of the task at hand as well as its inescapable common sense.

"What?" she eyed him suspiciously.

"I see it. No, really, I do," he said, sobering up. "I'm not laughing at you. I'm realizing how we must look through your eyes. We're so far, far away from any of this. You're right; we're following the MRP and constantly trying to adjust labor behind it. Fair enough, I can see how stabilizing value streams is something we should be doing. I can also accept that creating stable operator teams is my responsibility—after all this is how I organize my people. I can also accept that I haven't asked much of my supervisors at this stage. But stable workload! Do you have any idea how many references we have? And what our customers do to us? They can double orders from one day to the next!"

"Is that so?" asked the consultant, looking amused. "Let's have a look at logistics then."

"What a mess!" exclaimed Amy cheerfully. "Look at this!"

The warehouse didn't look particularly messy to Ward. It was a large building with alley after alley of customer container stacks—large metal or cardboard boxes piled three or four high—and rack after rack of pallets of components. In the courtyard beyond was the provisional tent that housed bags of plastic granules. The tent had been adopted four years ago as a temporary measure to give logistics space to breath, yet had become a permanent extension, and looked rather worse for wear. In the warehouse proper, forklifts were scurrying with reckless abandon, honking at each other at every intersection, and turning corners fast enough to make him wince.

"How many days of stock have you got in here?"

"Overall? About 20."

"Yeah, no wonder Phil asked me to have a look."

Amy moved along a rack, checking labels on the boxes, and then exclaimed, "Oh goody—parts produced three months ago!" Ward felt a mixture of chagrin and annoyance with her perky excavation into each new fault.

Chandon was just about to get back in the glass cubicle that she shared with the other logistics operators when she spotted the plant manager and the consultant step in through the forklift gate rather than take the long way around and use the pedestrian door. She shook her head in exasperation. Andy was fine as plant managers went—he was easy to work with, supportive, and not too demanding, but he completely lacked common sense.

"Andy! How many times have I told you to *please* not bring visitors unannounced in the warehouse!"

Ward turned around, sighing, and saw the logistics manager stomp her way toward them.

"Carole—"

"If she's saying it's dangerous," Amy picked up, "she's right."

"What did you just say?" challenged Chandon, switching to heavily accented English. She was not impressed with the American woman. She hated consultants in general. Seagulls who fly in, crap over everybody, and fly out again. How hard was it to explain that someone was doing something wrong? Let her see them do something right first.

"I said that I agree with you," repeated Amy with a toothy smile. "These guys drive around like it's, what, Daytona."

"We follow every safety procedure," she huffed.

Ward did not know whether to laugh out loud or run for cover. The two women were facing each other like prizefighters ready to attack. Ward noted to himself that they wore their hair exactly the same way: straight, shoulder-length, with a strand pulled back over the ear. It was funny because they couldn't otherwise look more different. Amy had a round face with strong features, a full mouth that easily looked pouty when she wasn't smiling, and large black eyes now looking far from amused. Chandon, standing as a mirror image, her blue eyes flashing, her mouth a habitual thin line of combative anger.

"Hmm," Ward cleared his voice, "I was mentioning that our customer demand varied significantly."

"That it does," Chandon agreed, raising her eyes in annoyance.

"Can you show me where you keep your highest-volume finished goods?" asked Amy.

"I'd have to look it up."

"In the computer?"

"Of course in the computer," responded Chandon. "We have hundreds of customer references here, far too many for me to know where each one is stored. That's why we have computers. The system allocates spaces to references according to where there is room."

"Well, it would make it easier, wouldn't it, if they were in fixed locations, no? Imagine going to the supermarket and having to look in the computer to find out where the milk is."

"Not the fixed-location discussion again!" Carole barked at Andy, as if Amy wasn't even there. "I thought we'd concluded that we simply don't have enough room to keep a space by reference in the warehouse. Now if you want to extend the warehouse ..."

"With all the stock you've got, you must be kidding!" Amy noted.

Chandon glared from one to the other, clearly furious. "Andy, you'll have to excuse me, but I have some real work to do. I do not have the time to listen to consultants coming in and criticizing without knowing anything about the work we do here."

"We're here to learn, Carole," chided Ward, both embarrassed and annoyed at the two women. "And it's not like we're a world-class benchmark in terms of inventory turns."

"Well, whatever it is," she persevered, "I would suggest you take this up with production because I can assure you we're doing our work here."

"I'm sure you are," said Amy sweetly, which seemed to infuriate the other woman even more. "And I've seen what I wanted to see. One last question. Can I see your last misshipments to customers?"

"Follow me, please," replied the logistics manager, stomping away. She led them to a large office at the end of the warehouse where the logistics staff was located. She sat irritably at her desk, and pulled out a file of computer printouts from beneath her desk.

"Here, we document every missed shipment."

"And?"

"And what?"

"You document them? Well that's fine and good—but what do you do about them?"

Chandon didn't answer, her eyes throwing daggers.

"Where is the analysis?" insisted Amy.

Ward knew there was none. He sighed deeply.

"Any of these high-volume parts?" asked Amy.

Andy grabbed the folder from Chandon's grasp, and quickly spotted some part numbers he knew well.

"The second on the list is a plastic cover. A worthless part in terms of value, but a very high runner. We're making it on a press that is clearly overloaded."

"Our customer asked us for 20 percent more parts than we expected," defended the logistics manager.

Amy said nothing, and smiled, like the cat that got the cream.

"I'm sorry about Carole," mumbled Ward, as they returned to his office. "She's really good at her job, but can be a bit of a pain to work with. In truth, she cares intensely, she always wants to do a good job, but that can make her rather defensive, I'm afraid."

That made Amy laugh. "Don't apologize for her, Andy. I sure don't blame her. Actually, we've been poking into all the areas of your plant, and she's the only one to actually show an interest at what the plant manager could possibly be doing there. That's a pretty healthy reaction. As for the rest, I can't begrudge someone what they don't know, can I? I'd be out of a job!"

"You were telling me there are three main components to stabilizing my plant," Ward recalled, subdued, trying to synthesize what they had gone over so far. "Would you mind going over that again?"

"Sure:
- First, stable product families going through clear value streams.
- Second, stable operator teams, working in production cells or zones.
- Third, stable workload."

"That's what I remembered. I think I can visualize the first two, but we didn't talk much about the third one. I really don't see how I can stabilize my workload considering the kind of customer variations we get."

"With stocks, of course. But that would require a completely different outlook on logistics. Before we go there, let's talk about the benefit of the first two items."

"I think I'm clear on that," Ward nodded, "in theory at least. If people work continuously in the same areas with the same parts, I should be able to rely on their brains to spot small problems before they turn into a full blaze—that's the main idea, right?"

"You got it!"

"I guess that's exactly what Phil has been trying to get us to do. But I still have no clue how to make this happen."

"Think it through," she said brightly. "You'll figure it out."

"Yeah," he doubted. "So you keep saying."

"Take your time to put your thoughts in order, and email or call me with what you want to do," she suggested.

"What about the workload thing?"

"Hey, when the glass is full, the water you pour in it just spills on the table. Let's call it a day, shall we?"

"How many consultants does it take to change a light bulb?"

"Huh?"

"One, but the light bulb has to really want to change!"

Claire laughed.

Amy had been regaling them with a string of consultant jokes. Ward had invited her to dinner on the spur of the moment, Malancourt being on the way back to Metz, where her hotel was. He'd had time to have second and third thoughts about it during the drive to the farm, but in any event, she and Claire hit if off at once. It turned out that Amy had a three-year-old daughter, and they launched immediately into one of these conversations about naptimes and cute antics that made his brain try to throttle itself. And so he prepared the food as Claire grabbed Charlie and took Amy for a grand tour of the riding stables. Another good surprise of country living in France was that he had discovered an unexpected passion for cooking. He now cooked most days when he came home early enough, finding the chopping and stirring a relaxing way to put the plant away and focus on his family. Being a plant manager could really eat you up if you weren't careful, with constant demands and a list of worries that grew faster than you could solve them.

"This is *so good!*" Amy exclaimed enthusiastically, helping herself to another portion of quiche lorraine.

"It's just an omelet."

"Don't listen to him," snorted Claire. "Andy's an excellent cook."

"You've got him well housetrained, I can see," Amy chuckled. "Mine's absolutely hopeless. Can't thaw a pizza in the microwave without carbonizing it."

"How do you deal with your daughter, what with being away with your job?" wondered Claire.

"I'm not away that much," said Amy, a bit defensively. "And Mike's very good with her. He teaches nearby, so he's got easy hours. He loves spending time with her anyhow, but that's about it. Of course he never remembers little things like baths and clean clothes. Every time I get back, he hands me a little street urchin, I swear. But I try not to be away from home too long. I'm just doing this gig here to help Phil out."

"Have you known him long?" slipped in Ward, as casually as he could.

"Phil? God, yes. That's how I met Mike; he's his best friend. Phil hired me as an HR manager for ILM, his previous company. It was just two plants at the time, of course."

"And how did you move to consulting?" asked Claire, clearly intrigued by such a different career path from hers.

"I was a fool, that's what it was," she replied brightly. "I met Mike because his dad was mentoring Phil in turning the company around with all this lean stuff. Mike even wrote a book about it afterward. In any case, I really got involved at the time, with *kaizen* and everything, but after a while, I felt I had nothing much more to learn. It was becoming too much like work, you know, not so much fun," she grimaced. "So I got a consulting job in a large outfit that wanted to start a lean practice. Now, that was no fun at all. I thought I'd discover other places, new industries, and so on, but it was all about politics and pretend lean. Yuck."

"I know what you mean," agreed Ward. "I did eight years in supply-chain consulting. But I didn't find it that bad. I got to travel, that was cool. And see many different businesses."

"You're right, I guess," Amy conceded. "It was just the wrong time. My boss was a real jerk, and, in truth, I just wanted to be home with Mike rather than spend weeks away doing *kaizen* events in podunk factories where the management couldn't care less."

She paused a while, staring at her wine, and taking another long sip.

"Mmm, this is delicious. You guys must come to California, we've got some pretty good wines there ... In any case, it turned out I'd completely missed the main plot. I thought that lean was all about hitting the processes with a few tools, and getting people involved, which I did really well, thank you very much.

"But in the meantime, Phil starts getting all excited about how lean is really a management method. A full business strategy, not a production tactic. Now, I'm sitting through dinners with Mike and Phil and my father-in-law, who's the original hard-ass *sensei*, and they go on and on about this, while I'm doing my no-hope *kaizen* events. That was a drag.

"Next thing I know, Phil hears about a factory for sale in the industry, and he and Bob, Mike's dad, come up with some crazy plan about how if they can triple the inventory turns, they should be able to liberate enough cash from the business to make the acquisition

101

almost pay for itself. Then I hear myself saying, 'And who's going to do the SMED workshops for you?'

"So Phil hires me back as lean director. Would you believe it? Mike and I even chip in some equity—nothing much, but it really feels different when you own even a small stake of the business, particularly after working as a consultant."

"Splendid!" said Ward.

"Awesome, you mean. In the end, it got crazy. We acquired a company each year for the next five years. The whole thing kind of ran away with itself. I'd work the just-in-time side, while Phil tackled the engineering bits—that's what he's really good at."

"And then," Claire asked, mesmerized. "What happened?"

"Nothing fails like success, I guess. From the start, Phil had equal shares with a friend of his, who'd been his longtime partner. They had a falling out, I've never exactly known on what, but in the end they decided to sell the company and go their separate ways. I'd never liked Phil's partner much, but he was a real salesman. He managed to entice two groups into acquiring ILM, and, in the end, the winner paid a fortune for it. The original deal called for the management team to stay on for a couple of years to make the transition, but the new management was so completely hopeless, they immediately started undoing everything we'd done—absolute morons. Mean, as well. So in the end, we just called it quits."

"And is that how you became a consultant again?" Claire asked.

"Sorta," Amy smiled wistfully. "When Phil got into this new scheme, he asked me if I wanted in, but I was feeling rather burned out from the frenetic days we'd had with growing ILM. Not that it wasn't fun, but it was work, I'll tell you. So with Andrea growing up, I wanted more time home. And we'd done really well, so there was no pressure to get another job immediately.

"But," she laughed, "after a couple of months at home, I got such a bad case of cabin fever that Mike begged me to find a job! In the end, I set up my shingle as an independent consultant. I mostly do jobs for

Phil and a couple of other guys I know from the old days. It's pretty cool—I only take the work I feel like."

"You've made it!" exclaimed Claire, sounding genuinely impressed, which, Ward thought wryly, didn't happen very often.

"So have you!" replied Amy, enthused. "Look at this beautiful place you've got here! And the work you're doing with the horses, it's so exciting. It's real. I love it."

"What a wonderful evening," Amy said, as they drove through the night, back toward Metz. "Thank you, Andy. And thank Claire. Her work with the horses—it's terrific!"

"Big dumb beasts."

"Get outta here! They're so beautiful. So powerful."

"They're pretty to look at," he conceded—and expensive as hell to keep up.

"Pretty? Pretty doesn't half say it. There was one girl practicing jumping, and I could feel my leg twitch every time she took off. I can't imagine what it must be to ride one. I know what I want for Christmas!" she giggled.

If only it was so easy, thought Ward bitterly. He wasn't about to tell her how much the stables depended on him feeding the family, but the thought rankled.

"Amy," he said after a while, "I don't mean to be a bore about this, but I need to understand what to do with our logistics. I heard what you said about how important the inventory was."

"Right now? Oh, all right. The first thing to do, you see, is to wean them off the computer. Before reducing stock, you need to understand how the stock behaves, and what generates it. So the first step is fixed single locations for each reference."

"But Carole is right—we'll never have enough room. The software maximizes the use of empty spaces."

"Blah, blah, blah. I believe that she believes it. But you have to try to find out."

She fell silent, and he worried he had little with which to go back to logistics manager Chandon.

"Look, the trick to logistics is first to put the stocks at the right place, then to stabilize the lead time, then to reduce the lead time, and finally to optimize the handling and moving costs. Start by visualizing your stock, and you'll realize you've got plenty of parts the customer doesn't want right now gathering dust—or worse, getting obsolete—and on the other hand, you're missing the very parts you need."

"What you were suggesting at the plant?"

"Yeah. Hinting. Listen, for my first job, before I got to work for Phil, I was a fast-food restaurant manager for a couple of years. I'd work there to pay for my tuition, so they offered me a job and I stayed on for a while. Now, that was real work.

"In any case, in a burger joint, you've got a small stock of the high-runners, those you put in the special offers, or the meal deals. When a customer asks for one, they get it immediately, as the counter staff turns around and picks from the stock. Then the people in the kitchen make one to refill the stock, and so on, yes?"

"I'm with you."

"But if you go in and ask for a special extra pickle but no onion, they'll say please have a seat, and we'll bring it to you. Now, of course, that is extra cost for the restaurant since the whole idea is that patrons help themselves. But these are low-runners. What then happens is that the guy in the kitchen finishes the last high-runner, puts it in the stock, and goes on to do your special order, which is then delivered to you. In *kanban* terms, the production *kanban* card for a low-runner is put directly into the launcher."

"Huh?"

"Never mind the *kanban*. The idea is that the MRP works on the basis that any gap in stock has to be filled in. The logistician believes that if she has all parts in stock at all times, she can't possibly be found short. But instead, this creates a situation where you hold many parts you don't actually need, and because of long batches and slow replenishment, you still miss deliveries of high-runners. The trick is to reverse that thinking and to keep a stock of high-runners, which you replenish daily, and deal with all the others as make-to-order."

"You're saying make-to-stock for high-runners and make-to-order for low-runners?"

"Exactly!"

"But I'm not sure we have that many high-runners—seems we have mostly middle-runners."

"Oh, give me a break. Let's make a bet. List all the references that make a cumulative volume of 50 percent of your total volume, and then prove to me that they're not more than 5 or 10 percent of your references."

"Do you really think so?"

"Never failed so far."

"I'll check that first thing in the morning. Stock replenishment for the high-volume and make-to-order for the low. Blimey!"

"But," Amy warned, "it's not so easy. You've got to learn to do it. So first make sure you visualize the stocks of the parts you're playing with so that you understand what happens. That's the whole point. Start with the top of the list and produce them every day."

"Every day? That's going to be a shock to the system."

"Yep—SMED. If you can't change tools in less than 10 minutes, you're not even in the game ... Hang on Andy—don't get lost in all of this. First, and most importantly, stick to what you're doing with the red bins, but *involve your supervisors*," Amy said emphatically. "The red bin is really nothing more than a tool to learn about the parts." She turned to him with her most serious face of all: "This is all about getting the line management to own their problems, and to have a daily opportunity to discuss with the staff specialists on what really goes on. That's critical—got it?"

"I think so. You're right. Carole was the only supervisor who showed up when we were in the plant. I think I might have a problem with the others."

"Good. Second, try to organize cells and operator teams so that people learn to work together. This is really, really important. Operators are essential to fighting the first sparks of problems before they grow into raging fires."

"Using all the brains in the factory, not just 10."

"Yes, but you've got to organize it. Third, *kaizen* is the key. Have you got a continuous-improvement officer?"

"I've got a young black belt doing six sigma projects."

"Four-month DMAIC? Define, measure, analyze, improve, control? Gawd!"

"What's wrong with it?"

"Nothing, as such. But it won't help you with involving your staff and line—one guy working in a corner and looking for brilliant solutions."

"It's not like—"

"Yeah, yeah. Lean is about learning by doing. There is no expertise in lean, only experience, as the *sensei* says. So it's about cycles. Your management team, supervisors, and operators all need to go through many, many cycles to figure out what continuous improvement means."

"Hmmm," he answered noncommittally, feeling lost.

"So get your guy to run three-day workshops, like *kaizen* events, on standardized subjects—line balancing, SMED, quality analyses, that sort of thing. One week the preparation, and one week the event. And on and on and on."

"That frequently?"

"Probably not enough. You want each of your managers to participate in at least two workshops a year, so how many does that make if you have one management team member per workshop?"

"Counting the supervisors, you're right, I'd probably need 20 to 40 workshops per year."

"And, ultimately, you want every operator in the plant to participate in a workshop in the year, so make the count ..."

"But that's—"

"Hey, you asked!"

"I did," he agreed, gritting his teeth. How on earth was he expected to ...

"Get to it then!" she gruffed in mock drill sergeant's voice—and then laughed.

"Phil's approach to production is pretty straightforward," she said as he parked in front of her hotel. They'd booked her in the most expensive place in town, a converted monastery with pretentious rooms overlooking a wide park.

"One, fix quality problems. Two, reduce inventory to free up cash. Three, lower costs by eliminating all the waste you've uncovered doing one and two. He's done it several times, so just follow his lead—he knows what he's doing."

"If only it were so simple from where we stand," he sighed.

"Listen, this is not rocket science. In defining their lean model, Toyota picked up on four simple obsessions. One is managing production sites through stable teams of multiskilled workers, so you get both volume and mix flexibility. Second is getting everyone—and I mean *everyone*—involved in quality. Third is just-in-time process control by continuously reducing lead time, which dramatically improves return on sales and capital turnover ratios, and fourth is all around cost reduction by eliminating waste. How hard can it be?"

"Yeah, real simple," he agreed with heavy sarcasm.

"It is, but you've got to figure it out by yourself. The trick is don't try to do it all on your own. You must involve everybody, every day, if not, you'll fail."

"Sorry for inviting her at such short notice," he murmured to Claire as he crawled into bed. She was half asleep, all warm and cuddly. She smelled like home.

"It's fine, darling," she yawned. "It was fun actually. She's an impressive lady."

"Yep," he sighed, burying his face in her hair.

"Hey, baby, don't sound so depressed. It went well, I thought—no?"

"Oh, yes. Absolutely."

"What is it, then?"

He turned away and let himself fall flat on his back.

"On the drive back, I realized something—and it's scary."

"Hmm?"

"This whole thing—it's not about the plant. It's about me."

"How d'you mean?"

"It's me! I've got to relearn everything I thought I knew if I want to do what they're asking. Everything. It seems I've got everything ass-backward all the time."

"Sounds like dressage," she mumbled, falling back asleep.

"Everything you thought you knew, you've got to relearn differently all the time. That's what makes it fun!"

"Aaaargh!" he complained to the night.

"They're right," he thought to himself, unable to sleep as thoughts whirled and crashed through his mind. "I'm trying to run the plant, I'm not managing people," he realized. Amy had hit a nerve. He now saw that he spent his day trying to keep things on a par, but he'd never considered having to manage all 450 people in the plant as *individuals*. He thought of them as staff, resource, not as *persons* who could help him service customers and make money. How does one directly manage so many? Oddly, he found the thought exciting, and even somewhat comforting after today's visit. Amy had been nice as can be and had tried to soften the blows, but he wasn't completely stupid, and he had felt on the drive to her hotel that she didn't have high hopes for the plant, no matter how cheerful she tried to sound. He'd felt really down on the way back, but now, at least, he had something new to work on. He also realized why trying to stabilize the work environment of each person should help. He also now had a better insight into why Phil had insisted so heavily on getting the *line* to solve problems rather than relying on *staff* functions. He didn't see how to do it yet, but he felt buoyed by the thrill of learning something new, something he'd never even considered before. Each operator mattered, every part mattered. Of course. But how?

Amy collapsed on the plush hotel bed with a deep sigh. It was still too early to call California, and she lay there moodily for a while, staring at the ceiling, feeling too exhausted to get ready for bed. They were nice folks. And that was the problem. Andy seemed really keen to do something about his plant, but he had such a long, long way to go that she doubted he could crawl himself out of that hole. She just couldn't picture how he would manage to both acquire a lean attitude himself and get his management team involved in time. She picked herself up and started unpacking her travel toiletries, wondering whether Phil had bit off more than he could chew this time around. Oh, sure, they had leaned more plants than she could remember with the rapid growth of ILM. But in every case, Phil had tackled the transformation directly with the management team in a "my way or the highway" style.

She knew he hated doing that. He was a great believer in developing people and moving them up from the ranks rather than the hire-and-fire, up-or-out bias of most senior managers. But still, he'd accepted from early mistakes that he needed to hit the business hard just after acquisition, and to push people to make a stand early. He'd come to agree that better no guy than the wrong guy.

With this new venture, though, he had been sucked in by the geography, with plants across the world, and tied up with so many issues that he'd found it difficult to apply his formula. Also, he hadn't been able to rely on the ranks of devoted followers as he'd had in ILM. In most newly acquired business, he'd always been able to staff a couple of key managers who had previously done their lean learning in their own operations, to sustain the transformation. With Nexplas, he had to build it all from scratch, and without the time or resources to do so. The day spent in Vaudon made her feel really low because Phil had asked for her opinion of the plant—would it cut it or not? She didn't know what to answer. Yes, they were trying, but they were also left out in the cold without the kind of support they needed to turn this one around.

Ward needed to stabilize the plant as well as learn to involve his middle-management in daily problem-solving, and all at the same time. It wasn't such a big deal when you knew how to do it, but having to learn this by doing it was a tall order. She felt guilty for not committing to help them more, but she just couldn't see herself flying to Europe every month.

In any case, she knew what Mike would say—they'd had this conversation often enough. Her husband was a social psychologist whose father was one of the first Americans to pick up lean from Toyota and who had become a lean *sensei*. Mike had introduced his dad to Phil and, together, they had turned around one company, then acquired others, and so on. He had focused his psychological research on trying to understand the human underpinning of the lean approach: why did it work so spectacularly when it did, but also so rarely.

She knew that the first thing he'd say was that the plant manager had to learn the stuff by himself—this was the essential bottleneck to the lean success. Managers, from the CEO down, and most importantly plant managers, had to learn this personally. They could not delegate learning. They could not purchase or hire it in. They had to go through the moves themselves, on the shop floor. From this premise, he'd argue that learning, as it was now better understood in the field, came from learning by doing, and then confronting one's perspective with others. Both of these were profoundly unnatural to traditional managers. First, they assumed that their job was to get other people to do things, and all they had to do is coordinate and motivate (ha!), and, second, they were very uneasy about actually listening to another point of view. They thought of their job as command and control, to tell other people what to do and think.

In her experience, managers who succeeded in lean transformations had the kind of self-confidence that allowed them to get involved personally with shop-floor experiments without feeling threatened by possible failure, and who also had enough experience to listen to other people's angle on a situation and take it in carefully without either dismissing it or overreacting. Andy seemed both open-minded and willing, but she really doubted he had the experience and self-belief required to take on the transformation. What a mess! Well, she wished them luck.

Chapter Three

GO AND SEE

"So, you've finally gone and visited a customer line, have you?"

"Um, yes, sir," replied Ward, awkwardly. "Great speech, by the way."

Phil Jenkinson frowned and muttered, "Public speaking. Hate it. Right up there with death and taxes."

Ward couldn't help but smile. The big man really had looked out of sorts. Unlike Jenkinson, Ward had never experienced a fear of speaking in public. And judging by Jenkinson's response, it looked like his anxiety was there to stay. Not that the speech wasn't clear—Ward had to admit that it was perfectly straightforward. The speech had, however, released other demons for Ward, namely a fear that Jenkinson's comments about moving production closer to customers' assembly sites could be bad news for Vaudon. Several of his products could arguably be relocated to Eastern Europe.

"I wanted to talk to you about it," said Phil, as if reading his thoughts. "You've got a few molds I'd like to move to Wroclaw."

Ward cursed to himself. He was learning to dread any conversation with bloody Jenkinson. Not so much because the man was unpleasant, but because of his abrupt way of springing unpleasant surprises on you. Having inherited his father's quirky British sense of humor, Ward found most people amusing in some way. But he'd yet to find anything remotely funny about his CEO. He was physically imposing—taller than Ward, and a much larger man—and hardly ever smiled, joked, or made inappropriate comments. He didn't even listen to himself speak the way these alpha power types tended to. While there didn't appear to be any meanness to the guy, he seemed to display an equal absence of tact. If he hadn't been scary as hell, Ward would have found the man dull. But there he was, wondering nervously what evil news was going to hit him, again.

"But, first, tell me how it went at the car assembly plant," Jenkinson went on, oblivious to how Ward might feel about his comments. Earlier, Ward had presented his plan for closing the plant to the executive committee, highlighting the difficulties of shutting a plant in France. No one had commented. Surely the CEO must realize that sending parts to Poland would send a strong signal that he intended to squeeze work out of Vaudon, one part at a time.

"Fascinating," replied Ward, managing to get his thoughts together. "Yes, *fascinating* in many respects. So I went to look at that complaint we discussed this summer, the scratches on the engine-cover part."

"I remember," nodded Jenkinson, sounding interested.

"Well, I had to admit that they were right about the part being visible. Although it was never described as such in the contract, the part does show clearly on the top of the engine as soon as you lift the hood. The scratches are visible."

"Customer first," Jenkinson shrugged.

"Indeed. So we got to talking about the probable cause and, came to the conclusion that this is a packaging problem—the parts get damaged during the handling, not in assembly. So we agreed to conduct a few trials to see if we can find a quick fix. In fact, we developed a promising solution—we need their purchasing guys to approve this plan, however, and that's a whole other story."

"Good work. Call me if things get stuck. Now tell me: what else did you conclude from that visit?"

"Well," Ward said carefully, "we—my logistics manager and I— had a disagreement with Amy when she came around. Amy seemed to think that it is our job to manage customer-demand variations. We argued that customer demand was so crazy and all over the place that no one could possibly *level* that."

"And?" the other man asked with an amused smile, as he seemed to picture the scene in his mind's eye.

"I asked the customer's production manager," continued Ward, gritting his teeth. "And he confirmed what Amy said. Their total daily production volume is completely stable within at least one month."

"But they've got mix issues?" suggested Jenkinson, looking knowingly at Ward over the rim of his glasses.

"Yeah. They shuffle cars around after paint as they select out the bodies to be reworked, and they also have missing-parts problems, which leads them to change the assembly sequence at the very last moment."

"So ... stable volume over the month, but variation with the daily mix? What was Amy's take on that?"

"I haven't talked to her about it yet, but I guess she'll say we should be able to *level* mix, right?"

"Absolutely. Do talk to her about it. She's got a boxful of tricks to make *leveling* work."

"I guess that you were right, after all," Ward sighed. "It turned out to be one of those 50 percent of the times when I was wrong."

"Congratulations, that's how we learn. Happens to me all the time," Jenkinson nodded, grinning briefly. "Just get used to it. But what other conclusion can you draw from visiting your customer?"

"The customer's always right?"

"Nope," snorted the CEO. "Thankfully, the 'wrong 50 percent of the time' rule applies to customers as well."

"Do what you tell me to do?" fished Ward, totally at a loss about what answer was expected of him. He really hated this question-and-answer game. The guy clearly knew what he wanted to hear, but he'd make him work for it.

"Ha! That'd be nice, for a change: someone who does what he's told!"

"What then?"

"*Genchi genbutsu*," explained Jenkinson, using the Japanese phrase. "*Go and see* for yourself to find out facts at the source to understand the true nature of the issue. This is probably the most important managerial practice in lean: *going to the real place to see the real thing.*

"*Go and see,*" he repeated earnestly, looming over Ward, "is the key to lean management. It's all about opinions in the end."

"Opinions?" repeated Ward, feeling the conversation had run away from him again.

"Yes, business is about opinions. Your opinion is correct, and you act on it, you make money. Your opinion is wrong, and you lose money. If your opinions about how markets behave are better than mine, you have the competitive advantage, right?"

"I guess."

"So the questions are: How do we develop better opinions? How do we develop judgment? And in this, there is no substitute for experience. As they say, good judgment comes from experience, and experience ...," he paused for effect, "comes from bad judgment."

"*Go and see* to the source to learn, is that what you're saying? So the whole debate about *leveling* isn't even the issue here—what really matters is getting any kind of answer by going to the shop floor?"

"Yes. Yes. The real place, the real thing, the real people. Data is clearly important, but all the reports in the world won't help you to truly understand anything as much as direct experience. Toyota folklore says that you must wash your hands three times a day."

"What? Wash your hands? What has that got to do with ... "

"You wash you hands before breakfast," smiled Jenkinson, "because you've gone to the shop floor and touched some parts. Then you wash your hands before lunch, because you've gone down to the shop floor and touched some parts. And you wash your hands before dinner—"

"—because you've gone to the shop floor before leaving the factory?"

"I used to think it was pure folklore, but if all my plant managers would simply go to the shop floor before checking their emails, at least half my problems would go away!"

"Not just the plant manager," agreed Ward guiltily, recognizing that checking his e-mails was exactly the first thing he did upon arriving at the office. "But all the other managers as well."

"And it doesn't apply only to production, but to sales and procurement and engineering as well."

"Is that why you think it's so important to visit customers when they have a complaint?"

"Yes. To understand the true nature of the issue. And also, of course, to develop relationships. See, there is a lot of anger in this industry," Jenkinson remarked sourly. "I find anger the most counterproductive behavior. In fact, I'm convinced that at the root of every angry discussion, you'll find a misunderstanding. People argue because they haven't got all the facts. They disagree about what should be done because they don't agree on what the problem is. So *go and see* is also about listening: listening to customers about how they use our parts, listening to operators about how they assemble them, listening to suppliers about how they produce them, and so on. You *go and see* for yourself, and you listen to the person who does the real job."

"Andy, hi—sorry to butt in," said Lowell Coleman, inching himself between the two. "Phil, can I have a word? Wayne has talked to Ford's Purchasing, and we need to discuss their position."

"In a moment, let me finish with Andy, and I'll be right with you."

"Andy, good to see you. I'll catch you later," Coleman said, pointing his forefinger like a gun, and turning the gesture into a salute.

Jenkinson blankly watched the older man retreat. Coleman was always impeccably turned out, with white patrician hair and fashionable suits. Ward gazed from one man to the other and could not help but notice the supply-chain manager looked far more the CEO than Jenkinson, who had turned up at the yearly corporate event in his habitual chinos and jean shirt. Did the man ever wear anything else? Probably not. He had most likely rationalized his wardrobe as he had everything else.

Jenkinson took off his glasses, and polished them on his handkerchief, looking far, far away. Knots of people were forming and unfolding as the best and the brightest from throughout the Nexplas empire gossiped over their buffet plates. Ward noticed that Jenkinson seemed to repel casual conversationalists, and that a vacuum had isolated them from the rest of the crowd.

"Go on," coughed Ward. "Hit me with it."

"Poland," said Jenkinson, looking up thoughtfully. "You ship a couple of parts to Mlada in Czechoslovakia, don't you? We'd like you to relocate them to the Wroclaw plant, which is much closer—they're right across the border."

"But—that would take a big chunk out of my sales," complained Ward, hoping he didn't sound whiny. "And the labor-cost difference with Poland is not so great any more."

"This is not just about cost," replied the CEO flatly, "but also about producing close to the customer."

Then do I get the parts for French OEMs in Flins or Sandouville currently being produced in the Czech Republic or Poland? thought Ward bitterly, saying nothing.

"The point is, I'd like you to handle the transfer personally."

"You mean, I get the responsibility to transfer the parts out of my plant into Wroclaw? I don't mean to be awkward, but shouldn't it be the other way around?"

"It should. Nevertheless, I'd like you to do it. Transfer has to be complete within the fiscal year—so up and running by March at the latest. Please."

Ward just nodded, wondering what could possibly lay behind *that* request. November, December, January, February; he'd better get cracking.

"I must really go, but there's a second thing," Jenkinson continued, making Ward almost wince. "D'you know Mark Neville?"

"Sure." Mark Neville was the plant manager for the U.S. Bethany site. He was a large African-American who must have been as wide as he was high. Ward still smarted from the first time he had met him, years ago, during his days as a supply-chain consultant for Coleman. Neville had made him look like an absolute fool in front of a training group. They'd met again at a corporate function, where they were seated at the same table, yet spoke little. Although they had been part of the same branch in the previous structure, Alnext's management style had never encouraged much plant-to-plant cooperation. Neville had been manufacturing engineering manager at the time, or production manager, he'd didn't quite recall. It suddenly hit him that Mark must be the guy to whom Jenkinson had given the Bethany plant after firing the previous site manager. Holy cow!

"If you can make the time," continued Jenkinson, "how about extending your stay here until Monday and visiting his plant?"

"If you'd like," Ward replied, raising a surprised eyebrow. He cursed inwardly at having to spend more time away from home, but he was pretty sure Claire would be okay about it. After all, she was the one encouraging him to react quickly to Jenkinson's "suggestions." "Give the guy a chance," she'd say. "I think he means well."

"Good! It's settled then," exclaimed the CEO, clapping his hands surprisingly loudly, making several suits look up. "I've got to go and see what's eating Wayne. I'm sure you can make the arrangements with Mark directly. And, Andy, ask him how much time he spends on his shop floor!"

As Ward settled in for the presentations, he thought wryly that there was a time when he used to enjoy these corporate executive conferences. At the time, he was the one talking the talk, and not having to walk the walk. Now that he had defected to operations, he had to admit how silly he must have looked with his supply-chain models, "master plan" theories, and talk, talk, talk. He picked fussily at his plateful of lukewarm plastic food, hoping the venue had been chosen for convenience and space rather than glamour. It was a drab hotel close to the massive Rexington plant where corporate had been relocated. Ward watched the execs mill around the buffets. There was very little ethos of teamwork in the division. He figured that the management of Nexplas would try to create more of a company culture now that they stood on their own, but he had not seen much sign of it yet. In the early days after the sale, there'd been a huge effort to create the proper corporate image with documents, a graphic charter for all PowerPoint slides, and a forceful elimination of anything with the Alnext logo on it. Since that initial push, there had been little else.

The CEO's presentation had been straightforward. They had shown a steady increase in productivity and a sharp decrease in customer ppms, although the trend was flattening out. They had taken a beating on inventory: after an early quick reduction, stocks had been crawling back up toward their initial levels. Many blamed this on the stock builds needed to cover for the summer, but Jenkinson had been forceful about this.

"Reduce your batch sizes," he'd repeated. "Read my lips: reduce batch sizes."

The real bad news was the sluggishness of customer demand. Klaus Beckmeyer, the newly appointed European regional manager, had presented the revised forecast. Many car models were selling at half the anticipated volume, if not less. This made Ward feel distinctly vulnerable. Before Jenkinson had taken a direct interest in the plants' operations, Kent Reed, the now departed branch manager, had twisted Ward's arm for an "ambitious budget" (read "ridiculous") with wildly unrealistic sales expectations. Ward thought about this in light of the bimonthly conversations he had started with Jenkinson. These telephone talks had focused on the operational life of the plant: complaints, ppms, headcount reduction, inventory, with little mention of the actual budget. Now, as far as Ward understood, Beckmeyer had budgetary responsibility for the European plants, which would make him Ward's boss—on paper at least. Ward felt Jenkinson was making a bad mistake in letting the budgetary process get out of line with his hands-on control of operational matters, but, hey, it's his company after all.

Ward also had been very interested on the status presentation on the Chinese plant. Right before the spinoff of the division, a coup of Wayne Sanders and the previous division VP had been to convince one of the Big Three to source one part family from China, where they found prices that not only defied any competition, but, some said at the time, defied the laws of gravity as well. The project was now ramping up, and the program manager had been trying to put a good face on it, but it seemed like Jenkinson had to be in China every other day. It looked like a real mess, and not one likely to be fixed by any "lean transformation." In any case, Ward smirked to himself, he had enough troubles of his own. Anything that would keep management's eyes away from Vaudon was music to his ears.

As they reconvened into the conference room after their ghastly lunch, Ward was looking forward to the next plenary talk. Jenkinson had asked his old mentor, Bob Woods, to speak about "lean management." Woods was something of a legend in the automotive industry—the first Westerner to have implemented a Toyota-like production system outside of Toyota. Ward had tried to spot him in the lunch crowd, but failed so far. From hearing Amy Woods describe her father-in-law, Ward expected some sort of cross between a beach bum and a Japanese *aikido* master. During the dinner at Malancourt a few months ago, Amy had regaled them with an impression of Bob Woods' first visits in Jenkinson's old plant. "I can see your warehouse, son," he had said right in the middle of the assembly shop floor, "but where is the factory?" According to her, after retiring from being an automotive exec, he spent most of his days tinkering with an old wooden yacht, which he occasionally sailed around the San Francisco bay. She had waxed lyrically about sailing under the rust-red pillars of the Golden Gate at sunset. Amy made them laugh recounting Woods senior showing up at the plant in his "I'm painting my boat again" clothes, which caused the operators to ask her what the new janitor was so riled about? He was rumored to have retained many automotive contacts and some influence in the industry, and it was apparently through him that the equity firm had hired Jenkinson as CEO for the Nexplas venture.

The man who eventually took the mike at the podium did not look quite the beach bum, more like the sailing master of a schooner from a 1950s movie. Ward noted that he must shop at the same store as Jenkinson, for he wore the same beige slacks and a naval-looking shirt with button-down pockets and shoulder straps. Woods stood ramrod straight, and glared at the assembled upper echelons of Nexplas with pale blue eyes under white brows. His face was tanned and weathered; a hard face with a hawkish nose and a thin-lipped mouth. He looked aged without looking elderly, and had an almost boyish habit of brushing back wisps of white hairs with an automatic gesture that was hardly necessary any more. As he started talking, you could hear there still was a good deal of fight left in the old guy.

"Lean management is radically different from anything you know." Bob Woods kicked in without a hello, thank you, or the obligatory after-lunch joke. He continued without pausing, indifferent to the people who clearly expected a colorful introduction and had not yet seated themselves. "Lean is about servicing customers better with less staff, less inventory, and less capital expenditure. You do this through managing your processes better, and with people who know what they are doing and create value, which means without the extra staff and buffers and waste of time and money."

He paused and looked at them all as if he was personally challenging each and every one.

"So it's not for the fainthearted. Phil's asked me to talk to you about lean management. I believe giving talks like this is a waste of time, because you either get it from doing it, or you don't. But I'll give it a go.

"In business, there are essentially three ways of running things. The first is having managers manage a department by getting their people to perform a number of activities. Do this or that project, whether the company really benefits or not, that's our job. Let's audit. Let's put out a newsletter. Let's implement a new software system. In some cases, this works really well. If you've got to build the great Western railways, you need to lay down so many miles of track a day and have the rails equally spaced. That's it. The rest is a matter of throwing people at it. But in most modern businesses, activities are not so simple, and simply insisting in implementing this system or demanding compliance to that procedure hoping it will help is a very, very wasteful way to work. No one wants to ask questions, because they're just a cog in a wheel.

"Many folks have realized the limitations of this 'throw people at it' approach, so we've invented a second way of running things, which is giving incentives for financial results. The thinking is simple: I don't care how you do it, but if you make the numbers, you'll get your cut. If you don't, well ... we'll find someone who does. This is overall more efficient than the first method because it at least motivates people to put in a lot of effort but is hardly more effective, and is wasteful of people's talents. Everyone does what they are paid to do, nothing more or nothing less, and as long as you hit targets and your boss gets the bonus, everyone is happy. Thinking is not in the bonus plan, and so it happens only when there is a fire to fight and then we all become geniuses. This is how most of us made our careers. Make the numbers, or else. Unfortunately, one individual's progress comes at the expense of someone else—which is also incredibly wasteful.

"Toyota has developed a radically different way of managing. Their approach is to blend both activity and results through *PDCA* thinking. The gist of it is to *get teams to solve problems together*. Toyota has identified a few typical problems, and drives people to solve these problems locally in greater and greater detail. This is important to understand if you want to do lean. There are no plug-in solutions. You can't purchase lean systems. You've got to motivate your teams to work things out by trying out new ideas, and testing hypotheses—constantly. It is about questioning assumptions. It's about asking questions. Eventually you get to stable processes that work well most of the time, and the exceptions are the basis for problem-solving and improvement. You also get people starting to turn on and use their brains, a rarely used commodity in our organizations today.

"To run leaner processes, you've got to get every one *thinking* about how to eliminate waste, every day," Woods said, challenging them all with an icy glare.

"What we've learned from Toyota is to deliver greater *customer satisfaction* through the use of the *Toyota Production System*, supported by the *Toyota Way* of management. I'll try to summarize these three themes for you. But keep in mind that it all really comes down to good common sense that, unfortunately, is not very common.

"No doubt you're all familiar with *customer satisfaction*. Let's define this: Deliver on time, good parts, and at the lowest possible cost. Work safely and maintain morale. Quality. Cost. Delivery. Safety. Morale. Now, the odd thing about Toyota's approach is that they truly believe that customer value is created on the shop floor, by all employees, and not just in engineering ivory towers and sales show rooms.

"Essentially, you're asking yourself two key questions:
- *Do our products or services consistently solve the customers' problems?*
- *Can our people solve their own problems to consistently ensure this?*

"Ultimately, I believe that the secret to lean strategy can be defined as disrupting markets by offering better products or services at a lower overall production cost—hence obtaining both growth and profitability, while locking out competitors whose replication of identical customer satisfaction would come at unbearable cost. I remember vividly when Toyota launched the Camry in North American markets. We all saw it as an 'over-engineered' product for the price range. The OEMs claimed that Toyota, not being burdened by the cost of pensions, had invested more per car than they possibly could. This may have been true, but it obscured the other part of the equation, which is that Toyota knows how to produce more variety and higher tolerances without suffering from the equivalent hike in manufacturing costs because of its mastery of production processes. The Camry was one of many market-disrupting products, as were the Lexus (which created a top luxury brand from scratch—outselling all luxury competitors from day one) or the Prius (which went against industry conventional wisdom by offering customers a 'green' response through hybrid engines), and now, the Scion. Such products are difficult to compete against because they hit the right spot with customers, and they have relatively low production costs that allow the company to price them competitively and still make a profit. As you can see, 'leanness' derives from a fundamentally different way of approaching business problems and going about solving them."

Woods paused for a while, taking the time to look the audience in the eye. Ward wasn't sure exactly where this was going, but it certainly put lean in a different perspective for him. He had always known lean as a bunch of techniques in the factory, like *"just-in-time delivery,"* not an engineering strategy. But, yes, clearly Toyota did not become No. 1 just by controlling costs. It made cars people bought.

"My Toyota *sensei*," pursued Woods, "worked directly for Taiichi Ohno, and he told me that Ohno was very uneasy with the idea that the *Toyota Production System* should be written down. He felt that it had to be lived every day on the shop floor by seeing waste and striving to eliminate waste. Documenting it, he felt, would only lead to misunderstandings and kill creativity.

"The ironic thing is that this is exactly what happened—not within Toyota, but within industry at large. To be honest, for much of my working life I did not 'get it.' When I did start to understand, I spent the rest of my career fighting the bureaucrats who wanted to make it into a documentation game. The one with the biggest training manuals was the leanest. In any event, eventually the *Toyota Production System*—TPS—was documented and came to be formalized in three large blocks.

"First is *auto-quality*, or *jidoka*: Stop whatever you're doing right now rather than producing a second bad part. This is a core notion in TPS, which goes all the way back to Sakichi Toyoda, who built automatic looms at the end of the 19th century. He was a genius who invented looms that stopped themselves when a thread broke. Stop and understand the problem, rather than keep running and sort out the bad parts. It's blindingly obvious, but even a century later very few people do it. Why? It's so incredibly hard to do. I was recently talking to a guy named Eric to whom I gave his first job in the bad old days, and who has since joined Toyota. He told me about becoming an assistant manager in charge of two assembly lines.

"You've all heard about the line-stop system. If an operator detects a problem that can't be fixed within a minute, the entire line stops. Music then starts and gets louder and louder until the line is up and running again, so that every one knows there is a problem. Eric's not been but a few hours on the job when the line stops. So he gathers the supervisors and one of his best engineers, and they go to where the operator signaled the problem. They understand the problem, and get the line running again. Then, because they're in Toyota, they start asking the first 'why?' Why did the line stop?

"They're still debating this when the assembly line stops again somewhere downstream. Two line stops in a short period, so Eric is really feeling the pressure and is about to rush his team to see what's going on, when his Japanese coordinator grabs him by the sleeve and says: 'Stay here, we have not finished the *Five Whys*. We still do not understand the root cause.' 'What about the line stop?' asks Eric. 'The line will start again without you,' the Japanese coordinator answers. 'More important that we understand the true cause of the first failure.' Meanwhile the team leader downstream puts an immediate countermeasure into place, enabling individuals to explore the problem.

"Now you're all production guys, and can appreciate how hard this can be. Let the fire burn—understand the true cause of the problem first. There are many ways to do so, but essentially, stop and understand what caused a defect rather than pass it down the line is a key pillar of TPS."

"The second pillar is the famous just-in-time system—JIT. Many people immediately think of this as trucks pulling up with parts at the exact moment they are needed with no inventory. It is actually more complicated than that.

"The real focus of the system is building to customer demand—which is represented by the *takt time* (how often should a part be produced within the available production time). The ideal way to do this is with *one-piece flow*, which means continuous movement of product without interruption, essentially building for customers who are pulling product when they want, in the amount they want. If you have too much variation in manufacturing—such as breakdowns, missing operators, bad components—or in customer demand, then you have to hold some inventory, but you hold only enough to cover this variation and then you keep on improving to reduce the variation.

"I still remember 20 years ago when I saw the first Toyota lines in Japan. They had different models go through the same assembly lines. Rather than invest in dedicated lines, and create massive overcapacity as we did, they calculated a *takt time* per model. One would be produced every two minutes, another every five, a third would only come once every hour, and so on. On average the line produced a car a minute, but as I watched the assembly sequence, I realized they had organized it so that operators could still follow a stable cycle, so low-work-content vehicles were interspaced with high-work-content and so on. I was fascinated. I said to them, 'I get it: long/short/long/short.' They said, 'Yes, and then we can use the *kanban* to get supplier parts.'

"What had *kanban* to do with anything? It took me a long while to figure it out, but in the end I realized the assembly sequence of vehicles was designed so that not only were the operator cycles stabilized by long/short/long/short, but the component pull on suppliers was stabilized by the way the *kanban* returned into the upstream processes.

The sequence was calculated so that a specific optional part would be assembled at a regular *takt time* as well, and so *pull levelly* on the supplying process. I was floored. These guys were actually thinking about the whole system and how it was all connected together.

"Not surprisingly, the supplying cells could work in single-piece flow, because they had such a regular demand. And it all came together because in working on one piece at a time, they needed to stop the process whenever they found something wrong with it.

"Continuous flow—stop for quality alert; continuous flow—stop for quality alert," Woods mimicked with his hands. "That's the core insight of TPS. Managing teams so they are obsessed with solving continuous-flow problems or quality problems. And to do so, you need stability. If the process is stable, then you can work on the deviations to improve the steadiness of the system. The stability depends on *standardized work*, which means having repeatable and commonly understood ways of doing things. You do it the standard way, then when a problem arises, you fix it, and then change the *standardized work*. So *standardized work* and *kaizen* are together the bedrock of TPS."

Ward had seated himself in the front row, curious about Woods, and now he found himself sneaking looks to his neighbors, hoping they were as lost as he was. He glimpsed crossed arms and deep frowns. Jenkinson seemed lost in thought again, as if he'd retreated to his own private planet, watching events unfold from afar. Ward was annoyed to see that Sanders, seated in the very front row, a few seats away from the CEO, was answering emails on his Blackberry. Sanders was a short, thin man with an overdose of ambition and charisma, which always made him look larger than life. Like Coleman beside him, he was always impeccably dressed. To him it appeared that business-casual meant no tie with an expensive Italian suit. He sported a permanent tan and the unyielding smile of the professional salesman. He had been the strong man behind the throne in the previous regime, and Ward wondered how he was doing with Jenkinson. He remembered that Amy had mentioned that Jenkinson had taken the Nexplas job because of a split with his own previous business partner, who she had described as the ultimate cheesy salesman.

"*Standardized work* and *kaizen* are the two sides of the same coin," continued Woods. "The palm and the back of the same hand. It took me a very long time to get this, but it is fundamental to understanding TPS. On the one hand, without standards, there can be no improvement. *Standardized work* essentially means that every work activity is broken down in a set sequence of actions. If people don't understand their work well enough to draw and follow the sequence, they'll never improve things. At best, they'll follow change for change's sake. *Standardized work* is not just about what we do, but how we do it, so that we get the expected results. To understand how, we must understand how people work, in practice. More importantly, we must look for the positive variance—the one person who carries out the task better and more efficiently than others, because they've found a useful trick.

"*Standardized work* is not about enforcing absolute compliance on workers. This is probably one of the largest misunderstandings I've come across in trying to apply TPS outside of Toyota. *Standardized work* is about agreeing how the work should be done best, to better see the problems. *Kaizen* is about encouraging operators and frontline supervisors to solve all the problems that appear as gaps to the standard: something that stops you from maintaining the standard cycle. This is a problem. It can be fixed, usually without investment, by using people's ideas."

Woods paused again, letting it sink in.

"But the real surprise is that standards cannot be maintained without *kaizen*. All the firms I know attribute their execution difficulties to the fact that people simply won't follow the rules or keep up standards. Fancy that! What a big surprise. Why should people follow rules? Why should they stick to the procedure, day in, day out, when local conditions make it close to impossible. The fundamental insight about *kaizen* is a human one: You can force someone to do something, but you can't force interest. You can't force people to think, they've got to be interested—and that's up to them. We are all natural problem-solvers. That's the key. By encouraging *kaizen*, we can wake up the problem-solver in everybody, every day. When people start getting interested in solving their problems, they also start sticking with the standards because they know it's the best way to work. Athletes follow rigorous standards, because they want to beat their best time, every time. They are *engaged*," Woods said excitedly and energized, the passion coming to life.

"And that's the true aim of TPS: making everybody engaged so that everyday problem-solving turns into everyday innovation, and, in turn, into more value for customers, which will bring mutual prosperity between the company, its employees, and society at large."

Ward squirmed in his chair. As much as he hated being preached to, he felt oddly moved by the old man's declaration of faith. But it was all a bit too much—he still had trouble with the notion that *kaizen* was necessary to engage people in following standards. Certainly, the French moral outrage to having to comply to *any* standard was not going to help, he thought wryly. The notion that he could engage French workers in *kaizen* made him smirk faintly. It was, however, a fresh perspective. And Woods really seemed to believe it.

"Lean management is about creating a system to make people think," repeated Woods. "It's about making people before making things. And better thinking leads to better products. This must be understood. For years we've tried to copy Toyota's lean tools looking for more efficient ways of doing things, and failing—not realizing that the andon system, or JIT for that matter, are no more than techniques, whose primary purpose is to clarify the fundamental problems of production. The tools are no more help in solving problems than a telescope is in stopping meteor showers or a microscope in eradicating viruses. The tools are nothing more than rigorous ways of highlighting issues in *normal* operations. The *sensei* have been saying it all along: true lean is not about applying lean tools to every process, but about developing a *kaizen* mindset in every employee. We fail to hear them because we don't want to hear them. You can't wake up someone who's pretending to sleep!"

"Now," Woods said, after another lengthy pause. "Toyota has been expanding beyond its home base for the past 20 years, and they've hit the same problems in getting TPS properly applied that we, in the West, have had in copying TPS. Like any other problem, they have been working madly to solve it by trying a series of countermeasures. These countermeasures have focused on culture—how people behave, which is the most difficult challenge of all, even for Toyota. Without the proper behavioral principles and values, TPS can be totally misapplied and fail to deliver results. Look how often Toyota's competitors have failed, often spectacularly. As one *sensei* said, one can create a Buddha image and forget to inject soul in it. As with TPS, the values had originally been passed down in a master-disciple manner, from boss to subordinate, without any written statement on the way. And just as with TPS, it was internally argued that formalizing the values would stifle them and lead to further misunderstanding. But just as they eventually wrote down the basic principles of TPS, Toyota put the Toyota Way into writing to educate new joiners.

"What they came up with, in the end, is a Toyota Way based on two pillars: Continuous improvement and respect for people." Continuous improvement breaks down into three basic principles:

1. *Challenge*: Having a long-term vision of the challenges one needs to face in order to realize one's ambition—what we need to learn rather than what we want to do—and then having the spirit to face that challenge. To do so, we have to challenge ourselves every day to see if we are achieving our goals.

2. *Kaizen*: Good enough never is, no process can ever be thought perfect, so operations must be improved continuously, striving for innovation and evolution.

3. *Genchi genbutsu*: Going to the source to see the facts for oneself and make the right decisions, create consensus, and make sure goals are attained at the best possible speed."

"*Respect for people* is less known outside of Toyota, and essentially involves two defining principles:

1. *Respect*: Taking every stakeholders' problems seriously, and making every effort to build mutual trust. Taking responsibility for other people reaching their objectives. Thought-provoking, I find. As a manager, I must take responsibility for my subordinates reaching the target I set for them.

2. *Teamwork*: Developing individuals through team problem-solving. The idea is to develop and engage people through their contribution to team performance. Shop-floor teams, the whole site as team, and team Toyota at the outset."

"Now," he repeated, "Phil has asked me to present the Toyota Way as I understand it and as closely as possible to how it was passed on to me by my various *sensei*. I am certain you're all sitting here thinking, 'What the hell does that mean?' I have great respect for Phil, but to be honest, I do not think this can be done. I learned only through years and years of doing and feedback, and eventually something penetrated my thick skull. In any case, I will try, but I can only give you my personal take on Toyota's values. They need not be Nexplas' values. In fact, I don't believe that values can be copied and pasted—they are the result of a common history, a shared learning. Phil's intention, I believe, in asking me to present the Toyota Way today, is for you to realize that there is a *management system* that underlies the *production system*. Toyota's own explanation of their success is that they make quality cars by applying the *Toyota Production System*, which is supported by the values of the *Toyota Way*. Both Phil and I believe that the entry point into lean is to realize that this is not just a production tactic, but a complete business strategy. I'm here today to get you to challenge your success at lean, and question your own management assumptions."

Ward felt the collective stir in the room. This was getting a little too close for comfort. What was the man saying? That the reason we don't get results isn't that lean is hard to do … but that we just don't *get it?* This, of course, was exactly what Woods was saying. and it was painful to hear.

"People come to me," he smirked, "saying, 'Sure, I'd love to do this lean stuff. But you don't understand. My customers are completely unreasonable. My suppliers can't deliver a good part. My management doesn't understand anything. My people never want to do what they're told. So please, go and talk to my customers and tell them to do lean, and then talk to my suppliers and tell them to do lean. While you're at it, how about convincing top management they should do lean? And my people as well.'"

Woods paused for dramatic effect, and resumed. "Life would be great if we could just place the blame on everyone else, but unfortunately the lean journey starts with you right here in this room. Each and every one of you. Many try, few succeed. Those who succeed do so spectacularly. They are the managers who learn to challenge their own management assumptions, every day on the shop floor, and who learn how to manage for lean. They learn to engage their people in solving problems all the time, so that processes can deliver more value to customers with less resources.

"To conclude, I don't like the word 'culture,' because it means something different to every one. Shared beliefs. Common behaviors. National quirks. All of the above, and none. Still, culture is the final frontier to create sustainable growth. Beyond lean systems, beyond the management behaviors supporting those, you need to create a lean culture, together. No two cultures are likely to be the same, but I have studied Toyota and been taught by their *sensei* for a long time, and I have learned a few things worth sharing.

"First, it's a culture where senior managers continually go to the work sites and listen directly to their employees.

"Second, it's a culture where the lean tools are used every day to visualize potential issues so that every one can ask 'Why?' until a root cause is identified and a countermeasure is put in place. Then they check until they're certain this is the right way to solve this particular problem.

"Third, it's a culture of 'problems first.' Senior execs get the bad news from their employees because they treat it seriously and respectfully. Staff are thanked when they surface a problem, not shot at or told to shut up and get on with their jobs. Try it someday: thank someone for bringing a new problem up.

"*Go and see.* Ask 'Why?' Show respect."

Woods paused again, glowering fiercely at all, until people started shifting in their seats, not quite sure whether he was done or not. He turned his hawk's face here and there, apparently intent on catching every person's eye.

"Phil thinks you needed to be told," he rasped finally. "I believe that those of you who'll get it will, and the rest won't, no matter how much it's explained or how often. Whatever you do, however, do not to try to cut and paste Toyota's culture. It's been tried before, never with much success. In any case, don't confuse Toyota and TPS. TPS is an ideal that Toyota strives for, and, in its best days, gets close to— which is why we want to understand why they do things.

"My experience of it is you have got to try, and try, and repeat to yourself the basic principles over and over again. Every time one of your employees solves a problem, they know more. Every time they solve a problem together, they not only improve their processes but they learn together as a team. Every time they fix a process or find something to add to a product, they build the success of your company. You're the management. You, here, all in this room. There is nothing else. If you work together to change your own behaviors to create a working environment where every employee can add value to the products, I believe you will profit as Toyota as profited. But it's up to you to find out how. Together.

"Thank you. Good luck."

Half-hearted and uncertain applause greeted Wood's conclusion. Ward was among the few who clapped enthusiastically. Everyone always complains that speakers at conferences never tell you anything new. Well, when they do, the audience doesn't seem to like it much either, he thought, sensing the unease of his fellow managers. As Woods stepped down from the podium, Jenkinson joined his mentor. Ward stepped forward to introduce himself, more out of curiosity than anything else.

"Bob, hey, this is Andrew Ward from our French plant," said Jenkinson, as several true believers (or corporate sycophants) fought for his attention.

"Ah," the older man said in immediate recognition. "The man with the ranch. Amaranta's told us all about it. This I've got to see."

"Um, more of my wife's place, really. And, not quite a ranch, more like riding stables?"

"Fancy that! A dude ranch right in the middle of France. Good wine country as well, she said."

"The best," agreed Ward, bemused, not quite knowing whether he was being teased. "Hope you'll visit us when you can."

"Be careful of what you ask for," the older man said with a sudden, striking smile, like sunshine across a rock face. "I might just do that. Phil keeps badgering me about doing a tour of his European plants. He mentioned you'd been progressing on quality?"

"Bad month in September," winced Ward. "We got surprised with a lot of claims from the summer months—"

"Too many temps?" interrupted Woods with a knowing nod.

"Not enough training," answered Ward ruefully.

"Believe it!"

"Hey, I might be slow, but I'm getting the message: *kaizen, kaizen, kaizen?*"

"You got it," nodded the old man. "The trick is sustaining *kaizen* over time."

"Still struggling with that one," Ward admitted.

"It's all about people!" said Woods. "And about being on the shop floor. It gets easier the day you accept you have to be responsible for everyone's understanding of their job yourself, personally."

Ward nodded. He agreed, on principle, but he struggled with how the hell he could possibly train more than 400 people himself.

"Go to *gemba*!" pronounced Woods cryptically, in true *sensei* fashion, using the Japanese word for shop floor. "*Gemba* is a great teacher."

"Andy, there you are!" exclaimed Coleman. "I've been searching high and low for you."

Ward looked up, startled. People were filing back into the auditorium for the next presentation—something about common definition of key indicators across the group—but he'd been deep in thought, staring unseeingly at his untouched cup of coffee. Woods' talk had reignited his sense of inadequacy. He thought he understood most of the words in the older man's presentation: all the basic lean concepts he'd heard about forever, even if the "Toyota Way" management stuff was new. But Woods' throwaway comment of "the shop floor is a great teacher" made Ward wonder if he really knew how to do any of this stuff on the shop floor. Sure, he had made progress on the quality issues. October had been much better. But he had to face it: He didn't have the first clue about implementing a just-in-time pull system. Or even about "stop-at-first-defect." How could you stop a continuous process such as injection presses in case of a defect, if getting them started again would only create more startup bad parts in the first place? Even in assembly, he feared that stop at first defect would mean his lines would be stopped all the time, which contradicted the notion of continuous *standardized work* for the operator. As for *standardized work* itself, he'd been trained to all the proper documentation but had never seen it actually applied anywhere, and, to be honest, had no notion of where to look. Maybe he could ask to visit a Toyota plant?

"Why the long face?" inquired Coleman.

"Just thinking," Ward replied, shifting mental gears. They hadn't found time for a real talk during the conference, and, upon closer look, his old friend looked tired. There was a trace of anxiety underneath the urbane smile and trademark affability. Ward had a lot of respect for the man, and believed he owed him his job. Coleman had always treated him like a protégé, and taught him much of what he knew about business on global markets.

"Don't beat yourself up about having to transfer parts to Poland. It was only a matter of time."

"Jenkinson really intends to close the plant?" Ward asked, suddenly alarmed. Coleman rarely told you things upfront—in this he was completely the opposite of Jenkinson. But his hints carried weight.

"It's always been the plan," shrugged Coleman. "And he tends to do what he says. But I haven't heard him mention it recently. He's fighting so many other battles in any case. Concerning the parts we mentioned: We are systematically reviewing how we move components across the world and trying to simplify our supply chains. I've been asked to halve the number of locations a product has to go through before it reaches a customer. The aim is lead-time reduction. As well as reducing unit cost at the same time, of course," he added wryly.

"Which ever way you cut it," Ward considered grimly, "it doesn't look good for Vaudon."

"Let's face it, old boy, you're stuck between a rock and a hard place. Sanders is still adamant we have to get out of high-cost areas altogether and migrate our European production East. Have you noticed how angry Beckmeyer looks these days?"

"And Jenkinson?"

"His worry is more about your customers. What are their mid-term prospects by the way? He sees an advantage having a French plant supplying French OEMs, but their sales haven't been too hot lately—"

"Tell me about it! I've had to revise forecast downwards twice this year," replied Ward.

"And it's hard to get into the German automakers. Production costs in France might be lower than Germany's, but they are still very high. You know that."

"Don't remind me."

"Be fair, Andy, you used to work those simulations with me. Don't take it so personally—it's only business. This benighted industry is getting tougher by the year. We need to cut costs drastically and hope we survive."

As Ward thought it over, another worry surfaced.

"Lowell—tell me one thing," he started uncertainly. After all, the last thing he wanted was to put the wrong idea in any senior execs' head, even his oldest ally. But in the end, asking is just a moment's embarrassment. Not asking can keep you embarrassed forever. "Remember when Kent Reed was still branch manager around this time last year? When we did the budgets?"

"Certainly. What's on your mind?"

"Well, with Jenkinson driving the U.S. so hard at the time, Reed had us all sign up for really ambitious budgets."

"Ambitious, yes, a bit—but that's how we move things forward. For all the good it's done him," he added bitterly. "He worked like a dog for the division for years, and Jenkinson ditched him without a moment's thought."

"You were there at the budget session. He held a gun to my head and forced me to sign off assumptions that'll never fly."

"It's how the game is played. We all know that. What's your concern?"

"Well, up to now I've been sort of saved because I've kept the Romanian parts that have been late in being transferred. But they're going as we speak. And now I'm losing parts to Wroclaw. I'm really worried about making the numbers in these conditions. And I've got no control over any of these decisions."

"Is that all that's troubling you?" Coleman dismissed his worry with a flick of the wrist. "Don't you worry about that. If there's one thing we can say in favor of our CEO, it's that he knows exactly what's going on in his plants. Everyone knows you're doing your best. You'll be right as rain, you'll see. Don't lose sleep over it."

Right as rain? Ward was often annoyed by Coleman's affectation for rare idioms. How right was rain anyway?

"You can't carry the weight of the world on your shoulders," Ward chided himself, taking a deep, deep breath. It was a beautiful Indian summer day, and he was lost somewhere in steep hills, overlooking a long narrow lake. About halfway to Bethany, he'd stopped the car at the Bald Eagle Viewing Spot and stepped out to stretch after several hours' drive. The light was breathtaking, unlike anything he'd ever seen in Europe, and the red and gold trees shone in full glory, resplendent against the cloudless azure sky. He opened himself to the feel of the woods, savoring the last days of pure sunshine after the first frosts, and before the hunkering down of the winter. The air was full of smells, a hint of a chill was stretching up from the lake's midnight-blue waters.

He'd chosen to drive from Rexington to Bethany rather than fly. He used to do that a lot, he recalled wistfully. In the glory days of consulting, he would rent cars in every remote site of his clients and stay the weekend after work for the simple pleasure of driving around in foreign locations. He remembered the excitement of discovery, blending with the nagging fear of the unknown, the unfamiliar, the unpredictable—as well as the occasional pure magical moment of stunning exotic beauty. He'd largely stopped traveling after settling down in France. Claire couldn't leave Malancourt very often or for very long, and when they did get away, it was mostly to visit his parents either in Richmond or in Aix. This summer's Greek getaway had been a rare treat. It felt good to be on the open road again, and, he resolved, that feeling good would be good enough for now.

For a short while, driving along the winding country roads, through small towns and red-barned fields, Ward briefly recaptured that feeling of contented carelessness. Right this second, he refused to own anything—child, marriage, plant. He let them own themselves and grow at their own pace, following their own path. For a while, liberated by the open road, he held on to his contrived mental freedom, like rediscovering an old friend.

Until Claire rang his cell and told him not to fret: Charlie was running a fever. Seasonal bug, the doctor had said. Should be fine by the time he got back. Nothing to worry about. Blast! Where had his life gone? Back in the car and as the song blared on the radio, freedom was, indeed, just another word for nothing left to lose. In a rare moment of insight, Ward realized why the stakes felt so high. He now had much that he cared about and so much to lose.

"I've got to ask," said Ward uncomfortably. "How much time do you actually spend on the shop floor?"

Mark Neville deadpanned him for a few heartbeats, making him feel like an idiot, but then suddenly smiled widely.

"Phil told you to ask me, am I right? I keep bitching to him that with all the corporate stuff we have to do, I don't have enough time at *gemba*."

Despite his imposing and somewhat forbidding physique, Neville turned out to be a genial man with a quiet confidence Ward both envied and resented. Neville was just a bit shorter than the Englishman, but bulky enough to hold two Andrews rolled into one, with space to spare. Impressive muscles jutted out of a short-sleeved white shirt that contrasted starkly with his dark skin. He had deep brows and wore a thick, black moustache that made him look more like a nightclub bouncer than a plant manager.

Meeting him again, Ward had vividly remembered their first encounter. It would have been what? Five years ago? He had been part of a group of trainees to whom Ward would impart the wisdom of superior supply-chain management in world-class manufacturing, no less, a consulting assignment for Coleman. In retrospect, he had to admit the whole thing must have sounded far-fetched to operational managers, not to say downright silly. When he had foolishly taken the group to task for not cooperating because all of this was, really, for their own good, Neville had glowered and snorted that the two biggest lies in business were "the check is in the mail" and "I'm from corporate, and I'm here to help," getting a cheer from the group. Ward's father had always maintained that, if you can't laugh at yourself, you're missing the best joke around, but he still felt guilty about the self-important nonsense he had dispensed during his consulting days to people who did know better.

"With all the reporting and stuff," Neville said, "I spend at least two or three hours a day in my office."

"Two to three?" checked Ward, astonished. "I'm lucky if I get to spend at least one hour in the plant every day. There's always something else to do."

"Yeah, tell me about it. Truth is, I go straight to the floor, and don't read emails until after lunch. Sometimes not at all."

"But, what do you actually do on the shop floor all this time?" Ward blurted.

"*Kaizen,* of course."

"You've lost me there. I thought that *kaizen* is about getting the operators to contribute to the processes and products. All I keep hearing is that I shouldn't just use the 10 brains around me and hundreds of hands but—"

"Every brain in the business. Yeah, that's a Phil soundbite. But that's the whole point. As plant manager you've got to encourage the *kaizen*. It won't just happen on its own."

"I'm not to be involved myself, but get it done? Delegate *kaizen* you mean?"

"Not exactly ... Listen, why not go to the *gemba*, it'll be easier to explain," proposed Neville as he drained his cup of coffee. Ward followed suit, blessing the man for having his own espresso machine. This was the first decent coffee he'd had all week, and for that he was prepared to be lectured and patronized until the cows came home.

As they entered the plant by the press area, Ward was immediately struck by how different this plant looked from his. Like Vaudon, there were two dozen presses from high to small tonnage, some assembly cells, and individual assembly workstations. Products were very similar as well—mostly engine plastic parts. Other than that, he felt he was on a different industrial planet. Strikingly, the plant was organized for flow. Parts flowed from the presses in a variety of cleverly contrived racks, either in containers or on rolling hangers, which reached the assembly stations directly. Ward was impressed to see how every flow system was built of simple white tubing cobbled together without any automation to be seen. The plant also looked far more labor efficient. Unlike every other plant he'd seen so far, Ward couldn't see people simply walking about. Here, operators were working at their stations. The plant seemed otherwise empty of staff.

Something else was missing ... Ward suddenly realized that there were no forklifts driving through the press and assembly areas. Instead, components and parts were supplied by small trains built out of white tubing. Unlike the forklifts that would deliver entire pallets of components occasionally (and even then rarely on time) at his plant, these trains circulated continuously, delivering small quantities constantly. Abruptly, Ward understood Jenkinson's comment about banning forklifts from the shop floor when they'd discussed the forklift accident during the summer. Neville confirmed that forklifts were restricted to the loading area for putting large customer components in the trucks. Ward noted that the area had been organized to maximize the forklift use by unloading the empty containers before loading the full ones. Every other material in the plant was moved by small trains.

He wondered how Neville had managed to coax a steady return of empties from his customers. In Vaudon, this was another constant hassle. Because the OEMs would not return containers reliably with every truck that came to pick up parts, they were constantly either short of customer containers, and had to work with cardboard boxes, or suddenly flush with empty containers they couldn't even store.

Another conspicuous difference was that, unlike Vaudon, there was not one operator per press taking the parts off the conveyor, fixing any small flaws left over from upstream in the process, and placing them in the proper packaging. Here, conveyors linked groups of presses where a team of operators picked the parts coming together on a single conveyor and placed them in the right container, and then placed the containers in the right supermarket lane.

"We try to group operators together," explained Neville, pointing this out with his huge hands, "to encourage team spirit, but also so that if we make a productivity improvement, we can rebalance the line with one less person. If they stand isolated in front of the press, no matter how much you improve the workstation, you can't ever take a third of a person out."

"You bet," agreed Ward, excitedly sketching the setup on the back of the travel information he had in his breast pocket. "Your productivity is twice, maybe three times mine. Wow."

"Yeah," the man shrugged self-deprecatingly. "Didn't happen overnight, I can tell you. Here we are, the Toyota cell."

Ward assembled the almost exact same part for a different customer. Again, his plant's assembly didn't look anything like this.

For starters, assembly wasn't in a single cell. French process engineers had separated some work done right at the press with the rest of the assembly spread across several workstations. Here, by contrast, all the assembly occurred in a narrow cell where three women worked with all the necessary components at hand, brought to them by various ingenious flow racks. Ward mentally counted the number of people involved in producing this part at Vaudon, and was horrified to reach six or seven, in a best-case scenario.

"Of all people," Neville muttered darkly to himself, astounded to see Ward show what seemed to be sincere interest in his plant. The guy was a Coleman protégé, and, as such, not to be trusted, Neville reminded himself. He still smarted from all the corporate crap he'd had to swallow over the years from fools like Ward and all the other consultants. As a young manufacturing engineer what seemed like another lifetime ago, Neville had had the opportunity to work on a Toyota-led project to develop a lean cell in the plant. Throughout the years he'd had to swallow his bile and watch one set of managers after another completely miss the point and systematically destroy value through the sheer arrogance of superficial reasoning and terminal short-termism. Jenkinson had been an unexpected breath of fresh air, but if Neville had been a gambling man, he'd put his money on Jenkinson failing at transforming this company—he did not realize what he was up against.

Now, irony of ironies, the same Jenkinson had sent the prime example of managers Neville detested to him for training. "Unbelievable," he sighed inwardly. Ward had had no operational expertise to speak of before being nominated plant manager, and even in his previous role as a supply chain whatever, he'd been a lightweight. Neville guessed Jenkinson took them where he found them, but if he based his hopes for salvaging the company on clowns like this limey, they weren't home free yet. He took a long calming breath, and wondered again how to explain colors to a blind man.

"This is what I do all day long," explained Neville, with the indulgent smile of someone who knows the joke is on you. "I just stand in front of a cell and watch."

Ward, looked at him, nonplussed, though the other man had turned his wide shoulder and was giving the cell his full attention.

"Hi, guys," he said offhandedly. "Hi, Sam, Brianna, Judy."

"Mornin', Mark," they waved back without interrupting their cycle.

Ward stared at the line, but found it so optimized he could hardly see any issues. He looked for examples of the seven wastes outlined by Amy Woods: *overproduction, waiting, conveyance, overprocessing, inventory, motion,* and *correction.* Yet he could not see any obvious break of flow in the ballet of work the operators were conducting before his eyes. The three women worked in a steady, coordinated way, without either rushing or waiting. It was amazing.

"Judy," said Neville, after several minutes of intense watching had gone by, making Ward realize he'd lost his concentration and was thinking of workstations back in Vaudon rather than, well, *seeing*. "It seems that when you grab the top part in front of you, you're hitting your wrist on the container. Does this happen often?"

The three ladies stopped what they were doing, turned toward the plant manager, then stared at the flow rack as if seeing it for the first time. Yes, it did appear as if parts arrived a bit high for the shortest team member.

"Could you show us?" asked Neville.

"Sure, Mark," she answered, picking up the component. Sure enough, she stretched her arm and banged the underside of her wrist while dipping in the box.

"It only happens when the box is almost empty—when it's full there's no problem."

"Judy, you know better than this. It still means you're banging your wrist several times an hour. You know how I feel about work-related injuries. I'd rather no one developed carpal tunnel syndrome."

"Aw, Mark, it's all right. Truly."

"No it's not. Tell me why this happens."

"I'm short!" she answered right away with a wide smile. She was indeed short, an Italian-looking woman with black curly locks, and neon-bright pink nail polish.

"You are," frowned one of her co-workers, a matronly woman with a pasty complexion and a rather sour face. "But I get the same problem. You have to stretch your arm more, which is going to cause fatigue, you'll see."

"So what's the problem?" asked the plant manager.

"Box too high?" suggested the third woman, a young, girlish blond.

"Flow rack at the wrong angle?"

"Yeah, but remember we had to put it there because otherwise it interferes with the machine."

"Or the container is too large, maybe?"

"Ladies—" started Neville, putting his massive hands up.

"Make a suggestion," they laughed in unison. "As always."

"Please make a suggestion," he agreed, nodding concernedly. "First talk it over with Pete, and then with Martha, will you?"

"Sure thing, Mark."

"Pete and Martha?" wondered Ward aloud, as they moved away from the line.

"Pete is the team leader for this cell and the next cell where we have three other operators. One guy didn't show up this morning, so Pete is replacing him. Otherwise he would have come around as soon as we did. Martha's the area supervisor."

"What's your ratio of supervisors?"

"It depends on the activity. Overall, I've got a shift supervisor for about 40, 45 people. But here in assembly, I've got assistant supervisors for 15 to 20 people. The ideal for a team leader is a team of five, but in this place I'm a bit under standard. One team leader will coordinate six to seven people.

"Wow, that's far more frontline management than I've got!"

"So everybody says," shrugged Neville. "But I find it worth it productivity-wise. And I've hardly got any structure staff at all."

"So, I'm just trying to understand. That's what you do all day?" Ward asked. "Walk around and ask for suggestions?"

"In a nutshell," agreed Neville with a superior smile. "When I'm not with a customer, at a supplier, or fighting it out with these fools in engineering, then yes. At the plant that's what I do. Surprised?"

"Um. Rather. I mean, the plant is very impressive. It's just that, well—that's how you got there? It is hard to believe."

"I guess. But it's essentially what I do. Look, to be honest, it's a bit more structured than just asking for suggestions. There are many other activities that must accompany this. I'll also go and speak to the supervisor, to make sure they see the problem. Their role is then to work with the team on the basis of *standardized work* and to get them to clarify the problem. Then, if a team member suggests something, the supervisor helps them to explain exactly how their suggestion would affect the situation. Once it's clearer, they agree on a time slot to try the idea out, with cardboard and what have you. Then, the supervisor helps the operator do the *check* of the *PDCA*. If the idea works, the operator has to convince the other members of the team. Then they need to convince the afternoon and night shifts as well. Only then do we consider the suggestion accepted. In truth, the suggestion process here is a large part of the work of the supervisor— and I keep checking constantly."

"You're getting them to do their own *PDCA*?" Ward asked. "They *plan* the idea, try it out, *check* on it, and *act* on it with the other team members, right?"

"Sure. It's not like I have anything better to do with my time?"

"Wow!" exclaimed Ward. "I wish I could do this with my guys back home."

Neville shot him a sidelong glance, but said nothing. He remembered all the times when everybody explained to him that he would never achieve Toyota's level of productivity because his employees weren't Japanese and had the wrong work culture or weren't selected as rigorously as Toyota did and did not have the right attitude or weren't Toyota trained on this or that and had some other character flaw. He'd realized back then that if employees conformed to the worse management expectations, they'd never disappoint. People were people everywhere. How long would it take management to understand this?

"You have no idea what the French are like," Ward added defensively, picking up on the other man's disapproval. "How did you learn to do this?" he asked as they walked back toward the plant's open-space office.

"This plant has a bit of history with lean. When I joined as a young manufacturing engineer, long before Alnext bought the plant, the original company had already been doing just-in-time—they had even gotten some kind of award for it. It was a much bigger site then, and they'd managed to land a few parts for Toyota's startup efforts in Georgetown. Headlights, mostly. At the time, Toyota had agreed to help us learn TPS, and they sent some of their senior engineers to work on the Toyota cell with us. They figured it was good training for them as well. I was the local manufacturing engineer who got assigned to the project."

"Twenty years ago?"

"Close," the man said with a wistful grin. "It was fascinating work. The guys had already organized the plant in rough cells, but this took us to a completely other level. The assembly cell still rolled the headlight covers in a protective wrap and then put them in large cardboard boxes that were forklifted away. Toyota had us purchase small plastic containers with special partitions, holding only five parts each. Then they told us that although the Toyota truck only came once a day, we would have to carry boxes to a special location in shipping every half hour, a few containers at a time. Finally, they wanted to have batches of 25 parts, and then change—no more."

"Twenty-five parts?" repeated Ward, astonished. "Five containers?"

"You heard me right: five containers and change," he emphasized with a chopping movement. "Five containers and *change*. But they wouldn't let us spend more than 15 percent of our production time in changeovers. It was a real brainteaser."

"How did you solve it?"

"Slowly. We fought a rearguard battle every inch of the way, but eventually we learned how to do it. And in the process they had us stop at every bad part to understand the problem. So here's the picture on the cell: They're withdrawing a fixed number of containers every half hour, but if a part is wrong they won't produce a second one until I've checked the line and figured out what went wrong. I almost lived on that line, I can tell you."

"What about your other work?"

"Well, that got to be an issue, for sure. But the management at the time thought it was important to learn this JIT stuff. They were mostly disappointed because all we did was very detailed work of which they didn't see the relevance at the time. For instance, we ended up modifying all the equipment so that the operators themselves could do the changes on the cell without relying on setters. It was such a big plant, no one realized the implications back then."

"Implications? Was there a bigger lesson?"

"You mean, other than produce just-in-time and stop the line rather than run with quality problems?" he chuckled. "Brother, the first thing I learned is how easy it is to say, but hard to do. Stop the line, for instance, easy to say. But at first, the line is stopped all the time and you don't know whether these are real problems or not. So you work compromises, you know, so many defects of this type and so on.

"But what I really learned was the importance of the team. This wasn't an easy lesson, understand. With everything we were doing on the line, if we changed one operator we had to start all the training and explanations all over again. Because Toyota's demand was so steady, we managed to have a pretty stable team in the end, and these guys were really committed, you know. They'd come in rain or shine. I remember one girl we had to send home because she'd come to work with a real bad fever. She didn't want to let the team down. In the end, I got the credit for many of the changes, but the management never realized that most of the ideas came from the operators themselves."

He paused, as they were about to reenter the management area. "Hang on," the big man said. "Let's go back to the line, I'll show you something."

Ward's mind was reeling, and he felt the now-familiar hollow in the pit of his stomach. How do you catch up to 20 years' experience? Neville had stopped the small-train driver to explain something that Ward could not spot.

"Anyway," Neville went back to his story as they walked back through the plant. "Management got really impatient, because although we made staggering productivity gains on the cell, we didn't seem to be learning any 'just in time' as it was understood at the time. We didn't really use *kanbans* on the cell, just pulled a fix number of boxes at a fixed time and so on. So they discussed this with Toyota, and they sent us a *sensei* from their supplier development center. That was something else. The guy came in and all he would say is 'cells.' We had to put the entire plant in cells. He didn't speak much English, so there was a lot of translation problems, but we sorta understood that he would not come back until we had the entire assembly organized in cells as we'd done with the Toyota line. So we did that, and I got put in charge of the whole project. It was a real ballbreaker; I had to fight with everyone, from management to supervisors to the union. But we got there in the end."

"Then?"

"Shop stocks," he sighed. "Each cell had to have its little supermarket of high-runners and a special lane for low-runners. The principle was clear, although it was a revolution: Parts had to be stored *after the manufacturing process*, not before. In essence, each cell had to own its own production, a little store of parts, if you will, and customer cells would come and withdraw at need. The main practical problem was that it meant getting rid of all the large packaging and move the entire plant to small boxes. This got crazy, so they abandoned the whole plant project, and made me module manager of a smaller area where I was given the go-ahead."

They were back at the cell, and Neville waved at the operators who looked up and nodded, but didn't interrupt their cycle.

"This was the big next step," he said, pointing toward a long tube where clipped *kanban* cards hung in a neat queue."

"At this point, we had been doing *kanban* boards, you know, putting cards up on a board painted green for okay, yellow and red for 'do some more.' Because we were pulling so regularly on the Toyota line, we never had really bothered, but in my larger area, the *sensei* made me put in all the paraphernalia of a *leveling* box, *kanbans*, and launcher queues, the whole shebang."

Ward looked at the hanging cards, trying to figure out what was going on. Plastic cards were clipped by packets of five, and arranged in a waiting queue.

"I get it," he finally said cautiously. "You're reproducing the sequence of consumption, is that it?"

"Pretty much. One box gets taken away from the shop stock over there, and the card gets placed in this batch building box here.

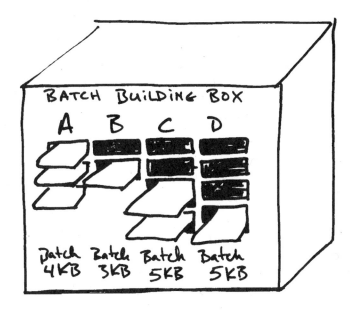

"Once the five cards have been reached, they're attached with a clip, and put into the launcher. We're not yet at the box level, but, yeah, we're trying to get as close as we can to producing in the sequence of consumption. The ideal is one by one in sequence."

He was back to watching the line intensely, and, again, Ward felt completely at a loss of what to look for, which was really disconcerting. After all, he'd been plant manager for three full years now!

"We were still in the middle of implementation when the site was sold to Alnext," sighed Neville with a frown. "So we join the Interior Parts branch and, at the time, that stupid fool Coleman was in charge—before they had the sense to kick him to Supply Chain. Geez, what an idiot."

Coleman? Ward looked sideways at the other man, trying to see if there was a pointed message there, but no, the guy was just reliving the moment, and probably would not connect Ward to Coleman. Ward was worried and intrigued to hear someone be so critical of his mentor, who he had not heard anything bad about before. He suspected Neville to be the kind of guy who'd nurse a grudge.

"So the fool sees all the small boxes I'd just implemented, and the fact that someone from logistics has to come and pick them up every half hour—true, we didn't have a train then—but in any case, he completely misses the impact of short batches, wouldn't listen to anything, and orders us back to large containers to minimize the wasted labor in doing all these trips.

"I remember a time before that when we were running with *kanban*. The machine breaks down in the middle of the night, and I get woken up. So I ask them how much stock they've got ahead of them to deliver to Toyota.

"At the time we're sending a truck every two hours. 'Three hours,' they tell me. So I kiss the wife goodbye, and while I'm not happy about it, head off to the plant, and try to sort the mess out.

"Same thing happens a few months later, when we've gone back to long batches. They wake me up in the middle of the night for another equipment problem, and I ask them, 'How much stock have you got?' 'Three days,' they say. So I tell them to 'Go to hell. Let me sleep. I'll see you in the morning.'"

He laughed unexpectedly. "Funny, no?"

Ward smiled dutifully, feeling lost at sea.

"In any case, I made such a nuisance of myself that they moved me back to manufacturing engineering. But then things finally got so bad with the new management that I simply quit. I'd had enough of production anyway, and wanted to try something else. Be my own man."

"Really? What did you do?"

"Oh, I started running a string of laundromats in town."

"Didn't work out?"

"Worked out fine," he smiled widely. "Just got boring after a while. Nothing much happens with laundry."

"So you came back to the plant?"

"Yeah. For my sins. In a way, I was really glad I'd left. Alnext management had cut the plant's crew by a third, and all these people were out of a job. Bethany is a real small town, and I knew all of these guys. I sure was glad not to be part of it when the word came down. But in the end, what remained of the plant was in a total mess, and they'd got some other incompetent fool to run it. So somebody remembers me, and they ask me whether I want to take over as production manager. 'What the hell,' I tell them—'Why not?'"

Ward found himself unexpectedly warming to the guy. This was a production chap, through and through—the real McCoy. While Ward had been playing consultant, enjoying the thrill of business-class flights, airport lounges, power breakfasts, and all the assorted ego trips of lording it over mere operational managers, Neville had been learning lean the hard way, apprenticed to the Toyota consultants, solving problem after problem, never being told what the big picture would ever be. He'd earned his plant. He cared.

And now, Ward realized that he, too, was beginning to care—and wasn't sure he liked the feeling. When he first heard that Vaudon's days were numbered, he had panicked and begged for time, certain that he would be able to tap-dance his way out of this mess. But the more he learned about Jenkinson, the more he became convinced that corporate dog-and-pony shows wouldn't cut it. *Pretending* to do lean was not going to be good enough, no matter how good a game he talked. So Ward had tried harder—and failed. And now that he could see a plant so much further along the lean journey than his own *tas de boue*—a mudhole, as they say in France. There was something to this lean thing that was hard to define, but defining at the same time. Something that gave Neville this outrageous mix of casual arrogance and deep humility. Something you had to earn, not something you could finesse. Bugger.

"And then you started lean again in the plant?"

"What?" asked the other plant manager, who was completely focused on the cell, his huge arms crossed.

"No, 'fraid not. They kept me running ragged with all the fires to put out, and all the corporate programs to implement. The big project was the new release of the MRP software. So I didn't even try. I focused on rebuilding cells, and stabilizing the operators in teams. In the bad years, they'd cut all the supervisors, and brought them down to one per day with huge areas."

"That's what I've got," agreed Ward. "To optimize the direct/indirect ratio."

"Yeah, all that jazz. So I gathered the remaining old-timers, and rebuilt a solid supervisory group; and then we tried to spread the ideas down to team leaders, but it was a day-in, day-out fight with the plant manager. There!" he exclaimed, nodding toward the team.

"What?" asked Ward.

"Bad part!"

Indeed, the operator had just put a part in the red bin, right in front of Ward's nose, but he had been so engrossed in the conversation he had not even seen it.

"And the team leader is making parts in the other cell. Gawd, one person missing and this whole setup goes to hell, I'll tell you. Normally, every time they place a bad part in the red bin, the team leader comes to have a look to see if the cause can be spotted."

"What happened?"

"We're not sure. We keep getting a few bad parts after the changeover. This team has a quality circle. They meet for an hour a week with paid overtime to try and figure out what makes the bad part, but we haven't found it yet."

"The changeover?" blurted out Ward.

"Sure, didn't you see them take another set of cards from the waiting file? Every time they do this, they have a changeover. That's what I wanted you to see."

Ward bit his tongue. In fact, he hadn't even noticed that they were changing production. He'd been watching the cell operate and entirely missed the production change. He wasn't *seeing*. When he thought of the rigmarole in Vaudon, where all the components had to be emptied of the old reference, and then filled up again, and then a setter had to be there to deal with the jigs and stuff, he understood why, but was nevertheless shaken by how poor he turned out to be at *seeing* the shop floor. If this man could do it, surely he could learn!

"No setters," Ward finally said. "But what about the components? Don't you have to purge the line of the components for the previous product before starting again?"

"Not any more," smiled Neville, clearly pleased. "Look, we have all components for all models on the line—"

"In really small boxes," completed Ward, slapping his forehead, finally seeing the line's arrangement. "Damn."

"You got it!"

"Damn, damn, damn!" cursed Ward, still completely shaken by the fact that he simply had not seen the change occur. He was on the shop floor, all right, but he was not even looking. "*Go and see,*" he blamed himself, not "Go and look like a bloody fool."

He turned back to Neville, "And all your cells work like this?"

"Not quite," Neville made a face. "But getting there. Slowly. Getting people involved in teams and finding the right team leaders and supervisors is still the hardest part of the job. Developing people takes time. And remember, I've only been really doing this for the past year or so."

"Jenkinson?"

"Yeah. When I heard we were being spun off, I was 'bout ready to quit again. The plant manager and I were shouting at each other constantly—I thought that yet another management change would mean even more cutbacks."

"It usually does," mumbled Ward, which got him another long, even look, but no other reaction.

"Then Phil Jenkinson walks in the plant with his man Bob Woods. The only thing Phil wants to see is what's going on with the Toyota line. Why are we getting so many complaints from them about shipments? The plant manager starts arguing that Toyota accounts for less than 10 percent of the plant's total volume—he doesn't have the resources to cater to their every whim. At which point the consultant, Bob Woods, says 'I don't have time for this—show me the line.'"

"He said that?"

"You've met the man? So I take him to the line, and we start discussing the work I had done on the headlights (when we still had them), and what I was trying to do with the existing cell. We get to the current Toyota line, which is another part, since we no longer did the headlights. And Woods starts bitching about the batch size. I start getting pissed with the old coot. Can't he see what we're doing? So I ask the guys to stop the line and demonstrate a changeover. 'There,' I tell him, 'Look. Under 10 minutes.' He just stares at me and says, 'One breath!'"

"One breath?"

"Yeah," he laughed. "Zero time, you know? The changeover has to happen while the team leader holds his breath. Woods saw that we were trying to do the existing change faster, *without actually challenging the method itself*. So, one breath. With this sort of equipment, the change should be instantaneous. That's exactly what we'd achieved with the Toyota consultants on the headlight cells all these years ago, so I just start laughing, and I ask him how he thinks it should be done. 'Don't ask me,' he says. 'Ask them!'

"Next thing I know, I get a phone call from Phil asking me how long it would take me to have the entire plant in pull system. 'Two years,' I tell him. 'You've got one,' he says, which is how I found out he'd sacked my boss and I'd been promoted to plant manager."

"Much obliged, Mark," Ward said, taking his leave. "I'm really glad I came. At least I understand why Jenkinson is so keen to close my plant. I'm utterly depressed—but much enlightened," he said, trying a bit of gallows humor.

"Phil wants to shut your plant?" asked the other plant manager, looking at him intently.

"And I now know why," Ward admitted ruefully. "I'm so far away from this it's scary. And I haven't been learning this for the past 20 years either. There's no way."

"Phil doesn't strike me as the kind of guy who likes closing plants."

"Well, he just pulled more parts out," Ward complained, not mentioning he had just submitted the full plan for shutting the plant down within the next fiscal year. "Sent them to Poland, you know, low cost," he explained lamely. "And look at the number of people he's fired since he's taken over!"

"Yeah," chuckled Neville darkly. "All you see on the websites are open positions. Although not so much now. You know his stand?"

"As in?"

"Better the no guy than the wrong guy," he smiled, obviously finding it somehow amusing.

"Talk about developing people!" replied Ward, sounding more bitter than he would have liked. But really, thought Ward, all this ado about "making people before making parts," and then the reality was they were cutting heads right, left, and center. Leadership, pah!

The other man gave him one of his long looks.

"I'm from right here, d'you know?"

"What, Bethany?"

"My hometown! Although in those days it was a much bigger place. It was also very much a right side of the tracks/wrong side of the tracks kind of place back then."

He cracked his fingers absently, looking far away for a second. Ward wondered where this was heading.

"Anyhow, I knew this guy at school. Bright kid, good at math and physics, really interested in engineering. Wanted to go to college. But all his friends were fooling around, and, well, you know how it is. He starts dropping out of classes. Still gets good marks, but doesn't show up too often. Then one day, he gets flunked at one of the key classes he needs for his college application. So he begs his teacher, arguing that his marks are not that bad, but the teacher is ticked off because he hasn't been showing up at class a lot lately. 'But I really want to learn,' the kid pleads. 'Yes, but will you let me teach,' the teacher says."

"Do you think that's what it is?" asks Ward. "Jenkinson tries to teach, but no one wants to learn?"

"Try it the other way around: You can't teach someone who doesn't want to learn. First you try to change the people, then you change the people," he growled. "About the parts to Poland? I hear what you're saying, but here, he's brought some parts back from China. The plant's fully loaded. When he gave me the job, we had a simple deal: I gave him productivity, and he gave me volume. He hasn't let me down yet."

"Will you do more work with Toyota?"

"Ah," he winced. "The jury's still out. They were considering us for the new SUV line, but Phil won't back down on price, which they consider too high. He told them he might lower the price on the smaller cars, but that considering the margin on high-range vehicles, he felt the asking price was appropriate. So they're not happy, and it's a big mess because our sales department had promised them a rock-bottom price for these parts, and now they say we're reneging, and this is bad for trust and so on. The long and the short of it is, I don't know. In the meantime, he's also asking them to help us push *kaizen* further on the existing lines. We haven't heard from them on this yet, but I do hope they'll send us someone. I'm reaching the limits of what I know here, and could do with being challenged again."

"Pity we can't level it out," grinned Ward. "Because I'm challenged plenty!"

"It's not that hard," Neville winked back. "It's just takes time. *Go and see. Kaizen.* One problem at a time, that sort of thing. Have faith!"

"Come on, Franck, red-bin time," stirred Ward. They'd been working for hours on their ambitious plan to convert the product flows into true cells. Franck Bayard, the technical manager, was from Strasbourg, close to the German border. Thanks to his fluent German, he'd spent his early years working with central manufacturing engineering in Neuhof. As a result of the various reorganizations, Bayard had returned to France to take the job of engineering manager in Vaudon, but he had never been happy with it. He was good at what he did, but getting bitter as time went on. Ward knew he had tried several times to find other positions, but without much success. The dearth of new products in Vaudon didn't help his mood or his prospects, and he kept coming up with increasingly esoteric arguments to retain his full engineering team. Ward suspected that he was partly tied to the place by the fact that his wife taught school in Metz, and as a state functionary couldn't move very easily. He was a quiet sort of chap, totally devoid of a sense of humor that Ward could detect, which made him difficult to work with. To be fair, he was a quintessential engineer. Give him a good, difficult technical problem that didn't require talking to anyone, and he'd gnaw at it like a dog with a bone and finally come up with an elegant solution. Getting him to do the red bins had been a sort of constant arm wrestling, which Ward knew he was losing.

Ward had been spending a lot more time with the engineer recently. Enthused by his visit to Bethany, he had decided to create similar production cells in his own plant, pronto. However, the product/process matrix had not been as simple to establish as he had assumed. They had created a few cells where products obviously went across the assembly hall and back through one station then another, but this lead to numerous volume problems. Some cells ended up being more than saturated with work, while others would only work one shift. By mapping the value streams for each product family and creating a product/process matrix, they had managed to come up with a grand plan to redo the layout of the entire hall, which Ward wanted to discuss with Jenkinson.

In the meantime, they'd succeeded in moving workstations here and there, creating a few complete cells. This had been much harder work than expected. Thankfully, Bayard had gotten very involved in the project. He split up his small team into working on problem-solving coming out of the red bins, and changed the layout of the factory. True to form, he tended to work on his own and would decree how the cells should be set up, which caused tensions with Olivier Stigler, the production manager—who would respond by dragging his feet in terms of committing resources or rescheduling production for the changes to happen. Ward eventually had to get more personally involved in the project than he'd planned. Not so much because he could contribute to the actual layout work Bayard was doing, but because he had to constantly intervene between Bayard and Stigler to make sure things got done. He'd hoped that by twisting both men's arms to be present at the reviews twice a day and work together on issues, they would develop a better relationship, but it hadn't worked out this way. Bayard simply became more withdrawn than ever at the reviews, while Stigler became more careless with his snide cracks about manufacturing engineering. People!

"Did you *check?*"

"Um. *Check* what, sir?"

"Come on, Andy, call me 'Phil.' Everybody does. *Check* whether investing in the new screws was the right thing to do. I paid for them, remember?"

Ward bit his lip, cringing unhappily. Wrong again! Of course he should have thought to *check*. He knew his boss well enough by now to guess he'd recall petty details like a few hundred thousand euros here and there. Bugger!

"It worked really well. Our ppm rate has gone done considerably," jumped in Stigler. Because Jenkinson had driven in from Neuhof that morning and gone straight to the floor after a quick glance at the plant's main indicators, Stigler seemed to be resolved to show off the work they'd done to the CEO.

"I'm glad it worked," said Jenkinson slowly. "But was it *necessary.*"

"Of course—"

"Hang on, Olivier," Ward cut in. "We haven't actually checked that. All we know is that we're making fewer bad parts on the two presses where we changed the screws, but we haven't really done the *check* of the *PDCA.*"

Stigler swallowed the rest of his argument, disappointed once more by the plant manager. "For heaven's sake, Andy, show a bit of backbone," he wanted to tell him. "Don't roll over like a good puppy every time the boss whistles. If we don't defend the plant, he'll shut us down for real." He was amazed Ward could not see the real danger they were in and the desperate need to stick up for the plant. He feared they would pay dearly for Andy's inexperience on this one.

"No time like now," said Jenkinson, taking his glasses off and rubbing his eyes. The jet lag must be getting to him, Ward thought. When he had spoken to Hans Ackermann about when to expect the CEO, the Neuhof continuous-improvement officer had gleefully told him that Phil's two-day visit had been as grueling as usual. According to him, Beckmeyer did what Jenkinson asked to the letter—but no more—and completely refused to interest himself in the spirit. Jenkinson kept pressing, but Beckmeyer did just enough not to be in formal breach of instructions. As a result, the plant visit was a long, frustrating process, one that Ackermann had compared to mental arm wrestling. "But at least I get more freedom to do things," said Ward's friend.

"Who would know?" Jenkinson asked.

After a quick discussion, they crossed the press hall to the maintenance department. Thankfully, it was impressive. Matthias

Muller, the maintenance manager, was a hard case, but he ran a tight ship. He'd scoffed at Ward's attempt to introduce 5S (again) in the plant in the past, but his own area was sorted out, ordered, clean, standardized, and disciplined. Jenkinson looked around and nodded, looking unusually pleased.

"Where's Matthias?" Ward asked one of the maintenance guys, who was sitting at the computer.

"650 tons is acting up again. He's having a look at the changeover."

They found Muller checking the connections of the waterlines, looking grim, as the two setters stood by. Ward cursed at seeing how unsafe Muller's approach was—he was literally halfway into the press checking the mold—but knew better than tell him otherwise. The chap would only laugh at him.

"Safety first, please," Jenkinson said with a sigh. "*Sécurité.*" He repeated in mangled French.

Muller, looked up, frowning at being interrupted.

"*M'sieur* Jenkinson?" he saluted, offering his wrist to shake, and then rubbing the oil on his hands over his jeans.

"Safety!" repeated the CEO.

"*La sécurité, oui,*" acknowledged the maintenance manager, looking annoyed. "I keep telling these guys to check that the lines don't ride the tie bars when they restart the press, but they never listen," he said as the two setters stared back sullenly. Muller was in his early 50s, and seemed to compensate for losing his hair by keeping it closely cropped and growing a salt-and-pepper goatee, which he would stroke distractedly. The guy was a good mechanic, but an absolute pain in the backside: stubborn as a mule, and not much more polite. He looked defiantly at Jenkinson, who was staring into the open mold.

Ward hastily explained that the CEO wanted to know whether, in retrospect, the investment in new screws had been necessary. He was genuinely curious to see how Muller would react. The taciturn technician did not respond immediately, but considered the question, rubbing his chin with his wrist. Working with Muller was like heating milk. The moment you looked away, he boiled over.

"Absolutely—" Stigler started, earning a raised eyebrow from the maintenance guy. No love lost there.

"For the 19, definitely," cut in Muller. "These cretins in engineering put a polycarbonate part on a press with a general purpose screw. I told them all along it would never work. With the short transition zone and high compression ratio, it shears the material and creates excessive heat in the transition zone through friction. The heat was causing us the 10 percent reject rate on the parts. The screw we've got now is designed for polycarbonate, and our scrap rate is down below 2 percent, so it was definitely the right thing to do. I've been saying that since the start of production."

Ward translated as best he could, as Jenkinson listened intently.

"As for the second," Muller thought out loud, pursing his lips, "I have to say I'm not sure. Reject rates have come down some, but not as much as I'd hoped. I was pretty sure that all our problems came from the screw because it looked badly used, and we had bad parts with every mold we used. But we fixed that, and still one mold is giving us most of the scrap. So I'm trying to figure out what is going on. We get a lot of flash still."

"Have you checked the squareness of the platens?" asked Jenkinson when Ward had finished translating.

Muller did a double take, staring at the CEO as Ward translated the question and then grinned. "I should, shouldn't I?" he said slowly. Stigler stifled a long-suffering sigh.

"The question is," insisted Jenkinson, "did we invest needlessly in the new screw for the second press? I accept your argument for the first. But what about the second?"

Ward's translation triggered a heated debate between the production manager and the maintenance manager. In the end, Muller just shrugged insolently and shut up. Jenkinson ignored the byplay, and raised his eyebrows at Ward.

"You're right," he admitted. "We can't tell for sure. It has helped, but maybe it wasn't the root cause."

"Yep. You spent money before figuring out exactly what the problem was. Money you could have used elsewhere to better effect. Agreed?"

"*Plan, do, check, act*," agreed Ward. "We're okay with *plan* and *do*, but we keep flunking the *check*. It's irritating as hell."

"Rome wasn't built in a day," replied Jenkinson patiently. "To be sure, you should have planned the *check* at the *plan* stage. Mistakes are okay as long as you learn from them. Of course, in this case, your education was rather expensive," he smiled, taking the sting out of the remark. "Please thank Mr. Muller for me, and congratulate him on the neatness of his maintenance area. I have seldom seen one better organized. Now we need to convince him to use more visual management!"

"No problem," the man answered in English when Ward had finished translating, taking the praise expressionlessly, and hurrying away with a curt nod after asking whether they'd still need him. Stigler glared at the retreating back, but kept noticeably quiet. He had never been a very outgoing person and had a way of getting himself into a state, building his own anger into cold rages that would leave him withdrawn and testy for days on end.

To Ward's frustration, the production manager suddenly excused himself, claiming that he had a call scheduled with a supplier. Ward suspected the man had simply invented a reason to leave. Jenkinson watched him go without making a comment, yet Ward felt like he was failing some sort of test nonetheless. What the hell was wrong with these people, anyhow? It was unusual enough to have a CEO who showed an interest in production, let alone actually understood something about it. He could attribute Muller's reticence to his limited grasp of English, but Stigler's negative attitude was a letdown.

"I guess I need to know a lot more about these presses," he admitted uneasily. "I didn't think to check the platens' alignment." Ward had always believed that he could manage the plant without having to know too much about the technical details. He was becoming increasingly convinced that this approach simply wouldn't fly. It's not even like the subject scared him—after all, he was an engineering graduate. It was just that with everything else …

"Probably not the real cause," shrugged Jenkinson. "I suggested it just to make the man think. I've been working a lot with engineering on the new projects, and we keep running into these problems. The argument about polycarbonate certainly rang true."

"So," said Jenkinson, looking over the press area. "How are you doing with the plant?"

"Slow progress," answered Ward with a grimace. "I don't know if you've seen it, but we've put two central boards at the entrance of the hall: One reports the date of the last accident and the number of days accident-free, and the other is a 'wall of shame.'"

"Wall of shame?"

"Yeah, customer complaints, what caused them, what are we doing about it, by when and so on. On the basis of *go and see*, I now run a daily management brief on the shop floor, by the board, focused on customer complaints. Our ppms and complaints keep coming down, and if nothing goes wrong in the next couple of days, November will be our best month ever. Scrap is now less than 2 percent of our monthly sales."

"Down from 4 percent, well done. But—"

"Yeah, it's still very high, I agree. Worse, it's so fragile! To be honest, I'm a bit overwhelmed with everything we're trying to do. I listened to what Amy said, and so, now, after the morning quality management brief, I spend time with each of the supervisors. It's hard work. As a result of observing the Bethany plant, we're now trying to organize all our assembly processes into tight cells. I don't know if it's the right thing to do, but I've taken the tack of grouping operators together—even if it's only one operation and then off to the customer."

"Creating stable teams, that's right. It's obvious when the product goes through several workstations, but in many cases, it's not so easy. When it's a long production line, we end up breaking up the line in zones of five to six people. Conversely, with large automated equipment, defining the team is not natural, so working with zones is the right way to go."

"Great. We've put together a plan to revise the layout of the plant over the Christmas break. I can show you if you want."

"Ah. I'd rather you didn't do one big push," replied Jenkinson. "*Kaizen, kaizen, kaizen.* Step change is important, but only once you know exactly what you're doing. In my experience, if you try to change the layout of the plant completely before having *kaizened* each cell one at a time, you end up making silly decisions, which you then regret. Better to do one thing at a time and learn."

"Oh," exclaimed Ward, taken aback. "No Christmas layout?"

"No."

"Well, on the bright side, that means that I get a Christmas break!"

"In this industry," suddenly laughed the CEO, "not likely."

"My real problem is I'm all over the place," Ward explained. "I've done what Amy suggested, so now we have a *kaizen* event every three weeks led by our continuous-improvement chap—and yes, it is targeted to teach the supervisors to better understand their areas, so there is one of them sitting in every session."

"What about your own management team?"

"Um. Not yet. Should I make it mandatory?"

"That's up to you. But think about it: who do you need most to educate about *go and see* and *kaizen*?"

"Right," agreed Ward, clucking his tongue. "Then we have the red-bin reviews. And the cell creation. All of this, everywhere, and to tell the truth I'm feeling overwhelmed. We're getting quality results, for sure, and some productivity, but nothing like I saw in Bethany. As for stocks, the logistics manager is experimenting with pulling parts from one press, but that's like a drop in the ocean.

"I get your point, mind you," Ward continued. "We've got to be better with the *check* part of *PDCA*. Whereas right now we're doing all this crazy activity, but I'm not sure what results to expect on the numbers. And I don't know where to start in terms of *check*, either. There you go. Snowed under, so to speak."

"The trick," Jenkinson explained, "is to anticipate the *check* mechanism in the *plan* phase of the *PDCA*."

"You've lost me there."

"Consider everything you do as a scientific experiment. If you're testing a hypotheses, you know beforehand what you're looking for— before you run the experiment itself, yes? One of the key lessons about conducting *PDCA* properly is prepare the *check* as you are clarifying the problem and preparing your experiment. Rather than *do* and *check*, you're kinda doing *check* and *do*. Learning is as important as results. So when you *plan*, plan for the *check*."

"*Go and see*," Jenkinson said in his lecturing tone, "is more than just a useful thing to do. It's a management technique. Some people, like Mark Neville in Bethany, have been exposed to it their entire working life and couldn't think of doing anything else."

"Mark seems to be doing little else!"

"And he's got the best results of the group, keep that in mind. His plant is by far the most profitable one, even with products that are not priced well. *Go and see* is the way he runs the plant, and couldn't do it any other way. In fact, when forced to manage a different way, he resigned. *Go and see* is the entry ticket into lean management—what they call 'table stakes' in Vegas. You can't even get in the game without this, let alone compete. Without practicing *go and see* every day you'll only ever stay at the surface, and not get the results."

"I have to admit I find it difficult. Even when I do the *go*, I struggle with the *see*," Ward confessed, thinking to himself that even the *go* was a struggle: There were always so many other things clamoring for his attention. Countless meetings, new reporting demands from Neuhof almost daily, defaulting suppliers, people problems to solve, endless phones calls and e-mails. Every day Ward resolved to spend several hours on the shop, as Neville did, but he would inevitably find the day slipping away without having gone and seen.

"*Go and see* is a management technique," explained Jenkinson, "a technique with four clear dimensions:

First it's about *developing judgment by testing hypotheses. Go and see* is the only way to figure out whether we are right or whether we have misconceptions. The expenditure of the second press screw was a failure of *go and see*: you didn't have enough judgment to know whether it was the right thing to do or whether they should do more work to clarify the problem first.

Second, it's about *building consensus by getting people to agree on the problem* before debating the solution. Most conflict I see in business involves managers arguing about solutions when they don't agree on what the problem really is. As a result, the imposed solution pleases no one other than the one that championed it, and people resist implementation. If they don't share a common view of the problem, why should they buy into the solution?

Third, it's about *achieving goals at the desired speed by checking regularly where people are* in their implementation and helping them if they run into difficulties. In this way, we can learn to link high-level goals with detailed shop-floor implementation and find out where the real difficulties are. And we develop better judgment about where and how to invest resources.

Fourth, it's about *empowering people by involving them.* Involving operators starts by sharing the company's objectives with them and solving their vexing problems immediately. Middle managers' involvement can be seen at how well they maintain the visual management system. Very often, people in the organization get stuck by needing either an authorization or a small push that is easy for senior managers, but hard for them. *Go and see* is about thinking, 'What can I do to improve this workstation or unlock this situation?'"

"Look, you keep arguing that it's unfair to expect Bethany's level of productivity from Vaudon because circumstances are different, right?" asked Jenkinson.

"Well, um, yes, I guess," mumbled Ward.

"So let's practice *go and see*. Let us test this."

"How?"

"Let's *go* to the line that produces the parts you saw in Bethany, and *see*, shall we?"

This was the first cell Ward and Bayard had worked, trying to recreate what he'd seen in the U.S. Setting up this cell had been the source of interminable debates, largely because traditional Alnext practices held that operations must assemble in flow with the presses if possible. And Ward had deviated from this by separating the assembly from the pressing, and, as a result, the press operator was waiting much of the cycle, causing Stigler to complain, making the case that they were losing efficiency. Ward recognized that he did have a point. Ward's planned next step was to group operators at presses with the kind of conveyors he'd seen in Bethany, but he'd not opened this second front—yet. In the meantime, all the assembly operations had been grouped in a production cell, with five operators in the middle. Ward hadn't wanted to wait for a small train, so, in the interim, he had a sixth person loading and unloading the cell with components from an improvised supermarket close by. He realized this went against the basic principle of holding finished-product stock at the production site, but no more than an hour of components on hand. He expected Jenkinson to call him on it, but he hadn't seen any other way to create the cell in the few weeks before the CEO's visit.

"So, what should you see?" asked Jenkinson, as they stood watching the five operators move the parts in and out of the equipment. You'd think the man would at least congratulate them on actually having created the cell, Ward fumed, but no, not a word. "Good job!" simply wasn't part of his vocabulary.

"Seven wastes?"

"That's right. I tend first to look for:
- Foot motion.
- Hand motion.
- Eye motion.

"But seven wastes is fine. What's the obvious thing here?"

"We get all three," said Ward. "Foot motion: they walk quite a distance around their workstation. Hand motion: they have to stretch out to handle parts. Eye motion: things are placed all around the part position in the machine, so they have to look around all the time. I see it."

The operators were quite distant from one another, and although Ward had succeeded in getting them to work standing up, so that they could move freely within the cell, they'd all placed little tables between the process where they accumulated parts rather than handing them over to each other in *one-piece flow*. In fact, Ward had originally pushed to have the machines much closer together, as he'd seen in Bethany, but the operators rebelled and fought for their "space," arguing they needed breathing room to move, even though this created additional steps in their cycles.

"No *one-piece flow*," said Jenkinson, pointing at the stacks of in-process parts. "No *single-piece flow* makes it hard to see whether the line is balanced properly. But watch carefully."

"Excuse me a second," said Ward, as he went forward and explained in French to the operators who Jenkinson was, and that they were only watching the organization of the cell they'd just redone—asking them not to work faster than usual, please, but to keep on at their normal pace. The operators gave side glances at the big man, but then eventually settled back into their normal pace.

"Have you noticed how the third guy on the left is much quicker than the others?"

Ward had. Actually, he'd noticed before. The operator's name was Thierry Fernandez, a temporary worker. He'd been very participative during the creation of the cell, and Ward had considered offering a full-time position, but Jean-Pierre Deloin, the HR manager, had quickly shot that notion down arguing the young operator had social problems. Indeed, today he sported traces of a black eye.

"He's a temp," coughed Ward. "Good worker, but, ah, we believe his private life might be a bit rough."

"Does he turn up to work on time? Any last-minute absences?"

"Not since he's been with us," admitted Ward, remembering having the same conversation with Deloin.

"OK!" said the CEO enthusiastically. "Let's *go and see* then. Let's try this. Can you ask them to stop working for a minute and introduce me to this gentleman?"

"Ah, *le grand patron*," said the young man, shaking Jenkinson's hand hesitantly. He looked no more than a gangly youth with dark eyes and a crew cut.

"Are you trained at all the stations?" Jenkinson asked through Ward. The man nodded diffidently, unsure what was expected of him.

"For a few cycles, I'd like you to do the full part yourself, by carrying it through the entire process. I'll be timing you, if it's okay with you?"

"*Pas de problème*," answered the young man, as Ward started praying this would not trigger another union crisis. The whole timing and stopwatch issue was highly sensitive in the plant, and he had not been able to convince either Deloin or Stigler that this was a fight worth having. But with the CEO himself, *que sera, sera*!

"Andy, can you jot down the times as I call them?" asked Jenkinson as he started timing with his oversized Rolex. Twenty full cycles later, it was clear that Thierry Fernandez had produced 30 percent more parts than the average production total that appeared on the production board divided by five. From the corner of his eye, Ward tried to catch the reactions of the other operators standing there watching intensely, which ranged from blank to clearly disapproving.

"All right," said Phil. The average work content is 358 seconds. What's the *takt time*?"

"Uh, customer demand is 450 parts per day, and we're running two shifts. So *takt time* is 840 divided by 450, mmmm, 112 seconds?"

"So the ideal number of operators is *work content* divided by *takt time*, that's 358 divided by 112, about 3.2—right?"

"And we're running with five, yes," agreed Ward, gritting his teeth.

"And you don't think this cell can run with four," reminded Jenkinson with a slow smile. "Which is precisely what we've come here to test. So now I'd like to ask the team to work without Mr. Fernandez here, following strictly the *single-piece flow* rules. Can you explain that to them?"

Ward went to the team, and made very clear that this tall man in slacks and lumberjack shirt was actually the CEO of the company, praying that this gang wouldn't see this as a perfect opportunity to call a walkout and start a wildcat strike—which, given Jenkinson's plàns, would doubtless lead to the rapid termination of the plant. Trying to hide his concerns from his tone of voice, he explained that the CEO wanted to run the cell with only four people. Could they please do that? Then he carefully explained that they had to work *single-piece flow*. They had to take the parts from each other's hand, one at a time. If the person downstream was not ready, they were supposed to stop and wait.

"Now, Mr. Fernandez," pursued Jenkinson, blithely unaware of the tensions he was creating in the team and getting Ward to translate, "I'm going to ask you to stand within the cell, but not do any parts yourself, but to help out anyone who's struggling with the cycle. We'll run a few parts, and we'll discuss what we've seen. You can tell us anything we're doing wrong, or that is not right with the cell."

Fernandez looked thoroughly puzzled, but nodded all the same and said he'd try.

"Go!" cried Jenkinson, watching intently.

Startup was a big mess. Jenkinson would stop the work every so often and discuss with Fernandez through Ward what he thought was going wrong, and then ask Ward to continue to translate for the other operators on the line. Ward, translating back and forth, was astonished to hear how insightful most of the young guy's comments were. The other team members were clearly resentful to have to apply what Fernandez was suggesting, relayed through the very *grand patron*, the big boss, but they played the game willingly enough. As time went on, Ward worried about the social consequences he would have to deal with. But in the end, he resigned himself, it was Jenkinson's company, not his.

To Ward's further surprise, Jenkinson stayed on the cell the two hours needed to get production stabilized with four operators. In the meantime, Ward had called in the production manager and the maintenance manager. Muller got into the spirit of the moment and was fiddling with the equipment on the spot as they discussed improvements. More often than not, he was communicating directly with Jenkinson by hand movements. On the other hand, Stigler continued to look distinctly unhappy—probably feeling, just like Ward, that he would have to inherit the whole mess after Jenkinson left.

It was hard to actively dislike Jenkinson, just as it was easy to really hate Muller for his bloody-mindedness. It was quite funny to see them both argue with sign language and tinker with the equipment, while the operators made parts, and Ward and his production manager hovered on the fringes of the action. He'd not seen his CEO lose his temper yet, or be anything but infallibly polite. His very unflappability was unnerving. What scared him about the man was his take-no-prisoners approach to management. Right now, again, he was making a point by doing, not telling. Ward wasn't stupid. He was getting the lesson. But his gut twisted at the thought of all the uncontrolled consequences this new show of managerial grit could create: for the operators, for the plant, for himself. In his own quiet manner, Jenkinson was the worst bully Ward had come across so far in his career. He felt he was being steadily pushed to walk closer and closer to the edge, and too bad if he fell, bringing it all down with him. It was like being led by the hand toward a narrow bridge by a polite man hiding a gun behind his back. Ward was troubled to acknowledge that he feared his boss, not so much for his temper or for any of the usual blame-the-messenger reason, but for the irrevocable steps he was forcing him to take faster than he felt ready, from handling the mold transfer to Poland to this little showroom exercise right now. It's not what they make me do, said the puppet. It's their hands inside me.

Remember to force *one–piece flow in assembly to see variations in the process*, noted Ward to himself, and scope the real productivity potential. By doing this all over the plant, I could have an idea of how much productivity I've got underfoot.

"Thank you all, you're a great team!" finally cheered Jenkinson, beaming uncharacteristically to the assembled operators, who, smiled back at him, both reticent and amused. They knew that this only led toward more productivity, but Ward doubted that they'd ever, in their working life, worked alongside the company's CEO. Lord only knew what they'd make of it in the end, but as Fernandez returned to his place within the team, they were certainly making parts much faster, and Ward had taken reams of notes about the details they had learned during the exercise.

"So?" said Jenkinson as they moved away from the cell.

"Is it sustainable?" asked the production manager sourly.

"That," replied the CEO, turning suddenly on him and speaking with exaggerated care, "is precisely your job. The only debate today is whether it was feasible or not. I believe that we have proved that it is? Don't you?"

"You have," agreed Ward in deep thought. "We also need to think carefully about how we explain all of this to the operators."

"Of course you do," agreed Jenkinson breezily enough. "But again, isn't that what I pay you for?" he added callously. "Look, the easiest thing to do is to pull that young guy out of the line and to get him to work on another cell. He'll probably work faster there as well, and you'll learn from him."

"And make sure the remaining operators keep up the pace," concluded Stigler, still unhappy.

"It's not about them," corrected Ward hotly. "But about *us*. Have you seen the amount of variation on the line caused by stumbling blocks we put in there. The false positives at the test machine, the missing components, the distance, the welder that doesn't close. Come on man—this is our job."

"One thing at a time," said Jenkinson, raising a hand as the production manager spouted a lot of French at Ward. "Andy, we were discussing *go and see*. The first point of *go and see* is not passive—you go and find out whether you're right or not. It's about formulating hypotheses and then try, try, try.

"One of the hardest things to understand about Toyota, or any other exemplary lean company, is that its operations can be seen as a *continuous series of controlled experiments*. Whenever the company does something, it tests a hypothesis through action. It's the very rigidity of the operations that makes the flexibility possible. To do so, the company teaches the scientific method to its workers through *PDCA*, and so stimulates them to engage in widespread experimentation.

"*Go and see* is about working with the people themselves and trying things out. If you look foolish, too bad. You'll get over it. It's about involvement in developing knowledge. We now know a heck of a lot more about producing this part than we did this morning. This is what Mark Neville spends his days doing—trust me. He knows more about producing parts than the three of us rolled into one. He delivers miracles because he both knows *how*, and how to empower his people to do it. My point is that knowledge is scientific. It's empirical, generated at the real place, with the real people, and the real parts. And in doing so day in, day out, you develop judgment to make the proper decisions. You must go to the site and see the thing before making a decision. And what better way to see than getting involved? Remember: you can't be an engineer if you're not washing your hands three times a day.

"The key is to listen to the person doing the job, especially about the problems that they're encountering right now. If you make decisions by reading reports or listening to your staff's analyses you're likely to make mistakes without even realizing it."

"Like investing in two press screws when I only needed one?"

"Precisely. I'm not saying abstract analysis can't be important. But facts are key to understanding whether our analysis is correct or not. *Go and see* is about developing business judgment through first-hand, hands-on experience."

"The second aspect of *go and see* is *creating consensus about the problems we face*," continued Jenkinson as they traversed the press area. "For instance, what is the main problem right here?"

"Productivity," Ward answered immediately, thinking back to Bethany's system to improve dramatically the productivity of the presses.

"Maintenance," countered Stigler. "I'm constantly having to get these old machines working again. They're falling apart. There's been no investment in this plant for years now, and many of these presses are completely shot."

"And there won't be investment now, trust me," replied the CEO, though not unkindly.

"Personally, I think quality remains your number one issue," he continued. "Your red bins are overflowing with basic problems such as flash on the parts or missing materials. Quality and slow changeovers, which result in long batches and huge inventories. And we cannot increase the number of changeovers until you control quality better, because, if not, we'll have no end of bad parts."

"Three people, three opinions," observed Ward.

"What we need," interjected production manager Stigler, "is supervision software so that we can monitor how each press is behaving in real-time."

"There we go," clucked Jenkinson. "We're already arguing about solutions before we agree about the problem. I believe this plant has used up all its unbudgeted investment credits for the year, hasn't it?"

Ward would have kicked Stigler if he could. Get with the program, Ward thought. He wanted to scream at him that there won't be a dime spent in this plant until we've delivered visible results. He was bitterly frustrated: Stigler genuinely believed he needed new software and equipment and other gadgets and investments to make the plant work, but he seemed oblivious that every time he asked for money upfront, he cost them credibility in Jenkinson's eyes. On the one hand, Ward couldn't blame his production manager for being forthright, and felt loath to ask him to be more political (which would also taint him of boot-licking, the ultimate character defect from a French point of view); on the other hand, Stigler consistently refused to acknowledge that Jenkinson might be right.

"And if you think I'm going to invest a dime in this plant," added the CEO, as if he'd been reading Ward's mind, "considering how much overcapacity it's got, you're dreaming."

"How do we agree on the problem, then?"

"We *go and see.*"

They walked slowly through the area. Jenkinson stopped at every press, shaking the operator's hand, looking into the red bin, handling rejected parts, walking around the press, and stooping to watch the spills under the injection units, pointing at the tangled piping and messed up controls. As they did, Ward slowly came to see his presses in a new light. They were filthy. They were old. They were abandoned. Sure, most of them worked, but they looked dingy as hell. Even the paint was scaling on most of them. Stigler is right, he concluded in dismay. There's no way we can fix this without spending more money on these presses. We'll never get it signed off, though.

Jenkinson watched a robotic arm pick a part out of the mold, and then, like Amy had done previously, put his hand on the ejected parts on the conveyor to check how warm they came out of the press as a means of gauging the cycle time—typically, the colder they were, the longer they'd stayed in the press.

"What can we agree from what we see?"

"Other than the presses look pretty bad?" asked Ward.

"They do," agreed Jenkinson.

"But you keep cutting maintenance staff!" exclaimed Stigler, waving his arms around, exasperated.

"Shut up! Listen! Learn!" Ward finally snapped at the man, who looked at him stunned. Shocked at being yelled at, Stigler whitened and narrowed his eyes behind his ridiculous glasses, and then settled in a sulk with a deep offended frown. Ward immediately felt guilty for flying off the handle, but hearing his production manager essentially venting his own complaints triggered his outburst.

Jenkinson continued as if he hadn't heard anything. "Think back to the essential things we need to learn. Process and—"

"Results. Yes, I remember. Getting good results from controlled processes."

"Okay. In the case of the presses, can we say the *process* is controlled?"

"Not in detail," agreed Ward, trying to regain his composure. "Certainly not compared to Bethany. We can see the presses run, but it's hard to spot what is in control and what is not just by looking at them."

"And what about *results?*"

Ward thought about it. "We measure the presses uptime. But I know what you're going to say: in the computer."

Jenkinson grinned. "So we can't see at the press what the results are, correct?"

"That's right."

"Which means the people who work at the press can't see what the press' performance is either?"

"Yes, yes, you are right."

"Okay. We can't agree on the main problem because we don't have enough visual management. Visual management is about seeing together, so that we know together and we act together—from the operator to the CEO."

"What do I need to implement then?"

"The first thing we need is a visual tracking of how the press is performing. We can sketch out a production film like this."

TRACKING OF PRODUCTION

6:00	Production	Programmed Stops	Change-overs	Organization problems	Break-downs	Remarks
6:30						
7:00						
7:30						
8:00						
etc.						etc.
12:00						
12:30						
1:00						
1:30						
2:00 TOTAL						

Part #	Standard Cycle Time		# of Good Parts		Productive Time	
		X		=		+
		X		=		+
		X		=		+
				TOTAL		
				OEU		

179

"And so on ... In this way, the operator can track and explain what happens at the press in five-minute increments. The key thing is to get the people on the press to observe what actually goes on in really fine detail. Then we can start distinguishing, press by press, whether we lose time because of rejects, changeover, down time, lack of work, planned maintenance, and so on. With this, we can create weekly Pareto charts of causes of lost utilization *at each press*. So that when we do *go and see*, we can discuss what the problem really is."

"And on the other hand, we should be able to see if all the key metrics are under control directly on the press," chimed Ward.

"Precisely. We need to visualize both results and process, so we can clarify problems, and concur on the main one we need to focus on. Do we agree on this?"

"Of course we do, you're the boss," said the production manager resentfully.

What the hell was wrong with the man? You don't talk that way to your CEO. Ward was trying to control his irritation, and couldn't figure out why Stigler was being such a jerk. The guy wasn't the sharpest knife in the drawer, but was usually a good, solid worker. Why was he being so difficult? This was more than simply stating your case. This was downright close to being offensive.

"I am," affirmed Jenkinson, with a smile that wasn't all that happy. "And while I can force you to obey, I can't force you to agree. That's the point. I am in charge, so my voice will be louder than yours. But I will not force you to do something you think is wrong, and I *will* thank you every time you share a problem."

Stigler had the good sense to look embarrassed and say nothing. Ward exhaled, relieved to see the production manager let go of his fight with the company's top dog.

"In any case, I'm making the point that the second dimension of *go and see* is to create consensus around what the main problem is. As you pointed out," he emphasized, looking at Ward and Stigler in turn, "this is not a democracy, so management's say will always rule. But you have to look at it the other way around. If management has to force the issue, it means that management has failed at creating consensus: this is a clear management failure."

"Which makes execution difficult then," concluded Ward, "because people haven't bought into the need for change, right."

"You got it, Andy. Every time I force someone to do something, I lose their intelligence in the process. Which is tricky, because the only way to learn is to do, so I am pushing people into the pool to see if they'll sink or swim all the time. That's life!"

Ward was looking at the press area when he experienced a moment of clear insight. Right then he *saw* the people, not just the machines. He saw the operators at their stations, the supervisor rushing around looking for something, the forklift driver struggling to maneuver an awkwardly placed container, the technicians discussing a piece of kit. He saw them all. And he realized Jenkinson was asking him to take responsibility for their involvement, not just their compliance. He'd always thought about management in terms of making people *do* things, or *apply* systems. Now he had to make them agree on what the problem was. Which led to his next insight: he had no clue how to do that.

"The third key aspect of *go and see*," continued Jenkinson as Ward privately battled his fear of inadequacy, "is to make sure things are progressing at the right pace to achieve our goals. The plant's journey has some appointments on the road it can't miss. These are imposed by the business, not us. Customer deliveries, parts from new programs, budget reviews, and so on. Just as an interest payment has to be met at the bank, targets *have* to be met. This is a fundamental lean insight —you *will* be on time. Usually, management tackles all the projects it can think of at the same time, and then whatever happens, happens. Because we don't choose between projects, we try to push them all through the pipe, and, at the end, only a few are realized, and many fall by the wayside."

"I hadn't really seen it like that," laughed Ward uneasily, "but, yeah, we could say that. That's certainly what we discovered when we started with the red bins. There were so many things to do at the same time that we got completely bogged down, until we learned to redo the priority list every two weeks."

"That's clever," agreed Jenkinson, "but it biases action toward the urgent. We also need to keep what's important firmly in mind. It's not either/or. When I walk into a plant, I have two questions in my mind:

- What could be done to improve profitability *today*?
- What needs to be done to grow the plant *two years from now*?

"What you did with red bins certainly answers the first question, and should be generalized to flow and workstation improvement. But we need to also focus on the key project the plant has to succeed at. If not, it's history."

"Such as getting new parts?" wondered Stigler, reluctantly getting drawn in the conversation again.

"Absolutely. What do we need to do to get new parts? Who should we convince? Doing what?"

"Well," admitted Ward, "you've been pretty clear about this: the plant that achieves your target of 10 percent direct labor savings, 50 percent ppm reduction, 20 percent stock reduction, and 50 percent less capital expenditure, will get parts. I don't see how we'll ever achieve it, but if I follow what you're saying, we should *go and see* how we're faring in reaching these targets. Right?"

"Correct. Actually, just from this morning's *go and see*, I have some idea of how you're doing. If you continue your current efforts, I am confident you'll reduce your quality rejects by half in the course of this year, if not more. On productivity, you've delivered some numbers, but the work we've done on the cell tells me you're still stumbling in the dark, and so does our conversation about press utilization. As for capital expenditure, you've already used the budget for the year. What we now need to go and check is how you're progressing on inventory."

"Ah. Logistics."

"Let's *go and see*!"

"Listen," chipped in the production manager. "This is no longer my area. I've got many things to do. Is it okay if I leave you here?"

"No, it's absolutely not okay!" Ward replied angrily, staring at Stigler in total disbelief. "And no, you don't have anything more important to do than touring the plant with your CEO and your plant manager!"

Stigler looked like he'd been slapped, but then gave a very French shrug, and followed them into the logistics hall. Still gnashing his teeth, Ward gave a call to the logistics manager to tell her to expect them, wondering what kind of reception she would provide.

This was a day for surprises. After Stigler's sulky teenager act, Carole Chandon, the dragon lady keeper of logistics, received them like royalty. There was no denying her good looks, and Ward had a pet theory that she'd developed her brusque, unsmiling manner to earn the respect of the big, tough forklift drivers who shared something of a macho cowboy culture. Whatever it was, it worked. Once she was sold on something, she would keep on badgering until she got her way in the end. They'd had a long talk after Amy's visit, about how being rude to corporate or their consultant wasn't a really smart move, and she seemed to have taken it to heart.

After offering them some coffee, she took them to the end of the store where she had had a painted yellow area outlined on the floor against a far wall. Whether on purpose or not, she ignored Jenkinson's theatrical headshakes as they crossed the warehouse filled to the ceiling with racks and piles of containers. The famed Bob Woods' wisecrack, "I can see your inventory, but where is your factory?" came to Ward's mind as he contemplated the amount of stock they carried.

"Here," she explained, "we thought about the consultant's comments, and tried something different. This is a part that goes straight to the customer off the press, so there's no assembly."

"How many trucks a day?"

"High volume—two trucks a day, taking both references: left and right. Rather than put the parts coming from production into the space allocated by the warehouse management software, I've asked the forklifts to bring the containers right here."

"You consolidated the trucks in this area?"

"If you like." Her command of English surprised Ward. He had always dealt with her in French, and was astonished that she was so fluent. Granted she had a thick accent and odd phrasing, but her points came across clearly.

"What happened?"

"At first, it was clearly impossible. We were producing one part for two days, and then the other for two more days. The place overflowed all the time. Everybody complained."

"And? What did you learn?"

"It was bad," she said, pulling a strand of black hair out of her face in a very feminine, almost coquettish movement. "Although I had a lot of stock, I still managed to miss deliveries. Incredible!"

She started gesturing with her hands, miming an inventory being filled in.

"I produce rights for two days," she explained, moving her right hand up. "But at the same time, I'm sending lefts away in the trucks," moving her left hand down. "So at the end of the production run of rights, I've got plenty of those, but I'm almost out of lefts. So there's a changeover, and I start producing lefts," making opposite hand movements. "Same things happens, at the end of the batch of lefts, I'm really low on rights."

"Absolutely," agreed Jenkinson with a knowing grin. "Then what?"

"It's stupid. If something happens such as a late change, I can still miss a delivery although I've got an average stock of three days. So I started thinking, and I asked the guys in production to produce each part every day. At first they don't want. But I don't give up. Still they don't want. So we go to *M'sieur* Ward, and he says: 'Do what she says.'"

She starts gesturing quickly with her hands, demonstrating shorter batch sizes.

"Now, we have less stock, and delivery is more reliable, because I can create a bigger safety mattress. It all fits in the zone."

"Excellent," praised Jenkinson. "What's your next step?"

"Changeover once a shift—and then in line with customer trucks. But production doesn't want. And now production wants to go back to once a week—too many changes, they say."

"This is absolute rubbish," interjected the production manager in French. "We're doing more changes on this one reference than, well, I don't know!"

"Have we got a capacity problem on the press?"

"No, none. It's a 600-ton machine, and all it does is these two parts. I don't know why engineering didn't come up with a two-cavity mold as they usually do."

"So what's the problem with what Carole wants?"

"It's an organizational nightmare!" Stigler continued, his fury rising again. "The setters have to change this press all the time and, in the meantime, other changes are not getting done. I don't have enough setters to play these games just to please corporate."

"Let me guess," interrupted the CEO. "Not enough capacity? Not enough setters? Too many startup bad parts after each change?"

"Setters," confirmed Ward.

"*SMED*," Jenkinson told the production manager forcefully. "Single minute exchange of die. Reduce your setup times. Do it. And do what she says."

"Fine," answered Stigler, calming down again, though his expressive shrug didn't bode well, Ward noted. It read something like: screw up production, see if I care.

"Well done, Carole," Jenkinson said, turning to the woman, who actually smiled back—a smile from Chandon? "What is the next part you're doing this with?"

"Is this the right thing to do then?"

"Absolutely. When do you do this with a second part: dedicated storage area and daily production?"

"I don't know yet," she answered uncertainly, looking at Ward. "We still experiment with this. It is difficult with production."

"When did you start this?"

"After the consultant come? September?"

"How many injection references do you have in total?"

"About 300 running regularly," answered Ward. "And yes, 20 references make 50 percent of our volume. We checked after Amy left."

"I have to talk to her about not spoiling my fun," grinned Jenkinson with a rare show of humor. "She's giving away my punchlines. Five to 10 percent of your references amount to half your total is a bet I like to win. So, 20 references ... two months per reference, this means that I will have a working pull system for the high-runners before 40 months? Totally unacceptable. The future of this plant will be decided way before that. You've got six months at the most."

"Three per month?" asked the logistics manager, aghast, but quick on the uptake.

"You've shown me you know what to do—now it's a matter of will, no more, no less."

"Impossible!" exclaimed the production manager.

"There is *possible*," replied the CEO counting on his fingers, "there is *impossible*, and there is *not-impossible*. I'm telling you that this is clearly a case of not-impossible, because it's been done before."

"Don't tell me, in Bethany?"

"There, yes, and elsewhere. So, people, now's time to earn your wages. I want this plant in pull as fast as can be. And I want the resulting stock reduction. Figure it out."

Ward looked from Chandon to Stigler. She was smirking ever so faintly, and the other man was looking livid, muttering to himself. She was bright enough to figure out that whatever problems she would have with physically organizing her stock per reference—something she had adamantly refused to consider in the past—paled in comparison to having to change every press in the shop once a day, or more—once a shift even.

"This demonstrates the third aspect of *go and see*. We now have a goal, and you can come regularly to see whether this goal is going to be reached on time. Is that clear?"

Ward nodded dumbly.

"It's management's job to see if people are giving it their best effort, and to help out if they get stuck. Sure, sometimes these goals are ambitious, sometimes we try to get through a door that is just too narrow. This is when management has to intervene to help force the door open. *Go and see*."

"The fourth aspect of *go and see* is empowering people by involving them." Jenkinson said. "Managerial relationships are very strongly asymmetrical: As a manager you have the impression you see the people who report to you every day, but, individually, they see you rarely. As a result, when they do meet you, the moment is very significant for them—and so is your opportunity to trip up and slight people even inadvertently in a way that will irk and hurt. Like getting someone's name wrong. Or singling them out inappropriately, even if it turns out to be funny and not particularly mean. It can still rankle.

"*Go and see* is the moment to involve workers by getting them to understand the global objective of the company. It's the story of the stonemason by the side of the road who thinks he's either cutting a stone, raising a wall, or building a cathedral. Same action, different involvement. It's hard to discuss the topic at this stage in the plant, because the visual management system is still too weak to have in-depth discussions with workers about their own job."

"What do you mean? Isn't that what we did in assembly?"

"To some extent," answered Jenkinson, pushing back his glasses and actually looking embarrassed. "But I have to confess to some theatrics there as well. I was making a point. Having asymmetrical conversations with operators that are both instructive and don't put them at a disadvantage requires *standardized work*."

"How so?" asked Ward, truly perplexed.

"Well, one of the first things Taiichi Ohno did in his shop at Toyota was to post the standardized work sequence at every work station. You just pull a washing line across the station, and hang a sheet of paper with the standard sequence, *takt time*, cycle time, and standard in-process stock there. Hand me your pad. Something like this."

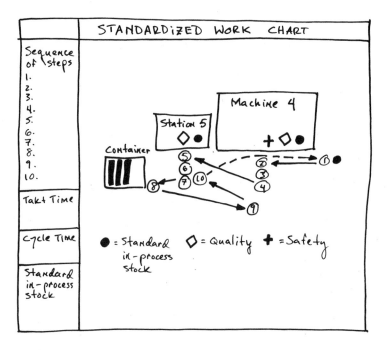

"You get the idea, but you'll come up with your own. Within the *Toyota Production System*, the supervisor's main job is to build these *standardized work* sheets with the operators. The point is that the document creates a basis for discussion with the operator. It makes the conversation simple. I can ask the operator why she didn't follow the standard sequence, and she can show that she's out of containers, so she has to walk around the workstation to get some. This creates the perfect opportunity for a deal: I solve the problem of the missing containers, and the operators commit to keeping to the standard sequence as much as possible and to contribute other problems and suggestions.

Jenkinson looked at Ward, Stigler, and Chandon, and saw their eyes had glazed over. It had been a long session already and they had much to chew on. He clearly hesitated about how much more he should discuss the topic.

"Let's leave it at that. *Go and see* is an opportunity for senior managers to establish direct relationship with frontline employees. This is as crucial for managers as for politicians shaking hands and kissing babies in an election year. To trust you, people have to know you. To see that you are interested in their job. That you *go and see* them, not just the machine they use or the parts they make.

"The basic *go and see* action is to address one problem for one operator every time you're on the shop floor. We ask these guys to do all sorts of things all the time, and the more we progress, the more we ask them to change, change, change, and get involved. The least we can do is solve some of their problems immediately. We can ask them what they need of course, but at first they don't quite know what to say. In order to help them see their own problems better we must first 'clear the window,' which comes down to creating a work environment where all problems are apparent. Kind of the opposite of what we have now in logistics around us."

"What ..." started the logistics manager, but Jenkinson, clearly tired now, pacified her by raising his hands defensively. The image was almost amusing, the blond giant retreating behind the petite brunette.

"Don't get upset. Look around you. I'm not saying it's mismanaged. I'm saying there's absolutely no way to see if there's a problem or not. These parts, for instance," he said, pointing to a dusty-looking cardboard box, "have been here for …," he read the label, "six months. Is it a problem or not?"

"I … don't know," she answered, biting her lip.

"Nobody does unless you *check*," he explained. "That's the whole point. To involve people we need to make it easy for them to *go and see*. We need to create the a visual environment where everyone can see.

"Visual management needs to answer four key questions:

1. Can everybody see if this is a good hour or a bad hour?
2. Can everybody see what the standard method is?
3. Can everybody see what the people who work here believe is their main problem?
4. Can everybody see what they're doing about it?"

"So," he spoke again after ordering his thoughts. "We involve people by telling them what our objectives are and by helping them resolve the niggling problems of their jobs. Keep in mind that these 'minor' issues might be really important to them as they are likely to occur every cycle. To do this, management's involvement must be to 'clean the window,' which they support through helping the quality of the working environment and the visual management. Okay?"

"Clear," agreed Ward dubiously.

"Finally, when we are on the shop floor, or at the customers', or the showroom, at suppliers, basically anywhere that work happens, we look for *people*. We are constantly seeking the positive variance, the guy who does something a bit more clever, who tries a bit harder. We look for people to develop. That is the ultimate key to *go and see*. We develop the ability see the people that we will need to grow, because their work and their involvement will sustain us in the long range.

"Thierry Fernandez," muttered Ward, with a flash of understanding.

"Or Mark Neville. Or many others. Regardless of where I am or what I am working on, there is always one thought on my mind: Who shows promise? Who shows up every morning? Who solves problems? Who thinks of something clever? These people are my future if I can involve and develop them."

Ward thought his boss had fallen into talking to himself. The managers of the French plant looked at each others as the CEO fell silent, lost in thought. The silence stretched and lingered, and they all seemed reluctant to break it. Finally a forklift honked them out of the way.

Jenkinson stirred and sighed, and said, "We should wear orange vests if we're going to be walking around in a forklift area."

"What about those who don't?" asked Chandon unexpectedly.

"Who don't what?"

"Show promise. Do what you said. Get involved?"

"We train," he answered resignedly. "We hope."

Will they let you teach? thought Ward, recalling Neville's schooldays tale.

Ward walked the CEO back to the front entrance. He had suggested lunch, but Jenkinson was worried about missing his flight. They stood by the glass door at the entrance of the plant, looking at the bleak, late-November day. A hard rain was beating down, and although just about lunchtime, outside it seemed dim as night. Jenkinson wore a very long, very black coat that looked terribly smart and expensive over his usual casual work clothes. Staring darkly at the rain-washed windowpane, it made him look vaguely sinister, like a character out of a *Godfather* movie, thought Ward irreverently, or Bruce Wayne—Batman in civvies.

"Thanks for the visit," he said. "You're sure you won't have anything before hitting the road? Cup of coffee?"

"I am fine," replied Jenkinson, though his tired smile said otherwise. "Have you gone to Wroclaw yet?"

"I was supposed to go last week, but then they told me to cancel because the plant manager had left the company."

"Yeah. We're bringing in an interim guy before we can find a new Polish plant manager."

"Do you still want me to go ahead?"

"Yes," he said, looking surprised that Ward should have second thoughts. "It needs to be done before year-end."

"All right," agreed Ward doubtfully.

"By the way, where were your supervisors today?" asked Jenkinson, bringing himself back to the plant.

"Um …"

"Remember what we talked about in Neuhof? You can't do it alone. Rely on your staff. You've got to involve your line. That's the key."

"I agree. That's what I saw in Bethany. Supervisors doing *standardized work* and team leaders rebalancing their lines once a week. *Kaizen*. Yes, it's just …"

"Look, the rest is fine as it is. You're learning, maybe not as fast as I'd like, but you are. But *you can't do this alone*. It won't stick. You need to develop a pyramid of competent, engaged people to sustain *kaizen*. It can't work any other way."

"I know," agreed Ward, close to admitting he just didn't have the knack. He didn't know how to do it. These guys, well, they just didn't want to get involved.

Jenkinson watched the rain pour on the factory yard some more, as if measuring the steps to his car and gathering his nerve to go and face a couple of hours' drive in this downpour.

"Andy," he finally said. "I know that you are trying hard. And I appreciate how much you want to save the plant. But don't lose your perspective. It might be too late already."

What the hell was he saying?

"I'm not saying it is," amended Jenkinson, throwing him a sideways glance. "But everything is very tense right now. So listen up. You're going after the step change. It won't work, not right away. You're going to burn yourself out, and keep building castles in the sand that will keep coming down. *Kaizen* first. Get more people involved. Get them to do the small stuff—red bins, *SMED, single-piece flow*, workstation improvement. Change *them* as you're trying to change yourself. Then the step change will come easily. Do you hear what I'm saying?"

"I think so," Ward answered uncertainly.

"We were always taught to go for the big change right away. To seek global solutions to global problems. But it doesn't work. We keep getting it wrong, because we don't understand the situation well enough. Not enough *go and see*. So think differently: Focus on *go and see*, and involving as many people as you can in *kaizen*. Small frequent steps. Ten times 10 percent rather than one times 100 percent. Try. Learn together. Quickly. Whatever happens, happens, but the learning will never be wasted, okay?"

And that's supposed to make me feel better? wondered Ward.

"What *is* wrong with you?" asked Ward irritably, as he ushered the production manager into his office. He had debriefed the CEO's visit with the team as best he could, frustrated at their lack of reaction. No questions, no suggestions, not even a snarky comment about the big boss. Stigler, in particular, had sullenly stared at his notes, refusing all attempts to establish eye contact. What was their problem? As the meeting ended not with a bang but a whimper, Ward asked the production manager to his office.

"Wrong with *me*?" the other man snapped. "Did you hear how you talked to me?"

"Did you hear how *you* talked to the CEO?"

"Of course," he said, with an ugly, sarcastic smirk. "So you're siding with him are you? Typical."

"Siding?" Ward repeated aghast. "You don't *side* with a CEO, you idiot. You do what he tells you to do."

"He's closing the plant anyway," Stigler retorted heatedly. "Can't you see it? You know it as well as I do. All this stuff, it's hypocritical bull."

"It might be—but we're still going to do what he asks, and to the letter!"

"Haven't you figured out his game?" pleaded the production manager. "He's setting us up! He's giving us impossible targets, and impossible actions *so that we fail*. So when he closes the plant, it's all on our head. Look at how he undercuts your authority with everyone. I don't know how you can be so spineless as to let him do this. No one talks to me like that in front of my guys."

His argument gave Ward pause. He suddenly realized that he didn't know Stigler as well as he thought. After four years of working with him, he couldn't tell whether the man was trying to cover up the gaps highlighted in his area, or was sincere in thinking this was all a big show.

"You just *can't do this* in a plant like this! He's just another bungling American who doesn't know the first thing about our labor relations," Stigler continued angrily. "Going directly to the operators, completely showing us up on our own shop floor. The man's crazy. How are we supposed to retain any authority after that! We're barely swimming, and now he's pushing our heads under water. I'm telling you: he's going to frame us for closing the plant."

"Why would he bother?" Ward asked. "Don't you think he's got better things to do than spend time in the plant if he's about to close it."

"Don't be naïve," he replied pityingly. "Talk to the old-timers. That's the first thing they do when they close a plant. Every one and his dog parades there to show the future is secure—and then the knife falls," he added with a jabbing thrust. "Ask around. You should know. We might not know lean production around here, but being shut down is one thing we're expert at. I bet everyone in this plant has been through at least one site closure. Everyone but you."

"Fine. And I don't intend to either," replied Ward, firmly, hoping he'd concealed how shaken he really was.

Malancourt, Malancourt, the name rang like a romance, and sometimes as a curse. Twenty years ago, Claire's parents had bought what had been a livable farmhouse, another large building, a derelict barn, and an assortment of ruined buildings, crumbling round towers, and remains of ancient walls. Claire's father had more or less spoiled the site by building a huge hangar to house 40-odd horses across the road, and a huge open air manège. And still the place retained a unique charm, which had grabbed Ward at once. After his father-in-law's accident, Claire parents had moved back into town, as he could now only walk painfully with a cane. Ironically, after surviving riding falls for years, he had hurt himself falling from a combine harvester helping a friend finish the season. At first, Claire and Andy had been content to redesign the farmhouse, by opening a large, loft-like living space, replacing the traditional tiles by floorboards, and installing new windows on the verdant western slope at the back of the building.

But, as time went on, Claire had imagined a full revival of Malancourt, in which they would transform the second building into a bed-and-breakfast, and upgrade the standing of the center in the hope of attracting more money. She'd been egged on, and eventually financially backed, by a wealthy childhood friend who'd learned to ride in this very place, and who had slowly drawn Ward into her vision for the place. He'd resisted at first, finding her near obsession for the scheme rather off-putting. But eventually, as Claire poured her considerable energy into beautifying the place, he'd relented, chipping in on weekends as well, until they'd started seeing something great emerge from the rubble of old stones and twisted ivy.

But the stark reality was that, in its current form, Malancourt belonged to the banks more than it did to them. The place was mortgaged to the hilt, and they'd taken on additional loans for the building projects. Ultimately, everything hinged on him being able to bring enough money home to pay off all the vultures. He had started looking around discretely in the area for other jobs after Jenkinson had told him he intended to close Vaudon, and it had become abundantly clear that his background qualified him either to manage another plant—which could be anywhere in France, though unlikely to be found in this downtrodden region—or at corporate headquarters in a major city such as Paris or London. Malancourt held him to the plant as surely as a large rock chained around his neck.

The main stables were dark as Ward stepped through the hangar doors. The building was little more than a huge warehouse made of concrete blocks: Two alleys of horse boxes facing each other covered by a corrugated iron roof; hot in summer, cold in winter. Claire's father had whitewashed the outside of the building, to make it look halfway decent, but never got around to the inside, where the walls still showed the depressing dirty gray of concrete blocks. A string of large bulbs dangling from a single wire threaded along the top of the boxes provided a diffuse, gloomy light. The thundering rain drummed a steady rumble on the tin roof.

"Hey, baby, you're early?"

"Yeah, Jenkinson visit. We're all shattered. I debriefed with the team and called it a day."

Claire was alone in the stables, leaning on a stall door and staring at the dark horse within.

"Come here and hold me," she said.

He circled her with his arms, kissing the crook of her neck.

"You're all wet!" she protested, but didn't move away. She smelled of honest work and horses.

"I think he's favoring his right hind leg," she whispered. "But I didn't find anything wrong. I'll have to see in the morning."

"You do this every evening?"

"Do what?"

"Check on all the horses?"

"*Mais oui*, I make sure the stall is set for the night, and I give them a good look. It's quieter then. I know what to check for during the day when they're being ridden."

The big bay stepped forward and blew its nostrils at them. Claire caught the large head and scrubbed the forehead absently. At least she didn't talk to them, like many of her clients did. She said she didn't have to, because she swore the creatures were telepathic. They could smell moods, she believed, and reacted strongly to whatever emotion was projected: fear, calm, anger, joy, haste, excitement. The mirror of the rider's soul, she'd once said.

"You should be doing my job," Ward suggested bitterly.

She laughed, and turned in his arms to look at him. In the dim light, her vivid blue eyes seemed almost black, and he wondered at how, even after all those years they'd been together, he could still get lost in her stare. She had perfect eyes. Her face was a bit too narrow, her features a tad too strong to be called beautiful, but her eyes, her eyes were mesmerizing.

"Silly! What makes you say that?"

"You'd be better at it than I am. *Go and see.* That's what you do all the time. I wish I could say I walk around my presses before going home in the evening and look to see whether they're working all right."

"That's not the same, be serious."

"Oh, I am," he said, bringing her against him, and tucking the top of her head under his chin.

She snuggled into him, burying her face in his chest.

"We've got to go and pick up Charlie at Madame Collet's," she mumbled.

"Yeah. Let's."

She hated hearing him sounding so down. It was so unlike him. He'd always tell the story about how he'd fallen in love with her at first sight and how she said the same, but he didn't believe it. What would such a woman find in such an average Joe like him? She'd never told him the truth. She'd never told him about the fear. The worry. Living among horses, loving them and loving riding passionately, but having to deal with the constant, nagging, obsessive fear of bad luck falls, of freak accidents, of her favorite mare having to be put down when she was 12 years old, of a rider not coming back from a simple ride through the woods. She knew she was attractive to many men. She had had them for the picking in London. Chew them up and spit them out. But when she'd met Andrew, she remembered being stunned, astonished, amazed. The fear was gone. Close to him, there was nothing but lightness. A steady effortless flow of good feelings. Nothing deep or profound at first. Something easy and sweet. The moment she met him, she felt like she was coming home.

She didn't dare say anything, because she knew it was for her he was working so hard to save a plant that didn't deserve it in the first place. But it was changing him. He'd lost his flippancy, the truant side of him that truly believed that good manners and a pinch of charm would get him through anything in life. He had started to care. She hated the way it sounded, but he was growing up. She prayed that it would not grow him too old instead. She couldn't bear that. Was Malancourt worth paying that price?

Chapter Four

MANAGING MEANS IMPROVING

"What are you paid for?" Bob Woods asked the production manager. Startled by this completely unexpected question, Olivier Stigler blinked several times without responding, his mouth opening and closing like a fish out of water. "And you as well, for that matter," Woods said, turning to Andrew Ward.

It was a bitter February morning, and the visitors had been four hours late in reaching the plant because of a bad accident on the autobahn. Jenkinson had finally convinced his *sensei*, Woods, to tour the European plants. They had stopped at Vaudon after visiting Neuhof, and would be on their way to Mlada and then Wroclaw. Woods, who Ward learned hated traveling, turned up looking his age and acting cantankerous as hell. He introduced himself to the plant team as a "lean consultant," period. For once, Jenkinson looked every inch the CEO, complete with a tailored suit and power tie. Ward assumed he'd been making customer calls. Woods, on the other hand, wore a tired old fleece and battered jeans. "California makes you forget what real cold is like," he kept muttering. He'd given one sour look at the plant, and apparently made up his mind that this place was hopeless.

"Nothing to say for yourself? What do you get paid for? Don't you know?"

Running the plant, what d'you think? thought Ward irritably, but said nothing. He had sworn to himself not to let them get under his skin this time around. No aggravation. One thing he'd learned during these CEO visits, he thought wryly, is to take a licking in public. Jenkinson was holding back today, leaving the floor to his mentor. If the others

199

thought Jenkinson was hard work, they knew better now. Woods was far worse. Where the boss was steady and persistent, like a mountain glacier rolling over a plain, the old man was harsh and abrasive, constantly challenging, and, simply put, a real pain.

Once again they were standing around a red bin in the press area. Unlike previous visits, Ward had gone over the top preparing for this visit. He'd made sure the three supervisors were present in addition to the management team. As the group shuffled behind the leaders, Ward was reminded of hospital rounds, with the crowd of students following the professor. The analogy was all the more striking now that he had recently imposed white work coats for management on the shop floor. Only Jean-Pierre Deloin, the HR manager, had ignored him. The supervisors wore gray shirts as usual. Ward planned to get t-shirts with logos for all the full-time operators, but the human resources manager had talked him out of moving too quickly on such personal issues. The French, he had argued, had different notions of what made their private space vs. their professional one, and would take offense at being told how to dress for work. Ward relented.

"I'm paid to make sure operators can do their work well," Stigler finally answered, telling them what they wanted to hear.

"Good answer," acknowledged Woods. "So," pointing at the red bin, "are we in normal conditions?"

"What do you mean?" Ward asked, jumping in and trying hard not to sound annoyed. The bin held no more than six or seven non-conforming parts, a total that reflected spectacular progress on this particular product. This victory had not come easy. When Ward gave Matthias Muller, the maintenance manager, direct responsibility over mold maintenance as well as machine maintenance, the established mold maintenance manager had felt slighted and in fact stopped coming to work, claiming a medically certified mental depression. This psychodrama had been disruptive for the three mold maintenance technicians, but Muller had attacked the problem with a vengeance, and helped calm everyone down by getting dramatic results. While the mold manager's departure left them short-handed, Ward was ambivalent about his return.

"How many parts do we see here?" asked Woods.

Stigler had the good grace to pick the parts up and pass them around for inspection. "Seven," he said.

"So … is seven bad parts normal conditions for this time of the shift? Or not?" Woods pressed on.

"What do you mean by conditions?" wondered Ward.

"Conditions," repeated Woods, shrugging irritably. "The state of something, you know, how it is regarding appearance, quality, working order—that sort of thing. Is seven bad parts from this press the normal state of this press at this hour? If not, what *is* the normal state of the press right at this time?"

Carole Chandon, who had a good relationship with the three supervisors, had been asked to translate. Ward hoped she would be sensible in how she phrased things. Denis Carela was a tough guy in his 50s, and seemed to be cast straight out of a black-and-white movie from his youth. He kept his thick gray hair in a short-gelled pompadour, and paraded his fit body with an endless collection of tight Harley-Davidson t-shirts. He spoke with a permanent ironic lip curl that set your teeth on edge. Ward had been told the guy owned two of the big bikes, and knew how to tear apart any machine inside out. He was an excellent technician and got on well with the maintenance manager, Muller, with whom he had worked with for years. Unfortunately, he had a strong antimanagement chip on his shoulder. Carela had taken the operators' side in every labor dispute since Alnext had acquired the plant, and Ward treaded carefully around him. He certainly didn't trust him one inch. Léa Mordant, the assembly supervisor, was a young woman in her early 30s. She'd been promoted to supervisor by Ward's predecessor, who had seen potential Ward hadn't found. A perpetually harassed mother of two, Mordant had dark bags under her eyes in all seasons. She got on fine with the assembly operators, who were mostly women, but Ward thought she exemplified resistance to change. At least, she had the good sense to ask Carela for help on technical issues. The night shift supervisor Afonso Sanches was Portuguese-born and came to Vaudon after working for the large chemical plant next door, which had closed. He was a short, thin man, with angry black eyes and a handlebar moustache. Ward's *go and see* practice had involved spending a few hours with the night shift at least once a week, which had revealed to him that Sanches ruled the night shift with the force of his personality, as long as nothing too technical occurred. He disliked tool changeovers, however, and Ward knew that would definitely be a problem.

"It's much better than before," said Carela belligerently, "if that's what he's asking."

"I'm sure it's better," replied Woods after listening to the translation. "But is it *normal?* Should I expect seven defects of this part at 3:00 p.m. every Friday? That's my question."

"We don't know, all right?" snapped Ward, exasperated. He hated the way Woods and Jenkinson would labor a point they all knew the answer to until someone actually stated it. "We're looking into the red bins once a shift, but we're not at that level of detail."

"Which means that this gentleman here," nodding towards Carela, who was now scowling suspiciously, "doesn't know whether he has to intervene or not."

"I guess not."

"You understand that no problem can be solved if it's not recognized as a problem," Woods said as both a question and a statement.

"But we did solve the problem," protested the production manager. "You have no idea how many bad parts we had before here."

"Who solved the problem?" inquired Jenkinson quietly. As Chandon translated the question, this created a flurry of discussion in French.

"Mr. Muller did," she explained. "Denis said they talked about it, but in the end it was Matthias who realized the mold vents had become filled with debris over time."

"Mold got hobbed?" nodded Jenkinson. "Constant clamping of the mold made the vents shallower, right?"

"Yes," Ward replied. "Maintenance cleaned the mold carefully and solved a big part of the problem."

"Cleaned the mold? Should it be maintenance's role to solve that kind of problem?" asked Woods of Ward.

"Ha!" exclaimed Muller, with an unusually satisfied expression.

Of course! Ward felt like answering, maintenance is supposed to maintain. But he held his tongue. Both Jenkinson and Woods kept going back to this theme: Who solves what problem? How? When?

"Do you mean production should solve this kind of problem?" he finally asked.

"Cleaning a mold? Hellooo—what do *you* think?" said Woods sarcastically. "Of course it's a production problem! Don't you think we could use maintenance technicians on more important tasks? Like actually fixing the presses."

Chandon dutifully translated, which triggered two equal and equally opposite reactions.

"Certainly, I can do it if I get the people," said Carela, with a smile that seemed to say this was an obvious point. He knew better than to expect anything sensible from management. He'd been there before— seen it all, done it all. Got the t-shirt.

"That's maintenance's role," said Stigler at the same time, looking outraged.

While Woods and Jenkinson looked at Ward, saying nothing, Ward was certain they had shared a whole silent conversation in the process.

"So," said Woods, after a long pause, turning the bad part he'd been handed over and over, looking at it from all angles. "What's wrong with this filter body?"

Ward examined the part over from all sides, and couldn't see anything obviously nonconforming. We have ways to make you speak, he mentally told the dull plastic. "What's wrong with it?" he asked the operator, who had been continuing to fill in the packaging from parts off the conveyor while keeping eye—and ears—on the proceedings.

"Traces of talc," the operator explained reluctantly, breaking his work rhythm to show a mild whitish streak on one side of the part. Couldn't they see it by themselves? "They can't seem to get the material mix right, and we keep getting these."

"And that would be a customer defect?" wondered Ward aloud. The operator shrugged and went back to his work, the parts continuing to fall regularly from the press. The less interaction he had with management, the better, as far as the operator was concerned.

"Quality?" asked Woods. "Is it a defect?"

Malika Chadid picked the part up gingerly, handling it as if it could bite. "I'd have to check," she answered in an unusually subdued voice. She was usually the dominant person in the room. Large and attractive, her buoyant personality generally took over, even a predominantly male environment. Ward rarely saw her so cowed. Where Chandon was ice, she'd be fire. Which would probably make me lukewarm water, thought Ward wryly.

"So the operator says this is a defective part—but you, the quality manager, *would have to check?*"

Her cheeks flushed and her lips tightened into a thin outraged line, but she didn't talk back. Ward had every reason to think highly of her. Customers liked her. They'd passed every customer or ISO audit without much trouble because of her hard work, attention to detail, and engaging manner. But since he'd been spending so much more time on the shop floor, he had to admit that he rarely saw her at the *gemba*, other than for the red-bin reviews. And even then he had to make a major fuss, pointing out that ensuring that the review took place on time with the right people was her direct and No. 1 responsibility. And so she followed these orders, in her steady, organized way but without much enthusiasm.

"Let me clarify this for all of you," jumped in Jenkinson. "Andy, if you would be good enough to translate.

"*Production needs to learn to solve its own problems.* You have many smart people here: operators, supervisors, yourselves. Get their brains working. Production solves its own problems.

"But to do so, functional experts must help individuals in production understand what is a problem, and what is not a problem. What I expect from a quality manager," he said, nodding to Chadid, who darkened further, "is someone who will tell me the exact difference between a good part and a bad part, and what in the process creates the problem. Operators need to be shown boundary samples. They need to be trained at parts inspection."

"*I* need to train operators?" she blurted out, her dark eyes flashing.

"Certainly. You and your team. You can draw a visual circuit of inspection," he said, grabbing Ward's pad. He drew a sketch of the filter and a circuit of quality parts to check in sequence.

"And, every day, come to the shop to check that you share the same understanding of what is a good part and a bad part with the operators. If we want to hear their ideas, we need to tell them exactly what we and them are looking for. Is that clear?"

"I'd love nothing more," interjected the press supervisor, bitterly. "But I have so much stuff to do. I like solving problems, it's interesting. But we simply don't get the time."

"What else do you have to do?" asked Woods, through Chandon, who looked more intense than ever. The work coat was at least two sizes too large, making her look oddly fragile. But she was following every exchange intently, biting her lower lip unconsciously in concentration.

"Paperwork, and bookings in the system, and shift planning, and dealing with materials, and—everything. Five or six years ago, they decided we should be 'autonomous,' which was just a way for them to dump the whole load on us. I used to spend some time with every person in the shift every day. But now I can't."

"Well?" asked Woods, turning to Ward.

The plant manager nodded thoughtfully. "We've got to look into it. Production solves production problems, is that what you're saying? Sounds obvious when said like this ..."

"You need to organize a *clear flow of problem-solving*," explained Jenkinson one more time. "Operators need to have a complete understanding of normal conditions, so that whenever there is a gap, they know it's a problem. *Go and see* is not just for the top management. It's for *everybody*. This means operators as well, in particular, how they learn to see the parts and see the equipment they use. How can all operators recognize they have a problem? The first indication that something is not right will be the moment that a part is defective. If the part is wrong, something is going wrong in the process. But have a look at the press. Is it in normal conditions?"

They all turned to look at poor, old press No. 7. This venerable old warhorse was beat-up, abused, and, Ward had to admit, none too clean.

"If the press looks like crap," sniped Woods. "How can I tell whether I have a problem or not? Of course I can't."

Ward half expected an explosion from his two tough guys, Muller and Carela. To his surprise, they looked upset, but said nothing. If anything, he thought they looked embarrassed.

"You're saying that—" said Ward, taking a deep breath, "that I'm paid to have everybody work in the right conditions—"

"So you produce good parts at *takt time* and minimal cost, yes. And safely as well."

"To do so, I need to organize a system where any one can see what are normal conditions, so that they can react to problems."

"Yes: a problem is defined as a *gap between the current situation and the standard*. Anything that is out of normal conditions is considered a problem."

"And production must learn to solve all its problems."

"All the time. Yes," nodded Woods. "That's the trick. Expert functions should be true experts, not just technical specialists. They help out when the problem turns out to be intractable—which is after we've made a practical attempt at solving it. I don't need maintenance experts or six sigma or engineering to tell me my molds are dirty. However, I need maintenance expertise to fix an unexpected breakdown or to help with major overhauls."

"All right, all right!" said Ward, raising his hands in frustrated resignation. "So help us out. How do we do it?"

"Take it easy, son," answered Woods with a tight grin. "You are doing this already. Some of it that is.

"Now, first of all you've got to be clear what problems you want operators to spot. Let's try these five ways of thinking about it:

First, *safety*—Are we working safely or not?

Second, *quality*—What is a good part? What is a bad part?

Third, *delivery*—Are we ahead? Are we late? Will we get to the appointment on time?

Fourth, *equipment*—Is it in good shape? Is it likely to break down? Do we take enough care of it?

Fifth, *productivity*—Can we hold a steady standard cycle without being interrupted? Are we doing any unnecessary work?

"So, safety. Are safe and unsafe areas visualized? Much like road signs. Then, quality. You've got the red bin in place, but it could be far more precise. You also need clear written standards about what goes into the red bin and what does not, as well as a continuous, on-the-job training plan for operators.

"Delivery. You're using a production analysis board with hourly objectives, but I don't see any comments that identify or explain the gap between target and actual. Also I don't see the planned time of tool change on it either.

"Equipment: the press has got to be clean and color-coded so that any one looking at it can spot abnormalities. We can all agree there's a lot of work to do there. You've started with the production films to visualize where the running problems are, but I've checked a few and there are almost no comments there. We want people's spot observations!

"Finally, productivity. The standard sequence of work should be drawn up by the supervisor and the operators and posted on the station. This enables anyone to see if the operator has to do unnecessary actions, such as trimming the part to take away the flash created by poor press settings, and so on.

"Of course, all of this would be a lot easier if your customers were pulling needed parts from each machine and cell. You'd have a supermarket at the end of each process, and the number of containers of each part would tell you whether you were in normal conditions or not."

"I don't think he understands our situation," shrugged the supervisor. "He wants us to solve problems—that's all we do all day. The issue is that problems don't stay solved. They come back, and they come back again, and so after a while, we learn to live with them."

"Precisely," exclaimed Woods when he got the translation. "That's the whole point. You work on problems all day long, but you don't really solve them. You go around the problem, not through it. Fixing the symptoms won't help. Until you've reached the root cause, it's certain that the problem will return."

"Okay then," challenged Carela. "When do you consider a problem is solved? In real life something always goes wrong."

"We agree," nodded Woods with one of those rare, toothy smiles that completely transformed him, scraping all the grimness away to expose the humor underneath. "Of course something always goes wrong. That's life!

"Problem-solving is about figuring out which *conditions* to manage at the lowest cost for the greatest impact. Greatest bang for the buck. There are two fundamental aspects of solving problems:

1. Reacting immediately so that the overall process returns to normal conditions, and

2. Finding the root cause of the problem: the factor that can be managed at the least expense (of cost and time).

"Heck, yes, something always goes wrong. Look, I can change the fuse every time it blows, or, instead, I can check that the pump is not overloading the circuit. One way of looking at the problem is managing fuse replacement—which does come back time and time again. Another way of looking at the problem is keeping the pump in good working conditions. We never actually 'solve' problems, we change which conditions we need to manage. In changing the fuse every time it blows, I spend time, effort, and material in 'solving' a problem that will come back. In managing my pump better so that the fuse doesn't blow, I invest *mental* effort in figuring out which conditions need to be managed rather than changing the part. Rather than managing the fuses, I manage the pump. To find the right factor to manage, I need to ask 'Why?' five times."

"Let's take your mold cleaning problem. What you're currently doing is managing a steady flow of *bad* parts," explained Woods. "This takes effort, organization, and in the end, people. Correct?"

"They need to be collected and counted," agreed Carela, after translation.

"And we need to make sure they don't slip through and reach the customer as well. It's all effort. Now, why do we get bad parts?"

"We went through this. The mold vents get clogged up through repetitive clamping."

"True, but stop and try to break it down, slowly. Why do you get bad parts?"

"Clogged vents."

"Why do you get clogged vents?"

"Repetitive clamping—which is inevitable with this kind of mold."

"So why?"

"Because the molds aren't cleaned often enough, or well enough," interjected Muller impatiently.

"Fine, we agree," continued Woods without faltering. "But why?"

"What do you mean why?"

"Think about it carefully. Why do we get bad parts *now*?"

"Because maintenance doesn't clean the molds regularly enough, obviously," answered the production manager, making Muller bristle. Ward quickly put a hand on the man's arm, to forestall another eruption.

"Why?" Woods carried on to Muller directly.

"Because we're swamped with things to do, that's why!" answered the maintenance guy angrily. "I wish we had the time to deal with such detailed stuff, but you just don't understand everything it takes just to keep the presses running."

"Aha!" exclaimed Woods, turning to Carela. "Now you'll understand. We have swapped a situation where we need to manage bad parts, to a situation where we need to manage cleaning the mold's vents. Do you see?"

"I think I do," answered the supervisor carefully. "The problem has not gone away, because it would mean redesigning the mold. But we can either deal with the bad parts, or deal with more precise mold maintenance. We're not managing the same conditions, as you said. Yes, I see your point."

"So, who should do it?" asked Woods.

"The fascinating thing," Ward thought out loud, "is that quality is dealing with the problem currently, as part of the red-bin process. But, in fact, we need to move the managing of conditions closer to the people who actually run the process. Production, right?"

"There is no cut-and-dried answer," concluded Jenkinson, "it all depends on how you allocate your staff. But ultimately, Bob's point is critical. Problems hardly ever get solved completely. But we can swap one expensive overall maintenance problem for more focused ones, which cost less overall, though they involve different people. Which is precisely why we need to work together at this."

"Managing a process means understanding exactly which *conditions* in the process need to be managed carefully," repeated Woods. "Good managers have a clear understanding of what makes the process tick, and hence can expend the least effort to keep the process running as best as can be. On the other hand, poor managers spend money and waste effort on the wrong conditions and end up with both poor performance and costly operations. *Kaizen* is the key to figuring out, by constantly trying and reflecting, *which conditions can be managed with the highest payoff*, and which don't matter nearly as much. Solving a problem entails learning to replace a *high-cost maintenance activity* in the process by a *low-cost one*. There is no miracle: Work remains work. But we can learn to work smarter by managing the right conditions. With the right pressure point I can leverage the world."

Ward had tried to translate Woods' tirade as best he could, and he didn't know how much of it had gone across, although Carela looked unusually thoughtful. For Ward, though, the switch had been flipped. He suddenly felt he understood what they meant by "visual management." When he looked at the press, he had no idea of *what* to check or *how*. He didn't have a mental pointer saying, "If you find flash on the parts, check the injection pressure here, the heat profile there, or the clamp tonnage over here." There were no reference standards to tell you what the correct parameters to control were, and what the correct values should be.

Of course he couldn't engage people in solving problems if problems were not apparent! And obviously he could not do it himself all alone, so he'd have to get his management team on it. He'd always thought of *kaizen* as workshop-type events where a group of experts with a few token operators would try to rapidly improve a situation. He'd never visualized *kaizen* as an ongoing activity, although that's exactly what Mark Neville had been trying to explain to him in Bethany.

"What was he paid for?" The question was not just for show. He suddenly 'got' that Jenkinson's and Woods' expectations of a plant manager's role *were* radically different from his own. They were not interested in implementing systems and doing reporting per se. Above all they wanted him to create the kind of working environment where problems could be solved by the people working in the process themselves.

Producing people before producing parts means getting everybody to solve problems every day. In order to solve problems, *people first have to be able to recognize problems,* Ward realized. Management's job was to highlight which conditions had to be maintained and to make this visual so that any one could check at any time whether *a process was in good conditions to run properly or not*—and if not, to know how to respond to return the process to a good condition. Brilliant. This new insight about what he was expected to do with his shop floor gave him a glimmer of hope.

"But what about the firefighting?" he said, interrupting whatever was being said as he followed his train of thought. "Doing all of this takes time and effort, and we seem to be putting out fires all day long."

"That's still your job, son," answered Woods with an amused grin. "Look at it this way. If you don't put out the fires, they escalate, and you get fired—no pun intended. That's a fact. But," he said raising a finger, like a preacher threatening fire and brimstone, "if all you do is fight fires, you'll have more of them, and bigger ones, and everyone burns out in the end."

"No pun intended," commented Ward deadpan before he could help himself.

"Managing a plant is a mix of fighting fires and improving conditions. Usually, plant managers spend 80 percent of their time running around being heroes, dealing with the big crises and saving the day, and 20 percent trying to improve things. The trick is to reverse the proportions. If you spend most of your efforts on improvements, you'll have fewer fires to fight, and they'll be smaller ones."

"All right," summarized Ward. "We visualize production, to make problems appear at all times, and then what?"

"Solve them one by one," answered his CEO. "Your rate of progress depends on how fast you can go through the *PDCA* cycles."

"Is stupid. Why not try to fix it all at once?" exclaimed Chandon. "If we know we have a problem. We should fix it immediately, no?"

"Except for *go and see*," answered Ward, wondering how his CEO felt about being called stupid—Jenkinson had not even blinked. "No big plans. No step-change. We need to take things one at a time because we need to understand the effects of what we do."

"Hang on, son," corrected Woods. "One at a time is one area, that's right. But don't let people think only one thing happens at a time in the factory. There's a lot of parallel work you can do, as long as one person tackles one problem at a time. Also, remember you need to react immediately to put the process back into good working conditions. This is not solving the problem as such, but getting back into standard."

"Of course. So, we reveal problems and then we solve them one at a time. Is that all there is to it? It sounds a bit ..."

"What?" asked Jenkinson

"I don't know," thought Ward. "Weak, I guess. Considering the battering we get every time you visit. No offense, Phil, but you do a hell of a lot more than reveal problems, you also give us a serious push."

"Okay—"

"What the heck is this!" barked Woods, staring at a press further down the line as the group was slowly drifting down the aisle."

"What now?" wondered the production manager sourly. Stigler was still not getting it. He'd been much more restrained this time, but still reacted to every question as if his competence—indeed, his honor —was being challenged.

"This!" shouted the old man, as if witnessing a major crime, pointing at an open press.

"Nothing," shrugged Stigler. "Tool change."

"You've got a press with its jaws open saying 'Feed me, feed me,' and you think it's nothing!" Woods hollered, scandalized.

"He's got a point," agreed Jenkinson calmly, cleaning his glasses and frowning deeply. "All I keep hearing is requests for more presses."

After a heated exchange among Stigler, Carela, and Muller, the production manager explained that the setters had encountered a problem with a connection, and they were working on something else while waiting for maintenance to solve the problem—which was unlikely to happen with Muller *not being available* of course. He couldn't resist the dig, insinuating that we could all be getting on with our jobs if we weren't forced to go through with this circus.

"And you agree with this?" Woods asked directly to the press supervisor. Carela got the point before Ward had finished translating, and with an irritating grin he shrugged majestically and said, "What can I do? The setters are not my responsibility."

"How come?"

More shrugging. More superior grinning.

"The setters report to me," said Stigler, abruptly.

"Oh, please!" Woods exclaimed. "I thought this plant had realized how critical changeovers were? And we let this happen! Phil, for heaven's sake!"

"I know, I know," agreed Jenkinson, rubbing his chin. "They're learning."

"Learning? At this rate, we'll all be dead before they do."

"We don't have to go through this," Muller shouted, red in the face, which made his goatee appear even more starkly white. "No, Andy, don't try to shut me up. I don't care who they are. We don't have to take this kind of abuse, not after the work we've been doing for the past months. I'm too old for this crap."

"You *will* shut up!" Ward heard himself yell, "and you *will* learn. Or you will be *gone!*"

Losing his temper was so completely out of character for Ward that everyone froze and stared at him gobsmacked. He could see Muller tensing for a fight, and if he knew his man, the guy would walk out on them. Muller opened his mouth to speak, but nothing came out. He stared wide-eyed at Ward, his eyes magnified by his lenses.

"If you turn your back on us now," growled Ward. "Don't bother coming back. And I mean it."

"No one talks to me like this, young man," Muller replied through clenched teeth. On the side, Stigler snickered silently. Chadid looked shocked, and stared in silent disapproval at Ward, as if seeing him in a different light.

"Well, you'd better get used to it, while you're behaving like bloody ill-bred brats," shouted Ward. "You all know the future of this plant is in the balance, and I've had enough, ENOUGH of all your histrionics whenever someone tells you something you don't want to hear."

He could see Muller was clearly taken aback by his outburst—this was the first time in all their years of working together that Ward had actually bitten back at one of Muller's frequent shows of temper. And in public, as well. For a second, Ward worried that mentioning the plant's closure in the open would have Lord knows what consequences, but right now he was just too fed up to care. Let them close the bloody site and fire him.

"Listen up," he said, "I've told Olivier before. We shut up. We listen. We learn. I don't care whether you like it or not, but you will pay proper respect to your CEO and his guests in this plant. Secondly, being scandalized because a press is standing idle, and the changeover has been interrupted is exactly how we should feel! That is certainly how I feel right now.

"We need to change our attitude, or to accept the consequences," he thundered, feeling anger coursing through his veins like strong liquor. He was so mad, he could feel his legs shaking.

"*Si on ne peut plus rien dire!*" said Muller *sotto vocce*, unable not to have the last word.

"Of course you can say what you want," said Ward in English, gnashing his teeth trying to cool down. "But you will say it in a calm, collected, and constructive manner. Is that clear?"

"Discuss, yes. Argue, no," added Jenkinson, cool as can be. "I will listen. But I expect all of you to listen to me as well."

"The setters are still not back," remarked Woods gleefully. "You can argue all you want, but the press is still idle, and you can convince yourselves as much as you want, but understand that you're not convincing us."

"*Et, merde!*" exploded the press supervisor, muttering something further in French that Ward vaguely understood to mean "where the hell are these guys," and stomping away to look for them.

"Look," said Jenkinson, taking back control of the situation after a few tense moments of silence, "Andy was just asking whether visualizing production and revealing all problems at all times was enough to sustain *kaizen*. As you've all seen, this is not enough. Management must *step in*, as well."

He paused, looking at each of them in turn to make his point as forcefully as he could.

"*Management must step in*, and make the right person aware of the problem they are facing. Here, we can see that we have several layers of problems. At Andy's level, I can see that this plant is not serious enough about controlling changeover time. There is no visible clock or timing, there is no quick reaction, I'm not sure that any of you take this situation as seriously as Bob and I do. Trust me: you should.

"Second, you, Olivier, are not focused enough on your changeover organization. Changeover, in a press shop, is the backbone of the activity. Don't kid yourselves. High-volume, easy parts I can put in China. I don't care if they spend months crossing the oceans in containers. They are high-volume parts, and easy to make. The only reason that I would consider making parts here is because I've got low-volume, custom parts that I need to deliver to a local customer, so it makes sense to have the production site close by. Got it? Increasingly, the only orders this factory will get are the low-volume, technically difficult parts. So listen carefully: *Changeover is your job*. This means that you need to be able to make the difficult parts with good quality. We simply won't be carrying massive stocks of exotics. So you'd better become experts at changeover quick."

"All the more so considering the overcapacity of the plant," completed Woods. "The only parts you're likely to get are the ones others don't want, which usually means pain-in-the-butt parts in short batches. As long as you think long batches and program your presses accordingly, you'll never fill capacity."

"Can you clarify that?" asked Ward, puzzled.

"Think about it this way," explained Woods. "What is your shortest batch size?"

"Some presses we now change once a shift," Chandon said. "About seven hours."

"So what happens if I have a part for you that is one hour's production a day?"

She thought it through carefully before answering, "I'll have to produce it once every seven days. Probably do once every two weeks."

"So you choose to carry two weeks' worth of stock although you have press overcapacity!"

"I do not understand."

"I think I get it," said Ward slowly. "Because we can't produce in slots of one hour at a time, we can't take small-volume parts easily, so we're stuck with our overcapacity. Is that what you're saying?"

"Bob's more right than you know," underlined the CEO. "The first thing I did when I took this job is to audit overall capacity. Managers are still requesting new presses, whereas we have capacity all over the place—it's just that no one knows how to actually use it. Whichever way you cut it, short batches are your job."

"In my previous job, on a good day, we could change a 1,000-ton press in eight minutes, and we ran batches of under two hours of production. We consistently ran changeovers between 10 and 15 minutes. For low-runners, we came down to half-hour runs," insisted Woods. "And that was more than 10 years ago."

"Blimey," muttered Ward, thinking that his average changeover time must be somewhere between 40 minutes and two hours.

"Let me get back to the main point," said Jenkinson steadfastly. "Yes, *kaizen* starts with making production visible to see all problems. But then management must step in to give definite tasks and to follow up—this is how *go and see* and *kaizen* fit together. You can't have one without the other."

"*Kaizen* takes several forms. The point is to get everybody, everyday, to contribute to improving processes and products. We've been discussing one form of *kaizen*, which is to react to every abnormal situation and to get the supervisors and the teams to solve problems one by one. A second form is the *kaizen* workshops we've all done: three days of a cross-functional group focusing on one specific problem."

"We're doing those."

"Yes, and this is what we'll *go and see* now. But first let me outline the four ways of organizing *kaizen* I'm familiar with:

1. *Reacting to daily problems* by visualizing problems and management stepping in to focus on key issues.

2. *Conducting cross-functional workshops* on specific subjects, with standardized formats, such as *one-piece-flow*, *SMED*, 5S, etc.

3. *Quality circles* bring together operators of one team regularly to resolve a detailed problem, coached by their supervisor and with occasional help from staff experts.

4. *Individual suggestions* by operators, coached and supported by their supervisor, so that they clarify the problem they're trying to solve, experiment themselves with their solutions, check the benefits, and convince all other team members.

"It's critical to understand that all four types of *kaizen* not only require *go and see*, but *teamwork* as well. *Kaizen* is impossible to sustain on one's own. *Teamwork*, both in terms of all functions working together and the hierarchy working together.

Jenkinson searched for his words a long moment, looking inward. He was a large man, and, on occasion, he seemed to both withdraw and grow at the same time, as if he'd cast some sort of shadow over them all. Ward wondered whether he was witnessing charisma. He'd calmed down, his breath coming easier, and his pulse no longer pounding. He really did not know what to make of his boss. The man was obviously ill-at-ease in public, a slow, plodding speaker with none of the energy of, well, Woods, for instance. But on the other side, he displayed some sort of steadiness of purpose that couldn't fail to impress.

"The arguments I witnessed today, I construe as a failure of *teamwork*. Functional experts passing the blame on to the others. Hierarchical levels unable to face their problems together without drama. Understand this. *Kaizen* will deliver the results you hope for, but only if you overcome your own difficulties with two key aspects of managing for lean: *go and see* and *teamwork*."

"Go on," said Woods impatiently, shuffling his feet. "Let's go and have a see at their *kaizen* workshops."

"What is the problem you're trying to solve?"

"We're implementing a *kanban*, sir."

"I can see that, I'm not blind," growled Woods. "But *what is the problem you're trying to solve?*"

"We've got this board, here, and every time a container is pulled from the cell's finished-parts supermarket, the card on the container goes here. When the cards reach the yellow zone, the operator knows he has to produce more of this reference."

"I've seen a few *kanbans* in my time, son. I can see what you're doing. But which part of the sentence 'What is the problem you're trying to solve?' is unclear?"

Sebastien Martin, the young continuous-improvement officer, stood frozen like a deer caught in the headlights, unable to reply. Woods' attack seemed totally unfair. Martin had been making a huge effort to expand his six sigma background, and was leading numerous *kaizens*. Ward had worked with him to define a standard three-day event, with a few slides of training for the group and then a set sequence of activities: *seven wastes*, *takt time* calculation, 20 cycles measurement, work-content calculation, cell redesign, and problem-solving with operators. The young man had conducted a grueling rhythm of one event every three weeks, with one week of preparation, one week of *kaizen* event, and one week of stabilization of the cell. He was a reserved, studious character who needed several iterations before he felt comfortable talking about any subject. Putting him on the spot like this would just make him wilt. Still, Ward figured that the best tactic was to let Woods make his point and then pick up the pieces afterward.

"Are you trying to solve a productivity problem?" asked Woods, with mock patience. "A quality problem? A stock problem?"

"Stock," the young man said hurriedly. "We're trying to reduce inventory."

"See? Now, in what way will this board help you to reduce inventory?"

This drew a dreadful blank from all, Ward included. He couldn't answer the question, and hoped that Woods wouldn't call him out.

"This is stupid," said Chandon in accented English. "We are trying to create a pull loop from logistics to here in assembly. Is it no good?"

"That's not the point!" snapped Woods. "We don't do things because we want to! We try to solve problems. If not, you end up doing silly things and wondering why the heck you don't get any results. So, again, what is the problem you're trying to solve? Inventory reduction? Fine. How does this reduce inventory?"

Deep, collective blank stares.

"Darn it, what kind of inventory does *kanban* aim to solve?"

Deeper blank paired with greater silence.

"What is the worse waste in lean? You've read the books at least, I hope!" asked Woods.

"Overproduction," grinned Ward. "I know that one!"

"OVERPRODUCTION! Yes! We are always tempted to produce faster than customer demand. It feels safer, in case we have breakdowns, bad parts, absentees, and so on. As a result, we use more manpower and equipment than we need, and since it's built-in to the system we cannot get it out. Correct? So, if we accept overproduction, we get ... your factory. More pallets and containers than necessary. More boxes everywhere. More forklifts. Larger warehouses, tents, everything. Ultimately, we can't do *kaizen* for real because overproduction hides all problems, which—"

"Makes it unlikely we'll solve them," completed Ward, nodding. "I buy that."

"I'd hope so," grouched the old man. "Now, how is your *kanban* going to stop overproduction?"

"Well ...," Ward thought out loud, "the operator can't produce more cards than he's got."

"Can't he? What would happen if he did?"

"Some of the other references would go into the red," pointed out the logistics manager.

"And then? So what? What if two references went into the red at the same time on the board?"

"He'd have to chose what to produce next, I guess."

"And this helps not to overproduce?"

"All right, not clearly," agreed Ward thoughtfully.

"Clarify the problem, Andy," insisted Jenkinson. "Bob is right. All these tools are supposed to clarify the problem—not to solve it. What is the problem you're trying to solve?"

"Right. What we're trying to do is to produce the five references at this workstation just in time."

"Which means?"

"Take one out, make one," said Chandon, frowning. "Stock replenishment."

"And? What's missing?"

"Sequence!" exclaimed Ward. "In sequence. That's what I saw in Bethany that I couldn't remember—it has been nagging at me all along."

"Yes. Stock replenishment in sequence. That's the principle. Produce one by one, in sequence."

"You can't overproduce because you visualize the waiting file, and so you know what you have to do next."

"What did Bethany use?" asked Jenkinson patiently.

"They didn't have this board," recalled Ward, closing his eyes and thinking hard. "They had some kind of tube on which they hung the *kanbans*. A queuing system."

Why did they keep tripping on their own feet like this? He'd seen this movie before, and it was starting to really get on his nerves. It's not like he didn't know the answers. It was just a question of connecting the dots. "We need to visualize the sequence of production, of course— this is what matters. And you're right, I did see it in Bethany. Why do I keep missing such obvious things, it's infuriating!"

"The real difficulty is asking oneself the right questions," agreed Jenkinson with a trace of exasperation. "What is it we always discuss when we look at any activity?"

"What results do we expect from it."

"Yeah. So if you'd asked yourself what results you expected from this stupid board—"

"We would have wondered what problem we were trying to solve. I'd have set inventory-reduction targets. We'd have questioned the whole principle of the thing."

"And you could have phoned Mark Neville, rather than waiting for us to show up and see this," groused the CEO.

"You, young man," called Woods, facing poor Sebastien Martin, who was reddening furiously. "Don't let your management do this to you. Whenever you need to run a *kaizen* exercise, go through the checklist:

1. What is the problem we're trying to solve?
2. What results do we expect?
3. What is the principle we should apply?
4. Did we get the results we wanted? If not, why not?
5. What did we learn? Where does this apply next?

Write it down, write it down now. You won't have your CEO holding your hand every day, you know."

"*Plan, do, check, act,*" muttered Ward.

"Of course, *PDCA*! What did you think *kaizen* workshops were about? Fishing for answers?" exclaimed Woods, rubbing it in. "Now will you boys and girls show me a workshop where you've actually got some results?"

"Over here," said Ward. "Here I believe we've done all right."

They regrouped in front of an assembly cell where three operators were busy assembling parts. The operators looked startled to see so many people for a second, but they'd been briefed, thank goodness, and didn't break their rhythm. Jenkinson made a point of getting into the cell and shaking everybody's hand while Woods looked on stonily.

"This part, here," explained Ward, passing a part around, "is very similar to one produced in the Bethany plant. Their cell works with three people. We used to have six. After Phil's last visit, we agreed that it was possible to improve productivity through *kaizen*, so we picked this cell because of the gap with Bethany."

"That is the right way to present a problem: a gap to a standard," approved Jenkinson. "Good. Please continue."

"Yes, our problem was clearly defined in terms of reaching the Bethany standard. But then we realized, after your last visit, that it wasn't only a matter of the number of people, but of following the actual customer demand."

"Sales pace determines production's pace," agreed Woods.

"First, we had to create the cell by grouping operations. We went from six to five people at that stage. Then we calculated *takt time*, measured 20 cycles of each operator, and drew a line-balancing sheet, which was posted for everyone to see."

"This showed a lot of variation in work cycles, mostly because of supply issues. When we created the cell, we set up a shelf to hold a small stock of components across the alley. Operators had to break their cycle to go and fetch parts. Also, as we discussed last time you came, by forcing *one-piece flow* on the line, we solved obvious balancing problems simply by discussing this with the people on the line."

"What happened to that young guy?" wondered Jenkinson, "You know with the—" he said pointing to his eye.

"Temp. A few days later he didn't show up. We never got anything out of the agency."

"Pity. He had potential."

Ward had never really found out what had happened, but suspected the other operators had given Fernandez enough of a hard time for showing them up in front of management that he'd preferred to go and work elsewhere.

"So, based on the *takt time* calculation and the cycle time measurement, we agreed on the minimal amount of workers needed. In the end, we got down to three people."

"I can't see the standardized work," said Woods, frowning.

"You're right," sighed Ward. "We haven't posted the standardized work."

"And I don't believe your targets represent the work content," Woods persisted.

"What do you mean?"

"Look at the targets on the production-analysis board. This is obviously a miraculous line, since some hours, the operators can beat the target. You said you've agreed on the minimal amount of work, yes?"

"We did. And that's what's on the target."

"So how come they can beat the target? Is it really the minimal amount of work?"

"Not quite," hesitated Ward. "We worked with manufacturing engineering who determined what would be a reasonable pace of work."

"So it's not the work content, agreed?"

"Um … If you say so," granted Ward, not quite sure what the issue was.

"So. Let's summarize," said Woods. "I can see the target is not based on the actual work content, and I also can see that there is no posted standardized work. How can you do *kaizen*?"

Ward looked from Woods to Jenkinson, feeling lost. For once, he'd thought he'd gone about it the right away. He was obviously missing something.

"Let me say this another way," the CEO waded in. "You made a productivity gain, yes?"

"We did."

"So when are you going to go down to two persons?"

"What?" blurted out Ward in total disbelief. "We've improved efficiency by more than 50 percent since we started working on this cell! You expect us to do more?"

"It's called continuous improvement," Woods grinned nastily, "not once-and-for-all improvement. There's a reason to that. Good enough never is."

"'Improvement after improvement,' my *sensei* would say over and over again," the old man pressed, jabbing a finger in the air, as they all stared back disbelievingly. "That's what the *kaizen* spirit is all about. Until you finally realize that *managing means improving* and then improving again, you're simply missing the whole point about lean management."

"Last time I came to this plant," said Jenkinson at the debriefing back in the meeting room, "we discussed the four dimensions of *go and see*. Let's see: You've improved customer service, quality, and you've done some efforts on productivity and machine uptime. But bear in mind that, so far, I'm not seeing any effects on your bottom line."

"Our volume—" complained the production manager.

"Skip it," said the CEO, holding up his hand. "We all have problems. I have enough experience with this to know the difference, and although I commend you for your activities, I'm not seeing results in the numbers. If we want to succeed, we need to develop the *kaizen* spirit in every employee.

This means understanding visual management:

– We visualize production
– To reveal all problems at all times
– To solve them one by one

– To improve management practices."

"This also means that management must *go and see* and step in when a problem appears, to involve the right people, clarify it, and make sure both an immediate action is taken *and* the root cause is pursued relentlessly. This is the first aspect of the *kaizen* spirit: making normal conditions visual so that anyone can see abnormal situations, and figure out immediately who needs to solve what problem. This will not happen if you, in this room, are not determined to sustain it, every day. So problems first.

"The second aspect touches upon the rhythm of *kaizen* events. Are you doing enough? Are you involving enough people? My rule of thumb is that every operator should be part of a *kaizen* event at least once a year. Be that as it may, the important thing is to understand that *kaizen* is not something we do on top of the job—it is the job. You've *kaizened* one cell. Very good. But should we congratulate you for just doing your job? The only questions are: Did it work? What was learned? By who? When are you going to do it again?

"Look, you may feel let down, and think we're crazy and expect too much. But let me tell you what I expect. I want you to realize that, in this company, *managing means improving*. Status quo is not an option, because every process unravels over time, and the competition doesn't stop. At the moment, I'm sure you feel that you are making exceptional efforts to turn around this plant. Please understand that I do recognize and value that. However, this is not what I seek. Your task is to reorganize your own jobs so that *kaizen* is the mainstay of what you do. *Managing means improving*."

"They gone yet?" asked Sandrine Lumbroso, sitting down heavily at the cafeteria table at break time.

"Think so," agreed one of the other operators. As the teams were slowly stabilizing, they'd started to sit by teams during the break, and they all looked up in surprise as the veteran operator joined them.

Cranky as she was, she was not particularly well-liked, though most people respected her as an old hand in the plant.

"Ha! You've had them on your back again. Ever since the first kaizens, they keep coming back to your cell."

"They're not too bad," answered the thin, middle-aged woman seated across the table. "They're full of hot air mostly—arguing for hours about the obvious."

"But what about the piece-rate increase? Since they've done these kaisens, none of you have any time to breathe."

"Oh, I don't know. They did improve a lot of things on the cell. Work is easier."

"I can't believe my ears, Sylvie! You're a union representative for Pete's sake!" Lumbroso exclaimed, raising her voice with a mean tone. "And you're defending productivity?"

"I'm not defending anything," retorted Sylvie Barras uncomfortably. "I'm here to build parts, and if we can make more parts without working harder I'm for it. This is what will protect all our jobs in the end."

"Not working harder, ha!" the other woman replied snidely. "As if. We always used to have time for a quick smoke and a chat. Now we don't see any of you guys anymore. And you want us to believe that you don't work harder. You've been had, that's what."

"Get outta here," intervened a younger woman. "I agree with Sylvie. We don't work harder, we just get a lot less interruptions. I mean, I don't see time go by, I swear. And I'm not so tired when I come home at the end of the shift. D'you remember how our shoulders used to hurt after a full shift?"

"Yup. And my wrist from having to bang these inserts in," nodded the union lady.

"Pah! I can't believe this," spat the older woman. "It'll end in tears, you'll see. All this 'improvement' stuff. I've seen it when I used to build TVs for the Koreans. It's just a way to increase productivity on our backs. Mark my words. You'll see, you'll see."

"If you say so," muttered Barras, picking up her tray and walking away. She'd never liked Lumbroso, but she was afraid the old bird had a point. She'd actually enjoyed the *kaizen* work done on the cell—and she could see the sense of it. Sure, it meant fighting with these blockhead engineers, but they tended to see the light in the end. After all, they were only men, so what did they know? However, she did worry where all of this would end. They'd made some rapid productivity improvement, and she did not dispute the need for cost reduction in the plant, but she wondered how fair it was, and whether anything would ever get back to the operators. She also knew that, as a union leader, she was inviting trouble by actively participating in the *kaizen* management initiative. Oh, well, she thought. As long as we're improving ergonomics.

As he drove the two men into town, Ward could not stop puzzling about the level of detail they got involved in at every visit. All he'd ever been taught about management was that one needed to distance oneself away from the narrow specifics of operations, to get the "big picture," and let subordinates get on with doing their stuff. But here, both the CEO and his consultant were spending considerable time going into a level of detail that took even the maintenance manager by surprise. He'd been trained to develop his general analysis skills—to look at the situation globally and find a general solution to a general problem. It was extremely unsettling to see these two attack issues with a microscope and tweezers, rather than the usual strategic pronouncements. In fact, he wondered whether Jenkinson had any strategic vision at all. The man seemed pretty clear on what he was doing most of the time, and certainly pushed the company in a deliberate way, but it was hard to see where he was taking them. All that detailed *kaizen* stuff was well and fine, but Ward could not see how this would turn the entire company around.

In fact, he wasn't even sure this would save his own plant. Although it had been on the tip of his tongue all day, he'd been very careful not to ask about the status of the termination plan for Vaudon. Jenkinson had not mentioned anything, and Ward was reluctant to get into this discussion for fear of precipitating events. But he was acutely aware that for all the hard work they'd been doing since the summer, his financial results did not show any spectacular improvements. Some of it was their own bloody fault. For instance, Muller had delivered a real improvement in press uptime, which convinced Ward they should be able to progressively eliminate the weekend overtime shifts. And yet, through a mix of miscalculations and misunderstandings between logistics programming and production scheduling, overtime was necessary every other week. To a large extent he tried to take hope from the fact no announcement had been made.

He'd also had to arbitrate a growing dispute between Franck Bayard and Stigler over what happened to all these people freed from the processes. With the support of the manufacturing engineer, they had delivered about 20 percent of the cell headcount at almost every *kaizen* workshop conducted by young Martin—even taking into account the precautions Woods had complained about. But still, this increase in productivity didn't appear in the numbers. Ward had started wondering whether production was playing a silly bugger's game of running the cells with the post-*kaizen* number of operators but not truly fixing the problems, thereby coming up short of parts at the end of the shift and catching up later with overtime. That would also explain the unreasonable resistance production was showing in stabilizing operators in fixed teams, as Amy Woods had explained. One more issue Ward needed to look into, which brought him back to the basic quandary that he could not do all of this by himself. Yet, maybe Jenkinson and Bob Woods were right. Maybe it was only by checking every singular instance in detail that one could really understand what was going on.

"You keep mentioning lean management," Ward said, "but all you ever give us are more tools. I thought it was not about the tools?"

Next to him, Bob Woods chortled.

"There's a Zen story that says that before you study Zen, you see the mountain as a mountain. When you've studied Zen assiduously, you no longer see the mountain as a mountain. But when you finally understand Zen, you see the mountain as a mountain."

"Bob," laughed Ward, "I'm sure it's real profound. But I have no idea what you're talking about."

"When you first study lean, it's all about the tools. Which is fair enough because you've got to get into the problem somehow. Then, when you've studied lean for years, you realize that it's not about the tools, but about a management attitude."

"Like *go and see*, and *kaizen* spirit?"

"Precisely. But then when you finally get it, you realize it's all about the tools in the end. Not the tools in themselves, but how you apply the tools to get results."

"The tools are a way to have a grip," added Jenkinson, "an 'in' into the problem. This is why applying the tools rigorously is so important. The tools frame the problem in a lean way. They don't give any answer, but if you use them with the proper attitude, they'll get you to clarify the issues in a way you hadn't before. On the other hand, if you use the tools with the wrong attitude, they won't deliver much."

"This is how you Brits conquered the world," threw in Woods. "The natives were quick to learn about muskets and how to shoot them, but they never figured out volley fire and the underlying organization that requires. So they never succeeded in outshooting the red coats—so all firearms brought them was to die out a bit slower."

"They were also far fewer than the white men," retorted Ward.

"Son, when the finger points at the moon, it's the moon you need to look at, not the finger," retorted Woods crankily. "Sue me for a bad analogy, but the point is the tools are the outgrowth of a way of thinking. If you use them with the wrong mindset, you'll get engrossed in the tools themselves, and not what they can bring."

"Focusing on the finger, not the moon it's pointing at," agreed Ward.

"Which we've all done, time and time again. But on the other hand, you've got to use the tools. You can't dismiss them—they're standard analysis techniques to attack repetitive situations. So of course it's always more tools, there are not that many ways of solving a math problem. If you don't know the standard technique, you can flounder for a long time before hitting the right solution by random walk."

"Amazing! Just like Amy said," exclaimed Bob Woods enthusiastically. "Would you look at that."

In the bright light of the brittle cold day, under a pale blue sky, Claire stood in a wide circle of dark wet sand amid the glare of the surrounding snow. Her tangled curls fluttering behind her, she stood very straight, in front of a huge, powerful stallion whose dark bay looked black against the whitened field beyond the *carrière*. The beast pawed the ground as she pulled the lead rope closer, the long whip held unmoving in her hand. Ward had seen this many times, yet never failed to be impressed by his wife's nerve in the face of the brute's might. He could well imagine how the "beauty and beast" image could affect their visitors, as she stood there, stone still, facing off the great horse whose gleaming flanks steamed with sweat in the freezing cold. They watched, mesmerized.

"Terango is the pride of Malancourt," he explained, holding young Charlie who, wrapped up in his winter outfit, looked like a small bear cub. "He's far too fine for a small outfit like this, but he belongs to one of Claire's good friends. Daughter of a local fortune, who married into yet more wealth. They were both taught to ride by Claire's father, and she wouldn't think of keeping him anywhere else. She's been very

231

involved with helping Claire work this place, and sponsors the yearly competition that puts us on the map."

"Incredible," exclaimed Woods as the horse reared up again, pawing the air. Claire was amazing, doing her thing. Standing, backing away, moving forward, projecting this implacable calm that would, Ward knew, have its way with the animal in the end. She'd been exercising him with the rope this morning, but now was the time to get in the saddle, and the prize-winning bay had always been tricky.

"Whoa! Easy," said Claire calmly as the horse shook his head side-to-side brutally, snorting plumes of white steam.

"They need to be exercised regularly," Ward explained. "Unfortunately, in the winter they don't get ridden as much as they should, so they're really frisky when you get them out."

The two Americans stood side by side in the bitter cold. A happy grin played on Woods' face, taking years off him. Jenkinson was looking his usual pensive self, only more so, incongruous in his black cashmere coat.

"Listen," coughed Ward, feeling chilled to the bone. "I've got to get this young man home and scrounge up something for our lunch. Feel free to stay. She'll ride it soon, and that's worth watching."

"We don't want to put you out," stirred Jenkinson, sounding ill at ease. "As we decided to postpone our trip to Prague to tonight, Bob insisted we came around this morning. Apparently Amy's been raving about the place. We don't want to impose. We'll be on our way."

"Nonsense," scoffed Ward. "This is no trouble at all. In any case, Claire made me swear I would keep you for lunch, she's eager to meet you both."

"Are you sure?"

"Certain. You know what they say?" joked Ward. "Never argue with a woman with a whip! Come on Charlie, stop squirming, we're going back."

"Here, that'll warm you up," said Ward, presenting both men with a cup of bubbly.

"Umph!" spluttered Woods, laughing. "That's a man's drink! I thought it was wine. What's in there?"

"I knew a Polish girl that had some for breakfast," winked Ward. "Local cocktail: We put a hint of *Mirabelle* liqueur in the white. Plum brandy."

"Excellent," mumbled Jenkinson. "Unfortunately, I'm driving," he said putting his glass down after a second sip.

"Well, I'm not," grinned Woods. "Good stuff."

"Your wife was awesome!" said Jenkinson admiringly. From the two men's comment, Ward got the feeling that Claire had put on a bit of a show, showing off her dressage skills. He knew how breathtaking it could be to see the big horse being taken through his paces up close, and was not surprised Jenkinson and Woods had been impressed.

"I stick to my guns," said Woods, his crinkly eyes sparkling. "Amy was right, this is a ranch."

They were sitting with coffee and drinks by the windows overlooking the back of the house. The view opened on a sloping meadow sparkling white with the night's fresh snow, which ran all the way down a gentle slope to a narrow brook lined with bare alder trees. On the other side, the field climbed slowly to the deep wood. At the far end, the trees made a dark bar between the snowdrifts' white and the hazy blue of the sky, lit up by a watery winter sun, blurring all edges into a life-sized watercolor.

"Floorboards," he said, pointing toward the floor. "I rest my case. I very much doubt we'd find floorboards in a traditional French farmhouse."

"Claire's idea," said Ward, nodding toward his wife who was now trying to persuade an overexcited Charlie that there was no escaping the afternoon nap. "She also had all the walls torn down to make it one room and all these windows installed on the back. When her parents lived here, it was all small rooms."

"Sensible lass!"

"Bob," hesitated Ward, pausing to shift the conversation back to work. "May I ask you something?"

"Go ahead."

"What did you mean about the targets we've got on our production-analysis boards. Why is having achievable targets a problem? I thought that all objectives had to be, let's see ..."

"SMART," chuckled Jenkinson. "*Specific, measurable, achievable, realistic, and time-constrained*, right? We can see how well this theory has worked for Alnext, yes?"

"Back to your idea that opinions matter?" asked Ward.

"That's right. But the truth is in this case that we also believe in specific, measurable, achievable, realistic, and time-constrained."

"Um," said Ward thoughtfully, "specific and measurable, I can see as they're at the cell. Time-constrained as well, since they're hourly targets. But you were complaining about them having been achieved."

"We have a different take on the issue," explained Woods, "which again is a matter of perspective and often hard to get across. To us these targets are not objectives as you think them. They are standards."

"*A standard is the best known performance*," continued Jenkinson. "So we take the time of the best operator over a few cycles like we did the last time I was here. Or you take the average of five straight times of the operators on the line. Or you take the actual work content: the sum of the minimum times of 20 cycles. Whichever way you chose to define the standard, the point is that you've got a realistic measure of the best time achievable with this cell in today's conditions."

"But how realistic is it to expect people to maintain that time for one hour straight? Or eight, for that matter."

"That's the whole point about *kaizen* spirit," replied Jenkinson, warming to the theme. "How can we reach our best time every cycle? Problems are defined as gaps between standard and actual, remember? So we need to see the standard at all times."

"That's a bit harsh, no?"

"You're not giving your operators a pay-per-piece bonus, are you?" asked the CEO, suddenly concerned.

"No, of course not."

"Then in that case, how is it harsh? The main problem is the 'shrug factor'—surely you recognize it at your plant! We need to develop *kaizen* spirit, all the time. It's sort of like jogging every weekend and knowing that, on average, you can run around the park in 30 minutes. On good days where the sun is shining and you're feeling wonderful, the run takes 20 minutes. On rainy days when the track is muddy and spirits are low, but you still have the gumption to run, it can take 40 minutes. No big deal. On the other hand, if you choose to run for competition, 'average' time is the worst possible target. Professional athletes try to beat their best time *every time*. The same principle applies at work. If five consecutive cycles reveal a potential of 1,500 parts per shift, then that's the target. Not a target for just the operators to achieve, but an objective for the entire team, supervisor, and plant managers to reach and beat. What can the plant manager do so that the team can reach its objective? Answers will come out of *kaizen*. But you must be on top of this: as long as everyone involved simply shrugs when it's a bad day, no lean tool in the world will be able to help."

"But what about all the things the operators don't control?" Ward asked. "There's always machine problems, delivery problems, and even tiredness."

"Andy, that's the point! If I take these into account and reduce the hourly target, then there is absolutely no incentive for you, the plant manager, and your team to solve any of these problems. The attitude is: here, we've taken all of this out of the target, get on with it and leave us alone. No. We want engagement! We want the management to take responsibility for achieving the targets—to see all the problems and solve them, working with people to better define the production processes."

"Visualize production," added Woods. "Yes? So we can see all the problems all the time. And solve them one by one."

"Agreed."

"But that's not the end of it," said Woods, leaning back to emphasize his point. "Solving problems one by one should lead us to *improve our management practices.* For instance, on the line we saw today, you attacked the problem of supplying the line and changing material during production changes by having an advanced stock of material and a guy there who keeps supplying the line. Did I understand it right?"

"That's what we did, to lower the variation on the operator cycles. And it works after a fashion."

"But did you change the plant's practice about handling material? Did you improve your own management standard?"

"What do you mean?"

"What's the principle for supplying parts and maintaining flow conditions?"

"Parts are kept at the place of production and delivered just-in-time. I know, the reserve stock shouldn't be there but in the warehouse, and I should have a train delivering the parts every 10 minutes, like in Bethany."

"Exactly. Think about this: You changed something locally, but you haven't drawn the full conclusion of your experiment. In this case, you did do the *check*, but you did not *act* on the consequences of your findings. Solving this problem should lead you to question the entire way you manage components in the plant."

"I've thought about it," muttered Ward. "Having a central area in logistics to prepare all components in small containers and delivering through a train to the lines, but ..."

"No buts. You've just got to learn how to do it. The point is that *kaizen* is about:

- One, visualizing production to reveal all problems.

- Two, solving them one by one.

- Three, improving management practice!"

I've heard that when Toyota builds a new plant, they start by developing the standards for everything by observing and documenting how their best plants around the world perform. Then it's the plant manager's job to achieve, and eventually surpass, these standards. Now, I don't know if that's true. It sounds pretty tough, but wouldn't surprise me. They *think* like that," declared Woods.

"The point is," insisted Jenkinson, draining the last of his coffee, "that having real targets on the hourly boards is not for operators alone. Let's take a step back. The first principle, of course, is that production pace should be equal to sales pace—or as equal as we can make it. No overproduction. So our *takt time* sets our demand. Then, according to the work content on the line, we can make a staffing decision of how many operators we need and what their hourly targets should be. The ideal number of operators is work content divided by *takt time*. The *lean* point is that work content is, well, lean. There is no slack in it. Work content is the minimum amount of work necessary to produce a good part. As I said, these numbers are not just for the operators: they are shared numbers to help *everyone* figure out how to reach them *together*."

Ward wrestled with this idea: "So we can never achieve the target exactly, because the moment we do, we *check* the standard again, and it's going to be higher."

"Yes, but the important point is that the target is achievable. It's not out of management's reach. It's an objective measure of a few cycles. Then you look at what needs to be done to hit it for one hour continuously, two hours, and so on. You see causes of variation, and you work on them. *Kaizen*.

"Look, we're constantly looking at *potential* rather than *average*. This type of focus gives a much greater importance to *normal operations*. Instead of being relieved that a process 'runs,' we invest our time figuring out what it's potential performance could be if it *always ran at its best*. As a manager, if you start asking yourself whether you are running your processes at their best every second, rather than just good enough, you'll naturally focus on *how the people in place run the process*. Clearly, a competitive sports team needs a different kind of management—coaching—than a weekend game. If we want processes to run at their best all the time, we need to focus on how front-line managers understand their jobs, the technical issues in the process, and how they coach their team to stay on top form.

"And so, trying to achieve the potential changes the 'if it ain't broke don't fix it' approach to most situations. Any sign of trouble must be investigated and fixed quickly because if not we'll never reach potential! Rather than just move parts down the process or customers down the line, we need to react at the first sign of something going wrong. Every nonconform is a harbinger of worse to come. Reacting at the first defect is the best way of seeing how front-line management works with their teams to keep the process at its potential at all times, and how they cope with difficulties *before* the real fire starts."

"Okay. It is a different kind of thinking," said Ward ruefully. "But every time I try, I hit this mental barrier. I just don't get it, do I?"

"D'you think any of us did overnight?" guffawed Woods. "It took me more than 15 years to even understand there was a problem with the way we thought, not just the way we applied tools. For years I was convinced that all I needed to do is figure out the lean tools and I'd beat Toyota at their game. I was sure we'd be able to leapfrog them. It took me a long, long while to figure out that we were simply not thinking along the same lines. Ask Phil."

"Yeah," Jenkinson answered. "Didn't come easy, or quick, believe me. I'm an engineer, so it took Amy to beat me into understanding that, really, it's all about the people, and how they attack problems. The truth is that, with hindsight, I realize we get very different kinds of solutions from doing *kaizen* than from asking the most gifted engineer in the world to come up with something revolutionary."

"We get something people can work with," nodded Ward thoughtfully, "because they've been involved."

"And also they do know a lot—they spend their lives with these parts and machines. Our problem is asking them the right questions."

"Hence, the production-analysis boards."

"And the call at first doubt, and stop at defect, and so on. The only way to really understand what goes wrong is to *go and see* and be there as it goes wrong. Say, could I trouble you for more coffee? This is really excellent stuff."

"We're talking a lot about reacting to problems, but getting to the root cause is just as important in understanding *kaizen*," said Woods, after Ward returned with the espresso. "Many years ago, I was industrial VP of a group similar to yours, making plastic parts and all sorts of automotive assemblies. We were trying to work closely with Toyota. I remember one part in particular we couldn't get right. We were throwing out one part in 10, and the *sensei* was beating us up for not finding a solution.

"Eventually he got us to set up a flipchart right next to the press and draw the entire molding process in detail. The question was, 'What do I need to get right to do a good part?' So we went over what we knew about basic injection. The he asked us to list all the possible factors that could cause the problem. It was a new press, so we went through all the usual things: pressure, heat, screw type, mold maintenance, the works.

"Once we had listed nine or 10 credible factors, he asked us to test them one by one. 'Invest one hour a day into testing,' he suggested, 'until you find the proper factor.' In some cases it wasn't easy, but by thinking it through, we managed to go through the list on the flip chart. Nothing came out conclusively. It got very frustrating, but then the *sensei* says, 'Just think of more factors.'

"Finally, someone thought of checking the incoming material in the silo. We hadn't thought of this before because it was fairly common high-density polyethylene, and Toyota did not allow regrind for its parts. So here we are digging for samples at different places in the silo, and, sure enough, we find out that the supplier delivered from a different source, which meant the material was uneven, which affected the parts. We had a big fight with the supplier, and the problem went away.

"But the funny part is, I then asked the *sensei* how long it had taken him to figure it out. 'Oh,' he said, just as casual as could be, 'I considered this immediately. In Toyota we always check the four *Ms: manpower, machine, material,* and *method.* There was nothing obviously wrong with your machine, so I thought about material. We've got a lot of problems because of material instability, which is why we don't let you use regrind yet. We will when you understand your process better.'

"'Why the hell didn't you say so right away?' I ask. 'We've been working on this for weeks. 'I know,' he answers. 'You've tried 11 factors that didn't work out, and one that did. If I'd told you right away, you would have learned one thing. In doing it this way, you've learned 12: you now know that 11 of these factors have no impact on this kind of defect, and that material homogeneity does. You've learned far more than if I'd told you right away.'"

"We only learn when we discover we're wrong," laughed Ward. "Is that it?"

"And we're wrong half of the time," agreed Jenkinson with an amused smile. "The problem is, we don't know which half."

"Harsh way to live, if you ask me," Ward complained.

"Who ever said lean was easy?" snorted Woods. "Lean is about beating competitors. Of course it's hard. But it's just work!"

Jenkinson shifted in his chair, making it creak loudly under his bulk. It almost seemed like a child's toy for a man his size. Ward had always wanted to find some old-fashioned leather club armchairs to have in front of the fire, but like so many other domestic things, he'd never got around to it, so they still made do with the used wood-and-straw chairs. If Claire had her way, she'd have the room looking like a Shaker interior. The first summer they'd spent together they'd taken a trip up the northeastern U.S. coast, where she fell in love with the carpentry. The first thing she did when they took over Malancourt was to scandalize everyone by radically redecorating the farmhouse. Seeing the CEO out of context, Ward finally noticed what bothered him about the man: He was slow. He spoke slowly. He moved slowly. Neither clumsy or gauche, but overly deliberate. That made him come across as a bit thick. However, Ward was learning that it didn't pay to underestimate Phil Jenkinson.

"The point of Bob's tale is not what you might think," Jenkinson explained in his plodding pace. "It's easy to dismiss it all as Toyota folklore, but the lesson in that story has been the hardest to learn, for me, personally.

"When Bob started coaching me on lean in my first company—"

"You kicked me out of the plant," interrupted Bob, grinning mischievously.

"As I was saying, when we first started, I saw lean with an engineer's eyes. We revealed problems, and we solved them. We were deep in a cash crisis, but it was a fairly small business then, so I could more or less get involved in everything myself. It was hard work, and really touch-and-go at some point, but we clawed out of the hole."

Claire had managed to get the kid to sleep, and joined quietly, bringing a tray of local pastries.

"Amy told us something about that," she said.

"Amy had left at that point, gone off to become a consultant. That really threw me at the time. I mean, we were having a ball. Finally we're out of the hole and sorting things out, and she'd been a huge part of it, and then she up and went."

He shook his head as if still dismayed by Amy's choice.

"Then, out of the blue, we got the opportunity to purchase another small company in the same field. It was crazy, of course, as we were barely out of our own mess. But, in the end, we went for it, banking on the fact that if we could turn them around the way we'd done with our business, the acquisition would more or less pay for itself. In the end, we hoped to double the value of our firm through the increased sales without being totally beholden to lenders.

"To cut a long story short, it worked out in the end, but again, there were some hairy moments—"

That made Woods guffaw. "The understatement of the day," he said, grinning.

"It wasn't that bad," smiled Jenkinson. "Anyhow, Bob had to hit me over the head more or less to make me realize I could not do this on my own. I had learned to solve problems and to get operators involved in *kaizen*, but I hadn't brought my management with me. I was still running everyone as if they were extensions of my will. I would create the action plans and control the execution. And I felt that whenever I was not involved personally, things would go wrong— which was a rational feeling, as they often did.

"Bob kept telling me I was managing too much, that I should have been teaching instead. How can one manage too much? It didn't make sense.

"Then, one day, I met a senior Toyota engineer at a conference. He was based in the U.S. and close to retirement. He was in charge of about 150 engineers, which would have been more than twice the engineers I had in both businesses. We were discussing how difficult engineers can be to manage. 'Herding cats,' he called it. Then I asked him how he actually spent his time. He told me he would spend about two hours per week dealing with administrative tasks. The rest of the time, he would get personally involved in problems."

"Kinda like Mark spending no more than two hours a day in his office or in meetings," interrupted Ward.

"Same thing. I was bowled over by how little time he spent on admin, but I agreed with getting involved personally in problems—if I didn't nothing got solved. 'Well,' the guy says, 'by the time the problems reach me, really they're people problems. Somebody doesn't know how to deal with this or that. So really, you could say that I spend most of my time teaching. That's what our system drums into us constantly: don't be *managers*, be *teachers*.'"

"I kept telling him so, but he wouldn't listen," cut in Woods, rolling his eyes theatrically. Away from the plant, he seemed like a different person. Sure, he was a crabby old man, but there was a deeper layer of humor that shone through, which made Ward feel better about him.

"It was an epiphany," Jenkinson continued. "I had to *teach kaizen*, not just practice it myself. I had to get my management line to understand *kaizen*. So after this meeting, I set about putting this idea into practice. The obvious thing was to do to my management team what had been done to me. So when I returned I gathered the entire management team of the acquired company to the shop floor, and we did a *SMED*. Then I told them that this was what I would expect from them, and they could take it or leave it. It was time to lead, follow, or get out of the way."

"Did it work?" asked Claire, intrigued. She had a way of focusing her total attention on people, just as she did with horses—although humans interested her far more rarely. Ward always found that quality hard to resist. It gave her a sort of shine, an aura.

He hesitated. "Nothing is ever simple, but, yes, in the end it worked. Then we acquired several more businesses, one a year on average, and they all got the same treatment."

"Managers must be teachers?"

"Let me tell you," chuckled Jenkinson. "That was something of a puzzler. I'm not the best people person, and I knew it. So I was stuck. I had no certain way to do this. In the end, I ended up making my own standardized work about teaching *kaizen*.

"It's beautiful here," he suddenly said, looking out of the window, probably distracted by the slanting sunlight bringing out a golden sheen on the distant trees.

"In the summer, we keep the colts in the pasture across here. The field on the other side of the brook is cultivated, so it gets real pretty come harvest time," Claire said.

"Will you tell us how you did it?" asked Ward, on the edge of his seat.

"My standardized work for teaching people? Not sure it would help you."

"Can't hurt, can it?" argued Ward.

"I call it *managing by problem-solving*, even though it does sound pompous," Jenkinson shared, seeming almost sheepish. "There are seven steps:

1. *Go and see.*
2. Visualize problems.
3. Measure local performance.
4. Standardize current practice and compare to best practice.
5. Teach basic analysis methods.
6. Experiment and reflect.
7. Draw the right conclusions for the entire system of operation.

"The first point, I guess you're familiar with by now: How much time do you spend on the shop floor these days?"

"A lot more than I used to. Not as much as Mark maybe, but at least half my day," replied Ward. "It might not show, but we've got so many shop floor projects going these days. And if I'm not there, nothing happens. I believe I'm actually getting in trouble with Beckmeyer, because I'm not phoning in at most teleconferences these days. Stigler stands in for me."

"Never mind that—and don't think I don't see the change in your plant. But I need results."

To be fair, Ward had been spending a lot more time on the floor. The change had happened gradually, not so much the result of a conscious decision, but more the effect of changing his work priorities. First, he'd finally resolved himself to the fact that he had to be present at red-bin reviews to keep them on track. From the reports he'd gotten when he was not there, the reviews would degenerate into constant bickering among his management team—to the point that the operators noticed, and commented about it, which couldn't be good. He'd also made a point of involving operators systematically in the discussion, which, for some reason, still made both Muller and Stigler uneasy. Probably the only point they agreed on these days.

In fact, he'd developed a personal interest in red bins. He was learning an awful lot from both Bayard and Muller. The manufacturing manager and maintenance manager seldom agreed on the cause of even the most banal problem, but it was an education. Only last week they'd been discussing the causes of splay on an engine cover part—silver streaking on the surface of the part. Muller argued that the barrel temperature was too high, which made the resin decompose and char or carbonize. The charred particles would then float to the surface during injection, creating the spray on the surface of the part. Bayard, on the other hand, believed the problem was that the mold gates were too small, which created restrictive friction to the flow of molten plastic, and so degradation of the material at that spot in the mold. Ward had no idea who was right and who was wrong, but it was fascinating. Now with Woods' technique for rigorous exploration of such problems, he saw a way of moving forward with clearer understanding and less wasteful arguments.

Certainly, these discussions had helped them with the *jidoka* part of lean. Woods' original definition of *jidoka* had been to 'stop whatever you're doing right now rather than producing a second bad part, and figure out what went wrong.' Ward had struggled endlessly with that, and taken Woods to task about it, until the old man took another tack. "Think of it as confirmation," he suggested. "Every step of the process has to be confirmed to be okay before moving forward, which is how we end up producing right first time. Every person—or indeed machine—who does any kind of work should be able to tell whether the outcome of the work is correct or not. When in doubt, the process stops, and someone comes to look in detail what is going on. That doesn't mean the process stays stopped until a definitive solution is found. A stop-gap countermeasure should only take a few minutes. It means that bad quality is not passed on to the next step. So work, confirm, and, if not, stop and reflect."

Working with Muller, Carela, and Bayard, they'd established a list of defects at each workstation that warranted immediate attention. And for infrequent defects less likely to happen, they set a clear number of consecutive bad parts that could be detected before a supervisor needed to intervene or stop the press. His only disappointment had been that neither Stigler nor Chadid had taken much part in these discussions. Indeed, he did not know how to resolve the growing rift in his own team, with the "technicians" on the one side—Muller, Carela, and, increasingly, Léa Mordant—and the "managers" on the other. He recognized the dangers of a divided leadership, but was completely baffled as to how to resolve the rift.

He'd also taken to heart Jenkinson's comment about washing his hands three times a day. Taking a page from Neville's book, Ward had stopped going straight to his e-mails in the morning. Instead, he visited the plant at a leisurely pace, copying Jenkinson's way of starting from shipping and moving back toward injection. He'd never admit it, but he felt proud of that. It took nerve. It did sound silly, but ignoring the morning batch of bad news from the U.S. or Neuhof was just as hard as giving up smoking. Woods' show about "what are you paid for" had rankled all the more, so that Ward felt he'd been far more engaged with the work, in a loose, unstructured way. He'd been walking through the plant every day. It had got to the point that he'd banned meetings in the mornings for all his management team, because he'd not been free to attend.

Still, in thinking through yesterday's plant visit, he'd come to realize the fundamental difference between "managing by walking about," which he had been doing up to now, and the kind of pointed lean management his CEO had in mind. Yes, he'd learned to spend more time on the shop floor. Yes, he'd tried to listen to what people had to say. This had indeed changed considerably both his management practice and his understanding of the plant. But it was still extremely vague. He did not know *what* questions to ask.

Woods' approach of using the visual management system to teach people to see problems and stepping in to support *kaizen* made a lot of sense. It turned "managing by walking about" from goodwill industrial tourism to a focused, action-oriented management technique. Ward had had many doubts about spending so much time on the shop floor, because most of the time he seemed to see the same things happening all over again without being quite sure of how to tackle them. He'd stuck with his visits mostly out of sheer determination, and much like the red-bin reviews at first, to show Jenkinson that he could stay the course with *go and see*, but he now realized that without the detailed practice of generating *kaizen*, his visits had been largely ineffective. The idea of teaching people to see problems and stepping in to help them resolve them appealed to him enormously, even though he felt largely technically inadequate to resolve them. Oh well, enough problems to keep life interesting, he reminded himself.

"The second point is *visualizing problems*," Jenkinson continued explaining. "This is unique to the lean approach and it's a tricky one, because there's actually technique to it. You must teach people how to visualize their problems simply. For instance, because we're chasing up all the cash we can, we've visualized unpaid customer invoices in accountancy, by simply piling paper against a wall. Red bins and shop stocks are only the start—any problem can be visualized without spending any money, but you've got to teach people clever ways of doing so. And I don't mean posting printouts from the computer on a board. It has to be physical, like a road signaling system. Something real—"

"You're doing it again!" scoffed Woods, interrupting him.

"Come on, gimme a break," replied Jenkinson. "Someone's got to."

"Won't do any good!"

"Bob keeps telling me I lecture too much," groused Jenkinson, sending a mock helpless look to Claire. "He believes in learning by doing and nothing else."

"Sounds like my father," she answered unhelpfully. "Keeps saying that horse riding can't be explained, it's got to be lived. He keeps making fun of me because I tend to lecture people about riding theory. He says there's nothing wrong with their brains—it's their legs that are the problem."

"Wise man," nodded Woods smugly.

"But I'd like to know!" protested Ward.

"Go ahead," sighed Woods theatrically. "But if I'm going to have to sit through this one more time, I think I'll ask you for some of that plum brandy," he said, turning to Claire with hands joined in mock supplication. She laughed, and went to fetch the bottle and the tiny liqueur glass set.

"Measuring local performance is a key step," continued Jenkinson, shaking his head at the offered drink. "Measuring the local gap between current performance and best performance, whether you gauge the best day, best hour, or the best seen elsewhere, invariably leads to a different, more detailed understanding of the problem; and from that a different way into solving it. Lean is a decentralized operation-control system, and measures are equally decentralized. That's why Toyota has developed different kinds of production-control systems over the years. For instance, every Toyota plant has a large electronic display continually displaying the shift's target, current situation, and what will be resolved at the end of the day by overtime. It's understood, a built-in assumption, that the plan *must* be achieved. You're familiar with the andon system: the same electronic board lights up with the station number when operators have a doubt and call management for help by pulling on a help button or cord. If the problem cannot be solved within a fixed time, the entire line will stop. The gap between current state and target accrues during this time. The point is Toyota conducts detailed analysis of the andon-cord pulls to understand the differences between shifts and stations, to analyze at a very detailed level where and who has the most problems. The idea is to measure the local performance gap between where there are more andon-cord pulls and where there are less, and try to understand the difference.

"From a management point of view, measuring the local performance gap demands another radical shift in practice, because managers must persuade teams to track their own performance and highlight their difficulties through the day. The benefits of this effort are enormous: operators will develop a true interest in developing their own understanding of their work and seek to achieve their team's objectives. But it's very tough, as management must be constantly interested and available. Production-analysis boards need to be checked at least once every hour by the supervisor and once a day by production management for operators to continue to see the sense in writing them up. My buddy Mike—also known as Amy's husband, by the way—is a psychologist, and he's quite convinced that self-measurement is the key to *kaizen*. Everyone knows that what gets measured gets done, so self-measurement is the key to self-improvement. But it's hard. The whole management system needs to support self-management at the *gemba*.

"The fourth point," Jenkinson continued steadily, "is to standardize current practice and compare with best known practice."

"The first thing Toyota supplier-integration folks ask when they start working with you," chuckled Woods, "is that you apply whatever method you've got consistently rather than to implement lean tools. That really throws everyone off. Where are the secret tools of TPS we need to solve our problems?"

"Tell them about the seats," suggested Phil.

"What seats? Ah, yes, the seating line. In my last years, I worked with an automotive group that produced seats. We visited a Toyota seat-supplier plant in Japan where the ratio of operators was one to our three. So we tried to copy the Japanese operation and organize seat assembly as a production line. Operators had traditionally built entire seats from scratch, each in their own way, which was felt to be the cause of the gap between actual seats-per-person conditions and what the Japanese seating plant was able to do. So our pointy-headed engineers came in, studied the seat-assembly operations, devised an assembly sequence, divided the operations by customer demand, and created a balanced line with operators organized in a line and each doing a part of the seat. Their calculations were correct. Unfortunately, the operators adamantly refused to change their working habits. They claimed that the line method would be not only dehumanizing, but would also create many quality problems as one person would lose the responsibility of doing one seat well.

"I asked my Toyota *sensei* to have a look, and he immediately berated us all for our wrong-headedness. The first thing to do, he suggested, was to work with each operator to standardize their own method—to make each operator build seats consistently. The second was to get the operators to compare their own standard methods with each other, and figure out the causes of the differences in quality and productivity from one person to the next. Many weeks later, he asked us to have the tough discussion with the operators about the benefits of working on a line—one with no interruptions due to missing materials because components could be brought regularly with a small train, and one where operators would help each other if they ran into trouble. In the end, the operators themselves contributed significantly to the design of the seating line, and the productivity gain was obtained with a quality increase through the development of the people."

"Once the gap in performance is measured and accepted," picked up Jenkinson, "people need to understand in detail what they currently do, and why this creates a performance shortfall. The third step in developing people is, therefore, not to immediately show them a better way, but first to make them understand their current method in detail, and compare it to best practice so that they themselves can figure out the problems with what they are currently doing. Again, the fundamental insight rests on the fact that people are natural problem-solvers: once we've understood the problem, our mind will flow seamlessly to adopting a solution. On the contrary, however, when a solution is forced onto us where we *do not see* a problem, chances are we will fight tooth and nail against it—no matter how clever the new approach really is."

"You say this," interrupted Woods, laughing, "but that has to be where we have the biggest fights."

Jenkinson made a face, shaking his head and mumbling, "I know, I know."

"These big bosses," continued Woods gleefully, "are so much smarter than any one else, they've always got the answer to every problem."

"Bob keeps reminding me not to think for my people," the CEO explained. "I've got to let them find the answer themselves. I can help with the problem definition, or outline broadbrush directions, but they have to find the specific solution themselves. It doesn't come easily to a trained engineer. In any case, the next point is—"

"Sweetheart," whispered Ward with an apologetic wince, "I think I'm hearing Charlie calling. I'd really like to hear the rest of this."

Claire had been listening intently and shot him an annoyed look. She cocked her head and got up. "Excuse me for a second, I'll see what's the matter and be right back—I really want to hear this as well," she said, shooting Ward an I'm-not-just-a-wife-and-mother glance.

"Please," said Jenkinson, exchanging an amused grin with Woods. Ward felt himself redden. He could take any embarrassment in the factory, but not a comment from his wife. Claire had always had this way of getting under his skin.

"Fifth, we have to train employees in basic analysis methods." Jenkinson picked up, when Claire had returned with a shy, sleepy little boy nestled in her arms, who looked at these strangers from the side of his face, hanging on to his pacifier like a talisman. "Obviously, visualizing problems is only half the issue: Problems need to be resolved, as well, and in a lean way—which means by using one's ideas rather than one's money. Chances are that if people knew how to solve all their problems beforehand, they would have done so already. Indeed, most operational problems are difficult to solve because it is often hard to distinguish cause and effect, and so breaking down the question into components parts for in-depth analysis is frequently complex. In the case of increasing press capacity without increasing investment, for instance, changeover time becomes a make-or-break issue. To help the plant reduce the time of its tool changeovers, the lean method is to separate internal (when the machine is stopped) from external (all the preparation that can be done while the machine is still operating) to reorganize tasks accordingly. If you don't know this, you're not likely to invent it by accident.

"Over the years, Toyota has developed a number of basic analysis methods to deal with specific subjects. Most of these techniques are based on the *PDCA* cycle, but are also specific to the type of problem at hand. More generally, Toyota has also developed an *A3 problem-solving* approach to tackle the most complex problems that do not fit any known form.

"The whole point of these lean analysis tools is not just to 'treat' problems with temporary fixes or workarounds, but to actually resolve them: to make sure the problem is fundamentally solved and does not appear again. To do so, the analysis techniques seek to identify root cause through a thorough examination of the question. The most basic analysis method, and also the hardest to master, is the *Five Whys* approach: asking why until the root cause appears. Although ostensibly simple, this technique requires depth of experience and a profound technical understanding of the situation. If not, the *Five Whys* can lead to endless questions all over the place, without getting any closer to the root cause."

"Don't be fooled by the simplicity of asking 'Why?' repeatedly," added Woods, sprawled back in his chair, sipping his brandy. "Asking 'Why?' is in itself a management act, not simply intellectual curiosity.

In truth, asking 'Why?' repeatedly, beyond the point of embarrassment where people actually don't know the answer, requires in itself a strong stand. In general, most of us prefer to sidestep any issue if we can and to go around the problem. All Toyota analysis methods are about tackling problems head on, and resolving them."

"I don't want to give the impression that lean management is overanalytical," pursued Jenkinson. "It is not. Going to see at the workplace; coming up with clever, simple systems for visualizing problems, such as simply drawing tape around containers; measuring local performance; and searching for root cause are all *actions*. Clearly, analysis is a more reflective state, but, again, Toyota experts rarely let that phase go on for too long. Soon enough, the supplier's engineers come up with working hypothesis, and the answer is invariably, 'Try it!'

"And so the sixth point is experiment and reflect. One of the companies we acquired had implemented a successful just-in-time pull system, where stocks were no longer held upstream of the process but in a supermarket downstream of the machines and cells. The downstream process helped itself in the supermarket lines of product through a *kanban* card system, and the cells would only produce what was being pulled out of the supermarket in the sequence in which it was consumed. All of this worked pretty well, but, unfortunately, the work-in-process stock remained quite high. I felt that problems were no longer being resolved. The plant's lean guys had been busy for several weeks trying to calculate and recalculate the exact size of the supply *kanban* loop to 'optimize' the system, but the problems weren't, in my opinion, being adequately surfaced and dealt with. So, in the end, I peremptorily announced they should halve the batch size and reduce the stock held in the supermarket by 50 percent, as well. They resisted and argued for weeks, but, in the end, I was their CEO, so they just did it. They encountered some problems, solved them, and continued to progress. They got there much faster than they would have by tinkering with their calculations."

"Is that what you did when you asked us to pull an operator right away from the cell?" mused Ward.

"Sure. You can run the cell for a shift with an operator less—if there is a real shortfall in parts, you can do some extra work. I tend to have the same approach to *single-piece flow* or component flat storage. Just do it! There are very few operational experiments which cannot be reversed quickly, and, hence, a bias to action is perfectly reasonable in routine processes. Analyzing is one thing, procrastinating another. However, direct action should not be seen as an end-all but as an experiment. We force *single-piece flow* to *learn* about the process. My real problem in the previous case was to keep the management interested in checking the results and to understand what they were doing to their process.

"The hard part of *PDCA* management, and more specifically getting people to do the *check* and *act*, is that it requires a radical transformation of managerial behavior," said Jenkinson. "First, problems have to be tackled one at a time, which involves agreeing with the persons or teams on which is the next problem to deal with, as opposed to producing pages and pages of action plans where everything needs to be done at once—and never is. Second, managers need to remain close to people as they conduct the experiments. They can no longer simply spread actions around or give assignments, and then move on to the next subject and disappear. Third, managers have to be maniacs about *check*. Every one wants to run off with the solution and tackle something new. Getting people to reflect on their experiments takes true management grit. And fourth, drawing the right conclusions from the experiment is often really tough. The final point is to improve management practices. But most policies have been set by the very managers who are now questioning them. In effect, it makes you publicly challenge your own policies, or your own assumptions. It takes a certain type of self-confidence to do that. Many managers are convinced that changing one's mind is a sign of weakness, and they are afraid to look stupid in the eyes of their people.

Nevertheless, the only way to become more competitive is to improve management practices and policies continuously. Improving doesn't mean random change. It means drawing the right conclusions from each experiment—which is a difficult skill to acquire, as it requires judgment. As I said before, managing means improving."

"I remember visiting a factory with the plant manager," recalled Woods, "and spotting one production cell where one shift was clearly doing better than the other two, both quality- and productivity-wise. I asked the team leader of the better performing shift how she explained the success of this cell. 'Easy,' she answered, 'I just make sure I work with the same people every day, and I stop them from moving operators around.' Interestingly, this is a core Toyota tenet about how to run operations: stabilize operators in teams so that they will know an area intimately. This is essentially a prerequisite to making people before making products."

"Yeah," nodded Ward. "Amy's explained that."

"She would," grinned Woods. "It's her latest big discovery. When I asked the plant manager why he didn't expand this to the rest of the plant in order to get the productivity and quality windfall, he got really upset and went on, you know, 'You don't understand. This plant has a lot of volume and mix variation. If I stabilize people in the cells, I lose all labor flexibility.' In essence, the plant manager is accepting a quality and productivity shortfall to avoid facing the fundamental problem of how to better schedule production while keeping people in stable teams and cells. He's got a successful experiment right in front of his very eyes, but refuses to draw the right conclusions."

"*Act or adjust,*" continued Jenkinson, "is a natural conclusion from the *check*, and where the true power of management by problem-solving lies. First, *adjust* is about challenging whether the observed results are up to what was expected, and, if not, understand why and what can be done to get to the objectives. Second, *act* means drawing the right conclusions from the experiment, and changing the way the system is organized to make sure the problem will stay solved, and to think about where else this learning could apply: *what did we learn, and what conclusions do we draw from this experiment?* Lean management is about learning and constantly creating working knowledge as a byproduct of any management act. This in turn, *builds the competence* of the people and *standardizes the processe*s on what works as employees start to share clear models of dos and don'ts in specific situations. Managing by problem-solving creates knowledge at the management level because managers are forced to develop a precise understanding of what their processes should do and not do in order to have the right conversations with their employees about which problems to solve—which creates a strong incentive for managers to get involved in the details of value-added work. Managing by problem-solving also creates knowledge at the employee level because solving specific value-added-level problems will increase the level of competence of frontline workers, as well as their mastery of their own processes.

"Finally," he concluded after a long pause, "this form of management also produces a different kind of organizational knowledge in strengthening the relationship between management and workers as they face problems together. This, in turn, builds up the intellectual capital of the firm and becomes the kind of competitive edge impossible to copy. That's true competitive advantage."

"Here's the deal," Jenkinson said, stirring on his seat in the silence following his long lecture. "Listen to me running off at the mouth like a know-it-all. If I was so good at this, we'd be lean already!" he sighed. "Andy, I'm happy with what you're doing on quality, and I hope to eventually see some results from your productivity actions. However, as we discussed several times, you're not improving flexibility fast enough. And this is affecting everyone. Right now, believe me, I need every cent of cash you've tied up in your inventories. So why don't you focus on reducing your batch sizes? As Bob pointed out in the shop today, the focus on mold changeover is ridiculously weak for an injection plant in a high-cost area. Good topic."

"But where do I start?"

"Tell you what," suggested Woods. "Let's see if Amy's willing to spend a week here working on your pull system. She's heard enough of Phil's managing by problem-solving theory to last a lifetime. She could take you through it on a practical case."

"Great idea," smiled Jenkinson, clapping his hands. "But who gets to tell Amy?"

"Hey, you're the CEO, fella."

"She's your daughter-in-law!"

"She could stay here," suggested Claire out of the blue, drawing an incredulous look from her husband. "We've finished the first guest bedroom in the building next door, across from the old stables. I'm sure she'd like it."

"She just might at that!" laughed Jenkinson. "I've been having a hard time convincing her to come to work in Europe more often. This sounds like the proper incentive. It's settled then!"

What about anyone asking me? thought Ward peevishly. Even his own wife was siding with the enemy.

"You're sure you won't have anything else?" asked Claire, putting down Charlie in his pen among a jumble of toys. Miraculously, fascinated by their two visitors the boy didn't protest loudly as he usually did. He stood tottering, holding the playpen's edge, staring at them solemnly and remaining timidly and blessedly quiet.

"No, thank you," answered Jenkinson. "Nice as this is, we've got to get to Frankfurt to catch a flight to Prague, and I'd rather drive by daylight."

"Claire," said Woods, "it's been a real pleasure. Riding that horse! That was really somethin'. I've been called a cowboy all my life," he joked, "and I have to come to France to see how it's done."

"Cowboy, my foot," laughed Jenkinson humorously. "You live in the Bay area. Claire, Andy, thank you, this has been a treat."

"And thank you for the lunch. Young man, cooking like this, you're wasted in industry. You'd make a fortune in the States," teased Woods.

"Well, I might still have a go at that, but I think my wife likes it here," Ward countered.

"Who could blame her, son. Who could blame her."

Ward used this moment of levity to switch gears. Taking a breath, he turned to Jenkinson and said, "May I ask you something? How is Nexplas really doing? It's hard to know from the front, so to speak."

Jenkinson hesitated visibly, but as Ward held his breath, the CEO replied calmly, "Difficult year. We'll know better in May after year-end. The first year was good enough to earn us some credibility, but that was mainly exceptional stuff, not operational results. This year is much harder. Customer demand is below expectations and Europe is, well, Europe, and is not delivering the results we've had in the U.S. And it accounts for a third of the business, which is why I'm here so often.

"In fact, my wife is complaining," he added as an aside to Claire, then continued. "With the price of oil like this, we're being hit by material price increases of all sorts. I'm trying to pass some of this to our customers, but they're pretty desperate as well, so price negotiations are really tough."

"I heard you're trying to move us down-market toward supplying parts for smaller vehicles."

Ward's comment actually made Jenkinson laugh quietly. "My, oh my, word does get around. That's not exactly true. Alnext's strategy was always to go for the expensive programs, the logic being expensive parts for expensive cars. As things went sour, they would bid below the competition, assuming that they would recover their costs through volume. Unfortunately, the volume has not been there in recent years, and because of operational difficulties we've paid for our quality in rework and quality inspections." Jenkinson paused for a moment, as if he were weighing carefully what he was about to say. He looked directly at Ward, and continued. "Ultimately, this is part of what brought them to sell the division. I have nothing against selling parts for top-range cars, but not at cut-rate prices. So I'm fighting to get prices readjusted up for this segment. At the same time I'm really uneasy about having all our eggs in the same market. So, yes, I'm battling with sales to get in the smaller-car programs. It's less profitable, but safer in the long run. Also it will challenge our engineers to come up with less costly processes."

"Thanks, it helps to know."

"April will tell," said the big man pensively. "April will tell. Which reminds me—you will have these parts transferred to Poland before year-end, yes?"

"I believe so."

"Been to Wroclaw? How did it go?"

"So-so. Plant looks a bit of a mess with the plant manager being replaced at such short notice."

"How's the new guy? Interim manager, can't remember his name."

"Brian Stonebridge? Seems all right," said Ward carefully. "Very energetic. Knows next to nothing about injection molding, though. He comes from a totally different industry."

"Don't know him," Jenkinson commented tersely. "Beckmeyer's choice. But we'll meet him shortly. We're going there after Mlada. What did you mean the plant looked a mess?"

"Well, um" hesitated Ward, uneasy about bad-mouthing another site.

"Out with it! Problems first, remember?" snapped Jenkinson, suddenly all business. "I don't hold it against anyone, and I'll make up my own mind. I am still interested in your opinion."

"OK. I was not impressed by their molding expertise. Particularly on the mold maintenance side."

"Specifically ...?"

"They outsource their mold maintenance to start with, which sounds weird. They get a lot of bubbles and voids, but don't systematically check the venting of the molds. Also, we discussed problems on the parts that they don't seem to link to mold temperatures. Same with sink marks, and they don't seem to think they can reduce the mold temperature on the side of sink and increase the temperature on the other side. I don't know. Maybe it gets lost in translation."

"Hah!" exclaimed Woods loudly, clapping his hands, surprising Ward. "I thought I'd got away with it," he laughed.

"Sorry?"

"We had a bet, Phil and I."

"Please—" said Jenkinson, actually looking sheepish.

"Last night at the restaurant," continued Woods gleefully, keen on mischief. "We disagreed about the plant. Phil, here, is a big softy, and thinks you're learning just because you listen to him. I was less convinced because I hadn't heard you get technical even once. You understand that's what it's all about in the end—the whole lean thing, right? We stop passing on our technical incompetence to customers, and we stop paying for our manufacturing incompetence. In a plant like yours, that means that it's all about molding in the end."

"And?" asked Ward, completely flustered.

"Son, you've just shown that there's maybe hope for you yet. You've actually learned something about molding, have you?"

Ward was about to protest that he'd already known, but realized with a shock he didn't. He'd let production get on with the technical issues up to very recently. Working closely with Muller these past months must have rubbed off on him.

"Son," repeated Woods, staring intently. "You've just stepped into a larger world. You've been running around doing all this lean stuff, and you've actually learned something about molding. Don't look like that—it's good. Just remember: One, *improve customer satisfaction by solving technical problems.* And two, *improve profitability by eliminating waste in the manufacturing process.* And three, *develop people by kaizen so that they know more.* That's my definition of lean! Truly! The challenge is to maintain the *kaizen* spirit." Unable to resist one last dig, of course, Woods added, as a parting shot, "Of course it would help if you had a working pull system—*pull* gives an architecture to *kaizen.*"

"Bastards!" was Ward's only thought as he watched the rented Audi turn out of the driveway.

"Hey, Mister," said Claire, putting her arms round him. "Bringing millionaires to my humble home? Your boss is not at all how I'd pictured him. Noticed how he helped me clear up? Would've been doing the dishes, too, if I hadn't stopped him. God, you're so tense!"

"Inviting Amy Woods to stay over? Don't you think I'll have enough of dealing with her at the plant."

"Don't be such a baby—she's sweet. I liked her. It's so strange to see how they all know each other so well, you know, your CEO, his mentor, the daughter-in-law who's also a consultant, and the wife of the CEO's best friend. It's hardly what I'd expect from the management of a large industrial group. Small town-ish, you know? What now?"

Ward sighed deeply, looking depressed again.

"I blew it, didn't I? I asked for it."

"Asked for what?" she asked, massaging his shoulders.

"That parting crack. Woods betting on me to fail. We were all doing fine, and then I brought it back to business. And bang, they hit me again."

"Hey, your CEO bet on you, didn't he?"

"Bastard."

"I don't know," she smiled. "I liked them. Phil is very impressive. So eager!"

"You don't know him. He'll sacrifice a battalion to save a division without second thoughts."

"You're being unfair. I'm sure he'd do it, but hardly without second thoughts. I think I understand them. Is it the rider? Is it the horse? Is it the course? In competition, this is all we think about, all the time. To you it's just a job. To them it's a competition. Different drives, no?"

"That's what he said, wasn't it? In competition you always try to beat your best time. We're just jogging along. Happy with average."

"There's a story we tell in France. It's about a little bird who falls from the nest. *'Piou Piou,'* he cries," she said, making the cutest face, her big blues opened in wide-eyed innocence. "Then comes a big fat cow and splat, she dumps on the little bird. So he's nice and warm, but still not happy. Doesn't like the smell. *'Piou, Piou,'* he calls. Here comes mister fox. The fox takes the little bird out of the cowpat, cleans him up delicately, and gobbles him up."

"So?" asked Ward, half irritated, half amused.

"There is a moral to this story: Those who put you in trouble are sometimes trying to help you. And those who get you out of it are sometimes trying to eat you."

Chapter Five

CLEAR DIRECTION

"That won't do," grumbled supervisor Denis Carela, taking Andrew Ward by surprise. It was early morning and Ward had walked to the shop floor rather than to his desk. Coming in from the rain, he'd breathed in the warm, familiar air with the faint smell of singed plastic. He'd found Carela standing by a press watching a changeover and muttering to himself. They'd been spending time together trying to figure out how to simplify the changes, but so far had had little success in significantly increasing the number of changes. Something always seemed to get in the way.

"Look, I know we've got no money to spend, only ideas," he added with his cynical, lop-sided grin. "But we've brought the molds to the press, so they don't have to cross the plant to get them. We've got preheating stations for them. It's still not good enough. Look at this!"

They were looking at one of the bigger presses where the fitter was struggling with a noodle mess of cooling hoses that needed to be fitted one by one on the mold. The guy was obviously having trouble, which took time and was dangerous as he clambered up and down the press.

"What do you suggest?"

"I'm sure we could create an attachment that locked all the hoses as a bundle. It can't be too hard, can it?"

"You're right," agreed Ward. "I'll talk to Olivier."

"Hah!" exclaimed the other man under his breath, looking away.

Ward wondered what that was about, but the last thing he wanted to do was encourage a guy like Carela to bitch about his boss. He stood awkwardly, as the setter continued to unravel the pipes and fit them one by one. It was painful to watch.

Carela shoved his hands in the pockets of his work jacket in true Carela style, like a grizzled James Dean. He wore the grey work coat open over black jeans, silver belt buckle, black t-shirt, collar turned up, every hair gelled in place. He made Ward smile. The man was a pain, but he had style.

"Is it me getting old?" the supervisor yawned, "or is it too early for work? Coffee?" he offered.

Ward nodded in surprise. This was the first time the other man had suggested anything remotely social. They walked back up the row of presses. Ward cursed inwardly at seeing the No. 7 still stopped, and an operator struggling to move a large container that had just arrived by forklift, while the forklift driver looked on placidly, from the high seat of his driving machine. Let us not confuse operators and drivers, shall we, thought Ward, annoyed once again at the plant's caste culture.

"Here," said Carela, passing a scalding plastic cup out of the machine. The rest area was empty at this time of the day, and looked distinctly shoddy. Ward felt he should do something about that—but with what funds?

They drank their drinks in silence. He was sure there was something on the supervisor's mind, but he was wary of losing the moment by pushing too hard, so he waited.

"This guy, Phil," Carela started slowly. "He's the big boss, right?"

"He *is* the CEO. Owns a bundle of shares. I'd say he's the boss."

"Doesn't look it, is all."

"No, he doesn't look it. But then again, things are hardly ever what they seem, are they?"

That made the man smile. "Guess not."

"What's on your mind, Denis?"

"Is he going to close the plant?"

"Not that I know of," answered Ward carefully, after a moment's hesitation the other man duly noted. "Why d'you ask?"

"You hear it a lot these days."

"Who says that?"

"You know," Carela waved his hand around vaguely. "People. Remember where we are, every plant around here has closed sooner or later. People talk."

"What do *you* think?"

"I don't know—that's why I'm asking. I've never seen a *patron* so involved in production. Remember the time before, he spent the entire morning on that cell. That created quite a stir. People weren't sure who he was. They talk. Léa has had to answer lots of questions. They are very anxious, very concerned. This makes the mood ugly."

"What really happened with that guy, what was his name? Thierry Fernandez?" asked Ward on the spur of the moment.

The other man looked away, shifting slightly. He pursed his lips, but didn't answer.

"It's not good, when people are this unsettled. They need to have a sense of what's going on, you know? If not, they think too much. About the wrong things."

Leadership lessons from Carela? Now, that was a first.

"Then, there is all this *kaisen* that you do," pronouncing it in a very French way, scorning the word. "Many changes. I think it's good, but, again, it's difficult for people. They ask questions. Why are we doing this? Why not the way it was before? It's all about productivity and productivity? Making more money for the bosses."

Hell, thought Ward dispiritedly. Crazy bosses on one side, and now mad workers on the others. Recipe for disaster.

"Phil seems a nice guy. I think he really cares about the plant," said Carela, looking Ward straight in the eye. "But with all this talk about shutting the plant, I don't know what to tell the people. Sooner or later we will have to say something, if not they will get stuck on the wrong idea and then ...," he shrugged again, looking away.

You and me mate, thought Ward wryly, considering his words carefully.

"Phil Jenkinson is not *nice*," he explained. "He's dead earnest. He's very serious about what he does, and he is the CEO. And owner. Because he is a serious businessman, he only gives work to plants that make money for him. End of story. He'd be crazy to do otherwise? If it was your money?"

Carela nodded slowly.

"On the other hand, because he *is* serious, he works hard so that all his plants make money for him. That's what we see—he works harder than any other boss we've seen, right?"

"Looks like it," the supervisor agreed cautiously.

"So where does that leave us?"

The other man took a last drag out of his coffee, thinking it through, and then crunched the plastic cup, chucking it in the waste bin with a theatrical swing of the arm.

"Out of the pan, in the fire," he nodded thoughtfully. "Site's not making money, so no new products, and no future. On the other hand, if we make progress quick enough, he won't close us right away."

"That's what I figure, anyhow," agreed Ward. "But I'm not in on the secrets of the gods."

Carela rubbed his chin vigorously, thinking hard, then unconsciously patted his hair in place.

"You're gonna have to talk to the people," he concluded, looking straight at Ward again. "Sooner or later."

Ward acquiesced uneasily. This was the first time ever he could remember the veteran supervisor giving him direct advice, and he could see how edgy the other man was about it. Jean-Pierre Deloin had mentioned that Carela had something of a story. As a young man, he had been committed to union work. He'd been working at a company that made home appliances and that had then been bought by a Korean group, which later relocated its production to China. The site's closure had unraveled in pain and violence, with the plant manager held hostage in his office, and, in the end, most of the laid-off people without any other work prospects, mostly because of the bad reputation the whole episode gave them. According to Deloin, Carela had come out of that losing battle bitter and cynical, determined never to involve himself too deeply in anything anymore. "This is just a job" was his approach to work, and Ward was surprised to hear him come forward, and not quite sure what to make of it. More than anything else, it was astounding that in nearly four years of working in the same plant they'd never had a heart-to-heart conversation.

"Another thing," added Carela with an unreadable expression. "I hate to be the one to tell you but … if this is all for real. If there is a chance for the plant, if we do what the *Americain* wants, yes?"

Ward nodded, wishing he could commit more clearly, but uncertain himself.

"You'd better ask yourself why Stigler's nickname is 'Dr. No.'"

Ward barely had time to think about the meaning of his chat with Carela, when Lowell Coleman called him on his office phone.

"Did you survive the CEO plant visit?"

"Got my hide tanned, as usual. But I'm still standing."

"Don't worry, all the plant managers feel the same way. Apart from that lickspittle Neville he's taken to, all of them bitch and moan about the visits. Not to worry, the guy doesn't have long to go in this industry!"

"How d'you mean?"

"He's seriously pissing off customers," Coleman explained to Ward, "which is a complete no-no in this business. The latest news is that Wayne had sold one of the OEMs on a dedicated plant in Romania. Big deal, an entire front module. And then this maniac Jenkinson flatly refuses to sign the deal. No exclusive agreement, he says. No dedicated plant to one customer."

"Wasn't there some sort of problem last time we built a plant for a customer?" Ward replied, "The Juarez plant?" He distinctly remembered hearing that the plant never made any money because the customer volumes had been much lower than initially expected, and that they subsequently rose much higher than plant capacity, which cost a fortune in exceptional costs; all of which was followed by an early dive in vehicle sales. Ward found it ironic that over three years the car had sold overall only 10 percent less than forecast, and yet the plant had lost money when it was under loaded, lost money when the demand was way over capacity, and lost money again during the tail of the market, when lower sales persisted for a good long while before being properly considered aftermarket.

"Sounds to me the guy is just sticking to his guns about flexible production, you know, fragment and mix?"

"That's not the point," replied Coleman testily. "Who cares about that lean crap? The point is that this is not an industry where you can say 'No' to customers. If the automakers blacklist you, you're dead. Let's hope that the Univeq guys realize soon enough what a loose cannon Jenkinson is, and teach him a lesson."

"Can they do that?" Ward asked, surprised.

"Why ever not? They're the majority shareholder. They decide who plays or who doesn't. They could even force him out of being CEO. He'd still be on the board unless he sold his shares, but he'd no longer screw us up the way he's doing now. This is no way to run a company!"

"Yeah, like we were doing so much better with Alnext," rejoined Ward sarcastically, wondering why he was getting into that conversation.

"Hey, whose side are you on, anyway?"

"I take it your project is not going well?" asked Ward, changing the subject.

"What makes you say that? No, actually, I'm working closely with purchasing and I think we're making progress. Which is why I'm calling. I need price and volume info from the plants. Could I get yours?"

"No problem, I'll tell Amadieu to send you whatever you ask."

"You're a star, Andy. Hang in there."

"Andrew?"

Franck Bayard, the engineering manager caught him at the front door as he returned from visiting a supplier, wanting to talk. The poor guy had never succeeded at his various attempts at quitting smoking, and now that the plant had become cigarette-free, he would regularly light up outside the building. While Franck was shivering in the gray March drizzle, he looked unusually excited. Bayard was unusually shy, thought Ward, and a dreadful bore. His geeky flattop and thick glasses didn't help matters. Ward knew him to be a family man, with four or five kids, but had fun imagining him with a wild secret life—no one ever saw him at any company events. Whatever it was, the secret was well kept.

"You'll catch your death, Franck."

"The cigarettes?" the man wondered, looking at the glowing tip of his smoke. "Yes, I know."

"The cold, man, you look blue."

Bayard stared flatly back at him, and Ward sighed inwardly—another attempt at levity that flopped miserably.

"Yes, Franck, what is it?"

"You were right," Bayard said seriously, squishing his cigarette in the ashtray. Having him come forward with as statement like that took Ward by surprise. The manufacturing engineer knew his stuff but assumed no one else did. He wasn't a bad sort as such, just extremely serious and self-absorbed.

"I was?"

"You were right," he repeated as if to convince himself.

"Um, what about?"

"Let me show you."

They went back inside and, to Ward's further surprise, Bayard led him straight to the shop floor. They walked straight through the press area (No. 7 stopped *again*!) to assembly. As they neared the first assembly cell where Jenkinson had done his show a few months ago, Ward was astonished to see Léa Mordant, the assembly supervisor, stopwatch in hand, frowning intensely at how the four operators assembled parts in the cell.

"Doesn't work," she said. "Was better before. Oh, hi, Andy."

"Let's get it back to the way it was before," agreed Bayard.

"Don't," cut in the operator. "It's actually easier to handle the part this way."

"D'you think so?"

"Positive. Let's see how it runs for a little while."

"Good work, guys," said Ward, not quite knowing what else to say.

"As I said, you were right."

"Terrific. About what?"

"You remember when we had this argument about averages and minimums?"

Ward didn't recall ever having had an argument with Bayard in his life, but nodded all the same.

"Well, I've changed my mind. Léa and I have reorganized this cell five times in a row now, and I've come to realize we never looked at handling the parts when we designed the process."

"Uh-huh."

"I thought we had to compensate for any difficulties in the work by building in a bit of extra time in the standard times as a precaution. But I now see the truth. It hides all the problems."

"That's what I said."

"I know, I know," the engineer's mouth twisted painfully, as if confessing a grievous sin. "I realize that now. We've been focusing on every handling movement, and it's incredible ... I had never looked at it like this before. There is so much to gain. Both in productivity and ergonomics. How could I have been so blind?"

"Good for you—you learned something."

Bayard threw him a dirty look, as if he'd been personally insulted by the very notion he had anything to learn. Ward sighed.

"How's it going, Léa?" he asked.

"Fine. This is really interesting. I think we need to create a central area for all components in logistics and deliver regularly to the line. That will make a big difference."

"I thought that was in the works. So what's holding things up?"

She gave him a sidelong look. She looked exhausted as ever, her pale face colored by deep black rings under her eyes. Mordant showed up every morning and was a hard, if uninspired, worker. Assembly was mostly composed of women, and somehow she managed to mediate the endless petty quarrels that he occasionally heard about. She shared with Carela a poor opinion of management, which seemed to be reinforced with every new event.

"Chandon and Stigler are still arguing about who should control the material handling."

Damn, thought Ward. Another issue he had not resolved. There were logistics material handlers to work in the warehouse and load the trucks, and production material handlers, who picked up containers filled with finished products on the line and brought components. He meant to put all material handlers under the logistics manager's responsibility, but both she and production had been resisting, so he'd not forced the issue yet. Couldn't they sort any thing among themselves, just once?

"I'll sort it out," he said wearily. "You're doing a splendid job here—keep it up."

She beamed at him, leaving him more perplexed than ever.

Jenkinson and Ward stood in the middle of the Wroclaw plant, watching the ballet of forklifts and people swirling through the presses. Once again Ward struggled with a puzzle from his boss.

"What do you see?" asked Jenkinson.

"What do I see? Honestly, I see many of the same things as in Vaudon. But I don't see a way to bring them under control."

"Let's take a step back. Forget what you know. What do you see?"

"The mess," Ward replied. "The piles of containers. The people walking about around the place. The forklifts running on empty most of the time. The stopped presses with nothing happening. I've got the same at home, but what is really frustrating is that hard as we try with *go and see* and *kaizen*, and we do make progress, we don't seem to be able to change this general impression."

"Has Amy come to Vaudon to work on the pull system yet?"

"She's coming over in a couple of weeks. We've been trying though."

Jenkinson fell silent a long time, just watching the plant. Ward wondered how he could look at operations so calmly when everything else seemed to be going south. They had come to the Polish plant to validate the product transfer. The molds had been in the Wroclaw plant in the allotted time, but now the plant could not produce a good part. Thankfully, Ward had built up his stock of parts, but that would only go so far. If they couldn't start churning out parts for real in the next couple of days, they'd end up stopping the customer, which would be disastrous.

Ward had been traveling back and forth to Poland far too often in the last few months, trying to meet Jenkinson's deadline for the product transfers. His first stay in Wroclaw had been something else altogether. At least there'd been a direct flight from Frankfurt. He'd landed in the middle of a snowstorm and, of course, the taxi booked for him had not showed up. When he had finally arrived to the plant, he found it a complete mess, until he realized with a jolt that the factory looked just like Vaudon before they'd started clarifying the flows and building cells.

Brian Stonebridge, the plant manager, was a genial forty-something Brit from Birmingham. He'd been working in flow industries most of his life, and had been seconded to a plant in Poland to start up a new project. The story fairly gushed out of him as they chewed on the stale pastries they had for lunch in his office. He'd met a *polska* girl, as he'd termed it, and decided not to go home, ever. Ward politely hadn't asked what "home" exactly meant, but the more the guy talked, the more he started worrying he might be witnessing a final meltdown. After pouring his heart out over sandwiches and coffee, Stonebridge had suddenly disappeared into a phone conference with Neuhof and left Ward in the hands of Tomasz Druks, the plant's production manager, a grizzled veteran who spoke hardly any English, and who seemed to be the real boss of the place. They'd gone and looked at the machines that had been designated to receive the molds, and although the presses were fairly new, Ward had been aghast at their state.

He'd spent the afternoon discussing the transfer plans as best he could, while Stonebridge rushed here and there in the plant, barking an equal measure of questions and commands, mostly in English with a smattering of what Ward assumed to be Polish. He'd wondered whether the man was not inventing a new pidgin right there and then. At five o'clock sharp, he stopped suddenly, like a mechanical toy out of spring, and dragged Ward out into town for drinks.

Ward had found himself in a café overlooking the old town's colorful main square, resolutely holding on to his beer as Stonebridge graduated to vodka martinis. When the girl joined them, he simultaneously thought that there was no accounting for female tastes and that maybe Stonebridge was the luckiest man on earth. She was quite pretty, a stunning redhead, tall, thin, and shapely, with emerald green eyes and milk-white skin. More than anything else, she seemed seriously taken with the man, which Ward found rather astonishing as he was a beer-barreled balding chap with black curly hair, a face to get lost in a crowd, and a loud, over-jolly voice. She spoke little English and they seemed to communicate on love alone.

Throughout the bizarre evening, Ward had politely declined meeting some of her friends, a midnight visit to the city's medieval network of underground passages—apparently, the historical curiosity of the town—and also had declined to disclose the salary Nexplas paid him to run a plant. He'd managed to return to his hotel room more or less in one piece, wondering whether the universe had always been this out of tilt and he too wrapped up in himself to notice.

What Stonebridge lacked in subtlety, he made up for in sheer presence. The next day in the plant, he seemed at one time everywhere at once, and then equally noticeably, completely absent, which was when the plant went back stoically to its daily business. Stonebridge had bent Ward's ear about all the exclusive Polish problems he had to deal with, such as 30 percent wage inflation and such low unemployment he couldn't recruit staff. The latter was great for the Poles, mind you, but made for a scarcity of competent technical resources. According to Stonebridge, the situation was further complicated by the fact that the previous plant manager had been dismissed by Beckmeyer upon discovering that he had an arrangement with the temporary labor agency and took a cut on each contract offered. They'd fired the man, but because of the full employment situation, had kept the agency, which, instead of keeping a low profile, was now agitating the workers for a wage increase. He expected a strike any day now.

Ward had returned home completely mystified. He did not know what to make of the man nor of the plant. He had established the necessary contacts for the transfer, but had a really bad feeling about this. And, yes, as he'd told Jenkinson, even he had been able to spot the thinness of their molding knowledge. As Claire's father often joked, he'd once met a cavalry officer that was such an idiot that even his fellow officers had noticed. The one inescapable conclusion from this first visit is that he would have to build a mountain of stock of the bloody parts to protect the customer from whatever disaster was likely to occur once the molds got to Poland. Not only was he losing a hefty chunk of business over this, but, on top of everything, he was going to take an inventory hit, which felt like adding insult to injury.

So far, his worse fears hadn't come true, but he'd been spending far too much time focusing on the transfer and away from his own plant. Jenkinson was driving him equally hard on setting up a working pull system in Vaudon as getting the transfer right. Ward had to admit that when the guy got stuck on something, he didn't waiver—he'd ride you until you got it done. On the pull system front, Ward had been talking with Mark Neville frequently in the past month, trying to figure out how to get it to work. The Bethany plant manager had been helpful, sending pictures and presentations, but the simple fact of building a leveling box had stumped the Vaudon team. It was always the smallest things that caused the biggest problems.

In any case, he'd moaned about the urgency of the Polish transfer with Neville, who had actually laughed. "Of course, they want it completed by year-end," he'd said. "Think about it: You get a real cost gain on transfers when you transfer from high cost to low cost. Say I send a part here to a place that can manufacture the same part for a 10th of the labor cost. Assuming they can build it, the selling price hasn't changed, so I pocket the difference. But customers aren't stupid. When it comes to renew the part contract in the low-cost country, they use the local wage rates as a basis for parts-cost calculation, and now you lose all the advantage. Plus add in all the exceptional cost you get with working in low-cost countries, expats, flow-in experts, and so forth. Phil's desperate for quick cost-savings, and we don't have that many parts left that haven't been transferred to low-cost regions. So that's what they're doing with your parts. Wayne Sanders is arguing for moving production to even lower-cost countries, now that Mexico, Poland, and the Czech Republic's wages are catching up. They're looking at Honduras and Costa Rica. Even Brazil is becoming expensive."

Ward didn't find any of this funny, but he could see the logic. He marveled how he had managed to survive as a plant manager for three years without figuring any of this stuff out.

"What you're seeing here is the real cost of making parts," said Jenkinson, jogging Ward back to the present to see the Polish plant's shop floor. Jenkinson took off his glasses and rubbed his eyes tiredly. He was definitely looking under the weather, and Ward wondered if the pressure was getting to him.

"The real out-of-pocket cost of operations. The system cost, in fact. Parts are usually priced on the basis of their unitary cost. On paper, it looks simple," Jenkinson reached for Ward's notebook and jotted down his points, saying each as he wrote:

- Cost of materials and components
- Cost of fabrication (i.e., milling, grinding, molding, etc.)
- Cost of mechanical assembly
- Cost of human labor in assembly
- Cost to correct defects, checking, and rework
- Cost of storing the part
- Cost of moving the part
- Company overhead attributed to the part (i.e., cost of design, management, etc.)
- Cost of disposing of obsolete units.

"And so on. What engineering does is try to minimize each of these items. But because optimizing several variables at a time in a connected system is very hard, these optimizing strategies have many side effects. I've talked before about the costs of so-called point optimization when it comes to making improvements—and how important it is to understand how changes and even improvements may generate savings in one area only to cause bigger problems elsewhere. Having clear purpose and shared indicators of success helps people see not just their own improvements, but how it ties into the bigger stream. For instance, engineers will entirely redraw a part every time in the attempt to reach the lowest material cost possible. In doing so, they generate a huge number of components for every product, which is incredibly complex to manage. Each new part requires new developments, creates stabilization issues at suppliers, delivery problems because of batch sizes, and so on. The overall cost of redesigning every part every time is staggering, and minimizing the material content hardly compensates. On the other hand, using standard parts as much as we can has huge system benefits, even though it makes the engineer's job harder. In my previous business this was widespread. We had to learn the hard way to use standard parts where we could, because we had already the benefit of the learning curve when we made them."

"Like making multiple cavities injection molds for large parts," muttered Ward. "If one part is bad, you have to throw away the three other ones, or get huge problems resorting them. And they're a bitch to change."

"Exactly. Or sourcing a part at the cheapest supplier, although you're moving the total product halfway through the continent and back."

"Changing suppliers purely on cost basis without looking at quality or capacity, and then being stopped by missing parts or defective ones," Ward replied, thinking out loud.

"Long batches to minimize the impact of production changes, which creates overproduction inventory ... We could go on all night. The point is that looking at this through a lean lens enables us to see the consequences of unit-price logic: the real cost that accrues to actually make and ship the products. To a large extent, lean is about discovering the *true* cost of making things: manufacturing stripped of all of this waste. Look at it, we can see it all: stop-and-go, overburden, seven wastes." Jenkinson reflected for a moment and added, "I believe Ohno himself defined the *Toyota Production System* as *making what you need, in the amount you need, by the time you need it—at a lower cost,* or something similar."

"So how come no matter how hard we work at *kaizen*, we can't seem to see an effect on the system cost, as you say?"

Jenkinson gave him one of his steady looks, and, again, Ward felt that he was being judged in a contest in which he still didn't know how to score points. This is not just about activity, he reminded himself, but about results. Doing the right activity to deliver the right results.

"In all fairness," Jenkinson said, "you've only started in earnest. I didn't find it easy, either."

Encouraged by Jenkinson's candor, Ward replied, "I'm fully aware the results of what we're doing are not showing up on the accounts, beyond the reduction of scrap. But I just don't understand why. It's not like we're not solving problems. We are, all over the place. But somehow it doesn't deliver. It's not just frustrating, but it's also difficult to keep people motivated."

"What your plant needs is *clear direction*," the CEO answered in his slow, let-me-explain-it-to-you voice. "You've learned to find waste in many activities, but now you've got to hold your team to a few clear subjects, and work at it until you get the results.

"If you're just solving problems without *clear direction*, you will suffer from the pillowcase syndrome: A site is an integrated system. When you squeeze at one end, it bulges at another, and you don't get the real gain. It's hard work to pull people out of processes with *kaizen* events. And yet somehow the heads remain on the books."

"Tell me about it," Ward countered. "We're trying to reconcile the people we've pulled out of cells with *kaizen* and the overall headcount, and I'm still not clear on what's going on. Look, I'm doing *go and see*, and I'm doing *kaizen*. I'm spending a lot of time in the factory trying to get people to fix the 'abnormal conditions' we identify. I still don't see how this is going to affect the plant's bottom line in the end."

"You're right—it won't," grinned Jenkinson, "but it's a start."

"What then?" asked Ward, readying himself for another lecture.

"*Clear direction*. Let's take this step-by-step. First, we agree that management happens on the shop floor, at the real place, with the real people, and the real things."

"Yes, I agree with this now. I'm trying to do it as well."

"Second, we've started to define management as problems to be solved, yes?"

"Absolutely. I walk around the shop and make people understand their problems and help them solve them."

"Now, in order to find out if we're right or wrong about what we're doing in the plant and to improve the bottom line in the process, we need to see the financial impact of our actions. At the moment, you feel you're doing a lot of work but none of this seems to be paying off. Do I understand the problem clearly?"

"Spot on," said Ward.

"So we agree that management is about framing the right problems on the shop floor for people in the processes to resolve them."

"That's the theory, yes, and I'm trying to do it. But the proof of the pudding is in the numbers, is that right?"

"Not all problems are equally important, Andy," explained Jenkinson. "We do define management as problems to solve, but not just *any* problem *anyhow*—that's just 'management by walking about,' which has never worked beyond window-dressing. Lean management is about setting *clear direction* on a few *typical problems* that have *typical solutions*. You've figured out that you need to solve problems, which is great. But not all problems have equal payoff, and as you've had occasion to find out, it's easy to get lost in everything that goes wrong every day."

"You can say that again," agreed Ward.

"The key now is to see that we're trying to solve a limited number of *typical problems*. For instance, in Vaudon, you're essentially working on solving quality problems with red bins and improving productivity through *kaizen* workshops. To these two problems, I've added creating a proper pull system in the plant, and the Polish transfer. Right?"

"Is that all I'm supposed to be doing?" Ward quipped. He felt his days were spent running like a headless chicken as every possible thing that could go wrong did go wrong, but he had to admit that when phrased starkly like that, those were the key points Jenkinson had been holding him to, day in, day out. "That's about it, I guess. I'd add spending time at customers and suppliers."

"Fine. Absolutely. My point is, those problems shape our mindset to a large extent. My friend Mike, Amy's husband, the psychologist, argues that our 'mental models' or worldview can be described in terms of the problems we find important, and the problems we decide we can live with. The trick is to clarify the important problems so we can lead people through them."

"Such as avoiding accidents, no quality complaints, and so on?"

"Yes, but in lean, we must be far more specific. Lean thinking is nothing more than clearly defining a few key, critical problems we need to solve. We never will 'fix' them all, but as we progress, we get better and better at it. So let's take a shot at articulating these core problems:

"One, *jidoka*: Don't let a bad part pass on to the next process. This is ostensibly a simple problem—but extremely complex to solve in practice. Machines have to be designed to recognize bad parts, just as people have to be trained to do so, and then the proper management procedures must be in place to sustain 'react at first defect' and so on.

Two, *just-in-time*: This breaks down into four basic problems:

- Mix and fragment production to get as close as can be to *takt time*, with any equipment. Toyota managers seem to have far more models of cars on a given line than any other automaker, because they're obsessed with *takt time* thinking.

- *Pull production* to avoid overproduction at every step in the supply chain.

- Manufacture parts in *single-piece flow*, one by one in the sequence of demand.

- Leveling production to avoid peaks and troughs, both on the line and at suppliers.

Now, these problems are pretty basic, but hard to solve. One never fully succeeds in leveling, but one gets better at it over time. The beauty of it is that if you can improve on these issues, you can stabilize the overall volume of your plants, while remaining responsive to the market in terms of mix. The savings in capital expenditure are staggering.

"Three, *improve your work practices and tools* without investment by involving people and getting them to improve their own working environment. Again, this is a pretty basic problem, which is hard as heck to solve. Hence *standardized work* and *kaizen*, and all the other techniques to do so.

"This is just for the production system, of course. At the company level, there are other big and relatively straightforward problems, such as designing products people will buy, keeping a full range of products, developing products today that will still be successful three years from now, keeping pace with the right kind of technology and innovation, and so on. The key is to be clear on how you define reality through *typical problems*, which have *typical solutions*. Archetypal problems, I should say, broad, characteristic problems that define our actions. These typical problems should reflect your business model, your opinions on how to make money in your market. The key phrase is to be able to say, 'If I resolve this typical problem better, I am getting closer to implementing my business model, and I will make money from this.' This is checkable, both in the financial results and on the shop floor."

"But how do we know that they are the right solutions?" Ward countered. "Or that we're solving the problems in the right ways?"

"Everything comes down to *clear direction*, and accepting that what gets measured gets done. What are the metrics? This is business, so you start with your budget, and then you draw a list of clear indicators that create a bridge between the financials and how good you are at solving these typical problems. So you establish a link between budget—indicators—and problem-solving.

"Indicators can vary locally, but, for plants, I tend to use more or less the same list all the time:

SALES
 – Customer parts per million (ppm)
 – Quality complaints
 – Missed-deliveries per million (mpm)
LABOR
 – Accident rate
 – Internal ppm
 – Parts per hour (pph)
 – Suggestions

MATERIALS
- Supplier ppm
- Supplier mpm

EQUIPMENT
- Overall equipment utilization
- Changeover time
- Number of changeovers

INVENTORIES
- Total percent of sales
- Days of raw materials
- Days of work-in-process inventory (WIP)
- Days of finished goods

"There. That's it," said Jenkinson, reviewing it for a moment while Ward's eyes moved up and down the list.

"People need to understand what they are trying to do every day. You can help them with this by helping them frame all their activities through the window of typical problems. What are the clear, basic goals they are working to achieve? This provides clean ways to mark progress, yet with no end in sight. This is what we call the '*North Star*' or 'True North.' The budget defines a target, but I also draw out a *North Star* with the rest of the team—defining the essential dimensions we need to improve and by how much. It doesn't define a destination as such, but a pace of progress."

"Fifty percent reduction in quality defects every year, 10 percent productivity, 20 percent stock reduction, that sort of thing?" asked Ward.

"Yes, and innovation, new programs acquisition, people development, and so on." Jenkinson paused for a moment, as if he were to comment on something he noticed on the shop floor, then continued. "Start with budget objectives, and then establish the operational improvements you need to achieve the budget numbers.

These improvements can be quantified through the indicators, which in turn correspond to *typical* problems.

"Targets will help you figure out if you are expending effort at the right place. For instance, you've been driving a lot of workstation *kaizen*, which I think is great, both for productivity and learning. But what I need from Vaudon right now is cash, and your inventories are not getting smaller. Are you increasing changeovers fast enough?"

"No, we're not," acknowledged Ward ruefully. "I can't seem to get moving on this."

"Because your team lacks *clear direction*. Without it, it's hard to focus efforts on what matters right now, even if it will change later on." Jenkinson looked at Ward and repeated, for emphasis, "People need *clear direction*. They need to know where you're taking them. You can be as open-minded as you like on the shop floor and change your mind often so long as they feel the overall direction is steady. Like tacking a sailboat, but keeping to the same general heading."

Ward continued to wrestle with this idea: "Reducing quality problems by half, inventory by 20 percent, and 10 percent productivity? Is that what you mean?"

"And with zero accidents. Yes. Let me put it this way. You showed that you know how to resolve quality problems. Are you doing enough of it? You've pulled a few of your references, proving that you know how to reduce inventory. When will you have the entire plant in pull? You've done productivity gains, we've seen that. Do you know how many heads you need out of the business to hold your objectives? The fundamental questions are always the same:

Are you doing what you need to learn, or just what you want to do?

Are you doing enough of what you've learned to get the results you need?"

"Look at the plant," said Jenkinson with a wide gesture toward the Wroclaw shop floor. "What you see now is the abundance of problems they have. It's all a big mess, and every mess hides a specific management problem, agreed?"

"Yes, I'm starting to see that now."

"The next step is to recognize what typical problems they need to solve in what order, and what kind of progress to expect on which indicator."

"I think I see where you're coming from. They could throw people at changing molds, for example. It would be relatively cheap, reducing changeover time by brute force, but they have so many mold upkeep problems that we'd need to focus on scrap."

"Yes. Something like that. Quality is always a good place to start, and, in this plant, I need a dramatic improvement of first-time quality."

Ward kept staring at the Polish plant, thinking it through. Stonebridge was rushing toward them in his usual state of perpetual motion. Ward saw Jenkinson notice the dark looks the man was getting from some operators. His own opinion of Stonebridge had not improved with practice.

"Did you hear he wanted to fire Tomasz?" Ward muttered.

Jenkinson didn't answer at first, but then said in a cold voice, "Yeah. I told him he'd go first."

By the time the two returned to their lodging that evening the weather had cleared up, and Jenkinson, looking exhausted, foreswore his e-mails for a stroll around the main square. In the brisk air they managed to catch the dying light on Wroclaw's colorful old houses, and a glimpse of ice melting in the Odra. Yet neither cared to brave too much of the chill, and they soon found themselves nursing drinks back at the hotel. One of the perks of traveling with the boss, thought Ward, was better accommodations. They were staying at a grand old place whose art deco splendor harkened back to better days long ago.

Yet the perks came bundled with drawbacks of course, one of them being occasional awkwardness. As Jenkinson sat at the bar with his laptop plonked on his knees and checking his e-mail on his Blackberry—falling back into his lack of social grace—Ward squirmed in his club chair, staring into space. He had left his computer in his room, and couldn't be bothered to go and get it. So he sat idly, trying to enjoy his single malt, thinking back to the thorny problem of getting these bloody molds to produce good parts. It was all the more vexing that, back at home, they'd not had any major problems. He'd been spending the day trying to apply Bob Woods' technique of listing potential factors with the Polish team, but, at that level, language was a problem. He had it narrowed down to three factors: injection pressure too high, incorrect heat profile, or improper clamp tonnage. These guys seemed to be telling him they were exact to the parameters, but he didn't know how to check. He'd sent the profile of the screw to Muller to see if he'd had any other—

"What the—!" Jenkinson exclaimed suddenly, so loudly he made Ward jump. The other guests stared their way. For several seconds Jenkinson sat absolutely still at his laptop, reading and rereading the document he'd just downloaded, his face a mask of shocked disbelief. Then he stood up abruptly and, clutching his blackberry, rushed to the middle of the lobby where he dialed someone intently.

Ward wondered what could have happened. He hoped no one had gotten hurt, and grew more concerned as Jenkinson spoke at length to several people. Ward thought about going back to his room, but in the end his curiosity had the better of him. He might never find out what had happened, but he would watch this little drama until the end. He felt more than a little foolish, pretending to be deep in thought watching the flames dance merrily in the fireplace while he spied on his boss from the corner of his eye.

"Ha ha!" said the big man finally returning to his seat with a satisfied clap of his hands. "Waiter!" he beckoned. "Another single malt, no ice, please."

"Good news?" asked Ward innocently.

"No," Jenkinson laughed happily. "Not at all. Bad news. Real bad news in fact!"

"Nothing personal, I hope?" asked Ward, thoroughly puzzled.

"Oh no. Nothing personal. Strictly business. Ha!"

Ward held his tongue with difficulty, desperately curious now, but not wanting to pry.

"The dirty dogs have shown their hand, finally" Jenkinson said, literally rubbing his hands in satisfaction. "D'you play chess?"

"Um, no, not really."

"Well, unless the other player is a real instinctive one, there's quite a long buildup of positions at first. And then you wait for the opening gambit. Until you've got that one, unrecoverable move, you don't know which way the play is going to go. But once the strategy is declared, then you can clear the board. Ha!"

"What happened?"

"Purchasing czar of one of the OEMs sent a letter to the lead partner at Univeq, asking for my head on the basis of my 'levity' in considering their demands, and insinuating we would be blacklisted in the industry if I persisted in my present course."

"O—kay. How is that good news?"

"Well," answered Jenkinson, draining his whiskey with a wicked grin. "To start with, the first thing Jim Mahoney did was to forward me the letter. Second, the author is a close personal friend of our pal Wayne Sanders, so finally the wolves are coming out of the woods."

"Sanders?"

"Yeah, Sanders. He's made a career of fawning on OEM purchasers, rolling over in every price negotiation, selling products that are impossible to build, and then blaming production for not delivering. He's developed such good buddies at our customers that when I asked him to put pressure on price, if only to pass on material inflation, he felt this would endanger his relationships. He's been doing everything he could to avoid facing the music without it actually showing, but he's finally been caught with a smoking gun. Ha!"

"Can't you fire him? You've sacked many others," Ward wondered, recalling that one of Jenkinson's first moves had been to take program management away from Sanders and to refocus it on engineering rather than sales.

"Hmm," Jenkinson took his second drink from the waiter. "*Dziekuje*. Difficult. He's got a good grip on the sales organization, and I'm not sure we could do without his contacts—yet. Also, he's the one who brought the division to Univeq. He plays golf with Mahoney. He's got a small stake in Nexplas as well."

"So he can do real damage, can't he?" floundered Ward, feeling way out of his depth.

"Possible. It's all a numbers game. If we hit our numbers next month, nothing much is likely to happen. The only thing liable to sway investment bankers in the end is the bottom line. Which brings us back to our discussion."

"How so?" blurted Ward like an idiot.

Jenkinson flashed another wolfish smile, which stopped Ward cold. He wondered how many people had underestimated him for his plodding style, Midwestern niceness, and overall nerdy behavior. He remembered Amy telling Claire how he'd started his first company on the basis of a patent he'd developed while still at university. The guy was outstandingly bright and, with hindsight, probably a very aggressive player, but he just didn't look it. Only very occasionally, when he'd warm to his subject, or just right now, could you peek a glance at the man inside, and realize he was so sharp he could probably cut himself.

"Let me put it this way. When the deal was put together for purchasing the division, I made certain assumptions. On the one hand, the equity guys value their investment at, say, five times the EBITDA, so to keep them happy, we need to keep growing the bottom line moderately. Considering they bought the division for peanuts, this is not necessarily the most urgent stuff. The other issue is paying back the banks, which requires cash. The main problem we're having is that the model assumed a sales-growth percentage that we're not delivering. Sales are barely holding their own at the moment because customer cars are selling sluggishly, and we're likely to go through a big slump before the new programs kick in."

"Is that why you're so aggressive in pricing?"

"Partly, yes. I need to get as much value as I can out of existing contracts. Also prices for materials have been rising steadily, and although I think we'll do better than expected on direct productivity, these gains still need to compensate for materials and components price increases. Now the Alnext old-timers don't see eye to eye with me on another area: They believe that their salvation rests in low-cost countries. I disagree. I don't believe in generalities. It all depends on the parts: Where is the customer? How technical is the part? What kind of demand pattern? You get the picture. By offshoring everything, we also lose innovation capabilities. On top of which, it's much easier to lean a factory in the U.S. or Europe than in China because, for the moment, manufacturing engineering is still based here and in the U.S. The main issue instead is the frustrating 'not my problem' culture, which is a pure management concern. It can be tackled. Anyhow, the two main challenges are new products and cash."

"Hence quality and inventories."

"Correct. Strangely, however, this is not self-evident in the industry, so I'm under fire for not doing enough on the cost strategy, such as not having moved Vaudon to Russia yet, and no one understands why I'm pushing so hard on engineering and manufacturing quality."

"I understand," nodded Ward. "You need quality gains to convince new customers and attract new programs, and productivity gains to offset the materials increase and pacify the equity guys ..., which leaves cash. Inventory reduction. Right?"

"Yup," Jenkinson laughed, still fired up by his political swash-buckling. "*Clear direction*. Vaudon is a thorn in my side because although the quality progress is encouraging, the productivity improvements are not offsetting the materials increase and it's not delivering the cash I need."

Ward's gut churned at hearing this cold appraisal of his plant, but hoped Jenkinson would stay in this unusually talkative mood.

"So we make you look as though you're not being tough enough on cost reduction."

"Exactly. I wouldn't be particularly worried if this wasn't such a political game. My best friend Mike keeps saying that the way people define reality has real effects, and you better believe it! It all depends on how Mahoney and the rest of the Univeq partners read the situation. They're in it for the money, nothing else."

"We've been pulling a lot of heads out of the processes," Ward noted, trying to lift his own spirits. "We have almost no temps left. I'm surprised about the material inflation being so high."

"It's what I'm being told stateside," Jenkinson shrugged. "And you've been losing volume."

Ward wondered how to interpret this as both men sipped their drinks, staring at the fire, lost in their respective thoughts.

"The real issue is capacity. At the end of the day, plants make money when they're loaded just right. Too much volume, and they crumble from all the associated costs. Not enough, and they don't cover their fixed costs. Certainly, we can do all we can to make our fixed costs more manageable. Many so-called 'fixed' costs are not that fixed, really. But still, there's only so much you can do. So you've got to load the plants. One way, of course, is to make them more flexible, which is why I'm getting so aggravated by the slow progress on batch-size reduction, and why it's so completely stupid to build plants dedicated to one single vehicle or customer. But the other issue is to pick market segments where volumes are steadier.

"The problem with going after SUV and pick-up parts is that although we get a good unit price for each part because each car is very profitable, the sales volume itself is very unstable and varies considerably according to context. For example, what if energy prices spike and the market tanks? This makes loading the plants tricky. Part of my problem is moving the group to supplying a full range of vehicles, not just the large end."

"I think I understand," Ward said. "If we supply a larger range of vehicles with flexible plants, we can bank on the law of large numbers, and keep the plants closer to capacity, is that it?"

"Law of large numbers, yes, you're absolutely right." Jenkinson was positively animated. "Every car model is an experiment. The more experiments we run, the more our real average approaches the theoretical average. Clever analogy. As long as we can build any model in any plant, which requires flexibility.

"In any case, that's the challenge—we need to be in all vehicle segments with flexible plants. Basically, strategy starts with your global volume broken down into mix, reference level, and the resources budgeted to produce it without any problems."

"And work content?"

"Absolutely. Then we can see all the exceptional costs that accrue as we hit problems—so we can better understand both our real cost and our standard cost. Even Toyota can get burned estimating global volumes, but at the plant level they've figured it out. They factor in 10 minutes a day for line stops, but if they haven't finished the planned number of vehicles in the shift, they do overtime right away and deliver the plan: *takt time* rules. In that way, they can see their costs and overruns on a daily basis.

"A large part of my problem right now is convincing the sales organization that we'll make more money overall if we go after parts for models where individual margins are not as high, but where volumes are higher, and which would complete our range. Uphill battle. But I'm convinced it's our basic strategic challenge. As well as shifting toward the transplants in the U.S., whose prospects look better whichever way you slice it."

"I see," said Ward, although he didn't.

Jenkinson suddenly looked at him over his drink, and Ward felt uncomfortably aware of the cogs spinning in the man's mind, feeling more than ever like a pawn on a larger chess set he had not even realized existed. Surprised at how detailed the CEO's interest had been at every visit, and how quickly he'd always reviewed the plant's financials, Ward had made the careless assumption that Jenkinson, as an engineer, was micro-managing with no global vision. He had to stop underestimating him. Whether he was right or wrong, Jenkinson certainly had a clear notion of the big picture. The challenging and somewhat confusing part was that, unlike all the other senior managers he'd come across as a consultant, Jenkinson communicated the master plan through the details—and not as "The Master Plan."

"Listen, let's focus on Vaudon. I think you've been doing really well. But simply spending more time on the shop floor won't cut it. Look at Toyota: Their ultimate strength is the ability to link their strategic deployment to shop-floor visual control. In effect, if the visual system is in place, you can *go and see* and *check* every day, at any moment, whether your strategy is being implemented. *Clear direction.* What methods are you using to keep the brains on the floor thinking about and doing the right thing? What you're finding out is that going to the *gemba* doesn't cut it on its own. You also need to establish a *clear direction* and make sure efforts are concentrated on high-payoff problems."

"Right," sighed Ward, feeling his mind was not large enough to take all of this in at once. "Again, where do I start?"

"Here's what you can do with your team:

- First, look at this year's objectives, whether you've achieved them or not, and then apply this to an analysis of how next year's objectives are set, from the targets I give you. You need to agree among your managers whether this is reasonable or not. I'm willing to listen on some items, and not on others, but we will discuss it. Remember, it's an unequal discussion, but a discussion nonetheless. And I won't force you to commit to something you don't believe you can achieve.

- Look at the improvement activities you've conducted over this year, and check the impact. Ask yourselves what worked, what didn't work so well, what you haven't been able to do at all.

- Then decide on the key activities for the year, and draw out a plan that can be deployed by topic or department."

"The fundamental questions are: *Are we doing enough to reach our targets? If not, what are we doing wrong?*"

"We can do that," agreed Ward, though he was unsure how his team would react to yet more pressure.

"So far, this is just an exercise on paper—it really changes how people work only when your visual management is firmly installed on the shop floor. If you've done the exercise properly, you should be able to check every day whether you're progressing on your strategy or not."

"From the visual management?"

"Sure. If you've got a ppm objective, you can see at every shift whether you're getting there or not just by counting the bad parts in the red bins."

"Hence, clarifying the maximum acceptable number of bad parts should be on the red-bin review during the shift," he thought out loud, remembering Bob Woods' comment, which he had found totally unreasonable at the time.

"That's right. Your shop floor is your greatest teacher. You have to work with your management team to *check* every day whether your strategy is being implemented."

"Is that what you do when you visit the plants?"

"The plants, engineering centers, customers. Yep, *go and see*. I know where I want to go, and so I go and make sure that things are progressing. Most of the time, they're not because every one interprets facts differently and every group of people is set on pursuing its own implicit goals, so I need to constantly educate them to where I want to go.

"It's not a one-way street, though. Remember I am wrong half of the time, like everyone else. Every time I visit the *gemba*, the people doing the work teach me something—even if it's rarely what they try to explain to me. There's always this tension between doing what is needed to progress toward the *North Star* and not doing anything silly by failing to listen to people's real problems."

A silence fell as Jenkinson's thoughts seemed to drift back to his larger battles, while Ward simply sat and tried to process everything. The larger man gave a sudden movement, shared what seemed to be a smile of encouragement, and stood up.

"Listen to me lecturing about listening to people's problems, when I've done most of the talking! You'll have to excuse me. It's late, and I still have calls to make. I trust that you'll keep this to yourself. And I will be back in Vaudon, where we can resume this conversation."

Ward was relieved to have a tutor he trusted to prepare for his next test. Amy Woods had returned to Vaudon, and this time, at Claire's insistence, stayed in the guesthouse. It was strange to have her at Malancourt, and as they'd drive together to the plant every morning for a week, he was sure the rumor mill was running full speed in the plant. Claire and Amy got on well with each other, and they'd hardly discussed lean back at the farmhouse. In fact, Amy was fascinated by the horses and had decided to learn to ride. Ward knew how it felt to start late, and winced in advance. But nothing stood in the way of the short woman when she got her mind to it. In this, at least, she and Claire were alike. Still, Ward was uncomfortable mixing his social and professional lives. Like so many other instances, Jenkinson's style in this was radically different from what he'd known before. His relationship with Bob Woods and Amy was more of a true friendship than casual getting on well.

Amy didn't seem to mind blurred boundaries in any way. In the plant she was exactly the same person that she was outside of it. As they worked through the details of the pull system with Chandon, Muller, Carela, and Mordant, she came across very differently from

Jenkinson's forceful, relentless push to do things and Bob Woods' abrasive criticism. She was happy to discuss issues over and over, doing as well as talking, invariably cheerful. She created an upbeat atmosphere by willfully ignoring work tensions. In the end, Chandon had become Amy's French mouthpiece, and the two women had formed a strong bond.

"What is hard to get one's head around," she explained as they reviewed all the parts of the system they'd implemented together, "is that the pull system is the backbone for *kaizen*. That's what gives small-step improvement the *clear direction* you need in a plant like this."

"I'm confused now," admitted Ward. "I thought the pull system was just a tool, and that *clear direction* came from management's attitude."

"Don't you see how they're the same? The Toyota tools are the practical reflection of management attitudes. And, conversely, they develop management practices from the continued use of the tools.

"But I can see where you're coming from," she acknowledged. "Most managers establish a simple divide between tools and principles. It's neat and easy. Staff specialists know all the details of the tools. Line managers tell them what to do, and never bother to learn how the tools actually work in detail—if at all. Consequently, most companies are disappointed with the results of their lean programs. Those who succeed in handling the tool and the management aspects simultaneously succeed spectacularly. You need both the tool, the *what*, and the method, the *how*. Not a big surprise, really.

"Let's look at this in practice. We agree that the top-down part of *kaizen* has two elements."

"Visualizing problems and stepping in, I got that."

"Actually three: *clear direction* as well—how should we move the problems forward towards resolution."

"All right—still fuzzy, as far as I'm concerned."

"Let's *go and see* and walk through the process then."

They stared at the warehouse, looking at the truck preparation areas Chandon had clarified under Amy's direction. There was a clear board identifying where each of the day's truckloads were being prepared in advance of the actual truck getting there.

At each truck preparation area, they'd created a small board displaying a list of parts that were supposed to be in the truck. Logistics operators would tick the boxes as they brought the containers to the area, which showed what was actually in the truck and revealed how fully the truck was packed.

Truck destination	Departure time	Preparation zone	Start of preparation time	End of preparation time	Status	Comments

"So what do we see?"

"We have immediate problems," Ward said, pointing to the status column showing that trucks were late, "issues that should be tackled immediately."

"And what about the larger issue?"

He looked at the area, trying to see it with new eyes.

"Overflow. We're pulling containers from assembly as regularly as possible, but we're not leveling customer demand, so we get accumulation of parts in this area."

"Which is a failure of what aspect of lean management?"

Ward looked from the stacks of containers back to the consultant, shrugging. He still had no handle on what customers did.

"Customers first," she said with a wide smile. "And *go and see.*"

"How d'you mean?"

"The imbalance between your *takt time* internal pickups and actual customer demand can be traced back to the fact that you don't work closely enough with your customers. You don't understand why they order erratically and haven't found the right person to talk to at the customer."

"Oh, for crying out loud!"

"Now, now," she said. "I didn't say you had to do it immediately. But let's be clear: defining the right problem gives us direction in terms of making sense of what we see here. Agreed?"

Ward sighed, crossing his arms in annoyance, and forced himself to nod.

"Let's move one step back then."

At the leveling box, Ward discovered that several cards had been grouped in the slots. This indicated that instead of picking up containers every half-hour, as they had planned, logistics operators had taken upon themselves to group the pickups so they only needed to do the trip once every hour instead of every 30 minutes.

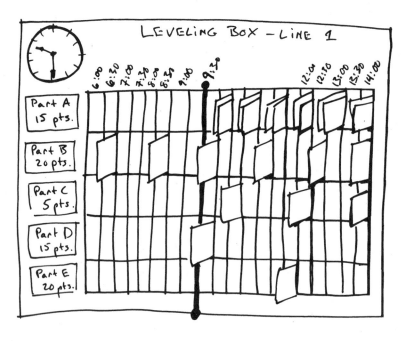

"And?" Amy just stood there and grinned at Ward. He felt a bit less annoyed than having Jenkinson or Bob Woods beat him down, but nonetheless he was frustrated. Amy continued, "What's the impact of this?"

"Production loses the rhythm of pickups. Which means that they don't physically see the pitch anymore."

"And?"

"It ties back to *kaizen*, right? How can they see they're not in a normal situation if the customer, which is logistics in this case, doesn't come and pick up the finished parts at the required time?"

"Absolutely. What else can we see here?"

"Some cards have not been picked up."

"Can we see why?"

"No ... We'd have to ask. So yes, this is a failure of visual management. We should be able to see right away what's going on."

"Uh-huh. Keep in mind's Phil's *managing by problem-solving*:

- One, *go and see*. What are we doing?

- Two, visualize the problem. We can see that cards have not been picked up.

- Three, measure local performance—"

"Yeah. We should have some kind of local tracking of how often we can't pick up cards, and a Pareto of causes and so on. Customer service for the leveling box, so to speak. On-time delivery of production to shipping. I can see that."

"Correct. Then four, standardize current practice. How does management respond when a card can't be picked up?"

"What do you mean?"

"The final aim of *kaizen* is to improve management practice. Do you get a phone call? Does Carole? Who knows about this, and what are we doing about it?"

"Right," agreed Ward rubbing his face. More work.

"Then we have to teach people a way to analyze this problem."

"But the problem is not here. It's likely to be in production, at the shop stock."

"Good thinking, let's *go and see.*"

Sure enough, the shop stock for the parts was empty. This particular part came straight from injection. They could see that the waiting queue on the launcher was full.

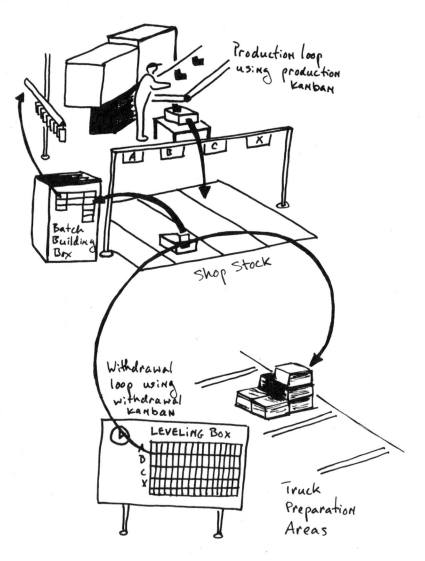

The press was indeed producing. Ward cursed as he realized the problem was that the parts being packed were not the parts waiting in the *kanban* launcher. He could see that the container being filled had no *kanban* card attached to it.

"Changeover hasn't happened on time," he said, looking carefully at the work area, "so production keeps filling in a container we don't need right now. It's overproducing."

"And not respecting the system: no box moves without a *kanban* card. So?"

"*Kaizen* again. Production management is not stepping in on this problem."

"And direction?"

"We haven't solved the fundamental problems of getting the changeovers to happen on schedule and on time. Bugger."

"And so?"

Ward could feel the familiar frustration rising once more. It was all there in front of him—but he couldn't just see it. If he couldn't make the connection between this specific shop-floor problem and the broader strategic challenge, how could he expect his operators to do this? He knew he was staring straight into both the gap between the cash he needed to generate to keep the plant alive and the current sad state of inventory. Finally he spoke, "We'll never reduce that blasted inventory—which means that we'll never deliver the cash Phil needs for the year-end. Yes, yes, I know. I just haven't been pushing hard enough. Hell."

Without losing her composure (was she ever anything but chipper?), Amy said, "Let's go through the steps again:

- One, *go and see*. Good. Here we are.

- Two, visualize the problem. The launcher does this for us.

- Three, measure local performance. We need to track changeover time and changeover duration at every press.

- Four, clarify existing standard practice. What is the setter organization?

- Five, teach basic analysis method. In this case it means the *SMED* methodology.

- Six, experiment and reflect.

- Seven, draw the right conclusions."

"We're doing plenty of experimenting," said Ward ruefully. "But not much reflection. That's the problem. So I need to keep working on this, keep thinking about this. And then I need to work with the folks on the line in producing smart responses. Okay, let's look at the batch building box as well.

"These batches are far too big compared to what we'd need to hit Phil's objectives. Jeez. I really need to get Stigler to crack this one. If it's *clear direction* he needs, that's exactly what he's going to get!"

"Hey, before you go, you must help me out about this *clear direction* Phil goes on about," Ward pleaded. "What's this about a *North Star?*"

"I wouldn't worry too much about it at this stage," chuckled Amy. "It says as much about Phil's problems as yours."

"How's that?" wondered Ward, taken aback.

"Well, you know, he's swamped with one crisis after the other, and on top of everything Bob keeps giving him a hard time about the need for *clear direction*—both for his sake and for everyone else's. Bob's take on it is that it's hard to keep people working on both large, challenging situations and everyday challenges on the smallest things, if they don't have a *clear direction.*"

"He gets my vote. That's exactly what I'm going through. On the one hand, this whole transformation Phil expects is daunting. On the other hand, they keep beating us up about such narrow details."

"*Clear direction* is all about maintaining one's bearing even when everything blows up all over the place. It's about following a guiding star regardless of currents and reefs and shipwrecks. That's why he calls it the *North Star.*"

"In our case?"

"Let's see. What was Phil's first task for you?"

"Fix quality," Ward answered immediately.

"Yup. And how?"

"Red bins."

"Sure, but more generally?"

Ward thought about it awhile, recalling his earlier conversations with the CEO. It seemed such a long time ago, although it couldn't have been more than one year. "Production must solve its own problems?"

"That sure sounds like Phil. So have you progressed on that?"

"Ah," hesitated Ward. "I ... think so. Certainly we understand better what our problems are. But—"

"You got it. Everywhere we look, we see that the quick reaction is not so quick, and we see that the root cause issues are not tackled either."

"That's harsh," Ward winced. "But I'd have to agree that's what we saw with the pull line."

"The point is that you are working on it, but how do you know if you're making headway? To do so, Phil defines a *North Star*. In a way, he's set the Star's main branches for you. Quality, certainly. What else?"

"Productivity at the cell level. Inventory reduction through a pull system. I think I see."

"What about your own challenges—would you have more?"

"Yeah, he's pushed me hard on customer relationships as well. And I've taken on board working with suppliers, although he's never asked for it. The Polish transfer, for sure."

"Any more?"

"Let me think," mulled Ward. "I'd have to add getting new products in the plant and developing individual problem-solving."

"Fine, this can be refined, but here's your first *North Star*," agreed Amy. She walked to the meeting room's whiteboard and began drawing it out:

- Improving quality through red-bin analysis.
- Improving workstation productivity through *kaizen* workshops.

- Reducing inventory through pull system.

- Developing customer relationships by visiting them at every complaint.

- Developing supplier relationships by visiting them to discuss problems.

- Getting new product in the plant—do you know how?

- Developing individual problem-solving by ...?"

"*Kaizen* workshops, I guess. Or quick reaction. No, wait, Bob's root-cause analysis."

"I'd argue for all three," said Amy. "Let's be broad and call it by 'managing by problem-solving.' How about safety?"

"Um. Of course. Safety—absolutely," Ward agreed, embarrassed that it had slipped his mind.

Improving quality through red bins.

Developing individuals problem-solving by one-by-one PDCA.

Improving workstation productivity through Kaizen workshops.

Getting new product in the plant — do you know how?

Reducing inventory through pull system and batch size reduction.

Developing supplier relationships by visiting them to discuss problems.

Safety first by daily checking safety conditions and immediate analysis of accidents.

Developing customer relationships by visiting them at every complaint.

"So, there you go, or close to that. You've got a *North Star*. It's got more branches than I'd like to start with, but at least you're clear on what you've got to do, regardless of all the firefighting."

"Is that it?" he wondered doubtfully.

"For starters," Amy laughed. "Then you can start quantifying each branch of the star. What is your objective for ppm reduction over this year? How much pph do you expect out of the *kaizen* workshops? How many *kaizen* workshops do you intend to run to get it? And so on."

"So that it gives me targets on Phil's indicator list?"

"Precisely."

"Okay. Just like that?"

"Not quite. Once you're clear on what you want to achieve, you've got to discuss it with your team until every one buys into it. Not necessarily that they will achieve it, but that it's achievable. The idea is: if we did everything right, could we get there?"

"I can always try."

"Who tries does," she winked. "The real benefit you'll get, though, is being able to measure whether you're progressing steadily on your goals regardless of all the crap that this industry is going to throw your way. Certainly, we all get off course. But if the *North Star* is clear, we can refer back to it and realize we're slipping. Are we doing what we'd planned? Is this enough to get the results? The beauty of it is that if you keep focusing your people on clear things, sooner or later, you'll gain their trust and everything will be easier. You won't have to fight them every inch of the way. This is definitely what happened with Phil's previous acquisitions. Once they were convinced he knew what he was doing because he kept at it through thin and thick, many of the debates simply melted away. Makes a huge difference."

"Amen to that," Ward agreed, unsure of whether he'd ever get that kind of clarity, or earn that kind of respect from his own people. You did ask, he chided himself. You should know better than expecting answers you like by now, he thought as he accompanied Amy down the stairs and to the taxi that would take her back to Frankfurt. After renting a car once, she'd decided once and for all that she would not drive on the German highway, not for love or money.

Finally Ward had something to feel good about. The *clear direction* exercise on the indicators with the management team had gone rather well, he thought, reflecting on the progress they had made on each of the topics on the whiteboard. Bayard had tackled the productivity issue, and was driving Sebatien Martin, the continuous-improvement officer, hard. Martin was running almost one workshop every two weeks. People were even starting to complain that they couldn't do their proper job anymore because they kept being pulled into these *kaizen* workshops, but Bayard didn't hear, and Ward supported him fully. Make them come, he agreed.

The other good news was that Muller had been working with Carela, and, as a result, press uptime had increased considerably. They had decided to take the red-bin approach to maintenance. They simplified the planned maintenance scheme to the large overhauls, and were now planning on a two-week horizon on the basis of a daily tour of the presses they did together, visually checking the machines and reading the production film. The impact on press availability had been noticeable, and because they had been able to cancel several overtime weekend shifts, bottom-line results were beginning to show an improvement. Good, thought Ward. Very good.

All that Ward needed to do now was bridge the gap between the shop-floor progress and the continued resistance he encountered with the very managers who should be supporting his efforts. He couldn't quite challenge them with this bold a statement. So as they gathered together, he started with clear, simple facts. Quality was still on track although they had experienced a bad February in terms of customer complaints. Immediately Ward found himself caught arguing with individuals over the wrong issues—blame, responsibility, you name it.

Jenkinson might be the most impolitic guy he met, but somehow his focus on facts seemed to eventually sway folks over.

"Two-thirds of them are mislabeling problems," Malika Chadid, the quality manager, said defensively.

"Fine. Are we clear on the problem? What's going on with labeling?"

"It's a production issue," she'd shrugged.

"It's a software problem," riposted Stigler. "If logistics can't edit the right labels, we can't put them on the right boxes."

Chandon's blue eyes had flashed angrily, but she hadn't said anything. She was forced to explain why inventory was so high. When he had the chance in Poland, Ward had asked the CEO whether he wanted him to perform the usual year-end raindance of reducing stock artificially by closing all the taps, and then reordering after year-end.

"How's that going to help you with your *North Star*?" Jenkinson had replied. "Get your inventory down, year-end or not—but do it sensibly."

"Are we doing enough *SMED*?" Ward asked.

"*SMED* is not the problem," answered the logistics manager. "Every workshop we've done is successful. As we agreed, I'm calculating production batches of 10 times the changeover time."

That was Bob Woods' advice: invest 10 percent of your press in changeovers. It worked out as a rough measure that you could simply multiply the changeover time by 10, and use this as a reference for batch size assuming there were no breakdown problems.

"But production is not following the program."

"I keep telling you we don't have enough setters!" exploded Stigler. "How can we increase the number of changeovers without more setters? Tell me!" He'd been very quiet throughout the meeting, and Ward wondered why he'd become more and more withdrawn.

"It's always production this, production that. We simply don't have the resources."

"Hear, hear," said Muller with heavy sarcasm, clapping his hands insolently. "Have you seen what your setters do all day? While we're hustling to fix things, they're having it easy."

"They keep having to clean up the mess your guys leave behind," rejoined Stigler angrily.

"Enough, gents," interjected Ward, trying to sound as calm as possible. "Let's understand the problem."

"Understand the problem, understand the problem," mimicked Stigler. "Parroting Jenkinson now, are you?"

"Now, now," said Deloin, looking up from whatever he was doing.

"You can play this game as much as you want, Andy. But you can't run production without investment. If it could be done, we'd know it by now," argued Stigler.

"You're not explaining what the problem is with the setters. Do we know how many changeovers we need per day with Carole's batch-size calculations?"

"About three times as much," answered Chandon tightly.

"That doesn't seem unreasonable. Olivier?" Ward asked. "Can we come up with a plan?"

"Come up with a plan yourself since you know it all now!"

"You're out of line, man!" snapped Ward.

"Am I? Why don't you fire me then," barked back the other man loudly, pushing his chair away in disgust. "Come on, do it! We'll see how good you are with production. Go on, take the setters away while you're at it! After the material handlers, go ahead. You're not fooling anyone, Andrew. You never knew squat about production, we all know that. And you were doing fine as long as you let us do the real work. But now, now," the man stammered, "with you bending over backward to lick Jenkinson's boots, you think you know it all. What a joke!"

"What the hell's got into you?" asked Ward quietly in the stunned silence that followed. They all stared at the production manager, who stood up and was now trembling with rage.

"What's got into me," he yelled, "is that I'm sick and tired of being the scapegoat for everything that goes wrong in this plant. You keep saying you want to help. Well help. Start by firing this bastard Carela for starters, he's been undermining me at every opportunity."

"Hey, you'll go before he does!" shouted Ward losing his temper himself. Even as he lost control he couldn't help but realize that he had sounded just like Jenkinson.

That shut Stigler up. He stood there white-faced, staring at Ward through his tinted glasses.

"We'll see about that, won't we?" he said in a harsh, low voice. "We'll see how long you can keep ordering us around as well, won't we?"

The man turned around abruptly and left the room, slamming the door violently behind him.

"Did that sound like a threat?" asked Ward aloud in disbelief.

"Or a warning," replied the HR manager unperturbedly. The old guy didn't seem flustered in the least. "Maybe he knows something you don't."

"Stéphane? Have you seen Olivier?" asked Ward later in the day.

Ward couldn't stop worrying about the scene. He hated conflict, and wasn't good with it. It gave him heartburn and nightmares. He finally decided to find the production manager and try to patch things up with him. Besides, he was anxious about that throwaway comment. He'd tried to think of all the possible things that could go badly wrong—and there were many—but could not come up with any particular one.

"He left, I think," answered the younger man, ill at ease. "I saw his car go," he said, gesturing vaguely toward his window overlooking the management parking lot. Ward had cancelled nominative parking and established first-come, first-served. But habits died hard. People still parked in their usual space, and the plant manager slot was always left vacant for him.

"We're all set for the year-end budget review, aren't we?" he asked, sitting on the corner of the desk. He thought the financial controller Stéphane Amadieu looked fidgety. Or was he becoming paranoid?

"All set. I think."

"And the situation is as we discussed? We're missing the budget, but not by much."

"Yes. Yes. Unless ..."

"Unless?" asked Ward, feeling his stomach tighten.

"Well," said Amadieu, passing a hand nervously through his dark, curly hair. "You know how the budget review is set up, right? We check sales against standard costs. Then we look at the variances line by line: purchase-price variance, material-usage variance, labor-efficiency variance, and so on. In the end we get the total cost of sales, the gross profit, and the margin."

"I know that, Stéphane," said Ward impatiently. "So?"

"So everything depends on the estimation of standard cost. We made the assumption that the previous budget had been built around completely unreasonable purchasing price reductions, agreed?"

"Yeah. I cleared it with Coleman. We don't control the price of materials, so we built the budget assuming central purchasing had succeeded in its cost-reduction actions. How are we to know whether they have or not?"

"That's the problem. We do know what we actually bill to suppliers. Coleman's office has been asking me for all that info in detail."

"And?" coaxed Ward, seriously alarmed now. He could feel the steel jaws of the trap closing.

"Olivier has asked me to recalculate standard cost using real-cost information from what we invoice. It appears that not only has purchasing not obtained the budgeted price reduction, but they've accepted suppliers' price increases. We're not passing nearly enough of that on to our own customers. So the net result is—"

"Our total cost is much higher than expected."

"Much, so our profit is—"

"Damn! Have you passed this on to anyone?"

"No, no" protested the controller. "Only Olivier."

"Bugger!" swore Ward. "Bugger, bugger bugger!"

"Hans? Andy Ward here. How are you, mate?"

"Andy! Good to hear from you. How are you doing? Long time no see." replied Hans Ackermann.

"Just a quick one. Do you know how the purchasing costs assumptions are treated in Neuhof's budget this year? Remember all the debates we had with Kent Reed at the time?"

"Ah ..." Ackermann hesitated, sending Ward's paranoia through the roof. "I would love to help, but I am not privileged to this information. I suggest you discuss this with Herr Beckmeyer."

"I'll do that," answered Ward, cursing silently. "You take care."

"I'm sorry, Andy," said Beckmeyer primly. "I understand you're upset, but there's nothing I can do."

Upset? Ward had spent the worst drive of his life getting to Neuhof. His mind wouldn't let go of the issue, and he had trouble concentrating on the road—nearly causing an accident and accounting for missing his exit. So much for "fun, fun, fun on the Autobahn." Upset? He was mad as hell. He stared blackly at his regional manager and the German division controller, who looked back, expressionless.

"What assumptions have you used for the Neuhof plant?"

"I don't know how that ..."

"Tell me!" yelled Ward furiously.

"You do not use this tone with me!" snapped back Beckmeyer, tight-lipped.

"Calm down, Andy. We've put in the original budget assumption," answered the controller calmly. "The purchasing-price variance is counted at European division level, and reflects the fact that purchasing hasn't obtained the hoped-for price reductions with the global price inflation. That is correct, I believe."

"But not for the Vaudon plant, right? You use a bogus, ridiculously low purchasing price for Neuhof, but the numbers you've just showed me for Vaudon take into account the real purchasing price, which is an order of magnitude higher! How correct is that?"

"What could we do?" Beckmeyer answered coolly. "You chose to communicate your figures directly to the U.S. without working through us. It's out of our hands. If you'd participated in any of the conference calls we had on the matter, we wouldn't be in this unfortunate situation now."

Was it a smirk Ward saw edging underneath the man's impassive countenance? "This makes Vaudon look like the worst plant of the group—no big deal, eh?" he seethed.

"You *are* losing money by any count, aren't you?" Beckmeyer asked arrogantly. The controller had the grace to look away, embarrassed.

"I'm screwed," he told his wife, gritting his teeth as the burning anger wouldn't let go of him, "Royally screwed."

"I don't understand. Money is money, *non*? All these games between top line and bottom line, what difference does it matter?" She had even cooked for them that night. Ward had returned from Frankfurt in such a state that he couldn't sit still for a full second without pacing around looking for something to kick. Preparing the evening meal as he usually did was not an option.

"If only it would be so simple! Sure, money is money, but most of what corporate does is spend time finding new and clever ways to allocate the blame. In this case, I'm well and truly skewered. This will probably cost me the job. I'm so sorry, sweetheart!"

"You've said that already in the past, and it hasn't happened yet. And even if you do lose this lousy job, we'd be fine, I'm sure."

"I could mop the stalls for you?"

"Too clumsy. And I couldn't pay you."

"In kind?" he smiled, trying to loosen his back muscles.

"Depends on how good a job you do," she answered coyly. "Here, have another glass."

"How come you always break out the champagne when I have bad news? Shouldn't it be the other way round?"

"Have you talked to Lowell about it?"

"That's the rub," he remarked, clinking her glass with his, and forcing himself to *taste* the bloody wine. "I'm not sure where he stands on this. Part of the problem is that his office got information directly out of the plant rather than out of central finance in Neuhof. Beckmeyer could be punishing me simply for not going through channels. But there could be a wider play going on."

"Don't get paranoid, darling."

"Hey, even paranoids have real enemies. I just don't know what to think. In Wroclaw, Jenkinson told me he was under pressure to cut costs more aggressively. It sounds odd, but I got the feeling he was being blamed for protecting Vaudon."

"Have you called him?"

"To say what? I'm not going to call my CEO to tell him I can't even calculate a budget properly."

Instead Ward called Neville for advice. They had been developing a good relationship, with frequent conversations about the headaches of Vaudon's budding pull system. Ward had come to find him increasingly helpful and level-headed. He didn't know the guy well enough to trust him fully, but, in this situation, his need for good advice outweighed the potential risks of opening up fully to Neville. He was very far from European operations in any case. Ward described the whole mess. At first Neville had chuckled, as he did, sounding like a minor earthquake. But then his tone changed, and he became irate.

"Coleman again! The guy is a real snake, a fixer. Did I tell you he got me to quit once? He came in with the Alnext lot when they acquired us. He's so good at worming his way into the good graces of top management. He knows everybody, and solves all the small problems quickly, making himself indispensable. But the man is a jerk, Andy. He keeps close tabs on everyone: He knows exactly which people owe him and which ones don't. And he's all about politics. He keeps moving his toadies up at every opportunity and stabbing everybody else in the back."

Ward had said nothing, making a face at the thought of having been a Coleman toady without ever knowing it. Sure enough, arranging him to become plant manager of Vaudon hadn't made much business sense. With hindsight, it was obvious. He'd been a consultant, for heaven's sake. But Coleman must have seen this as an opportunity to place one of his pawns in the job. Maybe Stigler had good reason to be so resentful, after all. Everyone had probably expected Ward to spend a few months, making a show of running the plant and then scuttling back to corporate as soon as possible. He probably would have done just that, in fact, if it weren't for Malancourt. Ward wondered whether he was moving out of Coleman's good graces.

"Should I bother Phil about this?" he finally asked.

Neville thought about it for a while, and then, unexpectedly, laughed. "I'd warn him, for sure. But I wouldn't expect him to be much help right now. He's got enough on his own plate."

What now?

"You wouldn't believe what the crazy guy's gone and done," chortled Neville. "He went to one of the Big Three, the one we've been having the big price dispute with, and held the gun to their head: you pay up, or we stop delivering."

"You're not serious!" exclaimed Ward.

"No kidding. I've stopped delivering a couple of parts already."

"You're not producing?"

"Of course I am—you think Jenkinson would stop leveling? No, I'm building inventory, all right. I'm just not shipping it," he laughed. "It's going to blow my inventory target for this month, that's for sure."

"And?"

"We won't know for a couple of days, while they use up all the inventory they've got in the system. Then we'll see. I've got their procurement guys shouting at me all day long, and our sales guys are screaming bloody murder, and there's all sorts of cutthroat maneuvering at headquarters, but you know what it's like. I'm just a production grunt, what do I know?"

"Bloody hell."

"Man's got guts, I'll give him that. So, yeah, I'd give him a quick shout, but I wouldn't expect much. My feeling is that you've just got to tough it out. I doubt Phil's the kind to get impressed with numbers game-playing, as you're describing."

"If he keeps his job!"

"There's that, yes," chortled Neville in a deep rumble. "Sure knows how to stir things up. Makes it more interesting, I say."

"I'm told there's a curse in Chinese," groaned Ward. "May you live in interesting times!"

"He wouldn't take the job?" Deloin said, stroking his beard. "Told you so. He won't take a management job. He's always said so."

"Damn!"

After discussing the issue with the HR manager, Ward had decided to offer Carela the production manager's job. A manufacturing engineering position had been offered to Stigler, who'd reacted to Ward's telling him he was no longer production manager by snickering meanly, repeating "time will tell, time will tell." Since then, Stigler had simply called in sick, and had not returned to the plant. Ward had eventually felt compelled to call Jenkinson, detailing the situation. The CEO had not said much, keeping the phone conversation short.

"He suggested Muller."

"Would he do it?"

"I think he would," offered the older man carefully. "But that wouldn't be to everyone's liking."

"In what way?"

"You know how abrupt and irritating Muller can be. It's made him many enemies in the plant."

"Would he do a good job?"

"Technically, yes. No problem. As for the rest …"

"We'll have to try it, then. Do you mind sounding him out about it before I offer him the job?"

"My pleasure," the older man answered with that creepy smile that made Ward's skin crawl. This was the kind of manipulative crap the HR guy truly enjoyed.

"What about having supervisors on shifts? Did you mention it to Denis? What did he say."

"Ah. I didn't. Better you talk to him yourself."

"What's the matter with everyone," suddenly fumed Ward, losing patience. "Every time I ask someone to do something in this plant, it's either 'No' or 'Get someone else!'"

The outburst only seemed to amuse the old HR manager. He gave Ward one of his avuncular looks that Ward hated, thoughtfully stroking his ridiculous collar of white beard. Ward had often wondered whether the beard was fake, and pictured ripping it off Deloin's face in one brisk move.

"Don't you think you should address plant organization matters directly with your staff?"

"I know, I know," accepted Ward, claming down and letting out a long-suffering sigh. "I really should talk to Olivier about it when he comes back, so that he'd pass it on to Denis. But I'm pretty sure he won't do it. On the other hand, if I go straight to the supervisor, I'm just going to get more grumbling about undercutting the line, undermining authority, blah, blah, blah. Olivier's become so prickly about everything."

Deloin looked at Ward in his superior way, shaking his head ruefully. "It's not about him as a person. It's about what you're asking him to *do*. You're pushing him in a direction he's very unhappy about."

"What do you mean?"

The older man looked at him ominously, and then, unexpectedly, suggested lunch.

"Separate the people from the problem," advised the HR manager. "You're getting your knickers in a twist right now because you think people don't want to do what you, the plant manager, ask them to do. But the truth is they disagree with what you want to do. They think it's stupid. So they'll be damned if they do it."

Deloin had taken Ward to the chic restaurant on the other side of town. A young couple had turned an old chateau into an expensive hotel, overlooking a wide lawn in which a medieval tower still stood, faithfully guarding a small stream. It was a colorful setting, but like many such places in France, hard to keep up. Ward had always preferred putting up visitors in central Metz.

"In truth it's quite funny," said the older man, looking anything but amused. "It's so easy to personalize these debates, but it's only a matter of perspective. I find it comical because, you see, your lot pushed us all out of the way."

"Our lot?"

"You, Olivier, Malika, yes. The systems people."

"You mean like the *Toyota Production System?*"

"No," the other man wheezed between a laugh and a cough. "No, I don't think so—I didn't mean that. I meant the IT systems, the quality systems, the HR systems. You know, workflows, processes, and the such. When we built the company that got acquired by Alnext, we had nothing of this. The president surrounded himself with a few men he trusted, rightly or wrongly, the plant managers did their accounts on the back of an envelope, HR was mostly pay and personnel files. Everything else was engineering and production. All that mattered was the bottom line. And to get it, we relied on everyone doing their technical job—you know, the operators operate, maintenance maintains, and so on. Budgets were scribbled on a single sheet of paper. The MRP was little more than a glorified bill of material. But we knew our job, so we were profitable."

"What is it Jenkinson says? Profit is an opinion, but cash is a fact." said Ward.

"Okay, so he's looking at a different measure. But in fact, he's a lot closer to the way we used to run things. That's part of the trouble. He's focused on customers and cash, and he's an engineer. But that's not at all what Alnext did when they acquired us. They forced their *systems* on us."

"The groupwide MRP system?"

"That was one," nodded Deloin with a wry smile. "But all the rest. There was the quality system, you know what I mean, with all the audits and reporting, and paperwork and so on. In HR it was the same. You know, I took the plant job because they kicked me out of the head office and I wanted to remain in the area. But it was crazy, all the procedures and red tape we had to implement."

"Like the supply-chain stuff I was doing for corporate?" asked Ward uneasily.

"Exactly. Systems. Corporate organizes the system, and the little people in the plant comply and all will go well."

"But surely, it works better than what you used to do, since you were acquired in the end."

"Wrong analysis," countered Deloin, an old resentment smoldering in his eyes. "With the way we ran things, we were far more efficient. What happened is that the president made a few very bad calls, such as acquiring more capacity in France when everyone started moving East—which is exactly why plants were cheap in the first place. No one anticipated what opening the French market to the Asian automakers would do to the home brands. But don't kid yourself, the plants were much better run. More profitable, as well. People knew what they were doing. Actually, look at who Jenkinson drives you to work with."

"The old-timers," Ward realized. "Muller, Carela, yourself."

"The guys who know the job, not the system. Why has Muller never progressed in the company?"

"Because he doesn't give a whit for systems," agreed Ward thoughtfully. "He just cares about fixing machines."

"Exactly."

"How does that affect Olivier and Malika, then?"

"Connect the dots. You, Olivier, and Malika were all hired to run the systems, not the shop. Better executive software, more quality ISO procedures, Stigler keeps asking for a computerized press management software. You were trained to run things through centralized IT systems. Stigler's dream is a computer screen in front of every operator that tells the guy what to do every second of the day."

"Yes. I can see that. And now Jenkinson is pushing us completely the other way."

"Jenkinson is asking you to decentralize management, yes. It's not the same as we used to do in the old days, because we relied mainly on line authority. From what I understand, Jenkinson wants to reinforce both authority and empowerment. In my day, no one would have considered asking operators for their input. They were there to operate, period. The widespread attitude was that when people begin to think, they start to disobey. This business of 'Let's figure things out together' is new to me, at least."

"*Go and see—*"

"And *kaizen*. At any rate, this is profoundly unsettling for your managers. For some reason, you don't seem to have a problem with it, but I'm telling you, *they* do. That's not how they see their job. When you force them to be on the shop floor so much, their 'proper' work accumulates on their desk. And spending so much time on floor means they have to deal with people directly."

"Isn't that what management is supposed to do?"

"Maybe, Andy. But why do you ask me to go and talk to Denis Carela for you? And how do you like working with Matthias? Or how do you feel when the CEO goes and talks directly to Sandrine Lumbroso?"

"Hate it, hate it, and hate it. I see your point. Still, I believe he's right. It's the people who do the work that matter, isn't it?"

"I'm not saying he's not," Deloin nodded. "I'm saying you've got to realize how difficult this new approach is for your management team. I'm telling you, you've got to separate the people from the problem. They are not resisting what you are asking them to do because they are trying to be difficult. It's simply that what Jenkinson's requiring of us is difficult—not to mention completely different to the way they were trained."

"It's his company," shrugged Ward with a grin. "Besides, he's a bloody pain, but I can't say that he's wrong either."

Deloin said nothing, concentrating on his food.

"What do you think, Jean-Pierre?" asked Ward, even though he knew better than to put the HR manager on the spot. "Is Olivier right? Is Jenkinson doing all of this to set us up to fail and close the plant? Or is he genuinely trying to help us?"

"When I was a young man," the old fox answered carefully, "we were all jealous of one of my friends who'd been able to buy a Vespa scooter—a real beauty. Everyone was envious and thought he was so lucky, but there was an old man who only said, 'We shall see.' Then my friend fell and broke his leg very badly, so everyone said the scooter had been a terrible idea, a curse in disguise, and the old man said, 'We shall see.' Then we all had compulsory military service in North Africa during the war, but because of his bad leg, my friend was exempted, and the old man said—"

"'We shall see.' So if I ask you whether you think lean management is good for the plant?"

"We shall see."

"You're sure you won't take the job," asked Ward, hoping he didn't sound desperate.

"No way," Carela replied, scratching his gray stubble and grinning. "I'm not crazy enough to be a manager."

"It's what you're doing now," pointed out Ward.

"Not the same," said the other man firmly.

"Not even for more money?"

"Now, *Monsieur* Ward," said Carela, looked at him down his nose, "I'll take that raise any time, thank you very much, but don't insult me. I won't take a management job, and that's final."

"Can't say I blame you," said Ward wistfully. "Can you work with Matthias Muller?"

"Me? No problem, we've been working together forever. Others, I don't know."

"I hear he's got something of a reputation."

The other man smiled again, but just shrugged.

"What about Stigler?" Carela asked.

It was Ward's turn to shrug, and not say anything. Ward wondered again how true was Stigler's accusation that Carela had undermined him in any possible way. He could easily imagine it.

At least Carela got his hands dirty. Ward had found him in the press shop building a flow-rack supermarket out of white tubing. In the old way, the operator at the press would stack up the containers of parts to form a pallet, which would then be picked up by forklift and pushed into logistics. They had agreed with logistics that a "small train" would come and withdraw the containers one by one from the press' shop stock every half hour for the presses in pull. The customer pallets would be consolidated in logistics rather than at the press. They'd spent hours discussing how to dimension the shop stock, but in the end had decided to follow Mark Neville's advice and just try it.

"Another thing. How would you feel about working shifts?"

This gave Carela pause. He looked up from his work, and thought it through.

"Fine with me. I used to like doing shifts, gives you more time to do stuff. Does that mean you're hiring more supervisors?"

"Two others, at least. We'll leave the night shift as is for the moment. Have you got any one in mind we could promote internally? D'you remember what Jenkinson wants us to do since the beginning? Production needs to learn to solve its own problems. This means organizing the problem-solving. So if we follow that direction to its conclusion, each shift should have a supervisor to support the team leaders in problem-solving. We'd need guys who can both solve technical problems and work with people. Teach, in fact." Ward winced, acknowledging as he said it what a tall order it was in their current culture.

"Let me sleep on it," Carela answered prudently.

"Take your time. I also would like to create proper team leader positions," continued Ward. "These would be operators with the additional responsibility for coordinating a team of five to seven people. They'd get a 5 percent bonus, but it's clearly an operating position. They'd be expected to make parts."

"Five percent more?"

"Well, I'd expect them to show up a bit earlier to handle the transition with the previous shift, and to leave a few minutes after the end of the shift, that sort of thing. Nothing 'managerial,' as you'd say. I'm really looking for reliable people who know the job well. I'm looking for people with perfect attendance and who get on well with others. Ideally, I'd look for problem-solvers as well but—"

"Top of my head, I can suggest Adrien Meyer and Mathilde Weber—big fan of yours," he added snidely. "As for the rest, I'd have to give it some thought and discuss with Léa. How many people are we talking about?"

"Five or six to start with. It's a new position, so I'd rather take it step by step. But ultimately, we'd want one for every five operators."

"That's a lot of people—can we afford it?"

"We're not increasing the headcount budget, if that's the question. We're going to have to liberate positions from the *kaizen* we're doing."

"Right," he answered sucking his teeth. "And you'd want me to be a manager. That'd be the day!"

Clear direction comes from working every day on a defined set of broad problems, thought Ward, *and focusing people on these problems day in day out.* If not, we'll all get lost in the small problems, the politics, the people issues. We've got to respond to our quality concerns quickly, fix our shop-floor organization for problem-solving, install a *pull system* to get us to reduce inventories and continue to *kaizen* workstations for better safety and productivity. And that's about it! This is what I need to work at every day. And screw the politics. If Jenkinson fires me, I'll thank him for it, he told himself defiantly.

"Hello, Denise," said Ward. He was surprised to find Claire's accountant still there when he returned from the plant. "Working late?"

"Denise's staying for dinner, darling," Claire said. "We haven't finished yet."

The long dining table was covered with a sea of small piles of papers, invoices, administrative forms, and all the assorted hassle that made running a small (or large) company in France such a bloody pain. After several unsuccessful attempts with other accountants, Claire had finally lucked out with Denise. She was both professional and friendly, and she'd lifted a huge load off of Claire by dealing with the endless state departments demanding money. Just employing one part-time worker to help had been a major headache and had added at least half a dozen more *organisms*, as the social services departments were called in France, to the already long list of bloodsuckers. At least the accountant was on the case now, which was one headache less for Claire.

"We've just finished editing the final accounts for last year," said Denise. She was a frumpy, middle-aged woman who looked, well, like an accountant. But she had an oddball sense of humor that had them in stitches as she gossiped about the extracurricular activities of Metz's bourgeois society.

"And?"

"Breaking even," said Claire with a face. "But I still can't pay myself any wages this year."

"*L'art pour l'art,*" smiled Ward, reading the disappointment on her face. "It's not like we need the money."

"Solène offered again to invest in Malancourt."

Solène was the owner of Terango. Very wealthy, and very bored.

"There is no urgency, is there?" he asked, trying to sound confident. "Trust me on this: You don't want to work for someone else. It's great that she's paying for exceptional stuff, but this is your center. Keep it that way."

She smiled. It all seemed so unfair. They worked hard for what they had, but it still didn't seem to get easier, and, for every step forward, disaster always seemed one step ahead. Andy often told her that doing what one wanted to do and working for oneself were the greatest luxuries she'd ever have, but evenings like this one she still had doubts. The fear, she realized, the damned fear was back. Ignoring the accountant who was putting away the paperwork, she closed on Andrew, relieved to see the magic still worked. He was no longer the happy-go-lucky, one-of-the-lads boy she'd met an eternity ago, but as she placed her hand on his arm, with a simple touch, the fear remained at bay.

"You really think it could go badly tomorrow?"

"They've sacked plant managers for less," he grinned.

"What about Phil? Wouldn't he help? He seemed nice enough."

"Don't confuse nice with soft," he said. "He's got everybody fooled. This guy is a poker player, all right. He bluffs without tells, and doesn't play losing hands. I just don't know which way he's going to jump."

The year-end budget review meeting was both anticlimactic and nerve-racking. Ward had slept little the night before and then left at the crack of dawn for Neuhof, driving in the gray early morning of a miserable wintry day. Claire had gotten up with him and, practical as ever, prepared him a full English breakfast before leaving. Ward's irritation had only increased at being mothered. He hadn't felt quite that anxious since his last job interview or exam finals. This was ridiculous. As he drove, Ward's mood swung back and forth between fear of being sacked on the spot and a simple urge to just get it over with. He gave himself a stern talking to—he simply couldn't let the job get him in such a state. What was *wrong* with him? Here's your *clear direction*, boy: This is just a job, he'd repeated to himself defiantly, like a mantra. Just a job.

Jenkinson had dragged the full executive committee to Europe for the European plant reviews, and had insisted on a quick plant tour before starting the meeting. Ward had not been in Neuhof for a long while, and was astonished at the changes. Ackermann had explained to him in muted tones, while touring the shop floor trailing behind the executive group, that he'd been given a full-time team of three people to implement a *pull system*, with some support from Amy Woods. And indeed, Beckmeyer demonstrated the full extent of *pull*, from the shipping area, to the *leveling* box, the withdrawal *kanban* loop, a massive stocking point that made Jenkinson frown, and then the second *kanban* loop of production instructions with the batch-building boxes and the launcher queues. A small train was delivering components to the lines and picking up finished product.

Ward was impressed. It was beautifully done, in true Germanic style, with shiny metal leveling boxes and color-coded plastic *kanban* cards. They'd opted for containers of parts stacked up three or four high on small wheeled trays, as opposed to the actual supermarket shelves Vaudon was experimenting with. Ackermann described *sotto vocce* how Bob Woods had given them a really hard time about it. The old coot had argued that instead of moving a pallet of parts at a time, they now moved a pile of parts at a time—which meant that they had made progress, certainly, but not much, and they had locked themselves into their solution, and could not fraction and mix picking any further. Ackermann explained that Beckmeyer had paid through the nose to install the whole thing, and had balked at the cost of installing a proper supermarket in front of each line. Indeed, if the thing had had to be as big as the alleys were, it would have been massive.

The entire visit was made without any comments by Jenkinson, who listened impassively while Beckmeyer explained this and that to his audience. But as they progressed, Ward started to see through his first impression. Clearly, the *pull system* clarified the *flow* in the plant, and it also made problems appear. Good. But, he realized, *these problems were not being solved.* The production analysis board had specific numbers corresponding exactly to the target for every hour. This was what Bob Woods would call a "miraculous line": There was no way operators would be able to hit the right number of parts on the hour every hour. Furthermore, Ward noticed, there wasn't a single comment on any of the boards.

He saw a red bin full of bad parts, although the cell was not running. Several lanes of the supermarket were empty, with no obvious response from the team. It would have been a very poor time to draw any attention to himself, but he itched to ask a thousand questions. The more he looked, the more his curiosity was piqued. He saw what looked like computer generated fabrication orders on a desk. It dawned on him that the German plant had purchased a surface layer of lean system, but not used it for *kaizen*. If he had not been such a nervous wreck, he might have found it funny. They had indeed built a Buddha image without injecting the soul into it, to use a phrase from Bob Woods' speech at the executive conference that seemed like an age ago.

The rest of the day was spent kicking his heels as each of the European plant managers stepped into the meeting room to face a court-martial-looking assembly of senior managers, each detailing the year and their plans for the coming one. He'd expected to meet Stonebridge there, but the Polish plant was represented by its financial controller, an edgy young man who kept reviewing his presentation on his laptop. Ward chitchatted nervously with the Czech plant manager whom he barely knew, a short energetic guy who had worked in the U.S. and spoke English with a thick Brooklyn accent and equally surprising colorful vocabulary. The Turin plant manager was a tall, elegant Italian who arrived late, missed the plant tour, and left immediately after his oral exam, so Ward had very little chance to talk to him.

In the end, his own presentation was a nonevent. Although he disclosed disastrous budget results, having missed his yearly objectives by more than a mile, the assorted bigwigs had nary a question. They listened absently as he groveled, obviously distracted by some other business. Jenkinson and Wayne Sanders—*the* Wayne Sanders—kept excusing themselves to take phone calls, and would whisper urgently to one another whenever they came back into the room. Ward had been surprised to see Lowell Coleman on the panel, but the older man had made no particular attempt at conversation beyond the usual niceties. Beckmeyer sat there as European regional VP, looking like he'd bitten a lemon, but, then again, he always looked bilious. He looked down his long, pinched nose at Ward saying nothing. Ward expected to be cut to pieces, but instead all he got was silence. He wrapped up his slides, and they all nodded abstractedly, thanking him for coming and so on. Jenkinson's only comment had been that his inventory targets for the next period were not challenging enough.

"Can you please tell me?" asked Ward, catching Jenkinson as he'd just hung up his cell phone, and was about to go back in the meeting room for the Czech presentation.

"Tell you what?" the CEO asked, looking genuinely surprised.

"Have I still got a job?" asked Ward, hating himself for sounding such a milksop.

"If you hadn't," Jenkinson smiled slowly, "I'd have told you myself."

"But, but," stammered Ward "What about my budget numbers? Vaudon is by far at the bottom of the list."

"Okay," said Jenkinson, sighing sharply with a glance at the meeting room, where he was being expected for the Czech presentation. "Variances don't mean anything to me. I can't change everything at once, but this next budget cycle we're going to be working from P&L and cash-flow projections, in plain English, so we can all understand each other and agree on where we're going.

"And I do care deeply about the budget process. Strong budgeting is absolutely essential to what we discussed previously—*clear direction*. I was not pleased at all to hear about the various fun and games happening with this year's numbers. Lowell Coleman has agreed to come here and take over the region while we look for someone local. Klaus can refocus on Neuhof. God knows the plant needs it."

Coleman? Ward thought, astonished. European regional manager? Instead of Beckmeyer? No wonder the man looked like he was sucking sour grapes. Even though he tried to be cool and steel himself from strong emotion—this was, after all, only work—Ward could not fight back the feeling of wild hope that suffused. He licked his lips irrelevantly wondering what people could possibly mean by the skin of their teeth.

"What happened with the price dispute?" Ward blurted out giddy with relief, realizing he'd blundered as soon as the words were out of his mouth. Jenkinson frowned darkly.

"How do you know about that?" he asked curtly.

"Mark mentioned it," stammered Ward, adding a serious *faux pas* on top of his original slip up.

"Mark talks too much," growled the CEO.

"It all worked out fine," he finally relented with a fleeting half-smile. "Situation's back to normal. And it was not what you think. In any case, I'd rather you didn't mention any of this, to anyone—and I mean it. The last rumor I need right now is how I strong-armed a customer into giving in on price."

"Sure," agreed Ward, trying to recover some of his aplomb. "I know nothing."

"And Ward—" added Jenkinson grimly as he went back into the meeting room.

"Yes?"

"Give me the inventory reduction. Show me the cash."

"You were right," Ward told his wife over the phone, elated. "I've still got a job."

He'd caught such jangled nerves from the review that he'd had to stop at a petrol station on the way, and was drinking an unidentified apple beverage and eating a soggy apple strudel with vanilla ice cream heaped over it.

"How did it go?"

"Zero drama," he said, still not believing his luck. "They all seemed preoccupied by something else. The big news is that Phil's taken Europe away from Beckmeyer and handed it over to Coleman."

"Wow. That's good news, right?"

"We shall see," he kidded. He'd told Claire about Deloin's scooter story, and she'd loved it, teasing him mercilessly by responding "We shall see" to his every pronouncement for the whole evening.

Hanging up, he realized that he'd never fully trusted Jenkinson until now. He'd always half-believed Stigler's theory that the lean stuff was the usual management posturing, and that at the first real opportunity Jenkinson would reveal himself to be just as driven by short-termism and number-playing as they all were. Now, he had to admit that even buffeted by all the storm winds of industry crises and internal politics, Jenkinson took them methodically to the shop floor, and tackled patiently the endless issues of quality and red bins, inventory and *pull systems*, and productivity and work-station design. It made the man no less scary, but at least you could rely on him to react in a predictable way, once you understood what he was about. And to some extent, that did make him trustworthy.

Ward had always thought of strategy as a destination, a vision of where one wanted to go. The idea of expressing strategy as key challenges was completely novel to him—and fascinating. The rare glimpse he'd had in his CEO's mind made him realize he didn't think in terms of having a grand vision, but of understanding fully the broad problems one had to keep working at. Alnext had, in the past, always pushed forward its leadership's vision—essentially increasing top line by making expensive parts for up-market vehicles and bottom line by producing in low-cost countries to drive costs down. Jenkinson clearly didn't think like that. He wanted to satisfy his customers by delivering defect-free parts on time. He wanted to keep his plants fully loaded without making inventory by getting them flexible enough to handle a wide mix of parts. He wanted problem-free starts of production to be able to renew products more often and less painfully. To achieve all this, he needed to develop the company's quality awareness and problem-solving capability. Ward realized with a shock that with Alnext's previous strategy, Vaudon had never had a chance—it had only been a matter of time. But if Jenkinson *did* practice what he preached, they did have a glimmer of hope, if they put their backs into it and finally got some budget-level results out of all their efforts. The CEO might be crazy, but there certainly was method in his madness: *Go and see*, demand improvement after improvement, give *clear direction*. Why had he never been taught this stuff?

Chapter Six

TEAMWORK

"We're just not good enough," declared Virginie Lesueur.

"What makes you say that?" asked Ward. Lesueur was a petite woman whose round eyes and round face made her look terribly young, a quality that seemed more pronounced as she stood between graybeards Matthias Muller and Denis Carela. The four of them were reviewing the quality analysis she was conducting on a flip chart. Malika Chadid had never fully committed to the full-quality *PDCAs*, delegating the work to Lesueur, a young technician she had recruited straight out of school two years ago. Lesueur was a local girl, having spent all her life in Metz where her parents ran a bakery. She'd studied chemistry and had taken to root-cause analysis like a duck to water, which served to show you just never knew. Still, her boss' apparent lack of interest had Ward wondering about Jean-Pierre Deloin's earlier point, about managing through systems vs. managing through getting people to solve problems. Chadid certainly did a great job at maintaining the plant's quality systems—but how much of that contributed to reducing complaints and ppms?

"Look at this. We've tried, what, five different factors? But we still can't figure out what causes the drool," said Lesueur.

"I'm telling you, the nozzle's shot," grumbled Muller, the newly appointed production manager.

"It doesn't drool on other parts—just this one," pointed out Carela.

"And it's not the melt decompression, we've checked that," Lesueur added, annoyed. "Let's face it, we're short of ideas."

"Well, keep trying?" suggested Ward, feeling slightly foolish for repeating the same things over and over again: "What is the problem? Can you clarify the problem? Keep trying." By now, technically, at least he had a vague idea what they were going on about. But this problem had caused another customer complaint, one that was significant enough that Lesueur had insisted on accompanying him to the customer to check it out. She'd gaped at the automotive assembly line throughout the entire visit. He couldn't hold it against her—he himself had seen more car factories than he'd ever wanted to in the past year, and was still awed by the scope of the installations and the size of the plants, larger than his own village.

"You don't understand—we're running in circles," she insisted. "We don't know enough! Factor analysis works if you've got some idea of what you're looking for, but here, we're just digging and digging and hoping to find something. We could be doing this forever."

"What do you suggest?" asked Ward, thinking of Mark Neville's practiced "Make a suggestion" line.

"I have no idea," she admitted, pursing her mouth. The two other men were not proposing much either, just looking at the defective part vacantly. "If only I could talk to Grimbert about it."

"Who?"

"Professor Grimbert. He used to teach plastic-parts manufacturing. He was really good."

"Not 'gateux' Grimbert," laughed Muller. "You can't be serious. He can't still be teaching."

"D'you know him?"

"Of course. Most of the young technicians we see over the summer from the Metz IUT discuss him. A real tough guy."

"He's fine," she said, sticking up for her old teacher, which was endearing. "Just doesn't put up with lazy thinking."

"Is he still active, do you think?"

"He was three years ago," she shrugged.

"Well, why don't you get in touch with him. If he agrees, we can offer him a day's consulting and you can look at this together."

"Oh, please," protested Muller, "What do we need—"

"Take it easy, Matthias," smiled Ward. "It can't hurt. All you ever suggest is we replace this or that. Let's use ideas—"

"Not money," snickered Carela good naturedly. "Consulting will probably cost more than replacing the nozzle."

"Yeah, but we might learn something. Can I leave that with you, Virginie? Let me know how it goes, and I want to be there if your chap actually does come."

The plant looked like a different place since Muller had become production manager. Sure, the guy would bark at anyone for anything at any time, but the shop floor had lost that sloppiness that had so irked Ward. He'd also attacked the setting problem head on, and asked Carela to time every production change personally. Carela had initially balked at doing it. He didn't want to confront the setters directly himself. After a number of run-ins with Muller, though, he finally agreed, grumbling. The new changeover times and number of changes improved at an astonishing rate, a fact that nearly changed Ward's mind about good old command-and-control approach to management. Muller was clearly not the empowering type, and he cracked the whip incessantly, but at least things finally worked. Olivier Stigler had not reappeared from his long-term sick-leave, which made the HR mutter darkly about harassment lawsuits. That was a problem for later. By now, Ward had resigned himself to take his disasters one at a time.

"We must be doing something wrong," Ward confessed to Jenkinson during one of their regular phone calls. "We've got a pull system in place, and it functions, but the results are catastrophic."

"In what way?"

"We've reduced inventory by about 20 percent in just two months, but our on-time-delivery has crashed. It's at the lowest level since Carole Chandon started fighting to fill truck by truck. She is now convinced the system doesn't work, and keeps bickering with the new production manager."

"Are you leveling?"

"We're pulling. Stock replenishment with *kanban* cards. As we discussed."

"Yes, but are you leveling?"

"I'm not sure what you mean by that."

"Look, I'm rather tied up at the moment, but I'll ask Amy if she'll come over and have another look. Would that help?"

"That'd be great."

"Any other problems?"

"One, actually," hesitated Ward. "I'm confused about something—"

"Come on, problems first."

"Well, it's about this idea of *clear direction*. I understand two important points in lean management are 'customer first' and 'developing people before making parts,' yes?"

"Indeed. So?"

"Don't take it badly, but all I hear about is fighting with customers and firing people, and well, it's confusing."

"Ah," said Jenkinson, falling silent on the other side of the line. Ward never knew exactly where he stood with the man. At one moment, he could be completely open and almost friendly. At other times he could suddenly clam up and make you feel like you'd just asked him the color of his underwear. Over the past year, Ward had come to respect his boss, for both his attention to detail and his strategic thinking. At the same time he couldn't rid himself of the fear, no matter how much the other man insisted on "problems first." If nothing else, the fear of sounding like a complete idiot. In the end, he'd concluded that asking Jenkinson would mean a moment's embarrassment while not asking would mean staying embarrassed for months.

"Do as I say but don't do as I do? Is that what you're thinking?" finally replied the CEO.

"Um. No, not as such, but—"

"OK. First of all, you're misinterpreting the incident Mark told you about. What really happened is that I had a deal with the vehicle's program manager. As part of a more global arrangement we'd been working out, she accepted a price increase on the remaining life of the model, that's all. This was partly to compensate for much-lower-than-expected volumes, and partly because we were costing the new model very tightly. I told her that I was willing to make an effort on price for the new parts, but that I needed cash upfront."

"I thought you were trying to renegotiate these parts up?"

"It's not black and white. Because this particular program manager knows what she's doing, we've been looking at the parts we're doing for her and we believe we can do a number of things to manufacture the parts cheaper. That way we'll split the cost saving. In the end, we're also doing more parts on her vehicle than before, so it's a win-win."

"So why the drama?"

"Internal fight at the customer. Their purchasing VP made a name for himself bleeding suppliers dry. He's actually driven a number out of business. So he told Sanders to stuff it and to forget anything we'd worked out with the program manager, showing who the big dog was. He and Wayne go way back, and Wayne knew his man well. For once Wayne got smart and kept me in the loop, so we called the guy's bluff. I never made the OEM *do* anything. I forced the purchasing guy's hand, and the program manager went to the CEO about how he was screwing up a relationship with a preferred supplier and messing with a bigger deal. The CEO sided with her, and the whole thing went away."

"I see. I only saw one leg of the elephant."

"As I keep saying, conflict is mostly misunderstanding. Complete waste of time. But that's not the important conclusion here."

"Uh?"

"The whole thing only happened because Bethany's quality is top notch, and Mark was awarded a top supplier award last year."

"Without that you had no leverage."

"Nope—without that I wouldn't have had a *case*," corrected Jenkinson. "It's all good business. The program manager wants to work with Mark on her next generation because she feels safe about the parts he'll deliver, and because she believes in the cost reductions we're suggesting. Her engineers will have to accommodate some stuff they won't necessarily like, but she trusts Mark's opinion, and can work with him and us. Which is why she was ready to go to bat on this instance. So customer first, of course, but not in just any way. We want to increase customer satisfaction and reduce costs. The issue here is having the foresight to realize that the *client*, purchasing, is not the *customer*: the program manager is."

"It's like when the line manager tells me his production program is completely steady, but the orders I get are all over the place," said Ward. "I'm delivering a stock managed by procurement, but my real customer is the production line. I get it."

"About letting people go, it's much the same thing. To develop people we've got to work with folks who are ready to cooperate in the first place, people who are ready to face their own problems and solve them jointly. You probably heard that Stonebridge is no longer in Wroclaw. He left the company because he couldn't work with the Polish team and was blaming every problem on other people. He was the plant manager, so the problems were his, period, even if they were created by others. It's the manager's responsibility to make sure his subordinates succeed at their job, end of story. And, by the way, I'd appreciate it if you continued to *go and see* at the Polish plant regularly until we've found someone who can do that job. Better no one than the wrong guy, but that can't last indefinitely."

"No problem," agreed Ward, wondering how Claire would feel about it. He'd been traveling more in the past six months than in all their years in France. He had indeed heard that Brian Stonebridge had been summarily dismissed, but he didn't know whether it was a Lowell Coleman or a Jenkinson decision, although he suspected the latter. He doubted the guy would be missed, but he couldn't help but have some degree of sympathy with the ex-plant manager, considering how he'd convinced himself it had been his head on the block at the previous budget review.

"We've discussed *go and see*," Jenkinson continued. "*Kaizen* spirit and *clear direction*. Another key dimension to lean management is *teamwork*, and by this I mean *cooperation across functions*. Because Mark works well with engineering, we can make smarter suggestions to the customer. Because I work well with the program manager, we can put together better deals. To answer your question, it can be confusing simply because win-win doesn't mean nice-nice, and sometimes you've got to knock people's heads together in order to get them to cooperate. But *teamwork* is the issue."

Ward was still mulling over the conversation as he walked to the self-service area for a coffee. Lately he had started a new habit. After his first couple of hours on the shop floor, he would eat a late breakfast at the cafeteria so as to catch the morning shift operators during their lunch break. They eyed him strangely at first, but got used to his presence over time, and would even include him in their conversations every now and then. Mostly it was about kids, school problems, weekend schemes, holidays, and the recurring concerns of living on a tight budget. Ward had learned not to feel embarrassed by such situations. He couldn't do anything about it—but the least he could do is listen and not close his eyes to the daily realities of the people he was living with.

That day, the conversation among the woman on their lunch break had been about a tragic news brief that had shocked the nation. A chemist had left his toddler locked in his car while he went to work, and the child had died from dehydration. Ward said a small superstitious prayer for Charlie's wellbeing and joined the idle chatter.

"I do worry about Maria, though, leaving her baby in the car like this," said one of them.

"Maria?" blurted out Ward, stunned. "Maria at the quality wall in assembly?"

The six women suddenly stared at him, as if noticing him for the first time. Ward suddenly felt embarrassed by their tight mouths and blank expressions, feeling like he had betrayed their trust by hearing something that was definitely not meant for his ears.

"Are you serious?" he insisted.

"Yes," said the one who had mentioned it, looking away, apparently conflicted about exposing her colleagues' behavior to the boss—who of course might just do something about it. "Just for an hour or so. She works the afternoon shift, and her husband works at the Lafalc plant on the morning shift. There's an overlap, so he rides his bike here when he's done, and drives the kid back with the car."

"The kid stays in the car?" Ward asked again, shocked.

"What do you think!" sneered another woman. "Many of the young girls do it, of course. On their wages, how could they pay for a babysitter? It costs more than they earn."

"Isn't there government help?" stammered Ward. "Some kind of a system?"

The women didn't even deign respond, looking at their hands, until Ward excused himself and left. Conversation picked up behind his back as if nothing had happened.

"For crying out loud," he told Claire that evening. "We make and ship parts halfway across Europe, but we can't organize child-care! How hard can it be?"

"Do it, baby, do it!"

"She leaves her kid in the car while she works," he repeated, hovering between outrage and disbelief.

"Do it."

"You're right. Denial is not a river in Egypt. I can't just pretend I don't know. I will get Deloin on it. Let's see if his vaunted city hall connection can finally be of some help. But how about you? What did the vet say?"

"The vet doesn't like the way the foal is positioned, but says we'll have to see how it goes when she actually drops," she answered, worry lines etched on her face.

Claire's friend had suggested that she let her prize stallion cover one of the mares for free, and Claire had high hopes for raising a colt she'd be able to sell for a good price as a yearling. She worried it was late in the season, and she might lose an entire year. Ward himself was a bit weary of seeing her get involved with horsebreeding, an even bigger gamble than horsetrading, but that had been this year's big project, and it was finally coming to term. All they could do now is hold their breath and cross their fingers.

"The problem is pulling without *leveling*," Ward translated as Amy Woods explained. They had spent the morning in the plant checking their makeshift *pull system*. "But to level, you need actual *teamwork*. This is not a problem any of you can solve on your own. So we're going to have to solve the *problem together*."

Amy was back again in Vaudon, and didn't appear to be too happy about it, either. Sure, she was her usual upbeat self, but there was a tension there as well. She looked preoccupied and unusually impatient. Ward wondered whether all was fine—no doubt he'd hear about it in the evening, as she and Claire would natter and share their news. The *pull system* they'd set up worked, sort of, but the results had been dire on the customer front. Stocks had plummeted, which was good, but so too had on-time delivery, which was unacceptable.

"Going back to basics," she gestured expressively. "Carole, when you run the MRP, do you agree that this takes the least amount of work, yes? You plug in customer demand into the MRP, and it issues production instructions."

"It's *a lot* of work!" Carole protested, outraged, a not unfamiliar tone for her. "We've got a lot of work to check that the MRP stock positions are accurate, and that the info on production capacity is good. But I agree that the MRP calculates what machine needs to do what."

"So how does the MRP think," explained Amy. "Essentially, it tries to hold enough stock of every product to satisfy customer demand. So when the stock level hits a trigger, it reorders a batch, and then routes this to the available production cell. Essentially, this is *a fixed-quantity, variable-time* reorder method. The order quantity is fixed, and the time it comes depends on customer demand. Because the batches tend to be quite large, there's also a long lead-time between the time you order and the time you get the parts. This would work fine in a stable environment, but the problem is that customer demand varies."

"Tell us about it!"

"So let's look at an example from another company, similar to what you've got going on here," said Amy, as she projected an Excel spreadsheet onto the wall in the logistics area.

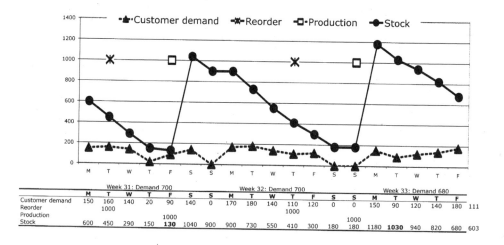

	Week 31: Demand 700						Week 32: Demand 700						Week 33: Demand 680					
	M	T	W	T	F	S	S	M	T	W	T	F	S	S	M	T	W	T	F	
Customer demand	150	160	140	20	90	140	0	170	180	140	110	120	0	0	150	90	120	140	180	111
Reorder		1000										1000								
Production					1000									1000						
Stock	600	450	290	150	**130**	1040	900	900	730	550	410	300	180	180	1180	**1030**	940	820	680	603

"Here you can see a few weeks of customer demand—the bottom line. Would you say that this is a realistic variation?" The group nodded.

"The squares show that the MRP reorders when the stock falls under 500 parts, at which point it asks for batches of 1,000 parts. This is pretty much what you had been doing. We can say that there is a three-day lead time. So the circles are the stock profile you get, which we're all familiar with.

"With this profile, you have on average about 600 parts in stock, but at its lowest point the stock has only 130 products in it, agreed? Now, when you implemented *kanban* on the high-volume parts, you radically changed your reordering procedure."

"We replenish what has been consumed daily."

"Not exactly, because of your batch sizes, you still have a two-day lead time."

"This is because we have so much trouble scheduling tool changes," protested production manager Muller.

"We'll get to that. Let's stay focused on the logic. Here's what happens to your stock.

		Week 31: Demand 700							Week 32: Demand 700							Week 33: Demand 680				
	M	T	W	T	F	S	S	M	T	W	T	F	S	S	M	T	W	T	F	
Customer demand	150	160	140	20	90	140	0	170	180	140	110	120	0	0	150	90	120	140	180	110.5
Production	160	120	150	160	140	0	0	110	140	170	180	140	0	0	110	120	150	90	120	
Stock	200	160	170	310	360	220	220	160	120	150	220	240	240	240	200	230	260	210	150	213.7

"It no longer has the classical profile, but oscillates randomly between 360 and 120 parts in stock according to customer demand variation. And the average is around 200, which is a third of what the previous stock had. So big improvement, right?"

"We have reduced inventory by about 20 percent," agreed Ward, "but something is going wrong because we're misdelivering a lot."

"Stay with the logic," Amy repeated. "This is a *variable-quantity, fixed-time method*. There is a daily delivery of products, but the quantity asked for can vary randomly, exactly following customer demand by two days."

"Yes, but it plays havoc on production," objected Muller, stretching out on his chair, and absently stroking his bald pate. He was worse at meetings than even Carela or Léa Mordant. The man was so full of restless energy he would often stand up and pace the back of the room before returning to fidget on his seat.

"Exactly," emphasized Amy. "Before, logistics was completely dependent on production, having to take what it received and store it. Now, production is a slave to logistics, and has to produce daily variable quantities. Which makes it very difficult to organize production. And so you guys keep arguing."

"But this is *just-in-time*, no?" asked the logistics manager tugging on an unruly strand of hair from her ponytail. "Production has to deliver what the customer wants? No?"

"This is *unleveled just-in-time*. It works, but at a high cost in both flexibility and capacity. At this stage, the problem is that the factory is not yet flexible enough to be able to cope—and probably never will."

"I just don't see how we can have batch sizes of 10 times changeover if we have to follow customer demand exactly," thought Ward aloud.

"Yes, this is the problem," Muller agreed, frowning. "I can't schedule production in any way, so we keep checking what is in the MRP and make choices about the *kanban* rather than follow the *pull system*."

"But you're supposed to follow the *kanban*!" exclaimed Chandon.

"If ... the *kanban* are leveled," explained Amy. "Look, let's follow this through to the end. Now the problem with exactly following customer demand is that you have a lead time because you can't organize production so that you produce exactly what you need daily—sometimes you should produce more than you can, sometimes less, so it's a mess, agreed?" Again, the group nodded.

"What we're going to do is think *takt time*. *Takt time* is really just customer demand, averaged over a period of time. Let's take one week. Over one week we can take the production hours we have and divide them by the total customer demand projected for the week. Like so.

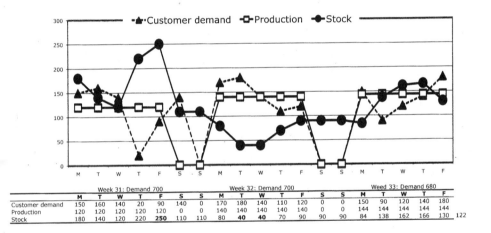

	Week 31: Demand 700							Week 32: Demand 700							Week 33: Demand 680					
	M	T	W	T	F	S	S	M	T	W	T	F	S	S	M	T	W	T	F	
Customer demand	150	160	140	20	90	0	0	140	140	140	110	120	0	0	150	90	120	140	180	
Production	120	120	120	120	120	0	0	140	140	140	140	140	0	0	144	144	144	144	144	
Stock	180	140	120	220	**250**	110	110	80	**40**	**40**	70	90	90	90	84	138	162	166	130	122

"So you're saying that I should average the customer demand over the week, with each day the same?" asked the logistics manager.

"Exactly. For a week, you order from production the same quantity every day, regardless of what your customer actually asks you to deliver. What we know about customers is that their total volume will be stable over one week, although their daily totals may vary considerably. So what they haven't picked up today, they'll add to tomorrow's orders. On average, it's stable. If you check your demand profile, I am certain that you'll discover this to be true."

"Hmmm, it could work ..."

"Now, in this example, average stock fell even lower, around 120 parts. But, it's also riskier, since my lowest point is only 40 parts. This is the lean method. It's much leaner, but requires constant attention. It's a *fixed-quantity, fixed-time* method. In production you can follow the *kanban* cues because the demand you get is *leveled*," Amy concluded, then jumped over to a white board. "Here. It's like this."

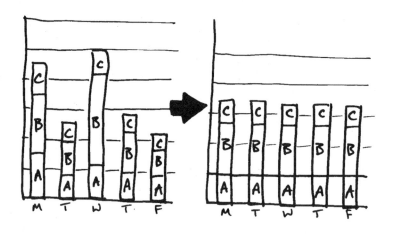

"I produce the same quantity every day for every day of one week?"

"Yes, so you can schedule the changeovers and control production tightly."

"But what happens in case of a problem?" asked Chandon, clearly ill at ease.

"This is where you must work together. Production and logistics must solve a common problem cooperatively. It can be done! Keep this in mind:

- First, every week you must agree on a leveled production plan that both of you sign—in blood.

- Second, you must constantly check whether the stock is behaving normally, whether it is overflowing beyond a boundary or whether it is under a lower limit."

"Visual control," exclaimed Chandon, snapping her fingers in comprehension.

"Which is why we need flat storage everywhere," Amy agreed. "Inventory points should not just be places where parts accumulate and wait, but a management tool to control the flow of parts and information through the factory. Let's get out of here and have a look at your stock."

Rather than heading toward the truck preparation area, Amy walked to the other end of the warehouse where all the supplied components were kept. The area was neat enough, and no longer had broken pallets and cracked cardboard boxes lurking in the corners, but it still looked cavernous—rack after rack of containers of all sizes and shapes, with untold numbers and variety of parts in them. Ward had to admit to himself he had no idea how to read this. He compared this to the shop stocks they'd set up in the plant, and saw the difference. The small supermarkets at the presses in pull could speak to him.

They said, "I'm full, so production is ahead or logistics is late," or "I'm empty, so production is late or logistics is unleveled" and so on. Here, in the warehouse, the stock was mute.

"We've started with a supermarket for key components," Carole said, taking them to an area where they'd put rollers on the floor and blue plastic containers were stacked up, neatly separated by rows. "Although that means we have to decant when we get large containers from our suppliers—purchasing doesn't want to hear about getting suppliers to change their conditioning policies."

"Same all, same all," smiled Amy, looking at one pile of five boxes of one reference. "So how many boxes should you have here?"

"I know," grouched the logistics manager, "it says three max on the label because we get these parts delivered every day."

"Uh-huh. So why do we see five?"

Chandon shrugged as they all looked at each other. Stuff happens.

"As for you, Andy, why do you let this process have two more boxes than necessary?"

"What do you want me to do?" he sighed. "Take them out?"

"Sure," she answered, picking up two small containers from the top and placing them in the alley in front of the location.

"I'm not going to do a Bob Woods on you, but do you remember ..."

"Yeah. Visualize the process to reveal problems at all times," preempted Ward. "To solve issues one by one and, in the end, improve management policies. Carole had visualized the process by creating a dedicated location for this component, but not revealed the problem by letting more boxes in the spot than was set by the standard."

"Dead right. And now?"

"Now that you've revealed the problem by putting the extra boxes in the alley," he grinned, "I've got to ask Carole how she's going to solve this problem. Which will probably reveal a management policy problem."

"It does," chipped in Chandon with a rare smile. "I keep asking you what to do about suppliers who do not respect our delivery requirements and send too much or too little! I'm still waiting for an answer!"

Amy laughed out loud at Ward's ever suffering grimace.

"I think that you've got the idea. If we're using a leveled plan, we need to have tight visual control to make sure the process is actually doing what we think it's doing. The trick, in management terms, is to force the process to perform at standard level, and deal with all the ensuing problems. But to do that, Carole, you need an overall storing policy."

"What do you mean. We've just done this. Is good, no?"

"It's fine, but what about the rest of the warehouse? You've started on the problem. We now have truck preparation zones for finished goods and the beginning of flat storage for main components. But what about the rest of the stuff—slow-moving finished goods that you store in here, and medium-runner components? The entire warehouse should be visual. For instance:

- A 'golden zone' where the most frequent items are stored in order to limit material handlers' movements.

- A 'dead zone' for all the dead stock—parts that haven't moved in the past months, with a clear policy of what gets stored there and when.

- Visualize the min and max on each location, as well as the resupply frequency, which will enable you to read whether we're in normal conditions or not.

- Track the warehouse's delivery performance to the factory, and so on.

"But ...," hesitated Chandon.

"Computer system," finished Ward, rolling his eyes. "Again."

"Clearly you're going to have to see how you work with the computer system," agreed Amy. "But keep in mind that in a *leveled pull system* you don't need to know exactly how many containers you've got at all times as long as you're within the min/max limits."

"Hang on," rephrased Chandon worriedly. "What you're saying is I should not worry about the stock level as long as it's within the upper and lower boundaries?"

"It's going to fluctuate randomly. This doesn't tell you anything—and in fact you need to keep yourself from overcorrection, which will simply create the old shower problem: You know, turn the hot water on but there's a long delay, so it's still cold, and then turn the hot water some more, and when it arrives it's scalding. So you quickly turn it all down, and now it's freezing again. As long as your finished-product stock is within boundaries, you shouldn't worry about it."

"Are you saying that we commit to an average quantity produced per day, and we try to stick to that plan as hard as we can, and we only have to make a decision when the stock is out of boundaries—upper or lower?" asked Ward.

"That's it. With the batch-building box, the *kanban* will do it for you. Essentially, the *kanban* will pull a fixed quantity at a fixed time if everything goes well, because as you're *pulling levelly* on production, the various references at the press will be pulled at a steady rhythm. As long as nothing is happening within stock boundaries in logistics, you're fine. When something does happen ..."

"We have to understand the problem and react."

"The good thing about the *leveling box* is that it helps you consolidate the customer trucks progressively, so you will see if you have a problem in production, because logistics will find an empty row in the shop stock, which indicates that something is wrong."

"I'm confused," admitted Ward. "I thought that we needed to put the customer demand in trucks in the *leveling box*."

"*If* the demand is leveled," explained Amy, raising an eyebrow. "If you're delivering to Toyota, it's no problem: their production programs are completely leveled. But for other customers, you need to put the leveled demand in the *leveling box* to protect your production and handle the variation with stocks in logistics."

"Right ...," he answered, confused. "The one thing I understand is that all variation should be handled in logistics, not in production— is that right?"

"Essentially, yes. Production copes with production-caused variation, and logistics with customer-caused variation. The first principle of *pull* is always to have the right stock at the right place. Each stock should cover one form or variation only, so that we can understand what goes on."

"So how do we do all of this?"

"I've told you last time I was here, but you haven't done it yet: *weekly production plan*. The first step is to get everyone here together once a week to produce a *leveled* production plan. You start with the high-runners and you work down the list of products. Once a week, with a calendar in hand, logistics produces a *level* plan, which is then discussed by production and maintenance until we get an agreement. This production plan is firm. You lock the door and no one comes out until you have an agreement. No changes, unless something major happens, and all the changes are logged."

"That part is easy. I'll authorize the changes personally," agreed Ward.

"The meeting is essentially about checking the consistency of the plan with what the customer is doing, checking the stock levels, and the availability of production. This is also a moment for *teamwork*. There are all sorts of reasons why the plan apparently can't be respected, from trucker strikes to machines that are down. The team must come away from the meeting with a 'plan B' to stick to the plan."

"How so?"

"It's a matter of pay *now*, or pay later. You either put exceptional resources in place now and stick to the plan—or you find yourself paying special transports later. The idea is to track special costs as they accrue."

"As doing overtime at the end of the shift if the plan is not respected?"

"Same idea. The plan reflects a normal level of resource. If we fear it's not going to be respected, we learn how to solve problems *now*! Not later when they blow up in your face. Can you do that?"

They'd moved to Chandon's office in the warehouse and Ward translated Amy's question into French carefully. Chandon and Muller stared at him, obviously avoiding looking at each other, which made Carela snicker. Jenkinson's comment about win-win not necessarily being nice-nice suddenly came to Ward's mind, as he realized he'd probably have to bang heads together to make them solve problems jointly. What Jenkinson meant by *teamwork* suddenly appeared in a different light. *Teamwork* was not a matter of people getting along, but of them solving difficult problems together. Logistics and production didn't need to be friends, they just had to be able to agree on workable compromises.

"With a leveled production plan, every week you generate the daily detail for the next week, plus the next 11 weeks to check that your assumptions are correct over the month."

Everyone nodded.

"Once a month," Amy continued, "you look a bit further out and generate a six-month capacity plan. We all know that each vehicle follows a certain life-cycle. Something like this.

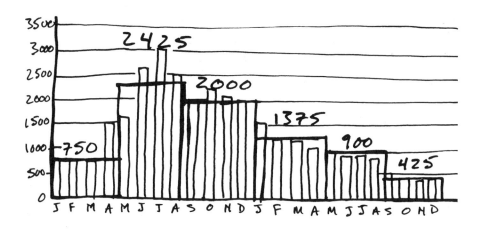

"But we don't exactly know how and when. How long will ramp-up take? When will the sales peak? When will volumes crash? So with sales, logistics, and production we generate a plan for:

- Monthly *leveled* volume by product family.
- Utilization of nondedicated equipment.
- Necessary labor.
- Target stock of finished goods and WIP.
- Target number of shifts."

"And we regenerate monthly the next six months?" asked Chandon.

"Absolutely. In fact, we keep checking our assumptions against real customer behavior."

"But that would lead us to create stock in advance," worried Ward. "Overproduction!"

"Good thinking! This is where it all gets interesting," smiled Amy. "There's a constant tension between *leveling* and overproduction, of course. No one said it was easy. On the one hand, plans are always wrong, and, on the other, planning is everything. What I usually suggest is that the person in charge of producing the proposed level plan also keeps a journal of planning rules, which are updated as we learn to plan more accurately.

"Don't forget that the other side of the story is *flexibility*. As you become more proficient at fragmenting production lots and mixing production batches to get closer to product level *takt time*, you will be far more prepared to cope with surprises. This is another paradox, but you have to live through it to realize just how true it is."

"What about suppliers?" interrupted Chandon. "We have absolutely no control over them—it's all central purchasing."

"Same debate," replied Amy brightly. "You have no control over suppliers, but you do have control over the information you send them. If one week you ask for 100 parts, and then the next for 600, what can they do? They'll deliver what they have in stock and reschedule the rest and ship it when they can. Or if you ask for parts twice in the same week, but then none in the next three weeks. You're doing to your suppliers what your customers are doing to you. You can decide not to do this: same quantities, same frequency, and warning them well in advance of plan changes. No scoop—that's the secret."

"If we create a *leveled* production plan reference by reference, it should be possible to break it down by component and send this to suppliers."

"Absolutely. It's called *a plan for every part*. In a lean supply chain, the customer sends the supplier their production plan weekly: a week's firm orders and the forecast for the rest of the month part by part. The point is to assume that every time a supplier misdelivers, *we* did something to make it impossible to deliver."

"How!" exclaimed Chandon, indignant. "Impossible!"

"*Si*, possible," fired back Amy. "Think it through. Imagine you haven't ordered a component for a long time, and you hit the supplier with a stock replenishment order for a huge batch. They'll send you what they've got in stock, and schedule the rest for production. But unless you're a very important customer, the chances are that your own batch will get into the queue with the others, and they'll take their sweet time producing it. On the other hand, if you expect the supplier to deliver the same quantity of parts daily and warn them well in advance of any changes, they have far less reasons to default. I'm not saying they won't, mind you. But you will find out earlier, and as you talk to them more often, you can figure out what to do quicker."

"*Teamwork* again," muttered Ward. "With the supplier this time."

"Why not? Mark Neville just got chastised by Toyota, who told him that 99.9 percent delivery might sound good, but to them that still meant 1,000 missed deliveries per million."

"You're kidding!"

"They're not. They gave a lecture on how we needed a stronger 'business interruption' risk-management system. Apparently, they're constantly watching out for reasons a supplier might have not to deliver. Poor old Mark got dragged to the plant at 11 p.m. the other night because Toyota worried the parts *might* not be in the truck. It turned out the parts were, but there had been a mixup with manifests, so they were worried. Toyota has three requests:

1. Bad news first—there actually is a "bad news" hotline.
2. Talk immediately and plan safety stocks.
3. People management.

"Listen, there's nothing miraculous about Toyota. They're just another big company with their share of issues. They're just more precise on many topics. They believe in fixing things *now*!"

"The point is we should take responsibility for our supplier's deliveries," nodded Ward thoughtfully.

"You're crazy!" exclaimed Chandon, raising her eyes to the ceiling in exasperation.

"Never stopped me before," he grinned.

Teamwork means getting functions to work together, Ward repeated to himself as he left that meeting. Sure, all the pull stuff was interesting, but this particular idea struck him as one answer to his management problem that was not just possible to achieve, but might have a real impact as well. He'd never seen *teamwork* in that light before, and the notion of extending this to both customers and suppliers was simply brilliant, if obvious. Getting them to work together meant getting them to solve problems together. Suddenly, he grasped why weekly production planning with all the key functions was so important. It meant creating a platform for the functional managers to work together on a recurring problem. Come to think of it, that's what a *pull system* did as well. He'd have to think of other instances where he could set up such occasions for his managers to work together. Finally, he thought, with a renewed sense of hope, finally he was getting somewhere.

"To foster *teamwork*, I've got to twist people's arms to get them to solve problems jointly, is that it?" asked Ward, testing his new insight, as they munched on their horrid sandwiches in the meeting room. The others had scattered to have lunch and check their desks.

"And *clear direction*, Phil would argue," answered Amy thoughtfully, as she picked the ham and cheese out of the bread and mayonnaise. "Diet time again," she explained, making a funny face. Ward kept his expression blank, biting back a smile. He'd been lucky to get his mother's gift for eating as much of any junk he wanted and never take on an ounce. Unlike his dad, who'd started piling on the weight come middle age. Or maybe he'd not got to that stage yet. In any case, living with Claire had taught him how deadly dangerous the "diet" topic was—next thing to religion. Don't go there, mate.

"Where does *clear direction* come in?" he wondered. "Problems come at us from every side, day in and day out."

"Yup. But to cement your team, you've got to pick a few typical problems they'll work on continuously."

"Such as *leveling*? This is what I was thinking," he said through a mouthful. "Baguette's the best part of a sandwich, by the way."

"Don't remind me," she sighed. "Yeah, *leveling*. In fact, leveling is one aspect of a larger problem, which is material stagnation. If we go back to basics and *value-stream mapping*, we can see that it takes about a minute to make a part on the press, and then a few minutes, tops, to assemble it. But if you run a four-hour batch, now it takes 240 minutes to move a part from the press to assembly and so on."

"I know, the value-added time is two minutes but the lead time can add up to days."

"From a lean point of view, your production lead time is made up of a few minutes of processing time and hours of stagnation time. The objective is to reduce stagnation."

"Parts stagnation—I guess I can visualize this."

"Bob usually distinguishes four typical causes of part stagnation:

- *The batch size*: Obviously if your production batch covers four days of consumption, which is, say, one hour of production, in terms of lead time we're looking at one hour processing time plus four days' waiting time. The last part of the batch will be used one hour and four days after being ordered.

- *Complicated flows*: In the same way, it happens if you've got a complicated flow. Say you've got a subcontracting loop in the flow and lots of different cells, the time it takes for one product to go through the flow is much longer than if it can move singly through the process. You've actually found this out when you created the cells. Basically, anytime you split and merge processes, you're creating stagnation, and when you've ordered a specific part it's hard to know when it will come out of the mess. The other problem, of course, is tracking quality issues through a complex process.

- *Lack of takt time thinking*: Another typical case is when production doesn't grasp *takt time*. Basically, they schedule production according to machine and operator availability and capacity. So we quickly produce several hundred parts of one type on a machine, then move the operator to do the same on another reference. This creates stagnation as it 'batches' parts again, even on dedicated equipment, rather than getting the machine to work at *takt time* and have one operator handle several machines at once. The typical problem here is that no one believes strongly enough in pacing production according to the sales pace—leveled sales pace, that is.

- *Poor transport and logistics*: If we can't move small quantities of everything all the time, we will group order, and, again, create stagnation. This is what happens when you pick up parts on the line every hour, but the customer's truck only comes once a day. Now say that, instead of having one truck picking up one part number at a time, a truck an hour picks up a little bit of everything. You've taken the stagnation away.

"We're trying to do bits of all of this," protested Ward.

"Not denying it," answered Amy. "The point I'm trying to make is that to create teamwork, you've got to get people together on *typical problems*. One such problem is stagnation, which can be broken down in various aspects, and then more and more detailed. This is why lean takes perseverance: It's a *system*, and it takes time to get it all to fit together. It takes teams to see the connections, and to address them not simply as points to be optimized but problems to root out and eliminate so work can flow. As you understand it better, you can keep your teams working on these typical problems."

"They'll never solve the problem completely, but they'll get better and better at it," thought Ward. "Back to sports again. The problem you need to solve tends to be simple, such as run faster than your neighbor, but to crack it you need to get into a more and more detailed understanding of what running means."

"Shared understanding. That's the key," agreed Amy. "As you create shared understanding because they've been at the front together, they also learn to stop throwing the hot potato at each other—"

"Like they're doing now!" sighed Ward.

"Yes, they do. *And* they start helping each other. Much like operators will when you've created a cell and you run it in *single-piece flow*."

"So it's all my fault again!" said Ward, chagrined. "I've been wondering for months what was wrong with them that they couldn't work together, passing the buck back and forth and casting stones in each other's ponds, and now you're saying that, as their manager, I haven't been able to define clear enough issues for them to work on together and—ha—bond. Wow."

"It's not just about comradeship and fellow feeling," she laughed. "Although that does matter. It's also a practical matter that people usually discuss information they all already know. Because we don't know how to disagree or how to listen, we keep rehashing what everybody knows. Party talk at work, sort of thing, like so," as she grabbed a pad and started scribbling:

"The trick is getting people to share information that only they know, and which is relevant to the others at that time. For this to happen, the group needs to be focused on getting one specific problem to solve."

"But why?"

"Hey, search me! I'm probably not explaining this right. You should talk to my husband, he's the expert on this psychology stuff. I'm just repeating what he says. Mike's view is that if I have special expertise, and mouth it off to you while your brain is switched on one of your own problems, you'll simply edit it out. He's got a great story about an experiment with seminary students. Two of his colleagues asked students at a Theological Seminary, as they arrived, to walk to another hall where they would be expected to give a talk on the 'Good Samaritan' parable. Along the way, the student subject of the experiment would stride past an actor impersonating a 'victim' slumped in a doorway. The experiment was set up so that subjects were either on time, in a hurry, or in a great hurry. Two-thirds of subjects that were in no hurry stopped to help, half of those in a moderate hurry stopped, and 10 percent of those that were in a great hurry stopped. Mike's point is that focus drives attention. Students with 'helping' thoughts are not any more likely to stop and actually, well, help.

"To a large extent this explains how many so-called lean experts can fully master the theory of lean—and walk past the most obvious wastes without noticing. Second, people in a hurry are less likely to help than others. In the lean context, this means that unless one makes a deliberate effort to stop rushing from one issue to the next and *look* at operations, one is very unlikely to see anything."

"*Go and see!*"

"Sure, but Mike says it equally applies to conversations. If we're not engaged in solving the same problem together, we won't discuss the information we each have and the other hasn't. By getting a team focused on a common problem, we can really leverage expertise by fitting the puzzle together. You know, like in the old war movies where all the experts hate each other's guts until it's time to blow the bad guy's base to smithereens, and then they coordinate perfectly."

"It all comes back to the use of expertise!"

"What else? This is industry, right? Making things starts with making people. So the trick to cooperation across functions is to get them all focused on solving a few typical problems in greater and greater detail."

"*Go and see* to share the understanding of the problem; *kaizen* to learn hands-on and challenge in solving it more and more precisely; *clear direction* to stay focused on typical problems; and *teamwork* to get people to cooperate across expert divides. Now I need to involve everybody all the time in the conversation. No way!"

"Guess what? It is a *management* method, ya know?"

"But what about individual responsibility?"

"What about it?"

"Well, if I'm focusing all my efforts on teams, won't people slack off? The one thing I'm not going to change my mind about is that things don't get done if you don't designate one person to get them done."

"You're totally right," she laughed. "Mike's got a few fun experiments about this, as well. Basically, if you hurt yourself in a crowd, no one will help you because they all think someone else will, and if there's only one person present, they'll be scared to get involved.

So if you twist your ankle and can't get up, the trick is to point at someone and say, 'You, sir, call an ambulance!'"

"If I'm right about individual responsibility, doesn't that contradict *teamwork*?"

"Not at all. You can still give one person the responsibility to solve a problem, but make sure they do so by involving the rest of the team."

"I thought there was supposed to be no 'I' in the word 'team'?"

"Consultant's blather. Listen, if you don't designate clear responsibility for problems, you won't get results. Teach people that they do not solve them on their own, but with all the people involved. In fact, you can give responsibility to solve problems to someone who has no authority on the subject."

"How can they have responsibility for a problem if they have no authority? They'll never get anything done!"

"That's where *you* come in: *teamwork*! You're the plant manager, for heaven's sake. Your continuous-improvement officer may have zero authority over the molding shop, but he still needs to coordinate the workshops and get the functional guys and the operators to collaborate to come up with a solution, doesn't he? How come?"

"If they don't," he grinned meanly, "I have a quiet chat with them about it."

"Don't even try to sound like Bob," she laughed. "But essentially, that's it. You've got authority to create *teamwork*, so you can give any one responsibility to problem-solve. They have to put the pieces together, talk to the experts, get them to agree on what the problem is, try out solutions, get every one to agree the solution is the right one, and so on."

"Like we're doing with Bob's quality analyses?"

"Exactly. Toyota's actually got a clear technique for it. They call it an A3 because it's supposed to fit on a sheet of A3 paper. Amy sketched out an A3, describing its parts as she went.

Title		DATE	Supervisor	Owner
Problem description		Root-cause analysis		
Grasp the situation		Countermeasure plan		
		Execution plan		
		Checking results		
Target		Follow up and learning points		

"*Title*: It might sound innocuous, but formulating the title of the *A3 report* is the first step to framing the problem correctly. The title must express correctly what the problem is in one succinct sentence. 'Machine X problem' is not the same as "Reduce grinder burn defectives from Machine X.

"*Owner*: Who's the owner of the problem? Who's the coach? Who's the supervisor? It might sound counterintuitive, but the A3 tool is not so much to solve problems, but to resolve the problem-solving/coaching relationship between boss and subordinate. *Teamwork* and developing individual competency go hand-in-hand.

"*Problem description*: Why is this a problem, and how big is the problem? The manager and the team member must agree on the scope of the problem. The employee must be coached to express the problem as a gap to a standard. For instance, the machine produces 3 percent defects, which is 10 times the production standard, and leads to an extra burden of so much in special transports, or extra costs, or ergonomic burden, and so forth. With the problem description, the employee has to quantify both the gap with the standard and the business impact of the problem in a way that talks to the manager. This might sound trivial, but in actual practice it is often difficult to do. The information needed to communicate this is rarely available, which forces the person creating the A3 to go speak with people about what's going on. The manager can coach the employee to seek the information outside of their immediate area, and scope the problem in a way to better understand the *importance* it has. By and large, if they can't come up with a historical series on one key indicator and compare it to standard, the A3 author hasn't understood the problem correctly.

"*Grasp the situation*: Properly grasping the situation means correctly identifying the *point of cause*: the exact place and the reason the process goes wrong. First you survey the landscape to find the real problem, then you keep digging down until you reach the source. Defects do not occur by magic. Defects are created because somewhere along the normal process some work is done wrong. Before trying to analyze causes, one has to correctly identify *where* the process goes wrong. To do so, the manager must help the employee draw out the technical process as it's supposed to happen theoretically, and then look at the reality of things, identifying all the places where things could go wrong. The employee must list each and every factor, and then experiment with each one until they find the one factor that accounts for the biggest chunk of the problem. A Pareto has to be drawn to show that coolant contamination is the No. 1 cause of the machine creating this specific type of defect. The point of cause is identified, as is the main factor affecting it.

"This is already quite a difficult analysis since factors must be tested one by one in real life, and many people think this is the end of the analysis: it's actually just the start. In doing this, the manager is training the employee to follow the scientific method of hypothesis testing. It might seem heavy-handed in industrial conditions, but that's exactly what any physics lab would be expected to do when exploring any issue.

"*Set a target*: Once the situation has been properly understood by having identified the point of cause, a clear target can be agreed upon between the manager and the employee. This target must be challenging enough to avoid simply working harder at the existing method—it must be created to encourage a radical rethink of the method, a stretch target that should still be reachable in one go. Setting the proper target to challenge the employee without completely discouraging them is a key managerial skill, and an important relationship-building moment. Again, the employee proposes a target, and the manager discusses it back and forth until they reach an agreement.

"*Root-cause analysis*: Having agreed on a target, the manager must now coach the employee in asking 'Why?' repeatedly until the root cause for the problem is found. Knowing that the coolant has been contaminated is the beginning of the analysis, not the end. Replacing the coolant is the immediate countermeasure. Learning why the coolant has been contaminated without anybody spotting it is the next question. The *Five Whys* exercise can be almost seen as a murder investigation: 'Why?' should be asked of the person who actually does this part of the work, which means following leads throughout the organization. *Teamwork*. There is one owner to the A3, but the only way this person will solve the problem correctly is that they speak to all the relevant actors. In the end, they might not be able to satisfy every one, but every opinion and angle has been considered seriously. Again, this exercise has as much to with building relationships as it does conducting clear analysis: in order to get the right facts the employee must speak with the people doing the work, find a way to get the meaningful facts from them, and learn to listen without bending the facts to their theories. Here the manager must help by opening the right doors and keeping the worker focused on the process as well as the results.

"So, you still with me on this," asked Amy, looking to see that Ward was keeping up.

"Yeah, yeah," Ward responded, nodding thoughtfully. "I think so."

"*Countermeasure plan*: Having identified a few root causes, the employee must now identify countermeasures to address the cause. This is another delicate moment, as the manager will accept no less than two or three possible actions for each cause. A single solution is unacceptable, and not just because it's likely to be obvious and costly: presenting *the one* answer contradicts the spirit of the scientific method. This is a key point. There are no 'solutions'—only hypotheses that need testing. In lean, as in the scientific method, every action we carry out is a hypothesis we test. In order to truly understand the problem, we should never have a single hypothesis—if we can't think of numerous viable alternatives, we haven't understood the problem fully. The team member must detail several countermeasures, and then explain their relative cost and effect on the problem to explain exactly why people should recommend one rather than the other. In some cases, we'll pursue different alternatives just to learn.

"*Execution*: Once the actions have been agreed upon, the A3 author creates an execution plan. The employee proposes a timeframe for the manager to challenge. He will also point out what practical steps may have been overlooked. Again, the best execution plan will surprise none of the individuals involved, since they should have been consulted as part of the process, and not simply assigned target dates and goals.

"*Checking results*: Once the action has been implemented, the results must be checked carefully. Again, this is a managerial problem: Employees would rather move on to something else. They find the *check* part of the *PDCA* particularly burdensome unless managers stress its importance. Two things need to be checked. First the effectiveness of the countermeasure on solving the initial problem, but also the impact on the cost of the overall process. Lean is about getting better results from fewer resources. So if the solution increases the overall cost of the process, it can't be very lean, can it?

"*Followup and learning points*: If the solution proves to be effective, chances are it would apply elsewhere, such as with new equipment or in the next parts design. The key to lean design is to weave shop-floor solutions back into the process or product for the next cycle. It's a powerful training exercise to get the employee to go and address the issue with engineers in terms of impact for the next generation of machines or products. Also, every problem solved often uncovers other issues, which can now be detailed for further consideration."

Amy paused. "In essence you create a communication protocol, sort of an like an internet protocol, so that every one in the company can read and understand what this is about."

"More *teamwork*."

"Bob's criteria for a good A3 is that you can read through it in a minute or less. His take on engineers is that they're only as good as their portfolio of A3s. I personally feel he's a bit extreme on this, but that's the idea. Think of it as a fashion model's portfolio for engineers."

"There's a thought," laughed Ward.

"Let me stress that, to me, the key thing in this format are these two little boxes, which indicate manager or mentor, and subordinate or mentee. Because the real paradox about teamwork is that it's all about individual development."

"You've lost me there," said Ward, making them two cups from the espresso machine he'd personally brought to work.

"*Individual development* is the ultimate aim of *teamwork*. Mike has all sorts of theories explaining this, but what it all comes down to is that we learn in groups far more effectively than we do individually."

"Is that true?"

"Why the workshops? Why the CEO visits?"

"You're right," Ward agreed thoughtfully, thinking of his own steep learning curve and how much he hated the CEO visits, but admitting at the same time how much he'd actually learned from them.

"We're apes with an overgrown forebrain, according to my husband. Thinking is a lot less fun than gossiping. Our social learning is far more developed than our intellectual one. So the trick is to create a social occasion of learning—solving problems in groups. Which is also a great setting for learning from other people's expertise and experience."

"We've got a good example here," noted Ward. "The young quality technician: Since she's taken up the quality root-cause analysis, she's progressed incredibly by working with Carela and Muller. Malika keeps having to call her in when we're discussing detailed issues."

"Has Bob ever given you his 'managers must be teachers' speech?"

"Um, no. Phil did."

"Yeah, he would," she smirked. "Took him long enough to get it!"

By now, Ward accepted that Amy had known Jenkinson before he had become the fearsome "lean manager" he now was. Nonetheless, he was continually surprised by how openly she spoke of Phil's challenges along the path. He found this reassuring in a way, since the fact that Jenkinson could learn this made the whole thing feel more approachable. And yet the closer he got to the mountain, the larger it appeared. The more he learned, the more he found there was to learn. There seemed to be no end to that stuff, which was probably the whole point, but it could get kind of overwhelming at times.

"Managers must be teachers. Sounds great, but hard to do, don't you find?"

"Tell me about it."

"Lean tradition actually has an implicit theory about it," Amy said. "One, *you learn by doing.* Two, *you learn better in a team.* Three, *teams learn if they try to solve problems together.* They learn by confronting each other's perspectives while seeking a common solution. *Teamwork* is about developing individual competence, because the skill lies in rolling the three together. Individuals will learn by being part of a team that learns to solve problems by trying and trying.

"I'll admit that I was an HR manager, so I'm biased, but to me the core of Toyota's success is that it continuously trains people so that they know more, and so that they are developed to the full potential of their abilities. By working with the front-line teams in solving detailed problems and drawing the right conclusions, it develops waste-free solutions to industrial problems, which over time, gives it an edge nobody can copy. It's not born of one brilliant individual's solution that can be copied and pasted. Their edge comes from the cumulative, shared experience of all their staff in running equipment and processes. Just try and catch up!"

"I'll show you something on your shop floor," she smiled, and made Ward wince silently, knowing he was in for another beating.

They went straight to the fateful No. 7 press, where an operator was picking up parts from the press conveyor and assembling a small insert in a large square machine before placing the completed part in a large container. Ward now fully shared the lean frustration with large customer containers—you simply couldn't do anything with these things. These large metal boxes blocked the proper design of the work cells, were impossible to move safely, and made the half-hour pickup of parts awkward. They were a royal pain in the butt. Why couldn't OEMs understand how much more effective small plastic KLTs would be on their assembly lines as well? Amy picked up the one part in the red bin, which was correctly marked as a startup part. There was nothing wrong with it, but the quality procedure said the first part had to be scrapped.

"How can I tell if it's a *good* part or a *bad* part?"

"I know what you're going to ask. When was the last time Jerome, here, was trained? He works on this station every day, you know. He could probably train us."

"So where are the boundary samples? How is this person being developed?"

"Ah, you're right. I've managed to get my team to stick to red bins and do some root-cause analysis but they've—sorry, *I've* not forced the issue on training."

"*Teamwork* works in both dimensions," she explained. "It means cooperation across functions and cooperation across the hierarchy."

"I know. I need to move forward with team leaders and supervisors."

"Team leaders are there to constantly show other operators what is standard and what is not. Supervisors are there to train operators to quality standards and standardized work—and to support *kaizen*. Training people to do the job well is our obsession."

"You're struggling with your *pull system* because you're so focused on fixing the parts flow, you haven't improved enough the *knowledge flow*. Lean is about walking on two feet: one foot is *improving the flow of good parts at lower cost*, but the other is *involving and developing people*. If you only hop along on one foot, sooner or later you'll fall flat on your face."

"But I am developing people," protested Ward. "We're doing workshops right, left, and center. We're involving operators."

"You still don't get it, Andy," she shook her head. "A few token operators here and there in workshops won't cut it. You're not addressing the problem. By setting up the *pull system*, you're organizing the flow of parts and the flow of information. But people-wise, you're still fixated on developing the 10 brains around you. You haven't created an organization that trains every operator every day. As a result, you're depriving yourself of both their involvement and their ideas."

"But I do work a lot more with the supervisors," Ward insisted defensively. "We've discussed Phil's *clear direction* idea, and we've decided to have quarterly plans by sector, and I do a daily visit with each supervisor to see how we're progressing. And we are making progress! It's finally beginning to show up in the numbers."

"You're not hearing me," she insisted with her classic toothy smile, taking the sting out of her tone. "You are involving your supervisors, which is great. But that's only two more people you've added to your small group of brains. We want them *all*! The factory looks like a different place, which is also great."

"Yeah, Muller is hopeless with the paperwork, but he's imposing a tough discipline on the place. We've got visual management now, too. Look over there: when one crate overbites the alley, we can see it. Excuse me."

There was indeed a large metal container half-way into the alley. Bloody containers!

"Hey!" Ward yelled, flagging down a material handler. "You just drove past this twice already. Feel free to straighten it up.

"How many times do I have to repeat …," he muttered, as Amy gave him a thoughtful look. Gone was the timid plant manager she'd first met. This new Ward had teeth, and both bark and bite. She'd tried to warn him that becoming a martinet was hardly the solution to the plant's problems.

"Visual management is much better," she agreed, "but you are not managing the training of *every* operator. You're obtaining discipline from compliance, not *teamwork*."

"I've got a plan," sulked Ward. "I'm just having trouble finding the people."

Actually, Carela had surprised him by coming up with half a dozen other names for possible team leaders. He'd also suggested an injection supervisor he knew as a possible supervisor. The guy was very experienced, and when his factory had been restructured recently, he'd taken the redundancy package. But he was now bored silly at home, doing construction odd jobs. Carela said he'd mentored him in his first job, before joining Alnext, and that the guy would probably be willing to take the job. Busy as he was with everything else, Ward had duly noted but not acted on any of it yet.

"There are two strands to the lean DNA, Andy," Amy said. "You organize the value stream of products, and you organize the value stream of people. If you keep hopping along on one foot, it won't be sustainable, and you'll get yourself into trouble. I've seen it happen before."

Amy had stayed over that weekend, but Ward hadn't seen much of her until Saturday evening dinner. Saturdays were by far Claire's busiest days, with all the weekend riders descending on Malancourt, and the nonstop riding lessons and jumping coaching sessions, particularly now that the competition season was about to start. Amy had spent the entire day at the stables, captivated by the club coming to life. It was as much of a social place as a riding facility, with clients spending as much time gossiping while they groomed their animals as they did riding them. Most of these people saw each other every weekend. They were a close-knit group who tolerated Ward as prince consort, but had nothing much to say to him. He didn't share their inexplicable passion for hoofed quadrupeds of the equestrian persuasion. And so Saturdays had become Ward's day with Charlie. He found having to spend the day with a two-year old brought him back to the basics of life on earth, but these days he found himself restless and impatient. Work was clearly preying on his mind more than it ever had. Claire had mentioned it a couple of times, and he'd refused to hear it, but the thought grated.

Amy had been very good about not bringing lean to the dinner table. She was brimming with her day with Claire, and they'd resolved that she have her first riding lesson the following day, when things had settled down at the club. In fact, Ward had been the one to come back to the lean topic, causing Claire to raise her eyebrows and take her leave, carrying a squirming, screaming Charlie to bed.

Ward also wanted to hear more of how three unlikely characters—Amy, Bob, and Jenkinson—had met. Jenkinson and Amy's husband Mike had been childhood friends. When Jenkinson had expanded his fledging first company and found himself in dire straits, Mike convinced his father to help out. Amy—fast-food restaurant manager and then HR manager at a dot.com company that had gone under—was hired by Jenkinson's business partner as HR manager of their vacuum circuit-breakers business. She saw Jenkinson as an overly bright guy who couldn't find his socks without his wife's help. Ward hadn't known this, but Jenkinson's wife Charlene had built a serious women's advocacy group from a home-based internet site she'd started when at home with their kids. Amy didn't sound like she'd warmed to the woman much, but she was certainly impressed by what she'd achieved—systematically highlighting salary differences between men and women in industry, and supporting women suing their employer for discrimination with expert advice and data.

"Phil just likes to solve problems," she explained, dismissing the topic. "He sees business as a big, fancy chess game. It's a live, complex moving game to him, and that's what he loves about the business: the challenge of making it *work*. It's both his strength and his weakness. He's constantly surprised by how *personal* it is to most people. He grew up without much money, and all he's made doesn't touch him much. He's just scoring points with it. Charlene's the spender."

"Tell me more about A3s?" asked Ward. "How do I use them?"

"There you go again," Amy laughed. "'Wow, new tool! How do I apply it?'"

"You know what I mean."

"I know exactly what you mean. And you know that's not the right way of going about it."

"Right. Um. Rewind, start again. What's the problem I'm trying to solve?"

"You got it! So what is it?"

"Developing my people. I understand that I need to develop the line's ability to solve their own problems, but I also have to develop staff's expertise, haven't I?"

"What we're trying to do is grow 'T' people. The horizontal bar of the T means we want to develop people's understanding on the whole process surrounding them. The vertical bar of the T is about developing their expertise in their own specialist field."

"'T' for Toyota?" he jibed.

"I prefer to think 'T' for 'team,'" she replied, rolling her eyes. "*A3 reports* structure the *PDCA* management relationship. As with targets on a production analysis board, the responsibility for coming up with a good *A3 report* is shared by the manager and the author. The person creating the report has to give it their best shot, but the manager must steer the process along, maintaining motivation and driving toward more rigorous and thorough work. The very rigidity of the *A3 process* is the key to its power to change minds. Employees remain self-directed, autonomous, and empowered in searching for the right answers to the right questions, but they are never abandoned. The manager's role is to coach and steer them through the process until their 'aha' moment. To a large extent, problem-solving is a misnomer. *PDCA* is as much a knowledge transfer method as problem-solving per se. The relationship is built up on the fact that the manager maintains the integrity of the principles while the employee does all the leg work to solve the problems of their detailed implications.

"The team notion is far more important than many people realize. There are two aspects to this. We're talking A3s, but really it's about the manager-employee relationship. If you, as a manager, are keen to create a stable team, then you're not so keen on hire and fire. You've got to work with the people you have—"

"Make up your mind. On the one hand, you say I need the *right* people on the team, and on the other, I've got to keep stable teams. Kind of contradictory, don't you think?'"

"Bob's take on this is rather extreme," she laughed. "As usual. He says he'd replace anybody tomorrow if he found a better person for the job. But no matter how green the grass looks elsewhere, finding better people is often hard and takes time. So in the meantime, you've got to develop the people you've got. And if you're successful in this, they get better than any one you find on the market quickly."

Ward busied himself with serving more wine to hide his embarrassment at realizing that's exactly what Jenkinson must've done with him. Trying to get him up to speed as long as he did not find anyone better to run the Vaudon plant—or close it.

"The two dominant people management models are either 'Do what I tell you' or 'Do as you think best as long as you get the results.'"

"Bit of both, really. On some issues it's 'Do as I say,' and when it gets tricky it's 'You're on your own mate, but make the numbers.'"

"Lean management is radically different. It's 'Let's figure this out together.' It's based on creating a mentoring relationship with employees. So you see them often, and you try to get them to see things as you do, and to learn by solving detailed problems. More often than not, they'll teach you something as well."

"Yeah—and repeat, repeat, repeat."

"There's that, as well," she laughed. "That's what we do. *Level, level, level,*" she imitated Jenkinson's drawl and his serious frown.

"*Kaizen, kaizen, kaizen,*" chuckled Ward.

"You build relationships through the number of *PDCA* cycles you've done with people, and you progressively reframe their thinking in doing so."

"But it can't work with everybody, can it?"

"Nope. There is no magic bullet. There are two things you can't put in the person: wanting to show up in the morning and work hard, and the desire—or ability—to learn. With lean management you need a healthy dose of both, because people get easily discouraged by the constant rehashing of problems."

"Tell me about it!" Ward snorted.

"It completely depends on people," she waved the comment away. "Some thrive on it, some don't. The challenge is recognizing which people are which. Most companies will hire anyone off the street, and then expect them to perform. If that person doesn't work out, we just let them go. That's plain crazy. The process cost of hiring someone is huge, for one. Phil's got me working to improve the hiring and training processes with Nexplas' HR department. It's a complete nightmare. They don't see people as individuals. They just stuff bodies into slots. They drive me nuts."

"To get back to *A3s*," jumped in Ward. "I can use them to get someone to tackle a problem that is not in their area of expertise, because producing it requires them to communicate with the experts and so on. Or I can use it to encourage them to go into greater detail in their own field. Is that it?"

"Every staff member and every line manager should be working on an *A3* at any given time, that's essentially it. Remember *go and see*? You take them to the *gemba* and agree with them on what the problem is, and then you check regularly and get them to reformulate their *A3s* until you're satisfied—"

"Or until they quit on you!"

"There's that as well, yes," she chortled. "In either case … problem solved! Actually managing someone else's *A3* is probably just as difficult as doing the analysis proper—perhaps more."

"Listen," she said after a pause. "I'm not worried about *A3s* right now. Unless you are using them properly—within the right context— they're still nothing but nifty tools. I believe you're still missing the importance of teams. People don't work for you or for their wages. You can demotivate them with stupid policies or not enough money or being unpleasant. But nobody knows how to motivate anyone. People don't work for you, they work for their buddies—for their teammates. That's their motivation. So start at the bottom. You've been very focused on getting your line managers involved, which is well and good, but until you've got stable teams on the shop floor you haven't got a proper foundation to work with. The work team is the basic building block of everything we try to do."

"You have no idea what you're asking!" grumbled Ward. "Production wants to shift around because of—"

"Lack of *takt time* thinking," she cut in.

"Then the people themselves! They keep bickering all the time. I just don't know where to start."

"I understand very well, thank you. I ran a burger joint, remember. We had all this, and more. People not showing for work in the morning, new know-nothing students to teach in 10 minutes flat, stupid management policies, you name it. But one thing upper management did understand was teams. 'Community of fate,' they called it. But they did try. And, with hindsight, the restaurants where the managers *got it* did well, and those where they didn't, did poorly. We had daily start-of-shift meetings to discuss problems, and we did team events and so forth, even with the turnover due to the nature of the business. The point is that in completely adverse situations, we tried to create team spirit. So get your HR guy on it. It's his job!"

"My HR guy," sighed Ward, visualizing Deloin and his reticence in the face of the numerous conversations they'd had about setting up a team structure. "You just have no idea." To be honest, Muller was just as much a roadblock. He remained determined to staff whatever process needed operators with whomever he chose.

"I don't give a damn about who said what to whom," yelled Ward, slamming the desk so hard he hurt the palm of his hand. He'd had enough with the all this incessant squabbling. "Carole, you *will* accept the parts if they correspond to the weekly level parts. And Matthias, you don't change the plan because you've decided to schedule preventive maintenance. That's what the planning is all about. You're telling me you can't see maintenance coming from one week to the next? People!"

"I don't know if you've noticed, but I'm being kept busy with production these days," countered Matthias angrily. "The maintenance guys are left to themselves, and I can't be everywhere at once."

"Fancy that! Then get one of them to sit in the production-plan meeting! How hard can that be?"

Once again they'd finished the weekly management meeting at odds with each other. Ward was reaching the end of his tether. He was failing to get them to work together, that much was obvious. It was slow, frustrating work, and it seemed to him they'd find the most far-fetched excuses to pass the buck. As a result, he was becoming snappish, and routinely fell into the trap of telling them what to do rather than getting them to clarify the problem and solve it themselves. He could see it happening, which added to his frustration. But it was so hard to resist just fixing things, especially right now when they were so close to actually making this plant work. For the first month, the year's hard work was finally showing in their numbers. They were now significantly better than Neuhof in total inventory days, and he was fighting every other day with central purchasing to get the supplier batch sizes down. But it felt like squeezing blood out of a stone.

"May I speak with you for a minute?" asked Chadid, as they stepped out of the meeting room.

"Sure, I wanted to talk to you, as well. How come we still don't have quality boundary samples and self-check training for operators in place? Carela keeps asking me when we'll start. Haven't you guys discussed it together?"

She gave him a flat stare, not answering, and then turned her back on him without a word, leading the way to his office.

"Here's my letter of resignation," she said, offering a folded letter, as she shut the door behind him.

"You're quitting?" he flailed, astonished. Of all people he had not expected that from Chadid.

"Found another job nearer to Paris. Brings me back closer to my parents," she replied.

"Oh, dear. I don't know what to say," he babbled, almost speechless. "Is it good?"

"I'm going to work at corporate for a big automotive supplier. They were impressed with the work we've done on red bins," she said with the thinnest smile.

"Yeah. Yeah. We're progressing. Why quit now?" Ward realized he hadn't actually talked to Chadid in a long while, well, not since Stigler had had his fit, really. He did see her at red-bin reviews and management meetings, but they'd hardly ever crossed socially any more. In fact, he'd probably seen more of Lesueur lately, who'd badgered him into tagging along for customer visits, chasing after quality complaints. She was fine as a traveling companion, but certainly nowhere near as much fun as Chadid had been. All the younger woman would ever talk about were quality concerns. He'd tried to get her to gossip a couple of times, but she'd just clammed up, so he'd given up. He'd invited Chadid along several times, but she'd always declined for one reason or other, so he'd stopped asking. He wondered whether she'd been actively avoiding him.

"So why?"

"You don't really want to know," she answered darkly. She was a woman of strong emotions, and he could see *something* ready to burst out of her but had no idea what. He could tell it wouldn't be good.

"I do, come on, have a seat. Please tell me."

"You've become impossible to work with!" she said feelingly.

"Virginie doesn't seem to think so," he'd answered defensively. "She spends more time solving problems than you do."

Her face darkened further, her large black eyes flashing furiously.

"See. That's exactly what I mean. We used to talk, Andy. Now all I hear is that I've not done this, I've not done that. I'm not a *tool*, I'm a *person*. I can't work in that kind of environment."

He stared at her, aghast. True, they hadn't been lunching together like they used to, but—

"And I can't forgive how you've treated Olivier. That was vile!"

"How *I've?*" he protested, stunned. As Deloin had feared, rather than simply resign and look for another job, Stigler had talked to the wrong kind of lawyer, and was now building a case for unfair dismissal. The HR manager wasn't too worried about it because he had not been actually fired. They had offered him another job, but the whole thing still weighed on Ward.

"We were *friends*, Andy. For three years we held this place together, and now you treat us like *this*? Olivier was right all along. He saw it coming first. You've taken on all these airs, now that you're hobnobbing with the CEO. Well good for you, but I've had enough."

"Hey! This plant is still open, you'll notice. We were that close to being shut down, you'll remember? That close!"

"Yeah, you're such a big hero," she said dismissively. "I'm sure that's worth trampling a few people."

They just glared at each other in angry silence. There was nothing much to say. His throat tightening, Ward felt hurt. She was being patently unfair. She was using their work on lean as a springboard to a better job, but still blaming him. She was using them, and making it seem like *he* had betrayed *her*! That was a bit much. And as for being friends, what an odd thing to say! They'd been colleagues, and sure, friendly, but this was work! Did the woman expect an apology for him asking her to do her job? In any case, she was hardly ever on the shop floor unless she was forced to it. She opened her mouth to say something else, but didn't, and turned around without another word, sneering at him.

"Good luck," he said to the retreating back, but he doubted she'd heard him. He wasn't even sure he'd said it out loud.

"Mmh," he mumbled as he felt Claire slip into bed. "How did it go?"

"We saved the mare, but lost the foal," she whispered dejectedly. He reached out for her cheek in the darkness and felt the wetness of tears running down her face.

"Oh, baby," he muttered.

"I'll be fine. It was a long night."

"What's Charlie doing here?" he asked, realizing that the little boy had squeezed between them.

"Woke him up coming in," she sobbed, hugging them both together. "That's all right. I want to be with my men right now."

"No, I'm afraid you can't replace either Chadid or Stigler right now," said Coleman dryly on the phone. "Phil is putting a huge pressure on reducing staff structures. You'll have to make do."

"Fine," Ward agreed reluctantly, not particularly surprised. No one could blame him for trying. "I'll ask Bayard whether he's willing to take over quality as well as manufacturing engineering. We still haven't got any new products on the pipeline either, so—"

"Don't lose hope on that front. Things are looking up," volunteered Coleman mysteriously. Their relationship had definitely changed since he'd moved to Neuhof to take over the regional management. Ward felt Coleman was colder, more distant, but maybe he was imagining things. He certainly didn't see much of him, as the man spent most of his time in Neuhof. Coleman had been a welcome change from Beckmeyer, inasmuch as he concentrated exclusively on coordinating the financial side of the division. He left all the operational matters to Jenkinson, which deflated the conflict and confusion Beckmeyer had caused trying to manage every other matter centrally.

"How so?" wondered Ward, hoping that something would finally come his way. He needed good news like winter needed spring.

"Have you heard that Wayne resigned?" said Coleman, with a hint of glee in his voice. "He remains on the board, but he's no longer on the executive committee."

"What happened?" wondered Ward, recalling how Jenkinson had rubbed his hands in satisfaction when Sanders had kicked off hostilities in the open. He'd had his pound of flesh in the end.

"Long tale, but to cut it short, back when Jenkinson took over, he spent months working with engineering. One thing he was doing was reviewing all the innovation projects. One of his pet theories is he wants to establish a *takt time* of innovation, whatever that means. In any case, some of the guys still located in Ann Arbor said they were working on a top-range dashboard skin that looked so close to leather it was almost indistinguishable from the real thing—but about 10 times cheaper.

It was real promising, though the guys felt they needed probably a couple more years' development work before it could seriously be considered for a customer program. Phil's got strong views on separating innovation from development, and part of the argument he was having with Wayne at the time is that he would not allow untested innovations in client projects. Off the shelf only. Well, somehow or other, Wayne heard about this magic product, and actually sold it to an OEM. Of course, when the customer asked for it, engineering was nowhere near ready, no prototypes to show, nothing. Made a big flap. In the end, Phil forced Wayne out. He poached a guy from Honda to take over sales."

"I hadn't heard," answered Ward cautiously. "I'm sorry for Wayne, but how does that help me?"

"You didn't know?" asked Coleman in mock surprise. "Wayne has been calling for Vaudon's closure all along. He's almost made it a *casus belli* with Phil, kept explaining to James Mahoney that there was room for only one plant in Western Europe. Everything else had to move East if we wanted to remain competitive."

"Isn't that what you thought, as well?" asked Ward, wondering why he was feeling so bellicose these days. He'd always known Coleman in the awed shadow of Wayne Sanders. Now Sanders was gone, and Coleman was European VP. Such was the way of corporate, but still, hearing him so pleased with himself irked.

"Me? For a while, sure. But Phil has shown us a completely different way to look at costs, hasn't he? In any case, that means you're off the hook."

"I'll be off the hook when I get new business for this plant," replied Ward sullenly.

"We've further reduced our defects with this," said Ward, showing Jenkinson a standard board they'd put in on every cell and workstation.

"When the operators take the workstation at the beginning of the shift or after a changeover, they've got to check that:
- The station is clean.
- The first part is OK.
- They've been trained.
- The parameters of the machine are OK.
- The first-level maintenance has been done.

If any of these items is not satisfactory, they've got the instruction not to start work until the supervisor has personally checked and told them to go ahead."

"Good," acknowledged Jenkinson. "And you've got supervisors working shifts?"

"Not yet, we're still looking for the right people. I've interviewed many, but I've grown cautious in hiring. Better no one than the wrong person, right?"

Jenkinson nodded assent, but said nothing. It was a warm July day, and the plant was hot, the smell of injection noticeable everywhere. The CEO was doing the plant tour on his own, in his uniform jean shirt and beige slacks, questioning details, arguing points.

"I'm very impressed with this quality kid—"

"Virginie Lesueur? Yes, she's turning out well. I still think she's a bit young to take over as quality manager, but I've got the engineering manager covering for both functions at the moment."

The plant looked good. They'd started the visit with shipping and spent a long time with Muller and Chandon discussing the detailed use of the *leveling box*. All in all, the system functioned. Now Jenkinson was pushing them deeper and deeper into understanding local causes.

"Good work," he repeated.

"Problem is," complained Ward, "that I think we're reaching the limit of what we can do here in terms of productivity. We've barely got any temps left. We're no longer doing weekend shifts. The presses still aren't loaded. I can't keep taking heads out of the business without starting to make people redundant. We've still got a couple of areas without proper team-leaders; since we've decided never to hire extra people for this position but use operators liberated by the *kaizen* process, I can still free up a few people to create the remaining team leaders, so the decision is not urgent-urgent. But sooner or later, we'll have to face it."

"We'll do it if we must," said the CEO, "but I tend to agree with you. Particularly in this social context. I'd rather not go to war over this right now.

"However, on the volume front, I think we can do something," Jenkinson continued. "First, I can now confirm you are getting the new diesel filter. Apparently, the OEM plant itself argued that they wanted to work with Vaudon specifically. They've had many problems, but they've been very pleased with how you've worked with them to solve issues. You can be proud of yourself on this one, since the plan was to take this part to Slovakia. The part stays here. You'll be working with their engineers and ours in Neuhof on the new model."

Ward could have whooped with joy. He'd been worried ragged about this one, waiting to hear the verdict with nail-biting anxiety.

"More immediately," continued Phil evenly, "we need capacity in the Czech plant. It injects a couple of parts without assembly for French final assembly. When you factor in the transport cost and the fact that the part has no assembly work content, it doesn't make any sense. So since you've got press capacity here, and we need some there, I think we're going to bring them back after the summer."

"Will the customer agree?" Ward asked, elated, but not daring to hope.

"I don't see why not. We're not changing the pricing, and they should make a saving on the transport cost since the parts are ex-works. Yes, I know they pushed us to put these parts in low-cost in the first place, but things have changed. Minds are changing as well."

"Brilliant. Brilliant," repeated Ward. It was an understatement: he was ecstatic. The proof of the pudding was in getting volume from making the plant more attractive, and finally, finally, all their hard work was paying off. What a relief!

"That's the good news," said Jenkinson, looking around at the presses. "Now let's go back to work. What are your main problems?"

"You mean, besides volume?" Ward replied glumly. He didn't want to do this right now. He wanted to celebrate success! Take a breather. Enjoy the moment.

"We're all right mostly," he said without much enthusiasm.

"Come on, Andy. You've only showed me things that've worked. How do you want me to help if you don't show me your *problems*."

"Right. Here's one. Our absenteeism is going through the roof."

"Is it? Why?"

"I'm not sure," shrugged Ward, having picked up the Gallic gesture for "out of my hands." "We've had a lot of overtime in June to compensate for all the bank holidays in May. It's sunny outside, people take days off. I don't really know."

"What does your HR think?"

"Ah," Ward acknowledged unhappily. "He thinks we're driving people too hard."

"And are you?"

"What do you expect?" he replied hotly. "We're completely transforming the culture of this plant. So, yes, we've got a zero-tolerance approach. Muller can be abrupt at times. But you have no idea how hard it is to instill a semblance of discipline in this place. Look around. Can't you see it?"

Jenkinson looked at the plant again, and he had to admit it was transformed. Most of the systems were up and working. The plant was orderly. Noticeably, there were no more forklifts in the press area, where trains now came by frequently to pick up small containers of parts. Ward had decided once and for all that he'd take the risk and the cost of double-handling of the parts in the logistics area to reconstitute the large customer containers. There were still a lot of discussions over this, but he thought it was worth it. He didn't mention it too loud, because he knew he didn't know how to be precise on the *check* in this case. On some issues, he was willing to go ahead on faith alone. He acknowledged this wasn't right, but, hey, sometimes you've just got to do what you've got to do.

"There are very few comments on the production analysis boards," Jenkinson pointed out.

Ward bit off an angry comeback. It was true.

"How about production films?" The data was collected, but yes, comments were few and far between. Jenkinson pursed his mouth disapprovingly, but said nothing for a while. Ward knew him well enough by now to know he was picking his words.

"Do you remember Bob detailing lean management a while back? At the convention?"

"Sure."

"Bob presented the two pillars of lean management. One was *continuous improvement*, the other was *respect for people*. I can see you've done a great job on the first one, continuous improvement. You're doing *go and see*, *kaizen* and giving the plant a *clear direction*. And this is paying off.

"But if you consider that only the left legs of the table are important and you ignore the right legs ... your table won't hold. You've got to do the work on *respect for people: teamwork* and *respect*, as well. Can you count up to two? One, *continuous improvement*, two ..." Jenkinson insisted, counting with his fingers and flexing his index in Ward's face, "two, people involvement. When do you intend to get started on that? Have you got a suggestion system in place yet?

"What is it with you people!" exploded Ward, suddenly furious. "It's always more, more, more, isn't it? You wanted results—you got them! What more do you want from me? No I haven't put in place any suggestion scheme!" he realized he was shouting.

"It's not more, it's better," answered Jenkinson calmly, his finger unconsciously pushing his glasses back on the bridge of his nose, his only sign of agitation.

"Respect for people! Hah!" Ward heard himself exclaim, unable to stop. "That's rich coming from you! You've been firing people all over the place. Use them up and replace them, that's respect, right?"

"What on earth are you talking about?" asked Jenkinson, looking genuinely puzzled.

"Take Wayne Sanders. Made this company. Made the whole thing happen. Put the deal together, but he gets in your way, and you coolly set him up until, good-bye, thank you very much, sorry about that old chap, sure you'll understand." Why the hell was he defending Wayne Sanders? he wondered, too angry to stop. Wayne Sanders, Olivier Stigler, Malika Chadid. How many do we have to lose on the way?

"I never wanted to get rid of Wayne Sanders," said the CEO with exaggerated care, taking his glasses off.

"The hell you didn't! We're all pawns in a game, aren't we? Tools to be dropped when a better one is found?"

"I didn't—" repeated Jenkinson raising his eyebrows, surprised Ward would think differently. When the man got serious, he had a tendency to get in your face, which meant that you had to look up to him hulking over you. "Wayne is an excellent salesman, and if you insist on talking chess, why would I want to lose such an asset, regardless of whatever else happened? The trouble is that he cut too many corners. He created too many problems with customers. Every new incident damaged our reputation, and hurt our future capability to sell. My job is not just to secure next year's cash flow, but a revenue stream for the next 10 years.

"Have you ever wondered why Alnext's automotive division got itself in such a bad shape?"

"Lack of productivity in the plants?" guessed Ward, trying to calm down, wondering what on earth had come over him. He had yet to see Jenkinson angry, and suddenly felt like he'd rather not.

"No more than most of the industry's players. Productivity is a large part of the issue, but not the immediate cause. What happened is that bad product launches cost the division its entire margin. Wayne's focus on selling anything to anyone and worrying later about whether it could be made or not cost the division millions he never acknowledged because it was all a production problem—leave all that to the plants. The reality of it is that launches start the moment you first talk to the customer.

"And productivity is a large part of the problem because until we've 'cleared the window' as you've done in this plant, it's very hard to understand in detail why launches are such a disaster. So you've done a good job, yes, but it's only the beginning, and you haven't even completed it, not by a far stretch. We need plants that sustainably deliver *kaizen* over time because *gemba* is a great teacher, and this is where we'll learn to make profitable products that start at the planned level of ppms and capacity, and which can be perfected as quickly as possible.

"So Wayne didn't go because he'd pissed me off or because he was in my way. Wayne left because *customers come first*. People who buy drills don't want drills: they want holes. Wayne is a gifted salesman but never understood that if you only focus on what people think they want and not what they actually need, you end up selling yourself into a corner. This is exactly what happened to Alnext Automotive, and it sure as hell is not going to happen on my watch."

"I don't know what's wrong with me," Ward told Claire when he got home, out of sorts and angry with himself. "Jenkinson is bringing business into the plant, and I jump down his throat." He'd returned home early, just after Jenkinson had left. It was a glorious afternoon, and Claire was exercising old Pagui in the pasture as Charlie looked on from the inflatable pool he was splashing in, naked as a worm in the summer heat. She unhooked the lead, and the gray horse immediately set down to graze.

"You just need a holiday, baby." She looked at him worriedly.

"Well, if he doesn't fire me for yelling at him, I think the plant's safe for the near future."

"Hey!" she smiled warmly. "You've done it! I'll get the champagne."

"I thought we only celebrated bad news," he grinned.

"Who says we need a reason?" she laughed.

She could tell how pleased he was, like a schoolboy with a prize. But she also could see the toll this year had taken. He'd started taking things so seriously lately, to the point of arguing in shops and restaurants, something he'd never hitherto comprehended about the French's God-given right to get upset with anyone anywhere. He'd even used what she called his "plant manager's" voice at home a couple of times when things didn't go his way. Not that it got him very far— you don't try a shouting match with a practicing *maître de manège*. Andy had always had an easy way with people because authority games simply didn't touch him. He didn't care. But turning this plant around was changing him. He had not taken any of his long walks through the woods in ages. She prayed that the pressure would ease off now that he'd finally been getting results. She never thought he would be susceptible to burnout, but he had her worried lately. He often joked that the only driving force of the universe he believed in was irony. Now, saving the plant only to crash and burn over it, that would be ironic.

Irony of ironies, he was succeeding. The latest concept they'd been discussing back and forth was Phil's singular take on *teamwork*. She'd always understood *teamwork* to more or less mean a strong version of "getting along." Certainly, *teamwork* at the center involved little more than sharing the chores and keeping a civil tongue even when the pressure went up, as during competitive jumping. But from what she heard from Andy, *teamwork* in Phil's specific sense meant to get different functions to work together at solving problems. In fact, as with the other key principles of *go and see*, *managing means improving* and *clear direction*, Andy generally felt he was floundering. Certainly, not one evening passed these days without him coming home overflowing with his difficulties and issues of getting his staff to work together. And still, little by little, she could see he was making progress. Many of the discussions, debates, and occasional arguments arose precisely because they were working together and strong individuals with set opinions rarely give in without a fight. People were solving problems together across job lines, and up and down the food chain, she could hear it. Yet, to Andy, headway always seemed dramatically slow compared to the constant effort he had to expand to make it happen.

She was not sure it was such a bad thing that Andy had finally blown up in his boss' face. From what she understood of the man, she doubted he would hold it against him. They'd discussed Phil often enough, once to the point of argument. It was funny how Andy simply couldn't fathom the guy. To Claire, the CEO wasn't such a mystery, like Amy had always said. He was a bright, deeply introverted guy who'd learned how to manage other people without having a natural knack for it. She could see how Andy could find him occasionally brutal, but she'd never seen any meanness in it, to her mind, more a difficulty to deal with emotional situations that made him direct, sometimes to a fault. She worried that Andy was absorbing too much of the pressure without letting it out—maybe blowing off steam would clear the air. She petted Pagui roughly as she clipped the lead back on, and the old gentleman turned his great neck to snort at her. It was a gorgeous day. Things would work out, in the end. She hoped.

Chapter Seven

MUTUAL TRUST

"The plant is on strike."

"What?" asked Andrew Ward dumbfounded. *"What?"*

Ward was in the Czech factory, looking at the parts to be brought back to Vaudon. He had never been to this site before, and was fascinated to see how they had responded to Jenkinson's pressure. Where Ward had tried to apply the full lean management system, and where Neuhof had installed a beautiful but superficial *pull system*, Petr Vojacek, the Czech plant manager, had taken a completely different tack. Vojacek, a forceful character, had not thoroughly bought into lean. He instead had focused narrowly on reducing batch sizes and controlling changeovers. As a result, he had created a specialized changeover preparation team, in addition to changer/setters. He started by setting a fixed sequence of production per press, say ABCDX, where X was an infrequently ordered exotic part, and progressively reduced the time it took to run through the sequence. At first, it took several weeks to run through ABCDX, but now they mostly did it within 24 hours. The parts were then pushed into logistics, which had to swallow whatever it received, and to ship to customers with whatever it could manage. The method was brutal, but Ward had to admit the stock level in the plant was remarkably low.

On everything else, however, Vojacek had made little progress. Red bins were in place, but it was clear they were not being addressed. The plant manager complained that Jenkinson was putting him under constant pressure to improve quality without giving him the means to hire more people to deal with his quality problems. He felt the CEO was being completely unreasonable—a sentiment Ward sympathized with. He had tried to convince Jenkinson he had a press-capacity problem and kept asking for new presses. Jenkinson's response had been that he would not get one more press until he reduced both his rejects and his down time, and that there was no way he was going to buy presses for a plant that did not know how to use them correctly.

In the meantime, solving the capacity problem was easy—he would transfer parts to Vaudon. That was the first time Vojacek had parts transferred out from his plant to a higher-cost country, and he simply could not believe the economic logic. Indeed, he felt he was being punished, plain and simple. Ward tried to explain that with oil costs fluctuating so much, transport costs had become a key issue, but the other man wouldn't hear of it. Vojacek wasn't unfriendly or unpleasant. He was just so totally involved with his production problems that he sounded like he was talking to himself most of the time, in his odd Czech/Brooklyn singsong.

What Ward would have given for Vojacek's problems right then.

"I said, the plant is on strike," repeated Muller on the phone.

"What happened?" asked Ward, stunned. He had run out of the press shop to the rest area to be able to hear something. He felt so short of breath he actually had to sit down.

"This afternoon, the shop stewards of all three shifts showed up, and told everybody they'd been had. They explained that they had discovered that corporate planned to shut the plant, and that all the productivity work over the last year was done to squeeze the very last penny out of operators' toil and sweat. They stood at the punchclock, and convinced operators not to clock in."

"I can't believe it," cried Ward. "How the hell did they get that report?" Just when he was actually bringing work back into the plant—now this!

"It's the same old theme again—no to plant closure."

Bloody strange way of going about it, cursed Ward.

"Listen, hold the fort, I'll be there as soon as I can."

"Phil? Bad news first, right?"

"Vaudon's on strike. I heard. Thanks for calling." When did the man sleep? Ward had waited for a decent hour in the U.S. with the time lag to call, but someone had obviously got there first.

"I'm at the Prague airport, and I'll be there as soon as I can. I'll need help with this," he admitted.

He waited for one of Phil Jenkinson's characteristic long pauses over the line as the other man was organizing his thoughts. Ward had learned to dread the pauses, and he now pictured the CEO calculating his moves by looking over his live chess set.

"I'm going to help," Jenkinson finally answered, "but you're not going to like it."

"When do I ever like your advice?" quipped Ward, aiming for flippancy but sounding resentful instead. He steeled himself for the worst.

"First, find out what the real problem is. Whatever the union says, something started this. Remember that the unions' interests are not the same as most workers. Find out what triggered the fire, what started it."

"All right. I can do that."

"Next, you're on your own with this one. You won't get any help from corporate. But I will make sure that they're not breathing down your neck and second-guessing your every move. You deal with your people, Andy. If you've got to make a deal, you talk to me directly, whatever the time. I'll let Coleman know.

"Now, listen up. This has to be very clear. One, the plant loses the Czech work. I am not giving business to a plant that goes on strike."

"What about the new diesel filter?" asked Ward, starting to panic.

"That is next quarter, and has been agreed with the customer, so there's no change there. And as for the Czech parts, we'll see how things turn out. But there won't be any transfers this quarter, and that's for certain.

"Second, if the plant stops a customer, I'll shut it down—whatever the cost."

"Come on, Phil!"

"No argument. Customers first. No Nexplas plant stops a customer because of an internal dispute. A plant that can't put the customers' interests before its own dirty laundry doesn't deserve to stay open. You've got safety stock, so you've got time—but this has to be crystal clear. I *will* do it."

The pawn would be sacrificed, Ward thought sourly.

It was drizzling when Ward arrived at Vaudon for the 5 a.m. shift. He had managed to get a couple hours' sleep at home after spending most of the drive from the Frankfurt airport on the phone with Mathias Muller, Jean-Pierre Deloin, and Carole Chandon. In the afternoon, Muller had lost his temper and almost got into a fistfight with the union leader. Daniel Petit was not a bad sort—in his daily role as a logistics technician Petit was just that, "small." But this was his moment of glory and he would not back down in front of his constituency. As a result, tempers were high and the situation had worsened considerably. During the night the unions had escalated the strike by blocking the trucks from leaving the plant. Ward knew that customers had parts inventories as well, but he had to sort this out today. That was it—today, or bye-bye, baby. The only glimmer of good news was that, according to Chandon, the strike was far from unanimous. Almost half the operators had chosen to work, which had triggered many heated exchanges between pros and cons. Naturally, Denis Carela was not answering his phone.

As Ward arrived, people were milling around at the entrance of the plant like lost souls in the false dawn. They parted to let him park his car. He got out under the glare of flat, hostile stares, feeling the blood coursing through his veins. His mouth felt dry, his bladder full, and his hands sweaty. He was not cut out for this kind of thing. Why couldn't people just get along?

"No to closure," a few voices chanted in the gloom as he approached, but the rhythm wasn't picked up very enthusiastically.

"Hello, Evelyne," he said. "Good morning, Marcel." One by one, he greeted every person he met, some responding naturally and shaking his hand, others muttering a diffident greeting. "Daniel! What is this all about?" he asked after deliberately greeting all the union reps. Only one of them refused to shake his outstretched hand. He wasn't about to be lynched that very second, he thought, relieved. After so many years working in France, he'd learned to take the handshake test at face value.

"We know all about your plans to close the plant. We will not have it!" shouted the union leader, playing to the crowd.

Ward stood there at a loss of what to do or what to say. He had worked out a thousand strategies on the way, but faced with all these people he knew and suddenly couldn't recognize, taken completely aback by the hard anger in their faces, he felt impotent, totally bereft of will. He just stared at them as an argument started louder and louder about something he didn't understand. You're panicking, he told himself. "What you need is a cup of tea," he thought he heard his mother say in her oh-so-reasonable tone whenever disaster had struck.

"What we need is a cup of tea," he said loudly. "Why don't we all get out of the rain into the cafeteria. Then we'll see whether we can straighten this out."

The union guys hesitated, but, heck, it was cold and wet, and nodding heads around the courtyard said that the cafeteria would be just as good a picket fence. As they filed in, Ward gave his key to the coffee machine to one of the operators, and politely asked her to organize hot drinks for anyone who wanted one. Then he started trying to talk things over with the union representatives and various people there. Over the years, Ward had come close to speaking French like a native, but he'd noticed that under stress, words would gush out in English and he had to concentrate forcefully on what he was saying, not to further inflame matters by reminding them all that he was a foreigner and, as such, forever on probation. The surreal feeling would not let him go. He was listening and listening, incapable of saying much. He heard about the detailed plans to close Vaudon. He heard about personal offenses and grievances, vendettas years old. He was lost in a sea of livid, sullen faces.

All of a sudden, it simply got too much for him. Here he was, trying to save a plant, and he'd been that close to succeeding, *that close*. And now the workers were intent on their own destruction, and nothing he had to say seemed to alter things one tiny bit. It all came to him in a flash. He could not do this on his own. He had tried hard, but it wouldn't work. It was only a job after all. They could close the plant for all he cared.

The irony of it made him laugh. It started with a giggle, but it soon bloomed into full I'm-loosing-it merriment. People looked at him in stunned silence, followed by furious murmuring as they thought he was laughing at them. The tension grew.

"So you think management wants to close the plant?" he asked as he'd brought himself back under control. "Well, maybe we should. This is so incredibly dumb. We probably don't deserve to survive."

More anger, reaching for him in waves, like surf breaking against a pier.

"Listen," he said, raising his hands palms out in a gesture of appeasement. "Please, listen. I'll tell you the whole story. But first I'd like to get every one else here—this concerns all of us, after all. Can someone go and fetch the colleagues at work and tell them I'd like to speak to them as well?"

The union reps complained loudly, but before they had the crowd under control, several operators had slipped out to spread the word to the workers who had chosen not to strike. One by one, they entered the cafeteria, looking suspiciously at their striking brethren, wondering what was going on.

Ward jumped on a table and gave them all a long look. He spotted Carela lurking quietly at the back of the room, refusing to catch his eye.

"I'll tell you what's so funny," he said loudly. "So *ironic*. You've just lost the plant a few million euros worth of business. I was in the Czech Republic to see about some parts Phil Jenkinson had decided to put back into Vaudon."

"You're lying," shouted one of the younger union guys. "We've got your own plan to close the plant! The presentation's got your name on it! Deny it!"

"Liar," echoed many voices in the crowd. "You're all liars and cheats."

"Let him talk," hushed one union rep, a hardworking lady he'd always found more constructive than others. She took her role very seriously in defending individual cases and rarely mixed politics into it.

"That's the funny part," he yelled. "There was a plan to close the plant. What's more, the decision had actually been made to close the plant. And because we've been working so hard for this entire year, Phil Jenkinson had changed his mind."

"*M'sieur* Phil?" someone asked.

"Yes. The CEO of this company. But now, because of this, he told me two things. First, we're no longer getting the Czech business. Finished. And second, the moment we stop a customer operation, he closes the plant, at whatever the cost."

"Liar," someone shouted again. "*M'sieur* Phil would not do that to us!"

In the theater of the absurd, things couldn't get much better, and Ward felt an almost overpowering urge to laugh again, his nerves slipping away from him. He was now being accused of lying because Phil, *Monsieur* Phil, whom many operators had taken a reverent shine to, would not do that to them.

"Yes. Phil Jenkinson, *the* CEO. He had decided to close the plant, but, by our hard work, we had persuaded him otherwise. Now we are telling him loud and clear that he'd been right all along. This plant cannot be trusted to deliver to its customers. Close Vaudon!"

"It's all a bluff!" bellowed the union leader. "He can't do it!"

"Trust me on this," said Ward more quietly. "He does what he says. If he says that he'll close, he'll do it."

"We hold the molds. He can't do anything without the molds."

"This is all bull," stormed the younger union guy. "The truth is these guys always aimed to close the plant, and they've been working us like slaves to get the most they could out of us while they did it."

"Fine," rejoined Ward. "Don't believe me. Continue to block the trucks, stop a customer, and see what happens. I personally don't care any more. I've worked for a year to try to save this plant, and this is where we get. So go ahead, close the plant. I've done my bit. Now it's your livelihoods, and your choice. Go ahead, do it!"

"You're bluffing! He's bluffing!" yelled Petit again, though the crowd seemed to waver.

"Hey, you don't want to believe me, fine. Ask Carela over there. He'll tell you."

"Denis?" asked the union lady, as all faces turned toward the supervisor in a slow movement, like the wind rippling through grass.

Carela stood against the wall, his arms crossed against his chest, his head bowed low, refusing to look at any one, more James Dean-esque than ever. He looked up slowly, his twisted grin in place, looking more sad than amused. Ward could see him torn between his policy of noninvolvement and the reality of the situation. He also realized for the first time the real respect the supervisor commanded in the plant. The entire roomful of people waited in hushed anticipation to hear which camp he would choose.

"Andy's right," he finally said. "Everything he said is true. Jenkinson gives business to plants that give him productivity. I believe that. I also believe that if he says he'll close the plant whatever the cost, he'll do it. This is not a bluff."

"What about the plan to close the plant?"

"There's always was a plan to close a plant," Carela shrugged. "And this one is a year old. I haven't heard anything about it since."

"Listen, guys," said Ward in the relative quiet following Carela's pronouncement. "Don't take the stupid risk. Stay on strike if you want, we'll work things out. But let the trucks go. Don't take the risk of stopping a customer line. It would just be so bloody stupid. After all the work we've done."

"Can we get the Czech parts back?" someone asked from the back of the room. It was one of the operators who had chosen to continue to work.

"I doubt it," answered Ward, from the top of the table. "Not right now, anyhow. I've yet to see *Monsieur* Phil go back on anything he'd said. We can probably change his mind again, but we'll have to work for it. Denis is right. He'll give business to plants that give him productivity. Period. So what'll be?"

"Bosses," yelled the angry young man. "They always get up to roll over with their fine words. Then who gets screwed in the end—we do! I say we fight."

No one echoed the rallying cry, not even the union leaders, who looked uncertainly at Petit. The union leader gave a blank look.

"Keep Muller off our backs, and we'll go back to work," shouted Sandrine Lumbroso, who'd been standing in the first rows. She was not a union rep, but she was a notorious barrack-room lawyer, and kept an unending tally of complaints for anyone foolish or brave enough to listen. Muller? That was something else again.

"He's driving us crazy," shouted another further in the crowd.

"The man's a real pain," agreed yet another.

Ward looked back at Petit, who seemed as overtaken by events as he felt.

"Muller, resign," yelled someone else. Soon enough the chant "Muller resign" was picked up across the cafeteria. Ward now felt totally foolish perched on this table, looking down at the screaming hordes. He had not prepared for that. He looked at Carela, who gave him his twisted grin and shrugged, opening his arms in a gesture of amused impotence.

"Sylvie?" he turned to the union woman, feeling he'd lost the initiative once again.

"Matthias drives us insane," she nodded, her serious face looking pinched. "We've got nothing against you, Andy. But all he does is yell at us all day long. That's a fact."

"And he forced me to stand up!" shouted a woman in the crowd.

"We don't want to work standing up," took up Sandrine Lumbroso.

Ward flinched. He had not realized that getting operators to stand had been such a sensitive issue. Trying to visualize single-piece flow in the cells as they formed and were *kaizened*, Ward had noticed that small contraptions would appear here and there to hold parts between workstations. After discussing it with Bayard and Muller, and then checking with Jenkinson, he had concluded that this was a result of operators working seated at their stations. Sure enough, when they got one of the seated cells to agree to work standing up, they reduced the surface of the cell by a further third, and managed to achieve *single-piece flow*. Carela had argued against it, insisting that the women in particular complained heavily about it. Ward had asked an ergonomics expert to come in to demonstrate that sitting and twisting to pick up components was far worse for their health than working standing. The debate had continued inconclusively for a while until Ward had told Muller to just do it—to have everyone in the factory work standing, no more arguments. In typical fashion, Muller had got the job done. And now Ward realized with horror that they were clamoring for Muller's head for something he had explicitly asked him to do, against both his and Carela's better judgment. It couldn't get much worse than this.

"All right," he said taking a deep breath. "Can we agree that you'll let the trucks go, and then we can discuss this calmly?"

Sylvie Barras looked at him intently for a long while, as if weighing his very soul.

"We can," she finally said with a firm nod.

"What d'you mean?" cried Daniel Petit. "We're not doing anything of the kind."

"Don't be a fool," she said urgently in a low voice. "I'm not gambling the future of the plant until we've talked this through."

"But—" he blustered, looking around and licking his lips, searching faces uncertainly for support, and not finding much.

"Listen up, everybody," she called loudly, interrupting the other union leader and highjacking his crowd. "Show of hands! Who's for giving Andy the benefit of the doubt? Hands up."

Hands came up immediately at the very back of the room from the operators who had chosen to work. Then, here and there in the front rows, more hands rose. And finally, as a swelling tide of fingers, a vast majority of people held their hands up. Andy quickly stepped down from the table, not wanting to ruin the moment and not trusting himself not to say something stupid.

"Okay, everybody, let's get back to work for the moment," she said resolutely, in a voice that brooked very little argument, and slowly, as if shuffling rank by rank, the cafeteria emptied as people spread out through the plants, leaving only the union leaders standing around Ward in the room, looking confused and angry, feeling cheated.

"Denis, would you come over here please?" asked Sylvie Barras, and to Ward's surprise, Carela, who'd watched all the operators file out from the back of the crowd, peeled himself off the back wall and reluctantly came forward, making a show of dragging his feet.

"Tell him," she ordered, her arms crossed beneath her bosom, nodding toward the plant manager.

"I've tried to tell you, Andy," said Carela, looking sideways. "Matthias really knows his stuff, but, ah, he's not good with people."

"Meaning what?"

"There've been incidents. You know what he's like when he loses his temper."

"The women, in particular," said Barras, "won't have it."

Here it comes, thought Ward, clenching his fists nervously. Is this the real issue? Or do they just want their pound of flesh?

"I can talk to him."

"Won't do any good," argued Petit. "We've worked with Matthias for a long time, and we don't mean him any harm. But we don't want to work for him."

"For him or with him?" asked Ward carefully.

"*For* him," repeated Petit. "No one would want him sacked. He's a fine maintenance manager. It's just that—"

"He's too harsh," finished Barras combatively. She would not back down from this. Ward knew he was snookered. He felt angry and confused. He'd put Muller in the production manager's job, and the man had delivered beautifully. He'd transformed the plant. Ward blamed himself for not having noticed that relationships had become so strained in the process. He hated the thought of throwing his own appointee to the wolves. It felt too much like a betrayal. What would Jenkinson do? He wondered. Sacrifice the pawn, he knew. Focus on the issue. You can't run a plant against its people. On the other hand, Jenkinson could've sacrificed him when Beckmeyer set him up—and didn't.

"I can't give you an answer right away," he finally said, feeling like a louse for not standing up strongly for his own guy. "I need to hear Muller's version first. Is that fair enough?"

The union reps hesitated a while, looking at each other, but the moment was gone. There was no reason to make an issue over this, particularly since they didn't seem vindictive toward Muller as such. In the end, they relented and Ward left them to it, nodding curtly to Carela on the way out.

He was not cut out for this job, he told himself again as he locked his office door, suddenly drained. He crashed in his chair, his legs still trembling from the adrenaline rush. He felt a sudden urge to resign on the spot. Get in the car and leave, and don't turn back. He knew it was nerves talking. He'd had a ridiculously happy childhood with well-balanced, easygoing parents, both quite successful in their own fields, if not very exciting. His father was a local branch manager and his mother owned a high-street clothes shop. He never had to make a hard choice in his life. He'd always got on fine with everybody, always had done well enough. And he liked it that way. He felt totally unprepared to deal with any of this do-or-die stuff. The more he thought about it, the angrier he got at the idea that he could let Muller down in such a way. He despised bosses who didn't stick up for their own subordinates. It felt like the worst form of cowardice: let someone take the fall for something you'd ordered them to do. Because, to be honest, he had been the one driving the production manager to step up the discipline. He'd been the one convinced that the problem of the plant was too much *laissez-faire*. And now it had come to this, letting someone else to take the blame for his own actions.

How was he supposed to maintain everyday rigor without brutal discipline? Sure he'd heard Amy and Jenkinson go on about working with people, not against them, but they didn't know this crowd. And, more to the point, if he disavowed Muller, wasn't he sending a strong message that he'd backed down? That it was okay to go back to the bad old ways. He thought several times about phoning Jenkinson to talk it through, but he didn't want to sound like a crybaby. Besides, ultimately, as Jenkinson had once told him, he was the help. He was the help sent to Vaudon to grow the plant. No one else. This was one decision he had to make on his own. He'd talk it over with Deloin when the man deigned to show up.

In the end, the decision was taken away from him. He'd been fuming for an hour in his office. He swung back and forth from self-righteous anger and a determination to show the union his mettle, determined to resign rather than let one of his men down, to a more nuanced, big-picture viewpoint that it was his job to make *teamwork* work. He thought again about Jenkinson's justification for pushing out Wayne Sanders: the man would not be a team player. The age-old management cop-out for shafting someone. And suddenly Ward had a managerial epiphany: if you want to be plant manager bad enough, sooner or later you had to take it on the chin. This is not just about me—it's about saving the plant; he told himself again and again. The weakest justification to sacrificing any one. A pawn in their game. He was going back and forth when he saw Muller get out of his car and approach the plant.

Ward rushed down the stairs, hoping to be the first to catch Muller, but he found him already in deep conversation with Carela. He looked pale as a sheet in the neon light of the lobby, with the deepest frown Ward had ever seen, the corners of his mouth turned savagely down. He took off his glasses and rubbed his face anxiously as Ward approached.

"You can have the bloody job back," he spat. "I never liked it anyhow."

Ward looked at him, and then at Carela. He wanted to protest that he would defend Muller if it came to that, but knew it was not true. So he just kept quiet.

"I've never been good with people," Muller said in a low rasp. "I know that. Give me machines any time—they don't complain, and they don't talk back."

"They just break down," said Carela with his twisted grin.

"Yeah. But I know how to deal with that."

"Can I have my job back as maintenance manager?" Muller finally asked slowly. Ward could see how much it hurt to ask. He knew the feeling. The man probably would have liked to throw the job in all their faces. Muller was a proud man. At his age, in this area, he probably needed the job, but would hate to beg. Grown-up time, Ward thought wretchedly.

"Of course," said Ward, feeling like a rat.

"And what about the Czech parts?" Muller asked. "Denis told me there would be no transfer."

"Not this quarter. This is Jenkinson through and through: tit for tat. The plant delivers, it gets business. It screws up, business goes elsewhere. But we can still convince him if we don't screw up again."

"What a mess," cursed Muller.

Ward was amazed that the guy still cared about what happened to the plant. He'd never understand people, he thought.

"Denis," he said, turning to the press supervisor. "Why didn't we see this coming?"

"How would I have known that the union had gotten a copy of the plan to close the plant?" answered the older man, deliberately misunderstanding the question. "My money's on Stigler. I wouldn't put it past him to have sent the PowerPoint presentations you guys put together for corporate to the union reps. No one told me anything."

"Don't be a bloody fool," said Muller angrily. "You always know what happens in the plant. You could've told us."

"I knew people were muttering about being worked so hard," Carela shrugged. "I had no idea they would actually walk out. I was caught with my pants down, as you were."

"Jenkinson once told me he believed conflict was usually the result of misunderstanding, and as such a complete waste. I tend to agree with him. We weren't listening enough?"

Carela looked at him in this way of his that told you loud and clear he thought you were a complete nitwit.

"What would you know about how operators feel anyhow?" he muttered.

"Well, if this is going to cost us our job," replied Ward hotly, "we'd better learn, shouldn't we?"

"Count me out," exclaimed Muller. "It's game over for me."

"Denis, you realize that you'll have to take over for Matthias."

"I told you 'No' before," Carela said tight-lipped. "It was 'No' then. It's still 'No.' Doesn't 'No' mean the same where you come from as it does in France?"

"As you just pointed out," pressed Ward regardless. "I'll never understand operators. You do."

The other shrugged it off, looking away and saying nothing.

"You've got to do it. Look how close we came to losing the plant—again! Four hundred jobs. Like you keep saying, we'll find work again. You and I. But what about Meyer? Mathilde? Sandrine Lumbroso."

"We've all lost jobs before," he rasped.

"Yeah, but who has been lucky enough to find work again? I listen to the stories. I hear what they say. Retraining? Temping? Come on. One in 10. That's 300 hundred with nothing."

"Do it, Denis," unexpectedly said Muller. "This is no joke, and you know it. We can save this plant, but we need to do it right. You can't continue to stand on the sidelines."

"Who's standing on the sidelines?" shouted Carela, suddenly looking distraught. "I've been working at this as hard as you have. And anyways, I didn't see the strike coming any more than you did."

"People listen to you."

"Because they know I'm on their side."

"So stay on their side!" insisted Ward. "It's not about sides, it's about working *together* so that we can all get something out of this mess. We know what we need to do. Jenkinson keeps telling us. We need to build an organization of supervisors and team leaders to take care of people's problems as well as drive *kaizen*. We haven't got that at the moment. Matthias and I have both failed at building it. So it's your turn to show us whether you're as good as you think you are."

"What do you mean by that?" jerked Carela, as if he'd been stung.

"Come on, Denis, the man's right. You know it."

"Listen, I gave up on union activism because it always fails in the end, but I'm not going to turn coat and take a management job. I swore I wouldn't!"

"It's time for everybody to grow up," growled Ward. "It's not about what you and I want. It's about working together to save this plant. And seeing how hard everyone is fighting against it, it sure doesn't deserve it."

"And then what happened?" asked Claire, holding her breath. She was seated on the floor, polishing a bridle, trying to coax some shine out of the worn leather. She had rather large hands with long fingers, rather at odds with her lithe arms. He'd often wondered how strong she was, lifting heavy stuff all day long, considering how thin her bones seemed, delicate, birdlike. She was looking at him in that intense way that, after all these years, still made him lose his train of thought.

"The strike just sort of went away. They got what they wanted. I gave them Muller's head on a platter. I spent the rest of the day pulling the plant back into shape, and not a peep from anyone. Almost as if they were feeling sorry."

"Maybe they are?"

"I don't know. That's the truth. I don't know how these people think. I've been lording over them for four years now, and I haven't got a clue."

"Hey, don't beat yourself up over it. You know them a lot better than you did a year ago. Gosh, Andy, you just turned away a strike. You deserve a medal for it! Sweetie, you did good."

"I sacrificed Matthias Muller for this, excuse me if I don't feel so hot right now."

"Will you stop acting such a baby! Muller's still got a job, no? The plant's still open, no? Your pride got hurt because you're not mister supermanager, well, so what? You know what my father would say."

"Back on your horse," he smiled. "If you can talk, you can ride."

"That's right. If you can talk, you can ride."

"No champagne for this?" he asked in the ensuing silence.

"Amy tried to discuss this, didn't she?"

"Yep. And Phil. *Mutual trust* ... although how the hell you develop *mutual trust* in such an antagonistic culture, I don't know. It's not like I can pay them more with our cost structure the way it is, and to tell the truth, I'm not even sure that would help. There's just so much bad blood there. Look at a guy like Carela—what a waste."

"Will he take the job?"

"Your guess is as good as mine!"

"The real question is: what conclusions did you draw from this experience?"

Ward blew air through his cheeks, not quite knowing what to answer.

"Don't become plant manager?"

Jenkinson actually smiled, shaking his head. "You'd never believe the number of times I've told myself the same," he agreed. "But beyond stating the obvious? What was the cause of the strike?"

"We'd been pushing people too hard, obviously. But beneath that, I think there was a failure to listen. You warned me, and so did Amy. But I thought the end was in sight. I wanted to make it work so badly. So I didn't listen. I am starting to come to grips with how much of a long-term project this lean approach really is."

"At first, you think you're in a sprint to the finish," concurred the CEO, "and then you realize it's a marathon."

"As you've said before, we can force people to do things, but we can't force them to be interested and engaged. I'm finally working with Denis Carela and Jean-Pierre Deloin to build a proper team-based organization. It's going to take the time it takes, but we'll get there. If there's one conclusion I draw from the whole ghastly episode is that, again, what we'd done was too fragile. It rested on too few people. But how does one change an entire culture?"

Ward and Jenkinson had found time to talk at Nexplas' third annual executive retreat. Ward had to credit Jenkinson; the company was changing. Many of Alnext's old-guard management had disappeared, replaced mostly from the ranks up, with a few new faces here and there. The firm felt far more like an engineering company as well. Most of this year's topics centered on product-development issues. Jenkinson's speech had mainly been about succeeding at product launches in the next year. What you need to learn rather than what you want to do. It seemed that what the company really needed now was to learn how to launch new products.

Jenkinson had paused to consider Ward's question. "'Problems first' is not just a phrase or even an attitude," he went on. "Like many of these Toyota-based aphorisms, we tend to dismiss them as folklore, until we realize they are management techniques. Like saying 'Thank you' every time someone brings you a problem. Technique.

"The core of *mutual trust* is that people feel that you take their problems seriously, and that you try your best to do something about it. Understanding doesn't mean agreeing. Like with *teamwork*, there are many issues in which differences are irreconcilable. But still, we can try to work across the divide point by point.

"*Mutual trust* is very long to grow, regardless of who you're talking about—whether between customers and us, or us and suppliers, or management and operators. Long to grow and, as you've seen, quick to damage. It takes hundreds of years to grow a tree, but a few hours to fell it. So *mutual trust* needs to be reinforced continuously. We need to listen and listen, and force ourselves to take everyone's problems seriously, to understand the problems and look for solutions, whether they are operators or neighbors. When someone tells you about a problem, you say, 'Thank you.'"

"Easier said than done." Ward couldn't help thinking that he hadn't heard Jenkinson thank him too often for all the problems he'd thrown on his lap. That is unless, "I expect much, much more" really meant "Thanks" in Jenkinsonspeak.

"Sure," said Jenkinson, "but what in lean is ever easy? When people come to you with problems, they rarely ask nicely. Usually, they've already worked themselves up, and they think they can force you to solve the problem for them in the way they want. So strike, yell, take it, or leave it. Taking anger on the chin and answering calmly, 'Thank you,' and 'Let's work the problem,' is never easy. Takes true grit. But it does come with practice. To a large extent, every time someone brings me a problem, I am truly thankful because it allows me to practice facing problems."

Ward thought snidely that if bosses were as good at practicing as preaching it would be a different world—immediately feeling guilty because he realized that he was probably doing just the same to his people in Vaudon. Damn.

"Without *mutual trust*, everything else we try to do is bound to fail sooner or later: *go and see, kaizen, clear direction*, and *teamwork* won't be sustained without constantly developing *mutual trust*."

"Something similar to what happened to you happened to me when we made our first big company acquisition," reminisced Jenkinson. The CEO had grabbed Ward at a coffee break to hear about the followup from the strike in Vaudon, and the big man nodded approvingly when Ward told him Carela had finally agreed to become production manager. Ward had been drifting from one knot of people to the next, exchanging a few words but not getting really drawn into any of the conversations. He'd been struck by the way the whole tone of the convention had changed subtly. He heard a lot less about politics, and a lot more about technical issues. He wondered whether it reflected a shift in his own interests, or whether he was witnessing a "Jenkinson effect," the unconscious alignment of people on their leader's personality and attitudes.

"We took over a company that made much bigger electrical equipment than we were used to," Jenkinson was saying, "and I attacked it head on with *kaizen, kaizen, kaizen*, and had a *pull system* in no time. Unfortunately, I didn't have Amy working for me anymore at the time, and I had to deal with the people issues myself. It was a disaster. I'd completely ignored the ergonomics problems operators were complaining about after *kaizen* activities. In my original company, products were different and this never had been much of an issue. Like all generals who lose wars because they keep refighting the previous one, I absolutely didn't see it coming.

"It ended up with a really tough fight, and the union took us to court. I was getting all steamed up and ready to dig my heels in and make a real stand when Bob Woods said, 'You know what? They're right.' I couldn't believe it. It's hard to accuse Bob of being a wimp in a fight. But he took me to the shop floor, and showed me, in detail no less, how the operators complaints were totally justified. So, in the end, we hired an ergonomics expert, and we started solving all the ergonomics problems as part as the *kaizen* drive. Everyone in the line management of that company became an ergonomics expert. It was tough."

"And?"

"Oh, like everything else, if you hang on long enough, after several *PDCA* cycles, a different kind of thinking starts sinking in. People see issues differently. They've worked together at solving problems so relationships change. To me, the core of lean management is being clear about what you want, and working with people at solving every problem, so that you end up developing a different kind or relationship with them, which is when *mutual trust* starts building up.

"That's when Bob taught me to say 'Thank you' to problems people would bring up. With the previous management, people had been taught that you either were part of the solution or part of the problem. Basically, the messenger kept being shot for bringing bad news. They learned to keep their heads low. We had to work with them on the shop floor for months to get them to start opening up. It was tough to cross that threshold of trust, but when we did—boy, did they tell us stuff. It came out raw and angry and bitter. I was close to giving up, but Bob told me off, arguing that anger was good—that it was all coming out. I just had to tough it out and prove to people that this was not a flash in the pan. Trust is slowly given, but quickly taken back.

"Treating everybody as an individual was the other thing we learned then. It sounds trite, but we don't really do it, in practice. Our equipment was awkward to use, and as a result we learned that different people had different problems. Sometimes these were physical, sometimes they were mental. At first, we wanted to push the first solution that worked on everyone, and we got into all sorts of trouble. But finally we got it—that is to say we accepted that every individual was different, and we started seeking individual agreement for everything we did. No two people had exactly the same problem, so, once again, we accepted that we had to work things out one problem at a time. The key thing is that we wanted to work with standards, both at the policy and the detailed work level. This, in fact, created different problems for different people. We learned that to maintain standards, we had to take into account individual problems—and help them to solve them. It seemed to take forever, but eventually we got there. I realized it was not just learning about the engineering that mattered, but learning about people, as well."

"Oh, come on, Phil—you can't mean that," exclaimed Ward, shaking his head as he got them both another helping of stale coffee. "We need rules, don't we? We can't tailor things to every single person. I understand all this business of *mutual trust*, but aren't you pushing it a tad too far?"

"Precisely," replied Jenkinson, wisely ignoring the filthy brew. "Because we need to work with standards, we need to understand the difficulties people experience with keeping these standards. Don't kid yourself, this is not about bleeding hearts and nicey-nicey—it's good business. Think about it, if everyone in the shop owes you something because you've helped them do their job, when any conflict comes up, you're in a far stronger position. The whole point about involvement is that you share problems with your operators: You get them to contribute to their workstations. You help out with their difficulties. They give you quality and productivity. Tit for tat. We can be lean precisely because we develop the *mutual trust* that all of us will do our best to serve customers with the leanest processes ever. You can design the leanest processes you want, if people are not engaged and don't give you their all to keep them lean, they won't ever work, and waste will keep reappearing.

"Here are the four key points we had to relearn, from the original Training Within Industry programs that Toyota used to build their own approach," Jenkinson summarized, counting on his fingers:

"*One*, let each person know how they're performing, and figure out problems with them. Problems first.

"*Two*, give credit when credit is due, particularly when you've found 'positive variance,' someone doing systematically better than standard and proposing a new standard.

"*Three*, let people know in advance about changes that will concern them—they need to understand why and be able to plan.

"*Four*, look for the best use of every person's abilities: There is no worse waste than untapped talent or motivation. It's our job to bring it out, or, at the very least, not to stand in people's ways.

"From the first lean turnaround I'd learned to have a *plan for every part*. Then I learned to have a *plan for every person*."

"What do you mean by that?" asked Ward.

"Who do you promote? Who do you have ready to step in? What role do you give them if it doesn't work out? How do you develop them? With engineers, we have a chat every quarter on a list of basic competencies—technical and managerial. Every three months, we choose problems to solve that correspond to areas where people need to be developed. Growing people takes time, but it's the only game in the end. To do so, however, you've got to treat each person as an individual, and take their problems seriously. No two individuals experience the same thing the same way. I've learned that now!"

"Let the *pull system* manage the process; don't let management manage the flow," explained Mark Neville good-naturedly. He'd changed his mind about Ward. In fact, Neville found he rather enjoyed his role as an amateur *sensei*. Besides, Ward's quirky sense of humor and off-the-cuff remarks made him laugh. The poor guy still needed every single thing spelled out, though. "Once you've got that figured out, everything comes together. Line managers are there to manage gaps to standard, not to make micro-decisions on the process. Level customer demand, then follow the *kanban* cards."

Ward had taken this opportunity to return to the Bethany plant before flying home. Neville had been keen to show him the work he'd been doing on component supply. His team had decided to store the high-running inbound components directly on trains lined up in the warehouse, rather than putting them in a supermarket first, and then on a train. As a result, several trains were prepared in advance without a tugger, which would move them. And as pallets arrived from suppliers, they were broken down and the containers were dispatched to their waiting location on each carriage.

"Look over there. We've created a full system of alarms to make sure the parts are arriving on the right truck. We've taken control of logistics from the suppliers. The truck drivers have to call us if there's a box missing before they leave the supplier, so we can call them back to ask what the problem is."

"How is your line organization working?"

"I've got an assistant plant manager who's effectively managing the supervisors. I've got a supervisor for every 30 operators or so—and they're the first line of management. Their main job is *standardized work* and all that goes around it."

"That's what they do all day?"

"That, and responding to alerts in the pull. My big thing is that a manager shouldn't have to repeat an instruction in the normal course of things. If they have to do this, there's something wrong with the process. We work hard at freeing as much time as we can from daily problems so that supervisors can focus on improving *standardized work*."

"In practice?"

"There's a training schedule for every operator. You can actually see it posted on each cell. Supervisors refer to the *standardized work*, train operators, and make sure it's respected. When they find problems, that's an opportunity for *kaizen*."

"And your team leaders? What do they do?"

"Mostly quality, though not everybody thinks like me. Team leaders are not management—they're operators. They're my first line of defense for quality problems. So whenever an operator has a doubt about a part, he asks the team leader who can tell whether it's a good part or a bad part and who can then check the *standardized work*. If they discover a real problem, they stop the cell and call the supervisor. Once a week, the team leaders also check the balancing of the line.

"Mind you, I'm nowhere near where I want to be in terms of reactivity. Every time I visit the Toyota plant we ship to, I'm humbled. Every time a Toyota operator stumbles on a problem, he pulls the andon cord and the team leader comes running. They have less than a *takt* to figure out whether this is a real problem or not. That's less than one minute. If they decide it's a real problem, they stop the line, and then the supervisor comes running. If they don't fix the problem quickly, they can be stopping the entire factory."

"Talk about pressure."

"Sure, but the thing is that the andon lights up every other minute. Even though this might mean shutting down the entire plant, it never does because of the rapid team response. Operators keep pulling the andon cord all the time. Talk about engagement. And that's my problem. I'm nowhere near that. At the moment, operators will call the team leaders once or twice a shift, but we're still miles away from doing it enough."

"Good topic for an *A3*," quipped Ward.

"How so?" asked Neville, looking at Ward as if he suspected his leg was being pulled.

"Um. Gap with standard and all that," Ward offered in the face of his friend's dark look. "Look at how often the cord is pulled in the Toyota plant, versus how often here. Ask what factors affect this gap and so on. You know … *A3*?"

"You son of a …," rumbled the plant manager with a deep frown, making the Englishman worry that he'd put his foot in his mouth—

again. "You know what. You're absolutely right!" he said laughing. "It's a perfect subject for an *A3*. I was wondering what to get my line manager working on."

"Do you use *A3s* much?" asked Ward with relief.

"All the time. But not at first. I'd been trying to get people to use *A3s* for years and getting very frustrated because nobody would. You know, 'Why don't they get it?'"

"Tell me about it!"

"Then, finally, I realized that I was the one not getting it."

"Tell me about it, as well," laughed Ward. "Sounds familiar so far."

"The thing is," Neville grinned ruefully, " I thought the *A3 process* was a great problem-solving tool. That if people followed the boxes, they'd get to the right solution. But, obviously, you don't know what you don't know. If you don't understand the problem, structured problem-solving is just a pretty way of showing off the wrong thinking. Then one day, completely on another subject, I came to the conclusion that I was pretty good at managing the floor, but really bad at managing my middle management. Talking about engaging them—I did not know where to start. And somehow I put the two together: *A3s*. The point of the *A3*, as I see it, is not so much for people to find the root cause of their problems, but to enable a coach to steer them through the process of solving their problems. See, each of the boxes in the *A3* allows me to *check* if they've really understood the problem—and that's the key. Shifting from applying solutions to understanding problems."

"*Check?*" asked Ward, genuinely puzzled. "For instance?"

"Well, if they can't describe the problem as a historical series on one indicator and its gap to standard, it means they haven't narrowed down the problem well enough. I can check the measure they've chosen and how they understand it. Then, if they can't come up with the point of cause in the process—if they haven't carefully tested their hypotheses—again it means they're going too quickly. Similarly, if they have a single solution per root cause, rather than two or three credible alternatives, it means they don't understand the problem well enough, and so on. The power of the *A3* is as much in the interaction between manager and subordinate, or mentor and mentee, as in the structured problem-solving itself. It's a management tool. And it's perfect for managing middle managers.

"Go on," urged Ward, thinking back to his bunch of knuckle-headed, stubborn, 'I am right and every one else is wrong,' irredeemable individualists back home.

"They do their job as they always did, but now each one of them has a running *A3* problem with me. And they have to coach their subordinates on one *A3* problem, as well. It's worked really well, and I have a much better idea of who they are and what they do since."

"Treating people as individuals?"

"You'd better believe it. Solving problems all the way to the root cause one at a time."

"What about team meetings?" asked Ward, coming back to the work cell. Back in Vaudon, he had been working hard with Carela at setting up the proper cell organization. But every time they resolved one issue, 10 more questions seemed to pop up.

"We do five minutes after each break. Mostly to talk about problems."

"Do you expect your supervisors to solve operators' personal problems as well?" Ward asked, following up on his previous talk with Jenkinson.

This made Neville laugh, and shake that big head of his.

"Listen, Andy. All problems are personal. What do you think? Our biggest problems are not machines breaking down or bad components from suppliers. We know how to deal with that. No, it's operators arriving late or not showing up in the morning. Then we have the problem of professional illnesses as well, and finding the right job for people who can't do certain operations—now that's a headache.

"Our biggest concern is team stability," continued Neville. "The moment someone's missing, the team leader has to fill in. As a result, they're no longer available for operators. When this happens, every time someone has a question, the team leader has to stop the cell. Since I don't want to stop questions, we take a real hit on productivity."

"Do you do this at every level?" asked Ward.

"Sure. Our policy is that the boss fills in for any missing employee, without fail. I thought we'd discussed that. Managers are responsible for their people's success at their objectives. That's a fundamental attitude, and it means keeping the process working on schedule even if someone doesn't turn up. We work also very hard at understanding why people show up late or don't show up at all. That's the supervisors' job—to get all the facts, understand the problem with the person, and come up with strategies to do something about it."

On the way back across the Atlantic, Ward forced himself to pick up a business book that Neville had pushed on him as he left the plant. He usually hated reading this sort of stuff, but found himself grudgingly interested in a massive study the Gallup organization had conducted exploring the link between motivation, performance, and working conditions. Sifting through its database of more than a million employee interviews, the researchers had looked for a way of measuring the strength of a workplace. Armed with the resulting questionnaire, they'd then asked 24 different companies in 12 industries to provide scores for performance (productivity, profitability, employee retention, and customer satisfaction) for 2,500 business units. They then looked for which responses related the most strongly with unit performance.

What they found was that performance varied more widely within individual firms than within the industry as a whole, and that the employees of the best performing units consistently ranked highly and responded strongly to the following six questions:

1. *Do I know what is expected of me at work?*
2. *Do I have the materials and equipment I need to do my work right?*
3. *Do I have the opportunity to do what I do best every day?*

4. *In the last seven days, have I received recognition or praise for good work?*
5. *Does my supervisor, or someone at work, seem to care about me as a person?*
6. *Is there someone at work who encourages my development?*[1]

Reading this, he understood why Neville had lent him the book. Neville's double setup—the *pull system* on the one hand, and the training at *standardized work* and *kaizen* on the other—fit well with Gallup's questions.

How could he have been so blind, he wondered, walking through the plant and hearing Neville detail this and that *kaizen*? He'd been told from the start: walk on two feet, continuous improvement, and people involvement. He'd really thought he'd had the problem licked, and it had almost cost him the plant. He started worrying what he was missing next! It's not the car that you see that makes driving dangerous, he reminded himself—it's the one that you don't.

Putting the book down, Ward had to admit that Neville was pretty unique in that he saw people making parts by using machines, rather than machines making parts, being loaded and unloaded by operators. Equipment is there to support people in their work. Automation is first used for dangerous or heavy operations, second for productivity. Why? *Because only people can improve their own processes.* This, he thought to himself, has to be the secret to lean processes. How easy it is from management's perspective to think that processes run people. He'd certainly gone by that mental model for ages without even realizing it. But really, he had learned through tough interactions with his people, that for everybody every day, people run processes. Lean processes are the results of the people who run them conducting *kaizen* activities. To do so, he had to create an environment where *kaizen* spirit could blossom. This meant forging a fundamental deal

1. Buckingham, M. & C. Coffman, *First, Break All the Rules* (Simon & Schuster, New York, 1999).

414

with every person working on his shop floor: You help me solve process problems, and I will help you solve your problems. We'll split the gains. *Mutual trust.*

As he drove back home from the airport, he had a short-lived, feel-good moment of believing that things were finally coming together. Trust: that would come if people realized that their concerns were listened to seriously and that earnest attempts to resolve them would be made. To develop such a culture, he would teach front-line management to resolve daily problems on the line through the use of visual standard conditions and *standardized work*. And he would train his middle managers to solve process problems by personally piloting A3s. This meant maintaining a continuous dialogue on problem-solving and improvement at all levels. That was the management method. There was nothing else. Teach rather than manage, indeed.

Calm had returned to Vaudon. Autumn had been pleasantly mild, with most of October sunny and cool. Absenteeism had returned to its normal level. Ward and Deloin began to interview every operator who took a leave or failed to show up, or, just as they had done earlier on, discussed accidents with them. Even tempered by the grating, limitless cynicism of the veteran HR manager, these interviews opened a fresh window for Ward on the lives of the people he worked with every day. He admitted to himself that throughout his early career he had been focused exclusively upward, impressed by the jet-setting glamour of top management. In his time in Vaudon, he'd simply not adjusted. He had surrounded himself with a small coterie of colleagues he thought of as friends, and delegated the day-to-day running of people and machines to his organization. His life had been centered on Malancourt, and keeping the plant ticking along, waiting for … for what, he didn't know.

The events of the early fall had finally drummed into him the obvious fact that each and every one of the people working in the plant were individuals, and the least he could do was to find out more about them. What he discovered was the rough reality of a region devastated by one economic recession after the other. The people he knew in Malancourt were mostly his neighbors, who tended to be farmers doing reasonably well, or Claire's clients, who were wealthy enough to indulge in such an expensive hobby as horse riding. But here, in the plant, he was discovering another reality. That of living in council estates, of scrounging a budget, of having trouble paying for the petrol to drive to work in the morning. Work for your pay, toil for your kids, sweat till you're wrinkled and gray. If he was honest with himself, he had to admit it had scared him. But now that he'd faced his own squeamishness, he also realized there was very little resentment against the unfairness of life. People got agitated over the small, personal stuff—petty jealousies, casual meanness. Some slights rankled even years later. Ward learned this from spending more time with Deloin. The old fox, deputy mayor of Vaudon was a terrible gossip. He could trace the genesis of any incident back three generations.

In the plant, through trial and error, Ward was learning what to involve himself in, and what to ignore deliberately. He'd also gotten better at handling his shop-floor presence. He'd figured out that, as plant manager, just being there mattered, somehow. It changed things. People behaved differently. Most of the time now, he would simply watch and listen, finding out that as he did many thorny problems would unravel by themselves, as people heard themselves spell them out. One Sunday morning Claire had made fun of him for watching a riding lesson with his *"gemba* face."

"*Gemba* face?" he'd asked puzzled.

"You know, that look of distant concentration. Captain on deck!" She'd kidded. "Don't expect me to salute, though."

Of course there were problems a-plenty in the plant. What worried him the most was that Franck Bayard continued to drive *kaizen* workshops with the frenzy of the convert. He was still as withdrawn and self-absorbed as ever and could hardly say two words in a row to anyone, but people didn't seem to mind him. He was forever fiddling with this or that workstation, slowly involving the supervisors and the operators. They didn't need to discuss much. They'd gotten used to his way of working with them and often contributed clever suggestions. The real problem was that Ward was running out of slots for staff operators who had been liberated from existing processes. He'd almost got a full complement of team leaders, and asked Carela to train them using red bins and *standardized work*.

The new production manager was now spending one hour a week with each shift's team leaders working through the basics of 5S, *standardized work*, and quality boundary samples. Carela and Ward also had agreed to spend Wednesday evenings with the night shift for the first four hours. The plant was another world at night, and they had managed to train the night shift to the day's changes. Ward had also reinforced the setters team with two more operators, and one had been promoted to maintenance technician. Ultimately, there would be a limit to where he could staff the full-time employees released by *kaizen*, and he was approaching this faster than natural attrition. He needed volume badly, since he was determined not to make people redundant if at all possible: not only would the fragile *mutual trust* established in the plant be severely damaged, but after what they had been through, Ward felt a duty to do all he could for his troops.

Similarly, between themselves, Carela and Muller had managed to fully liberate two presses through shorter batch sizes and clever mold allocation. Jenkinson had been pleased, and hadn't asked to move them to another site yet. But he knew that it was only a matter of time. Ward dreaded the moment he'd have to ship a press out of the plant. This would surely get the unions agitated again, but, hey, they would cross that bridge when they got there. Strangely, although he felt he had developed a better rapport with the operators, his relationship with the shop stewards seemed to deteriorate. Carela surprised him again by convincing Barras to take a post as supervisor. Ward had balked at first, suggesting she would have to choose between her union involvement and a supervisory job. To his further surprise, she had, which meant that he lost a friendly bet with Carela, who had told him he'd be damned if he was the only one to abandon his principles in the plant. "Don't let them make you an officer," he'd grumbled. "But if I'm going to do this, I'm not going to do it alone."

Barras was turning out to be a godsend as a supervisor. Ward had expected others to resent her lack of seniority, but so far everything had gone well. Léa Mordant had the morning shift in assembly, and Barras had taken the afternoon. The unexpected downside had been that Ward had lost the voice of reason amongst the union reps, and without Barras' down-to-earth influence, the guys seemed to be far more radical. "You're missing the point," explained the HR manager with his usual jaundiced view of things. "They're seeing what's happening. Operators are going to Sylvie or Carela when they have problems, and even directly to you. So the union's losing its grip. They're hating it, and they'll be trouble before long." Shipping presses out of the plant was exactly the kind of thing that could spark a repeat of September's events, and Ward was really not looking forward to it.

Ward told himself once more to stop being surprised by the man's insights. Carela had clearly taken on-board *standardized work* as a way of getting the supervisors to work with the operators daily.

"I understand better why we need stable teams," Carela mused one evening, as they were trying to figure out why the productivity of one shift in assembly was clearly below the other two. "Look at this: the two other shifts have a stable team here, but for the afternoon shift, the people keep changing."

"And?" asked Ward, puzzled.

"Getting them to follow *standardized work* is impossible. Look, the great thing about this *standardized work* approach is that you can focus on how people do the work, not just what they have to do. This is the key to productivity and ergonomics. I wish we'd done it before!"

"How do you mean?"

"Do you see these little plastic clips the operator has to insert over there? When we started taking times with Léa, we realized that Sandrine was going far quicker than anyone else. Then we also saw that all the other operators had their hands covered with tape to protect their fingers—but not Sandrine."

"Are we talking about Sandrine Lumbroso?" checked Ward in disbelief. He visualized the morning-shift operator's hunched shoulders, sour face, and constant whining. Among the operators she'd been one of the most opposed to supervisors systematically using stopwatches to establish the *standardized work*. Now it was revealed that she'd been far quicker at her workstation than any of her colleagues.

"Yep, Sandrine Lumbroso," chucked Carela. "Go figure! In any case, we noticed that she was twisting the inserts in rather than hammering them straight on as specified by engineering. Her method is far better for the operators and quicker, as well."

"Great."

"Little things like that, we can spread real quickly within a stable team. But whenever we deal with temps or new operators, it takes forever to get them up to speed."

"I've finally worked out what autonomous teams really meant," Carela said one day out of the blue.

"Autonomous teams?"

"Before your time. The previous management had this theory that every area had to be completely autonomous. As a supervisor, this meant that we were suddenly saddled with all the admin, procurement, and so on. No more time for manufacturing parts."

"We've taken all of that out, haven't we?"

"Oh, yes. That's not what I meant. See, when I was a supervisor, I spent most of my time deciding what part to run when on what cell, and then looking for components."

"Not with the *pull system*, I hope."

"That's my point. Since we've got the *pull system* working, the teams know what they have to produce just by following the *kanban* cards, and the train delivers components straight to the workstation. So they don't need the supervisors to be there to decide about changeovers. They can do it on their own. Which is how we can have the supervisors spend all this time on *standardized work*. Our teams are far more autonomous now, but it means something radically different from what I thought. 'Autonomous' means they know what to do when precisely because they don't have any production choices to make. They can focus on their jobs, which is producing good parts. I could kick myself!"

You and me both, mate, thought Ward, deeply pleased to realize that Carela's understanding of lean was beginning to overtake his own. The HR manager kept saying, "We shall see," with his knowing smile. Of all the changes Ward had made over this eventful year, the one he might have been most pleased with was convincing Carela to take over production.

Ward remembered a point Amy had made about management styles. Before being hit over the head by the threat of closing the plant, he thought of himself as an empowering manager. But the reality is he let people get on with their jobs without interfering, believing strongly that trust was the best policy. As a result he had isolated himself from the plant by buffering himself with "trusted lieutenants" as the plant continued its downhill slide toward closure, like so many other industrial sites in the region. Then, driven by Jenkinson, he'd done a brutal about-face, ordering people to perform and constantly complaining about why people would not simply *do as they're told*. In Muller, he'd found the perfect sergeant-major, and together they'd kicked the plant into shape—leaving most people behind and generating festering resentment in the process. The smoldering fire had inevitably sprung out and almost consumed them all. Now, in hindsight, he understood Stigler's meltdown and Chadid's resignation much better. It had turned out that Stigler really did have a breakdown, and Deloin was still trying to negotiate some kind of settlement with the man. Deloin was now convinced Stigler had mailed the plant closure presentation to union rep Petit. Ward's complete turnabout would have left his right-arm guys out in the cold, feeling betrayed. He'd been so obsessed with what he was doing at the time that he could never have seen this, but he'd done it all the same.

The strike had shaken him to his core. Probably even deeper than Phil's announcement that he had intended to close Vaudon. The threat of the plant closure had made Ward take results seriously, whereas before he had thought it was only a numbers games at corporate— games in which he had participated. But the strike had made him take the people seriously. People were not just numbers on the spreadsheet—they were indeed his most important asset: they made good parts every day. Slowly, painfully, he was discovering the hard truth of lean management every day. Not "Do as you think is best," nor "Do as you're told," but "Let's figure this out together." It was demanding because nothing in his education as a manager had prepared him to know how to do that. And he had to find out every day.

Ward had decided to call it a day early, and drove home through the winter dusk, as dark clouds rolled over land, at the edge of the trees. Today had been a good day. Mathilde Weber, now team leader in assembly, and Barras had approached him that morning about an idea one of the operators wanted to try out. Barras had asked if she'd stayed on with Weber after work to try things out with the girls of the second shift, would that be considered as overtime? Ward had kept a straight face although he felt like doing a high five inside. An hour a week, he'd agreed. They could involve as many of the morning-shift operators in the team that wanted to participate. *Mutual trust*, he smiled to himself, I'll help you to solve your problem, and you help me to solve mine.

Then, of course, it dawned on him. He really needed to get the suggestion program up and running. No more notes and discussion; *he* had to move on this. Suggestions were bubbling up throughout the plant, like the one from Weber and Barras, but there was no method in place to evaluate the merits of the ideas and put them into action. And if implemented, how to recognize the effort. Some people argued that suggestions were essentially part of the work and should be free (not surprisingly, these opinions was more prevalent among managers), while others argued that any operator contribution should be compensated. There was an old suggestion scheme as part of Alnext Business System, which involved a locked box at the entrance of the plant and a considerable cash prize for each idea. Ward had let it fall into disuse because it seemed to create more tensions and petty jealousies than foster team spirit.

Ward believed that Neville's suggestion system in Bethany could work in Vaudon. He resolved to test this system, running a U.S. hypothesis up a French flagpole, so to speak. In Bethany, each cell had a board showing the evolution: suggestion made, validated within the week, waiting for validation for more than the week (mostly because of an expenditure request), or refused. Neville personally checked that most suggestions were validated by supervisors within one week of having been made. He could manage that. Neville rewarded all suggestions that were accepted by giving small gift coupons, and had a competition for all accepted solutions based on cost impact, with more substantial rewards. Vaudon had progressed in terms of management responsiveness and operator involvement, but Ward wasn't sure they were quite ready to guarantee all operators suggestions would be considered within a few days; ready or not, though, it was time to *do*. He'd know if they were ready when it came time to *check*. Neville had always insisted that the suggestion system was a key way of putting pressure on his middle managers to make sure they take care of people. Operators help managers. Managers help operators. *Mutual trust.*

Chapter Eight

CREATING VALUE

"Let's have a look, then," Ward said. While delighted with what he saw, he did his best to keep a poker face.

"Solange, why don't you show *M'sieur* Andy," suggested Mathilde Weber, nodding to the operator who had come up with this idea. When he first arrived in the plant, Ward had insisted that every one call him "Andy." Years later, while he felt more at ease on the shop floor than his early days, this request still caused no small amount of confusion with the French shop-floor etiquette rules.

"Here," explained Solange Fabre, a quiet, middle-aged woman who was forced to return to work for family reasons. Apparently her no-good son was back home and needed help. Fabre, who rarely volunteered more words than strictly necessary, was an unlikely candidate for a suggestion. But there she was, demonstrating the changes they had made to the jig. "Before, we had to take the part like so, which was a really awful movement, and then we had to hit the part so. My hand always hurt at the end of the shift," she explained, showing the side of her well-worn palm.

"With the new jig," explained Weber, "the movement is much simpler, and we don't get any more rejects at the automatic testing machine."

"Well done," congratulated Ward, looking carefully at the fixture. "And did Franck validate it?"

"He did," Weber beamed proudly. "Not at first—you know what *Monsieur* Bayard is like when it's not his idea. But we conducted some tests, and he told us it was so smart, he should have thought of it himself." She was clearly pleased, and Ward, amused, fought to keep a straight face. He could just visualize the scene with Franck Bayard.

"But that's not all," continued the team leader, prodding the operator.

"Well, sir," the older woman said timidly, "I don't understand the part. See, we need to assemble this and that, but if they'd made it like this—see—this operation could be completely canceled."

"Good point," Ward answered carefully, suddenly feeling out of his depth again. He hadn't felt this particular emotion for some time now. Over the past year he had certainly improved his process expertise considerably, which only brought him here: a shop-floor reminder that he had not involved himself with the details of part design—not yet, he sighed. But this also reminded him that the long-delayed suggestion system was, indeed, up and working; it was grabbing ideas from those most in the know—the operators—and, just as important, it was teaching the supervisors to respond quickly to operators' suggestions by first implementing them (or if not, explaining why), and, second, by supporting the operator in implementing the suggestions themselves (or at least a mock-up before full implementation).

"What does Franck say about this?"

Bayard was, after all, a manufacturing engineer and probably had some notion of whether this was a good idea or not.

"He agreed," replied the team leader. "But he said he couldn't do much about parts design at this stage. Suggested we mention it to you, though."

Ward thanked both women, who had submitted their suggestion and placed it on the board. It had been picked up on right away, but the supervisor also told Ward that he would be interested by this idea. He reassured them that he was interested, and they had done the right thing. Ward told them again to never hesitate to bring anything to his attention—whether a new idea or a problem. Fabre went right back to work, mumbling that the team was waiting for her. Ward was pleased to see that they'd held to the *one-piece flow* and all stopped to watch while she demonstrated her idea.

"He was right. He was right—good going, ladies. Congratulations."

"*M'sieur Andy…*," interrupted Weber as he was about to turn away.

"Yes, Mathilde?"

"We hear there's an important visit next week. A potential customer?"

"The week after," agreed Ward, wondering how the word always got around so fast. He'd only talked to Phil Jenkinson the previous week. "A Japanese firm is looking into starting a joint-venture in Europe, and they are considering us. Phil is showing the European plants to one of their bigwigs. I'll make an announcement next week."

"The Japanese, they're really strong on cleanliness and so on? No? That's where the 5S comes from?"

"Absolutely. We'll give the plant a good clean before they come."

"Well, see, some of the girls were talking, and, if you want, we'd be willing to come over on the weekend to have everything shipshape."

"That's great, Mathilde," answered Ward too quickly, startled. "But we've stopped all the weekend shifts months ago, and it's no longer in the budget."

"Oh!" she cried embarrassed. "We didn't mean it like that. We all know the plant really needs the work—which means *we* really need the work. We are happy to come over anyhow. Make it look good, like."

"Great," said Ward, not quite knowing what to make of it. "Let me think about it. And thank all who suggested it. I really appreciate this. I really do. We'll make something work, I'm sure."

"They want to do what?" exclaimed Jean-Pierre Deloin, startled. To Ward's secret delight, the HR manager seemed to be caught completely unaware. "Come over on the weekend to prepare the plant for the visit? In the 20 years I've worked here, I've never heard the like."

"A little window dressing for the visit couldn't hurt. Jenkinson says that a Toyota supplier wants to penetrate the European market as well as supply Toyota over here. So they're doing it the way they've done it in the U.S., by starting with a local joint-venture to learn local business conditions."

"Wouldn't they steal the business from us afterwards?" objected Deloin.

"Exactly what I said," grinned Ward. "Jenkinson thinks that getting parts now and getting into Toyota's sphere is worth the risk. 'Competition is good for the soul,' had been Phil's precise words. They'll learn from us, no doubt. But the question is: can we learn from them? They're looking for somewhere to build a plant as well as comanufacture some parts."

"I'll tell you what," said the older man slowly. His face suddenly lit up with devious cunning, wrinkles and all. "You know the field behind the plant?"

"Sure, what of it?" asked Ward, wondering what was coming next. He'd gotten used to working more closely with the HR manager, but hadn't come to actually *like* the man yet. He felt like counting the fingers on his hand every time he shook Deloin's hand.

"We actually own it. And it's part of the industrial zone."

"Do we? Is it?" asked Ward, surprised that after four years he still discovered *details* like this.

"It was all before your time. There was a plan to expand the plant then, hah!" he snorted. "Right before Alnext bought us. In any case, the building permit was filed with the town council, and is probably still valid."

"So—are you saying Vaudon could propose an instant location to build a new plant?"

"I have to check. But it should be possible."

"Blimey. I have to let Jenkinson know. He probably could do something with it."

"About the other matter," continued Deloin, mulling things over. "If people really want to come and give a hand to prepare the visit, why don't we turn it into a social event?"

"What do you have in mind?"

"How long do you think it will take?"

"Hmmm," thought Ward. "More than half a shift, but probably less than a full shift. Let's say from 10 in the morning to around 4 p.m. with a short lunch break."

"'Yes, that sounds about right. You know, I could probably get hold of the *Salle des Fêtes* at the *Mairie*, even at such short notice. We have nothing major scheduled for the coming weekends. Maybe we could organize something, like a barbecue?"

Ward looked at the HR manager in amazement. Throughout the painful last year of profound transformation, Deloin never once left his posture of amused spectator. He was much like Carela in that regard. The odd thing about Deloin was that, in his own inimitable way, the man seemed to understand what Ward was trying to do. Interestingly, he had kept in touch with a young engineer who had been recruited by Toyota in the early days of the Valenciennes site. As a result, Deloin probably knew more about Toyota's *de facto* practices—as opposed to the lean mythology that had developed around the company—than most. Still, he had always refrained from getting involved, or even making positive propositions. Not that he'd been resistant, though. Whereas Ward had often expected him to react like the old guard in the plant, Deloin was often helpful and of sound advice on most things Ward attempted. Ward was confounded by Deloin's refusal to ever take the leadership on any of it himself. Fundamentally, it appeared, the older man held to the notion that believing in the worst would never disappoint, whereas Ward himself was, in the end, a cockeyed optimist.

"Could you set it up?"

"Can the plant afford it?" Deloin asked with heavy irony.

"Come on Jean-Pierre, of course we can."

"I'll see what I can do."

"Is that Denis Carela?" asked Claire, staring ahead as the production manager rode his Harley right to the front steps of City Hall. He killed the roaring engine, eased it on the kickstand, and mock-saluted toward Ward, taking off his helmet and loosening his vintage leather jacket. His passenger strode off from behind him, showing spectacular legs tightly shrink-wrapped in blue jeans. The girl took her helmet off, and shook a full mane of blond, curly locks. Carela turned to tell her something, and she beamed a wide smile at them, lighting the sullen January evening with her stunning beauty.

"Close your mouth, dear," said Claire, giving Ward a sharp nudge in the ribs.

"Um. Yes. Hi Denis," stammered Ward reddening. "This is Claire, my wife."

"Pleased to meet you," answered the familiar lop-sided grin, with a hint of pride shining through. "Here's Jennifer, my youngest daughter. She was curious to see her old man's workplace, so I just took her to the plant."

"What do you think? Will it pass inspection?"

"The paint should have time to dry," Carela laughed. "But we've done good. And I've changed my mind. We should go for white work clothes."

"We can always start," agreed Ward.

Ward was pleased: pleased with the plant cleanup, and pleased with the informal event afterward. A surprising number of operators had shown up, and not necessarily those he had expected. Most of the team leaders attended, and they'd taken quite naturally to organizing their team members in various cleanup tasks. Ward took this as a sign that teams were indeed continuing to gel. The weather had been too dismal for a proper barbecue, so they did a simple buffet instead, and opened this up to family members, as well.

Ward had balked at a plant visit at first, but Deloin had been unexpectedly insistent, and, in the end, they'd organized a regimented tour of the site for interested family members. The mayor had even showed up, this being a small town after all. And best of all he had refrained from making a speech.

"So?" asked Ward anxiously. He was driving Jenkinson to Metz, where they would be entertaining their Japanese guests before the CEO took them on to Neuhof the next day.

"I'm optimistic," answered Jenkinson calmly. "Their CEO just asked me to congratulate your plant again for the welcome. Good job, Andy, you did well there."

"We all did," agreed Ward. He'd thought the visit had gone well. They'd started with the safety and quality boards at the entrance of the shop, explaining how they dealt with each customer complaint, starting with visiting the customer's operations. Then Ward had shown off the large electric panel he'd had installed hanging from the ceiling at the entrance of the press area. It had the press numbers set as columns and four rows of lights:

- Operating.
- Changeover.
- Not loaded.
- Breakdown.

At the moment the board clearly displayed that the plant had free capacity, and that they had never managed to get number No. 7 working consistently. Ward had been surprised to see that the Japanese CEO asked many pointed questions about how they handled the *kanban* cards. "Why 30-minute pickups and not 10?" He also pointed out that the train was late.

"In Japan," the older gentleman explained in slow, arduous English. "There is gate. At time, gate opens and train goes," he said, gesturing with a karate chop. "At end-of-round time, gate closes. If train late, train cannot enter station. Supervisor come and unlock gate, and ask why train is late."

Ward had nodded dutifully, with a mental sigh. At least the bloody train was *running* that day, albeit a few minutes late. While the CEOs discussed the intricacies of the *pull system*, the rest of the delegation had spread about, taking copious notes about the parts and the processes. Ward was uncertain how open he should be, but Jenkinson had remained totally unperturbed. It was his company. In the end, the Japanese visitors had made a great show of bowing and clapping, congratulating the operators for their good work. And Vaudon had looked good—extra stock and obsolete parts were carefully hidden away in short-term rental at an external warehouse (he'd cleared it with Jenkinson first, who had just smiled), the alleys and passageways carefully touched up, and even the odd wall painted white. So what, thought Ward, a little window dressing couldn't hurt. In any case, his number one worry that the union would stage an impromptu social action had been unfounded. If anything, the operators had seemed proud of showing off their plant.

"We'll see how it goes," concluded Jenkinson. "And please thank your HR manager for that info on the available building plot. It could clinch the deal. For some reason they're in a hurry, and I hear some noise that they're having trouble finding potential partners. They really wanted a European automotive supplier, rather than a U.S. operation, but, on the other hand, they know us from stateside. We'll see. Now—"

"Before you ask about my problems, of which I've got many," grinned Ward, "there is one I'd like to talk to you about—even though I can't say whether it's in our scope."

"Go ahead."

"It's about Bayard. My manufacturing engineering manager. You know he's involved himself heart and mind into *kaizen* activities, especially for assembly."

"Yes, he's doing a good job," agreed the CEO. "And stimulating some suggestions, you mentioned."

"Indeed. The problem is with the part renewal for the French OEM. He's kaizened the cell repeatedly, and is now arguing daily with

the designers in Neuhof. He knows many of these guys pretty well—
he used to work there, actually, and speaks German."

"Good. The problem?"

"The problem is that he disagrees on both the part design and the
process. He's not the easiest person to work with, and tends to dig in
his heels when he thinks he's right—which is often. But we're talking
about a line he's kaizened seven times in a row, and where he's reduced
the labor content by half. So I believe he has earned himself a say in
the matter."

Jenkinson still said nothing, but from the corner of his eye as he
drove the car, Ward could see a wide smile on his face, making him
look almost boyish. "What now?" he wondered silently. When amused
Jenkinson tended to create major headaches for those around him.

"In any case, Beckmeyer called me to tell him to back off. I argued
the point with Lowell, who said I should go directly to you with this
one. I realize you can't get involved with every little bicker—"

"No, no, that's fine," said the other man. "You're absolutely right
to tell me about this. I'm actually very pleased to hear it." He did
sound pleased, and Ward remembered the look of furious glee that had
crossed the other man's face after reading the letter the sales manager
had made the customer's purchasing czar write. For a moment Ward
feared he had stumbled into one of Jenkinson's political schemes.

"Why don't you bring Bayard to Neuhof tomorrow afternoon? Our
friends have a 2 p.m. flight for Tokyo, so we should be finished early."

"No problem," agreed Ward, outwardly calm, yet wondering what
this was about.

"Did Mark ever tell you why he's so set against Lowell?" asked
Jenkinson out of the blue, after they'd driven several miles through the
bleak winter landscapes in silence. The sun was setting and the
temperature was dropping rapidly, with a cold fog seeping out of the
damp fields.

"No, not as such. He mentioned he'd resigned once because of
Lowell, but never got into specifics," answered Ward, surprised by this

new tack. He rarely heard Jenkinson gossip, although the man obviously knew more about what was going on than he let on. And though Ward almost did a double-take when Jenkinson spoke of Neville's grudge against Coleman, he realized that Jenkinson had been spending more time in Bethany than he had in Vaudon. And very little escaped the man.

"Mark had worked as a manufacturing engineer on a part for Toyota, who helped guide him through the process. On the strength of his performance, management promoted him to module manager and asked him to implement the full system, as he's done now. When Alnext acquired Bethany, they put Lowell in charge of the branch. He didn't understand anything Mark was trying to do, so they fought over it until Mark was finally shoved back into manufacturing engineering."

"Yeah, I sort of got that picture."

"But that's not what made Mark quit. As a manufacturing engineer, Toyota had requested that Mark be part of the team redesigning the headlights the plant was doing for them. It was a bit like what's going on with Franck: They felt that they had trained him to understand the parts and the processes well enough to be part of the team. So off goes Mark to explain to the Ann Arbor engineers how to design a better part with a better process that had higher quality and, oh yeah, cost less too. Naturally they didn't get along. They had pegged him as a production grunt who knew nothing about product engineering, and he thought they were ivory-tower prima donnas who understood nothing about design for manufacture. When Lowell sided with the engineers, Mark resigned."

"I didn't know that. Do you think that's what's happening with Franck?"

Jenkinson didn't answer, but chuckled to himself. "I've got a few magic moments in lean implementation," he said. "Clear events that tell me I'm progressing. The first one is pretty obvious: it's when I see managers and operators discussing how to improve the line in a *kaizen* workshop. Usually, this happens quickly, but it's still not a given."

Ward thought of the fights in Neuhof. Ackermann had finally been made area manager for paint and final assembly, and was trying to do things Jenkinson's way. But Beckmeyer still had not participated in a *kaizen* workshop. Although Jenkinson insisted that all plant managers participate in *kaizen* workshops, and drag their management teams in as well, the German plant manager still thought he was above such things. Beckmeyer had compromised to the extent that he now held a monthly inspection of the *kaizen* efforts, going around the shop floor with all his staff and looking at brief shop-floor presentations made by the supervisors.

"The second magic moment is when a line manager starts doing *kaizen* regularly on his or her own initiative—that is, when they start using *kaizen* as a normal way of doing their work."

"Managing means improving?"

"Exactly. Some people can implement the full visual system if we twist their arm hard and long enough, but still never get that *kaizen* spirit. Others get it right away. And I've learned that you never really know who will do what—or at least I keep being wrong half of the time."

"Carela was certainly a surprise in Vaudon," agreed Ward. "And so was Sylvie Barras for that matter."

"The third magic moment is when learning from *kaizen* gets applied to a new process. Again, this is a clear-cut event, usually around parts handling. But at some point, the engineers change their design to take into account something learned by making existing lines more effective. This is a real stepping-stone on the way to lean thinking.

"And the fourth is when *kaizen* leads to redesign the product itself. This is my ultimate aim. Lean doesn't succeed because we simply cut production costs. It succeeds because it delivers better products to the market. At the end of the day, it's all about the product. Product, product, product."

"I'm confused now, I thought lean was all about people, people, people?"

"Making people before making things, sure" chortled the CEO good-naturedly. "Because better thinking makes better products." The talks must have been going well because the man sounded in a good mood. "Ultimately it's products we deliver to customer, products and their usage. Think about it, most of what we've done with the red bins and the *pull system* and the *kaizen* workshops is to reveal our understanding of the product. By following the problems in the *pull system*, we looked differently at workstations, but more importantly at how we build and design the parts. We learned something about the parts themselves, which could have an impact at the customer."

"The products?"

"Yes. We started this whole transformation process on the idea that production must learn to solve its own problems. More fundamentally, what I'm trying to do is create the kind of organization where knowledge flows up and down the line. Process knowledge, product knowledge. Making people before making parts means developing more knowledgeable people who will design better products than the competition from the customers' point of view and with leaner processes that the competition can't match cost-wise. Sustainable competitive advantage."

"I see," muttered Ward, blowing his cheeks, cursing inwardly: the big picture still did not come easily him.

"Nexplas will be a lean organization when every person in the company can contribute directly to improving the products."

"Show me again how you're suggesting to modify the part design?" asked Jenkinson of Bayard through Ward. Bayard spoke very good German, but, unfortunately, very poor English. Having to explain his ideas in front of the CEO and his German colleagues—who to a person were giving him icy stares—was making him twitchy and uncomfortable.

"Look here," explained Bayard, pointing at the drawing of the part. "With the existing part, this section is very weak. It often cracks during final assembly on the line. We have endless claims, but the problem is built into the design. We've tried everything we could locally, but we still can't fix it in the process. Now we could slightly increase the material thickness and the radii without changing the functionality of the part. This would considerably improve its quality."

"Good thinking," agreed the CEO

"Not me," said Bayard embarrassed, switching to halting English. "Operator suggestion."

Jenkinson nodded thoughtfully, and Ward thought he saw a hint of a satisfied smile in his usual expressionless countenance. He sighed, and stretched up, looking at the assembled team of engineers and managers.

"Gentlemen," he said slowly. "First of all, the target cost for this part is totally unacceptable. I expect a 30 percent reduction in total cost. This part must be manufactured in a high-cost area at a competitive price, so please rethink the project that way. We've been comparing our parts costs with our Japanese competitors, and we're up to 40 percent more expensive. Part of that is overhead: A Japanese supplier would be expected to have less than 10 percent overhead in the part cost, whereas we have at least 20 percent. So I will continue to drive overhead reduction in the company. We need to challenge the overhead structure, and reduce project management costs. But, most importantly, we need to eliminate scrap costs, which is why I'll ask you to take Franck's recommendations very seriously."

This caused looks all around. "Overhead" was clearly a buzzword in everyone's mind for "me."

"So, first, I'll ask you for a study of every detailed cost to achieve a minus 30 percent cost target. Please break down the cost problem into clear components. We need to explore many more options. For instance, our mold manufacturer in China is proving to be extremely reliable delivering simple molds, and vastly cheaper."

"Second, I'd like you to provide cost projections for different volumes. We need to understand cost in rampup, in full volume, and in tapering down. This way your process proposals will take the entire life-cycle of the product into account."

More aggrieved stares. Jenkinson was pushing them far out of their comfort zone. The CEO had spent months working with engineering in the U.S., but clearly far less here in Neuhof. Ward could pick up the mental shrug of disbelief from some of the engineers. He could let them know what they were in for. But even if he told them it would be a rude awakening for which they hadn't bargained.

"Third, having looked at your proposed assembly, I'd like you to work with Franck, here, to propose a minimum capital solution. Less automation, not more—understand? Simple, standard machines. No conveyors. I'll let Franck explain, but I want a proposal within the month. Is that clear?"

"So, gentlemen, right now, you have to work together to solve two problems. I want to see your target ppms for this part, and how you intend to achieve it. And I want to see a plan to reduce the cost of making this part by 30 percent. Any questions?"

"You think they'll do it?" asked Ward, trying to hide his skepticism.

"They'll have to," answered the CEO. The difficult meeting didn't seem to have affected his unusually good spirits. "Sooner or later, most of a product's costs are determined at the product engineering phase. Typically, engineers will try to stay in a safe area, and let any risk spill over to manufacturing. And yet, *kaizen* spirit has an even greater impact at the engineering phase than in actual production. The key for us is to realize that we must feed the experience of production back into designing every next generation of product. It's not easy, but they'll learn."

"I'd like to believe you, but my experience of them so far hasn't been one of open minds."

Jenkinson gave Ward one of his long, weighing looks that made the younger man squirm inwardly, wondering what he'd said that was so totally foolish.

"Because Franck Bayard is ... open-minded?"

"Franck," laughed Ward in earnest. "No, not really. Well—"

"He's learned, hasn't he?"

"Yes. Yes, he has, but—"

"So. Tell me which experiment that we conducted actually made him learn and change his mind. Not that he'll think he has changed his mind if you ask, probably, but in practice?"

"Actually," said Ward, recalling a conversation about a year ago, as the manufacturing engineer was catching his death smoking outside the plant's entrance, "he mentioned changing his mind through *kaizen* workshops."

"Every action we take should be taken as a hypothesis we test through experimentation," preached the CEO one more time. "What's the hypothesis, here? And what should be the experiment?"

"The hypothesis is that ...," thought Ward carefully, "we can develop *kaizen* thinking in engineers by getting them to participate in *kaizen* workshops. Franck got his insight because we had no new products on the drawing boards, so he had little else to work with. So ... the proper experiment for the Neuhof engineers would be to participate in *kaizen* workshops, right? But if that's the case, then why didn't you tell them to do so?"

"Why didn't I?" the CEO wondered aloud, with a tired smile.

"Aaaargh!" complained Ward, who even to this day thought occasionally of responding to the *Five Why* exercise with a *Five Because*. "Because, because ... because you first need to convince their boss. Of course."

"And who was noticeably absent in the room today?"

"Neither Klaus not Mario were there," answered Ward, thinking of Mario Klöch, the European engineering manager. "I see. You've got a problem," he grinned impudently.

"I have indeed," agreed Jenkinson. "In the meantime, I'd like you to visit Bethany with Franck Bayard and get Mark to show you around what he's been doing with engineering. I believe you'll find it interesting."

"I'd forgotten what it was to work with a *sensei*," laughed Neville, as he welcomed the bedraggled Europeans to the plant. The winter journey had been horrendous. In addition to the annoying processes for simply taking an international flight, they had to deal with a canceled flight and Bayard's lost luggage; he had trusted his personal bags to the hold so he could use his carry-on allowance to carry a couple of prototype parts for show in Rexington.

Neville had been explaining how Bethany had been chosen by Toyota for another round of supplier development. Two other non-competing suppliers had been picked by the automaker to develop their lean level, and a Toyota *sensei* had started doing visits with both plant managers in turn.

"The first time the *sensei* comes, I'm really fired up to show him the milkruns I'm doing with suppliers."

"Milkruns?" asked Bayard, looking completely baffled. He had already been complaining throughout the trip that American was even harder to understand than English. Ward had quipped that English and American had everything in common except, of course, language—and the other man had given him a comical, quizzical look. Ward thought that he should have known better than try an Oscar Wilde witticism on the manufacturing engineer. The man didn't improve with prolonged contact. They'd all been surprised to see his wife and four boys show up at the 5S party. Even his family was nerdy—four identical flat-topped clones with glasses.

"Yeah, we're organizing transport so that our trucks pick up small quantities of every component several times a day according to a fixed route among suppliers. Sort of working like a post-office van doing the round of mailboxes, or a milkman delivering full bottles and picking up empties. It helps us both with inventory and control of supplier deliveries. We are having trouble filling the trucks consistently beyond 60 percent and, with the price of oil, I'm really keen on optimizing the transport cost—"

"But—" started Bayard.

"I'll explain later, Franck," said Ward gently. "I'm curious to hear about the *sensei* visit."

"Yeah," chuckled Neville. "So I start talking about my truck problems, when he asks … well, what else? 'What about quality?'"

"Quality's not a burning issue, I tell the guy. We're at nine ppms overall, way below industry average."

"Wow!" exclaimed Ward. "We're nowhere near single-digit. We seem to be stuck at around 40."

"The *sensei* asks, 'Nine ppms?' Since you have so few bad parts, he adds, they must be really interesting. They must really highlight the clear breakdowns in the process. Please show us the bad parts you have, and tell me your standard management process for reacting to them."

Ward laughed with Neville, but one more time felt the familiar irritation at being constantly mentally wrong-footed. First quality, then lead time, then costs. The sequence of Toyota interests was systematically the same, and, yet again, his mind had drawn a blank when he'd asked himself about what the *sensei* would be interested in. Almost two years down the line, he should know better, right?

"I take him through the kind of ppms we get and how we treat them, and I get a lecture on, can you guess?"

"*Go and see*, probably," joked Ward. "Though I'm not sure how it applies."

"Bingo!" grinned the huge man, shaking his wide face in disbelief. "'*Genchi genbutsu*,' the *sensei* starts explaining. '*Go and study. You must visit the source of the problem and see it for yourself.*'"

"But you do! You've got the closest system to stop-the-line I've seen in the group."

"Yep," agreed Neville with a wistful smile, "but I had understood only half the point. You see, at first I'd understood that *genchi genbutsu* was for management responsiveness—that it would get us on the shop floor as close as can be to the moment a bad part was being produced, so that we understood what went wrong in the process and would work on a way to fix it."

"We all agree on that."

"Then I learned the hard way that *genchi genbutsu* was for *operators*—that it was there to teach operators to recognize a good part from a bad part, and to support all the training work we did with the team leaders about boundary samples and self-check visual circuits."

"We're still struggling with this one, but we're working on it."

"But here the *sensei* opens another angle—an obvious one—but, hell, I should have thought of it before. As we look at our remaining ppms, and I'm explaining this and that on why we can't make a good part, it becomes clear that in these cases we've done about as much as we could in production. Now we're really surfacing some basic flaws either in parts design or in the manufacturing process. As these are more or less set throughout the program, even with *kaizen* we get to a stage where all we're doing is inspecting the parts out of the process. As we look into the red bin, he asks, 'Is this an operator problem? Is this a process problem? Is this a product-design problem?'

"'Red bin teaches you about the product,' explains the *sensei*. 'Engineers must practice *genchi genbutsu* to learn about the *product*.'"

"Of course," muttered Ward. "That'd be the day."

"Yep. In any case, as we're in the process of redesigning a Toyota part for the next program, he gets involved with this and divides by half our target of startup ppms. That went over well, as you can imagine. Product engineers crying for their mommas! Can't be done, not at that price, and so on. So where do we start?"

Ward shrugged.

"*Genchi genbutsu*," laughed Neville. "We need to understand customer use better. Which enables us to better understand how the parts react to the process. The fascinating thing about this is that we find the same principles in engineering as in production."

"And what about manufacturing engineering? Did you hear what I heard?" asked Bayard with a snigger of badly hidden satisfaction, which made him look even geekier than usual.

"About what?"

They'd been debriefing the plant visit all through the long drive back to the closest airport.

"Manufacturing engineering. This 'genchi whatever' thing."

"*Genshi genbutsu—go and see* for yourself at the real place."

"Well, apparently, in Rexington, Jenkinson won't allow the engineers to start drawing up a new process if they haven't improved the existing one's performance by at least 10 percent."

"I missed that," admitted Ward. "But it does sound like him."

"Can you picture the hotshots in Neuhof being asked to demonstrate their right to design new equipment by first improving the old?"

"That *is* funny," laughed Ward, picturing the scene in his mind.

"I'm going to enjoy this," concluded Bayard, with righteous anger. Ward sighed loudly at the idea that he'd have to find a way for all these divas to work together. *Teamwork*, sure. Easier said than done.

"So, that's the war room I keep hearing about?" asked Jenkinson with his usual poker face as he looked around the empty meeting room, peering at the charts pinned on the walls.

"This is it. Each section of wall is dedicated to a product project. You can see the project timetables as well as up-to-date estimates for actual delivery dates. You also can see all open problems, as well as supplier problems, and so on—everything that is needed to visualize how the project is going and the issues that need to be tackled to move things along as a team. But, um, why? What have you heard about it?"

"Oh, nothing short of cardinal offenses. You want them to change their design process, is that it? You've ruffled a few German feathers there, Andy. Talk me through it before they all walk in with the pitchforks and the sharp sticks."

"That bad, huh?"

"Yep, you've got them stirred up for sure," drawled Jenkinson with a slow smile. Even after all this time, Ward never knew exactly where he stood with the boss. But he'd learned not to care as much, and shoot straight with him.

"Franck's been working with Mario. Apparently they've got some ridiculous process of 20 gate reviews for each project. My understanding is that at each of these gates, there is a go/no-go decision. Essentially what happens is the project is presented to senior management at the gate, who then makes their objections. Then the project has to solve the problems until the gate is passed. As a result, projects take forever, and there are still many problems when they arrive at the factory. Although the process solves some concerns, they're not necessarily the ones we worry about at the customer or in production. This goes back to your point of developing an understanding of what you're testing for before you begin designing—not after."

"Uh-huh," nodded Jenkinson noncommittally. "And you suggest?"

"Four or five clear milestones at natural steps of the project, such as concept, system design, detailed design, prototype, and preproduction. At each of these steps we would try to identify the main problems that would affect the downstream stages, and try to solve them. The idea being to work problems upstream."

"I agree."

"Mark also mentioned something about developing a number of different solutions even though we knew only one would be picked in the end, for learning purposes. I see the logic of that, but think that in practice it would be far too advanced for us right now. Our main issue right now is to get the engineers focused on respecting deadlines and identifying problems early."

"I'm not surprised they're up in arms," grinned the CEO. "I didn't think you'd have the gall, to be frank."

"Well," shrugged Ward, "you gave me license to stir the pot. Besides, with what I've just done in Vaudon, this isn't that scary."

"Anything else I should know about?"

"No, not really. I finally shut down the MRP for all internal transactions, so we only work with the *kanban* cards and the *pull system* within the walls of the factory now. No more computers on the shop floor."

"And?"

"It might be easy for you," laughed Ward, "but it was one of the hardest calls I've made. I can't tell you the panic when we unplugged the damn thing. We were all convinced the plant wouldn't produce a single part the next day."

"I'm laughing with you, Andy, not at you. I've been there, and, yes, it's a scary moment. What happened?"

"Nothing, of course," sighed Ward. "The *kanban* cards work fine. They've been doing so for a while, in any case. It was all in our minds. As always."

"Good, but don't forget the key rule about a *kanban* system: the cards are reviewed monthly, and you try to take some away every month. *Kanban* is a tool for *kaizen*, right."

"Right," agreed Ward, adopting what he realized was a poker face to match Jenkinson's.

"Anything else on the development project before we let the wolves in?"

"One thing. I'd like to ask you for some training budget to train all the engineers here to use *A3s*. I think it would be really helpful."

"Bank's closed, Andy. Not a dime. Do what you can," Jenkinson answered grimly.

"Are we in trouble again?"

"I'm not sure," answered the other man slowly. "The bank that helped us set up the company has been acting weird lately. We've been able to pay back some of the loans with the stock reduction, but not as fast as I'd hoped. And with the way that financial markets have been behaving ... . I don't know. I've got a bad feeling about this."

Ward stared mutely at Jenkinson who was standing in front of a project display without looking at it, lost in his thoughts. Ward felt the conversation was way above his pay grade and had picked up an unusual note of uncertainty in Jenkinson's voice.

"In any case," rejoined Jenkinson, gathering his thoughts. "Strict diet for the company until I figure out what's going on. Inventory reduction remains a priority, and let's keep the spending to a minimum, shall we? I agree with the idea of *A3* training for the engineers, but let's figure out a way to do it on our own resources for the time being."

How easily one forgets, Ward smiled to himself. The meeting had gone badly, reminding him of that very first session in Neuhof where Jenkinson had made Beckmeyer cut his quality department staff. He was a fool not to have expected it. It came to him that much of that early resistance to change had disappeared in Vaudon. Sure, people were still slow to do the work, and he had to be constantly on their case to keep up the *kaizen* rhythm. More than anything else, getting his staff to follow up with the *check* of the *PDCA* remained an uphill struggle. But by and large, they'd learned to accept being challenged, and they didn't question the fact that a gap in performance could be linked to a problem in the process. In many instances, he even had to cool their ardor at changing the entire process before improving the existing one. Phil's insistence on improving the existing equipment before designing or purchasing new equipment made more and more sense. Indeed, the only way of proving that you've grasped a problem was to improve the situation, even if in just a minor way. Improving current conditions proved that you understood the process. *Improvement after improvement* was slowly being accepted as a normal way of working in his plant.

Ward swore as he almost missed the airport exit on the autobahn once again. He'd never get used to that one. He was dropping Jenkinson at the airport, after which he would drive home.

"Don't you get that feeling of déjà vu?" he chuckled.

"How so?" answered Jenkinson slowly, deep in thought as usual.

"I was remembering that time I drove up to Neuhof to plead for the plant."

"Turns out you did the right things. And I'll admit that it was one of those times—half the time I am wrong. I had made up my mind about closing Vaudon."

"Yeah, I'm relieved that this Japanese joint-venture deal got signed, because the way volumes are these days, jury's still out on whether the plant would survive further demand drops."

"You've just got to love the automotive industry," grinned the CEO wryly. "I suspect you're going to hear a lot more about *kaizen* when they start showing up."

"That's already started," laughed Ward. "They're complaining that our ground is neither flat enough nor horizontal enough for the machines they want to install.

"To be honest, back then," he added after a pause, "I was just buying time. I didn't think I'd succeed in making a difference."

"You've done good, Andy," approved Jenkinson. "And you've come a long way. Sometimes buying time is all there is. I agree with you that this joint venture is a huge relief. No matter how much *kaizen* the plant does, if we don't have enough volume to put in it, keeping it open remains dicey. But, then again, the deal came together precisely because they saw what you were doing with the plant. Success isn't always a function of how aggressively you pursue one thing: sometimes the best you can do is put yourself in the position to succeed. Serves to show it's not over until it's over."

Jenkinson paused for a moment, then turned to Ward. "You know, Andy, we keep discussing all the various aspects of lean management. Maintaining the *kaizen* spirit, keeping a *clear direction*, encouraging *teamwork*, developing *mutual trust*. It's all very powerful stuff, but never lose sight of the fact that the real secret to lean leadership is *go and see*. To do any of the rest, you've got to be there. At the real place, with the real people, looking at the real parts—finding out the facts. Whenever there's an operator with an idea, you've got to be there. Whenever there's a customer unhappy about a product, you've got to be there. Whenever your own management team comes up with some thoughtless policy that is going to cheese off customers or operators because they haven't thought it through or some needless investment because they haven't understood the problem, you've got to be there. You've got to be there and teach.

"I know what you'll say. You can't be everywhere at once, all the time. And the bigger your responsibility, the harder it sounds—look at me with operations on three continents. But that's not the point. People need to get on with their job, and you can't be holding their hand and looking over their shoulder 24/7.

"*Go and see* is about making sure you visit every department regularly, and check that people are doing what they're trained to do and understand correctly what we're trying to achieve as a company. And sometimes you spot problems they can't see because you've got a wider perspective. You can pull the andon cord, and say, "Stop and think again. Look into this more deeply. Understand the problem, find other options.'

"But the entry ticket is *go and see*. No matter how pressing all the other issues. No matter how urgent the politics. To practice lean management, you need to wash your hands three times a day. Meet the people, touch the parts. Ultimately, that's what distinguishes those who 'get it' from those who don't. It all happens at the *gemba*. As my *sensei* taught me long ago, the secret of lean leadership is no secret at all: *Go and see*. Ask 'Why?' Show respect."

EPILOGUE

Andrew Ward was enchanted. He'd never sailed before, and sitting on the wooden deck of the old ketch as it flew under the red ochre pillars of the Golden Gate beneath an azure sky had him spellbound. The sailboat was a thing of beauty: all varnished woods and polished bronze, pure pleasure to the touch. Bob Woods stood at the wheel, grinning like a maniac, his sparse white hair flying in a halo around his hawkish face. His son Mike sat across from Ward in the cockpit, engrossed in typing on his laptop, rarely looking up at the astounding beauty of surf and rock cliffs that unraveled around them. Mike looked like a pudgy, scruffy version of Woods, the hawkish features mellowed by longish hair and shortish beard. He looked the very image of the Berkeley radical, and Ward guessed he was one back in the day.

The past two years had been tough. First, oil prices had skyrocketed, and with them demand for smaller cars. For a few months, Phil Jenkinson had been hailed as visionary CEO for his efforts to shift Nexplas from its focus on SUV parts to smaller vehicles. Ward knew better—that he had not anticipated oil prices to move that far up, and was simply trying to broaden his market range. But better lucky than smart, right? Then the global financial crisis had hit, and the bottom had fallen out of the automotive industry. The equity owner had found itself in trouble and dragged Jenkinson through the mud for not slashing costs as rapidly as the situation warranted. They had trouble making their numbers for a while, but, then again, who hadn't? As markets slowly and painfully returned to normal, the partners finally accepted that the company had remained strong through the worst of the meltdown and had, in fact, emerged as one of their solid remaining assets. Jenkinson's personal ratings were up again. Amid the crisis, Nexplas market share had increased, and the company was now seen in good shape for the recovery. Even hard-nosed financial analysts had admitted Jenkinson's lean strategy had paid off.

Loafing on the deck of the *Felicity*, Ward mused idly upon the unlikely chain of events that had led him there. On one of his visits, Jenkinson had asked whether any one in Vaudon was ready to take over the plant. Fighting a sudden, panicky surge of adrenaline, Ward had suggested that if Denis Carela would agree to take the job—which he doubted—he would do fine; or, failing that, Carole Chandon would probably be a good plant manager if she got sufficient coaching on the technical side. In the past two years she'd worked well with Carela, and if the two continued to work as a team as they'd been doing, Ward believed she could take over the plant's management. He'd been increasingly involved in engineering issues the last year, and delegated much of the administrative functions to Chandon and the financial controller. But why the question?

"I'd like you to consider taking over the job of European regional manager," Jenkinson had dropped, casual as can be.

Ward had felt himself freeze in both excitement and terror. This was a huge promotion. He'd never thought of himself as ambitious, and, clearly, the past three years had shown him that more clout meant more problems, but also a greater ability to steer things in the right direction and get things done. "What about Coleman?"

"He'll be returning shortly to the States. It' still very hush-hush, so please don't spread it around, but we're considering our first major acquisition, and I need Lowell on this. The European job had always been temporary—although it lasted longer than we'd planned."

"Would I have to move to Neuhof?"

The question had made the CEO smile, not unkindly. "Up to you. I'd expect you to spend a couple of days a week there, but I understand you'd probably rather stay where you are. I don't have any problem with it as long as you spend the time it takes to *go and see*."

"I'd love to have a go. I need to talk it over with Claire first."

"Sure thing," had answered Jenkinson. "There's no real rush."

Which is how they'd ended up in California. Claire's first reaction had been to break the bubbly out (and when Andy asked again if this were good or bad, she joked, "We shall see") and then declared that they needed a holiday to think it over. She had stayed in friendly contact with Amy Woods over the course of several return visits to Malancourt, each time sparking a genuine invitation for a visit to the States. After the success of his book on Jenkinson's lean transformation of his previous company, Mike had moved to the business school where he was now researching and teaching lean full-time. They had a lovely house within walking distance of Haas, with a distant view of the ocean on those rare days without fog. Amy had been visibly pregnant when they'd arrived, and in very high spirits. On the day of the scheduled sailing trip, both she and Claire had chosen to respect the sea by staying on land.

"Is it always like this?" wondered Ward aloud.

"It can get awfully foggy," answered Woods senior.

"Lean implementation, I meant. Does it ever get stable? Or do we continue to face problem after problem forever?"

This made Woods guffaw, and his son Mike looked up from his laptop with an amused grin.

"It's when you run out of problems that you're in real trouble," laughed Woods. "No problem is your biggest problem."

"What do you mean by that?" wondered Ward, puzzled.

"Big company disease," explained Woods junior. "We keep expecting Toyota to regress to the mean sooner or later, to become just another automotive company. Up to now, though, they've kept facing and solving their problems, even though those problems continue to evolve all the time. For instance, they're now dealing with all the problems caused by their rapid expansion, such as training enough people quickly enough, and the overcapacity caused by the financial collapse—even if they aren't as badly affected as many others, they still lost money for the first time in 50 years. Their senior management has always been weary of catching what they call 'big company disease.' They are determined to keep the *kaizen* spirit alive."

"You've done the easy part," agreed Woods. Before Ward could protest, he added, "No, really. Up to now, you've faced known problems. But at some point, you will face a tougher problem, which is that of reinvention—finding a problem where none exists."

"A lean organization is one where every one adds value to the products, is that it?" asked Ward.

"Partly. That's Phil's current bee in his bonnet," said Woods. "I have a different take on it. It is all about the operators in the end. This has always been the hardest lesson for me. With every new tool we'd introduce, my *sensei* would ask, 'What is the mission of the operator with this tool?' We knew how to work with foremen and team leaders, but we always got caught short at the operator level. The truth is that much of lean is about teaching people to change, from the shop floor up."

"Change?"

"Yep, change. But not in a wide sense, not 'makeover' or 'transformational' like we tend to think of when we say change. I mean practical change in three specific ways: Volume changes, which means rebalancing to the new *takt time*. Mix changes, which means frequent production changeovers. Product change, which means successful launch of new products. These demand real *mental* skills beyond knowing how to make good parts—and they apply from operators to the CEO: How do you deal with demand fluctuation while maintaining full utilization of your capacity? How do you use the same lines to produce different products? And, finally, how do you frequently introduce new products that people will buy? This is not about reorganizing or reshuffling the deck. This is about learning a real practice of change. And the core insight they've hit upon is that you do it by balancing *standardized work* and *kaizen*."

"Sticking to standards to learn change. That's a bit of a paradox, don't you think?"

"Which is why no one's getting it. It only makes sense when you practice it every darned day. *Standardized work, kaizen, standardized work, kaizen,* until you improve your management practice and know more about your customers, products, processes, and people."

"Isn't there an end to this process? Surely, there's a point where you can't squeeze any more out of people and machines?"

"Interesting question," answered Mike, who'd put away his Mac in the cabin as the ocean spray had started to wet the deck. "Much debated. Is lean mean? We hear all sorts of cases where lean tools have been applied mindlessly and only resulted in further exploitation of workers and conflict with management. My colleagues and I have been studying the employee's perspective. What's in it for them? Is a constant drive for improvement engaging or simply stressful?"

Apart from his academic tendency to lecture, Mike had none of his father's abrasiveness. He was an easygoing chap, easily diffident, with an oddball sense of humor that had surprised Ward until he'd learn that Mike's mother was indeed British and that he'd been raised mostly in the UK, where his father had been working at the time.

"The basic insight to the motivational aspect of *kaizen* is that it's relatively easy to get anyone to do anything if you've got authority and push hard enough, but you can't force *interest*. Lean managers try to get their employees to use their minds and hearts as well as their arms and legs, and you can't coerce someone to think. Thinking can only come from interest and paying attention. By studying how people feel at various points of their working day, researchers have found that people feel happiest when they're totally engaged in a task, much like athletes finding the elusive 'zone' of their perfect game, regardless of the nature of the task—whether doing a crossword, checking ball bearings to see if they're perfectly rounded, counseling others, or solving quantum equations in nuclear physics. Flow—but a very different type of flow than the one in lean. This one referring to a state of mind. This feeling of total engagement tends to appear when we find ourselves balanced between the challenge of the situation and our competence to deal with it. Too much challenge, and we panic; too much competence, and we're bored. Obviously, this 'sweet spot' remains elusive because challenge and competence evolve randomly in work situations unless carefully managed. Interestingly as well, when people feel totally engaged in a task, the one thing they hate is being interrupted by anything that breaks their mental flow.

"What's more, *kaizen* gives employees a greater degree of control over their own work than any other organizational approach. Ultimately, there's nothing quite so depressing for a human being than having absolutely no control over their circumstances. In lean, operators can stop the line if they have a problem. Operators participate in the design of the workstations. They make suggestions. In general, they have some degree of control over their environment, which is a huge bonus. Additionally, the more they have been involved in the design of their working environment, the greater ownership they feel and the deeper a commitment they develop for the job. Finally, team-based problem-solving is a strong promoter of *esprit de corps* and fellowship within the working team."

"That's what I've found out the hard way. I've tried forcing the changes on people, and it blew up in my face."

"In the end, that's the thing," shouted Woods, yelling to be heard against the breeze. "Because we're so biased by 'results, whatever it takes,' and we don't instinctively understand the parallel Toyota makes between process and results, many companies find it relatively easier to adopt the continuous-improvement tools, without focusing equally on involving and developing people. So rather than walk on two feet, they hop along on one, hoping to win the race. Invariably, they fall flat on their face. And we've all learned this the hard way. Not just you—everyone I know who has succeeded at lean has had to discover that respect for people was just as important as continuous improvement. To satisfy customers, we must certainly practice *go and see*, *kaizen*, and challenge ourselves continuously, but if we don't encourage *teamwork* and develop *mutual trust*, we keep rowing against the tide—no matter how fast we progress, the goal post keeps slipping away."

"One further reason lean management works," added Mike pensively, "is self-measurement. When people measure their own performance, they improve their practice. Not when their boss measures them, nor when staff guys do it. It has to be themselves, to be truly engaged. When it's the boss, they soon measure how to best please the boss, which is often another matter altogether. However, self-measurement is so psychologically painful that management needs to maintain constant pressure for people to do so continuously. Essentially, this is what lean systems do: they visualize hourly self-measurement. As soon as management stops showing interest and helping to solve problems, people stop, and processes go downhill. As long as people are kept engaged in measuring their own performance, they'll improve it.

"Combined with learning by doing, and learning by working with others, through *kaizen* and *A3s* and so on, this creates a very powerful learning environment. I'm writing a paper about this right now. Self-measurement, learning by doing, sharing experiences, and challenging others with your perspectives. That's my theory about *kaizen*, anyhow. To answer your original question: No, there isn't any predictable 'end' to the process, simply because there is no end to human ingenuity. But to get there, the real challenge is to start thinking in terms of understanding problems rather than jumping to solutions. That's the really hard part: What is the problem you're trying to solve?"

Epilogue

"Hey, here it is, look," shouted Claire excitedly, having run down as soon as they'd docked the yacht, waving a magazine in the air. Amy followed in a more stately manner, with one of her brightest smiles. Claire scrambled on board, and shoved a glossy page in Ward's face. He stared at a picture of himself grinning like an idiot and with an appalling haircut, boldly captioned, "The Lean Manager." Someone had contacted Jenkinson about writing an article on lean transformations, and he had suggested they interview Ward. Pleased despite himself, Ward looked at the silly photograph, astonished that, against all odds, maybe the horse had learned to sing after all.

ACKNOWLEDGMENTS

The characters and the situations in this novel are entirely fictitious. Although we have based the story on our experiences on the shop floor and the teachings of our *sensei*, the book does not pretend in any way to be a description of either the Toyota Production System (TPS) or the Toyota Way. References to TPS or Toyota Way in the book reflect only our understanding of their application outside of Toyota and in no way claim to represent the position of Toyota Motor Corp.

Heartfelt thanks to the book's chief editor Tom Ehrenfeld, who has done a superb job of coaxing this book into being. The idea of this sequel to *The Gold Mine* started years ago when our publisher Jim Womack encouraged us to write a followup novel, going deeper into the management issues of lean transformation. The book's storyline was first suggested by Pat Lancaster, who regretted we'd not written the previous novel from the perspective of the plant manager—to convey both the excitement and anxiety of having to carry out the transformation in practice. Years later, Orry Fiume made the same comment, and we started scoping out together a business case for a lean transformation. In writing the story, we have relied on the experiences of many managers who do this every day at the *gemba*. More particularly, we owe a large debt to Nampachi Hayashi both for his shop-floor teachings of TPS and deep insights into lean management according to the Toyota Way. Thanks also to Tatsuhiko Yoshimura for his insightful presentation of key ideas in Toyota's management approach. In the use of these principles to transform the business culture, we have been fortunate to work with successful executives, such as Pierre Vareille, Jean-Luc Vidal, Theo Benz, Christophe Baron, Jacques Chaize, Frédéric Fiancette, Evrard Guelton, Patrick Thollin, Jean-Paul Guyot, Jean-Baptiste Bouthillon, Jean-Claude Bihr, and many others, as well as expert lean officers, Alain Prioul, Philippe Pull, Yves Mérel, Paul Evans, Eric Prévot, Philippe Grosse, Marc Mercier, and Marie-Pia Ignace. Much of this book draws from discussion and support within the lean community, principally with both Jeff Liker and Dan Jones, who have helped structure its core ideas all along, and many inputs from conversations with other leading lean thinkers, such as Art Smalley, Durward Sobek, Pascal Dennis, David Meier, Mike Hoseus, and René Aernoudts. Other Toyota experts such as Jim Womack, José Ferro, and Gilberto Kosaka have generously contributed their time and experience.

Many others have sustained us with advice and inspiration, and we are grateful to Godefroy Beauvallet, Neil Harvey, Philip Cloutier, Laurent Bordier, Christian Amblard, Steve Boyd, Patrick Labilloy, and Sara Bienek for their valuable input.

Technical injection details in the book are mostly borrowed from Douglas M. Bryce's *Plastic Injection Molding* (Society of Manufacturing Engineers, 1996); Bernie A. Olmsted and Martin E. Davis' *Practical Injection Molding* (CRC Press, 2001); and Glenn L. Beall and James L. Throne's *Hollow Plastic Parts* (Hanser Gardner Publications, 2004). All mistakes and inaccuracies are our own. Many thanks also to the Lean Enterprise Institute team involved in the production of the book for their dedication and hard work: Michael Brassard (who suggested the title), George Taninecz, and Thomas Skehan, and to the reviewers who made many thoughtful comments: Peter Willats, Cindy Swank, Mark Graban, and Matt Zayko.

Finally, we would like to thank our family for their support and patience as they've often had to sit through more lean talk than anyone in their right mind would want to.

Lean Enterprise Institute

Continue Your Learning

The Lean Enterprise Institute (LEI) has a wide range of learning resources, all with the practical knowledge you need to sustain a lean transformation:

Learning Materials

Our plain-language books, workbooks, leadership guides, and training materials reflect the essence of lean thinking — *doing*. They draw on years of research and real-world experiences from lean transformations in manufacturing and service organizations to provide tools that you can put to work immediately.

Education

Faculty members with extensive implementation experience teach you actual applications with the case studies, work sheets, formulas, and methodologies you need for implementation. Select from courses that address technical topics, culture change, coaching, senior management's roles, and much more.

Events

Every March the Lean Transformation Summit explores the latest lean concepts and case studies, presented by executives and implementers. Other events focus on an issue or industry, such as starting a lean transformation or implementing lean in healthcare. Check *lean.org* for details and to get first notice of these limited-attendance events.

lean.org

A quick and secure sign-up delivers these online learning resources:

- Jim Womack's thought-leading e-letter delivered monthly to your inbox.
- Use of the Connection Center to network or benchmark with fellow Lean Thinkers.
- Entry to a range of Forums where you can ask questions or help others.
- Access to the Lean Road Map for customizing and tracking a personal learning path.
- Use of the Lean Notebook for saving and sharing important articles.
- First notice about LEI events, webinars, and new learning materials.

About the Lean Enterprise Institute

The Lean Enterprise Institute, Inc. was founded in 1997 by management expert James P. Womack, Ph.D., as a nonprofit research, education, publishing, and conferencing company. As part of its mission to advance lean thinking around the world, LEI supports the Lean Global Network (leanglobal.org), the Lean Education Academic Network (teachinglean.org), and the Healthcare Value Leaders Network™ (healthcarevalueleaders.org).